Field Guide to Child Welfare

Volume IV

Judith S. Rycus & Ronald C. Hughes

CWLA Press
Washington, DC

Institute for Human Services
Columbus, OH

CHILD WELFARE LEAGUE OF AMERICA, INC.
440 First Street, NW, Third Floor, Washington, DC 20001-2085
Email: books@cwla.org

CURRENT PRINTING (last digit)
10 9 8 7 6 5 4 3

Cover and text design by James Graham
Photographs by Jeffrey A. Rycus

Printed in the United States of America

ISBN # 0–87868-620-7

Rycus, Judith S.
    Field guide to child welfare / Judith S. Rycus & Ronald C. Hughes.
        p.   cm.
    Includes bibliographical references and index.
    ISBN 0-87868-617-7 (v. 1). -- ISBN 0-87868-618-5 (v. 2). - - ISBN
    0-87868-619-3 (v. 3). -- ISBN 0-87868-620-7 (v. 4)
        1. Child welfare--United States.   2. Social case work with
children--United States.   3. Family social work--United States.
I. Hughes, Ronald C.   II. Title
HV741.R94   1998   98-4701
362.7'0973--dc21   CIP

CONTENTS

Volume IV

PLACEMENT AND PERMANENCE

VIII. ATTACHMENT, SEPARATION, AND PLACEMENT

A. Attachment and Attachment Disorders

B. The Effects of Traumatic Separation on Children

C. Placement Strategies to Prevent Trauma

A. ATTACHMENT AND ATTACHMENT DISORDERS

1. Conceptual Framework

2. Application

Conceptual Framework

Abused and neglected infants and young children are at high risk for developing insecure or maladaptive attachments. Early, prolonged, or traumatic separations from the primary caregiver have also been highly correlated with attachment disorders in children and youth [Levy & Orlans 1995; Bowlby 1973; Maccoby 1980]. When these attachment patterns are observed in infancy and early childhood, they tend to be durable, sometimes persisting through adolescence and into adulthood [Levy & Orlans 1995; Mussen, Conger, Kagan & Huston 1984; Maccoby 1980; Cline 1992; Isabella 1993].

Many children and youth who experience severe maltreatment and/or repeated or prolonged separations from their caregivers during early childhood exhibit serious attachment disorders. These disorders are characterized by an absence of meaningful attachments; superficiality in relationships; a vigorous avoidance of intimacy; rejection of overtures of affection and caring; a pervasive lack of trust; a strong need to control and manipulate others; and behaviors that include volatile anger, hostility, and cruelty to animals and other people [Levy & Orlans 1995; Cline 1992]. Attachment disorders and their associated behavior problems can seriously interfere with family adjustment in both foster and adoptive placements, and greatly increase the risk of placement disruption [Katz 1986; Pinderhughes & Rosenberg, 1990; Fahlberg 1991; Levy & Orlans 1995].

Some children who have experienced relatively deprived environments during infancy retain a capacity for recovery, and can develop healthy attachments, if they are provided with a permanent, nurturing caregiver, and a stimulating environment early in life [Mussen et al. 1984]. Even children with intractable attachment disorders can sometimes be helped to learn trust and to develop meaningful interpersonal relationships with the proper therapy and the constant support of permanent, giving, and patient caregivers [Cline 1992; Levy & Orlans 1995; Fahlberg 1991].

Because the quality of early attachments has such a strong and enduring influence on children's social and emotional development, child welfare workers must be vigilant in identifying signs of attachment problems in children who have experienced maltreatment and/or separation. There might be attachment problems in children living with their own families, or in adoptive, foster, or relative placement. Workers should include interventions in family case plans that promote and strengthen healthy parent–child attachment, and that provide specialized therapy for children with attachment disorders.

HEALTHY ATTACHMENT

An understanding of the importance of healthy attachment to all aspects of child development will further our understanding of the potentially traumatic consequences of maltreatment and traumatic separation on development.

Infant attachment refers to the earliest enduring social and emotional relationships very young children develop with the significant people in their lives. The propensity to develop attachment is a fundamental and inborn human trait. Positive attachment is widely believed to form the foundation for many aspects of subsequent development [Maccoby 1980; Mussen 1984; Gardner 1978; Damon 1977; 1983].

An infant's first attachment is formed with its mother or other primary caregiver. Infants rapidly develop other attachments as well, usually with fathers, siblings, and extended family members. Attachment between a mother and her infant is a reciprocal process. The mother's caregiving behaviors of feeding, holding, nurturing, smiling, cuddling, and talking to the infant reinforce the infant's attachment to the mother. The infant's responses to its mother's care, including cooing, smiling, cuddling, and becoming quiet when held, strengthen the mother's attachment to the infant.

Children develop their strongest attachments to caregivers who are sensitive and quickly responsive to their needs. The caregiver recognizes and knows the meaning of the infant's verbal and nonverbal cues, and knows how to respond to these cues to meet the infant's physical and emotional needs. This includes feeding the infant when it is hungry; assuring the infant is warm, dry, and physically comfortable; and comforting and soothing the infant when it is distressed or frightened. When infants are tired, hungry, or distressed, they often cannot be comforted by anyone other than the caregiver who has historically recognized and responded to their signals of physical and emotional need. As they get older, children with healthy attachments can also be comforted by other supportive caregivers.

Engaging infants in play and other pleasurable social interactions also promotes the development of attachment. This is often the basis of attachments formed by infants with siblings, grandparents, and others who do not generally provide primary care. Nurturance and pleasurable social interaction are both necessary predeterminants of attachment. Infants are also more likely to approach persons with whom they have attachments for play and interaction.

There is congruence in the literature about the effects of early attachment on many areas of child development [Ainsworth et al., 1978; Bowlby, 1970; Maccoby 1980; Mussen et al. 1984; Gardner 1978; Damon 1977; 1983].

First, a child's early attachment experiences have a profound effect on the child's later ability to form and maintain healthy interpersonal relationships. According to Erik Erikson [1959; 1963], the primary milestone in emotional development during the first year of life is the development of "basic trust." For Erikson, trust refers to infants' perception of the environment as a positive, generally responsive, nurturing and dependable place, as well as their sense of competence and confidence in their ability to act upon the environment to assure that their needs are met. The degree to which caregivers positively respond to cues and meet an infant's needs has a significant influence on both aspects of trust. For Erikson, an infant's early and continuous attachment to a dependable and nurturing caregiver is the single most important factor in the development of basic trust. Erikson also believes that infants' experiences with attachment influence their "world view," or basic attitude toward the world, which sets the tone for all future relationships and interactions with the environment. Thus, if early attachments are absent, unpredictable, or a source of pain, a child will be more likely to avoid intimacy in future relationships.

Healthy attachment promotes the development of language and other communication abilities. Social interaction between infants and their caregivers stimulates the development of both verbal and nonverbal communications. Babbling, cooing, vocal interactions, and eye contact with caregivers are precursors to language development. Infants develop communication skills at an early age. Crying is an infant's first and primary means of communicating distress or discomfort. Within a few months, the infant's cries become differentiated, and most mothers can recognize tired cries, angry cries, frightened cries, or cries for attention. Timely nurturing responses by the caregiver to these and other cues from the infant further reinforce the infant's attempts to communicate. Children who have been neglected, abused, or abandoned by caregivers are often delayed in their development of language and other communication skills.

The nature of a child's attachments can affect the development of self-esteem. Through relationships with important others, a child learns that he is valued, worthwhile, and wanted. He is positively reinforced by the affection, caring, and protection he receives from those with whom he has close attachments. These positive relationships are critical in establishing the foundations of the child's sense of self. Healthy attachment is viewed by developmental psychologists as one of the most important foundations of healthy personality development. Children who do not feel loved and important often develop low self-esteem, and perceive themselves as inadequate in many ways. Children also identify with persons to whom they have close attachments. This is a primary way that attitudes and values are transmitted to the developing child.

Proximity to a primary caregiver affords a sense of security, which reduces anxiety in stressful situations. Infants and young children have few skills with which to cope with life stresses. As children grow, they develop more sophisticated coping strategies, and greater self-reliance in mastering life's tasks and challenges. Infants and young children, however, must rely on the adults in their lives to protect them, and to remove the sources of stress. Children depend upon their primary caregivers to feed them, keep them warm, comfort them, reassure them, and protect them from harm. The child who has developed a strong attachment with a caregiver has a dependable source of security, which frees the child from unnecessary anxiety and fear. Children who are deprived of this security may display strong anxiety reactions to even minor stresses. If the anxiety state continues for a long period of time, it can interfere with the child's development in all domains.

Considerable early learning takes place through play and interaction with primary caregivers. Play stimulates a child's cognitive, physical, and social development. Children develop social skills such as sharing, cooperation, and negotiation through play with parents and siblings. Children are also encouraged by parents to learn and to repeat new skills and activities. For example, many children would likely never attempt to ride a two-wheel bicycle without training wheels were it not for a proud, cheering, encouraging parent. The child's trust in, and wish to please the parent, both aspects of healthy attachment, are significant factors in motivating the child to learn.

Finally, healthy attachment fosters the development of self–reliance and autonomy in children. The secure emotional base derived from healthy attachment promotes exploration, experimentation, and the development of self–confidence and self–reliance.

MALADAPTIVE ATTACHMENT

When the caregiving environment does not consistently meet an infant or young child's physical and emotional needs, maladaptive attachment is likely to result.

Ainsworth and her colleagues [1969; 1978] conducted seminal early research on variations in attachment behavior in infants using a technique called the "strange situation." One–year–old infants were observed first at home, and then again in a laboratory setting, where they were subjected to brief separations and reunions with their mothers. Their behavior in response to this separation was assessed. Most of the infants studied were found to be securely attached to their mothers. They related to their mothers in warm interaction; they used the mother as a safe base for exploration; they protested and cried upon separation; they showed pleasure when the mother returned; they were easy to console; and they clearly preferred the mother to a stranger.

However, some infants displayed behaviors that suggested their attachments to their mothers were quite different in nature. Ainsworth et al. [1969; 1978] described these attachment styles as anxious and insecure. Insecurely attached infants were divided into two categories; avoidant, and ambivalent or resistant. These insecurely attached infants demonstrated a variety of behaviors both in the presence of their caregivers and when separated from them. For example, the avoidant infants explored independently, but they did not use the mother as a safe base; they tended to ignore her. They showed little protest when separated from the mother, avoided contact when she returned, and did not discriminate between the mother and a stranger. By contrast, the ambivalent/resistant infants did not explore the environment at all prior to separation; they became severely agitated and anxious during separation; and they simultaneously sought contact with the mother and pulled away from her upon her return.

Ainsworth et al. [1969; 1978] noted correlations between the caregiving behaviors of the mothers and the attachment styles displayed by their infants. Mothers of securely attached infants tended to be warmly responsive and available to their infants, and they attended readily to their infants' cues. Mothers of avoidant infants were more likely to be unresponsive and rejecting with their infants; they appeared to lack emotional warmth and expressiveness, and they avoided physical contact. Mothers of ambivalent infants tended to be inconsistent and unpredictable; they were available and responsive on some occasions, but not others.

A fourth style, labeled "disorganized–disoriented" was later described by Main and Soloman [1990]. The attachment behavior of these infants was confused and often contradictory. They approached the parent, but with a stiff body; they expressed intense anger, followed by a sudden dazed appearance; they failed to seek out the mother when frightened; they attempted to leave with a stranger rather than remain with the parent; and they often showed fear at the sight of the mother upon reunion. Lyons–Ruth et al. [1993] found that disorganized attachment patterns in infants increased in frequency as the severity of social risk factors increased in their families. Carlson et al. [1989] found that 82% of infants in their study sample of maltreating families exhibited disorganized-disoriented attachment. Crittendon's [1985] study results identified that mothers of disorganized-disoriented infants were often abusive or neglectful toward their infants, and Main and Hesse [1990] identified that many of the mothers of disorganized-disoriented infants had themselves suffered physical and sexual abuse as children.

Some children with organic or neurological conditions may fail to develop strong attachments. Examples are children with autism, and some children who have been prenatally addicted to drugs, such as crack cocaine. Some children with organic problems are believed to be unable to accurately perceive, understand, and respond to external stimuli. They may not be able to signal their needs; they may experience excessive discomfort despite parental intervention; and they may not respond positively to their caregiver's interventions. Their caregivers often do not feel reinforced or competent in meeting their child's needs, and the child's unresponsiveness may contribute to emotional withdrawal by the caregiver.

While mental retardation may have an organic origin, we must not presume that children with mental retardation, even at severe or profound levels, cannot form attachments. Most children with mental retardation have the same needs for nurturance and affection as do all children, even though their manner of expressing and responding to such nurturance may be different from that of typical children.

The long–term effects of early attachment problems on later adjustment and behavior are not fully understood. Several studies have found sufficient correlations between early attachment style and later behavior to suggest that children with maladaptive attachments are likely to have a wide variety of behavior problems during preschool and school–age [Lyons–Ruth 1993; Maccoby 1980; Levy & Orlans 1995]. Insecurely attached children are more often socially withdrawn, hesitant to participate in interactions and activities, and less curious. They are easily frustrated in response to problems, seldom ask for help, and may be hostile and aggressive toward other children.

However, caution in interpreting this data is warranted. For example, while Lyons–Ruth found that 71% of preschool children with serious hostile and aggressive behavior had been classified during infancy as "disorganized" in their attachments, this group of highly aggressive children represented only a small percentage of a larger group of children who had been classified as "disorganized" in their early attachments. Even grossly pathological care does not always result in the development of attachment disorders. Some children are known to form stable attachments and social relationships even in the face of marked neglect or abuse [American Psychiatric Association 1994]. An appropriate conclusion is that maladaptive attachment increases the likelihood of later emotional and behavior problems, but does not, by itself, always cause them.

Mussen et al. [1984] also suggests that while the general classifications of insecure attachment may be accurate, several factors may reduce accuracy in determining the attachment style of any individual child. These factors include cultural differences in the expression of attachment and emotion; children's temperament and their general vulnerability to anxiety; and whether the parent supports autonomous and self-reliant behavior in the infant, or is highly protective. As an example, if an infant failed to react to brief separation from the mother, and also failed to respond to her upon return, the infant would likely be classified as avoidant in attachment style. An alternative explanation might be that the infant is sufficiently autonomous and secure in his attachment not to be threatened by a brief separation. Or, the child may have attended day care and may be accustomed to being left by the parent. Mussen et al. [1984] also noted that children's attachment styles often varied during the first year, and the exhibition of certain "insecure" behaviors did not necessarily mean a child was insecurely attached. In order to accurately identify children with insecure attachments, the parent–child interaction should be observed over time, and in a variety of circumstances.

Research has also attempted to identify the relationship between caregiving behaviors of mothers and attachment outcomes in their infants. The results of these studies strongly link sensitive and responsive maternal caregiving with secure attachment in infants [Maccoby 1980; Mussen et al. 1984; Isabella 1993]. The precise relationships between other maternal styles and attachment outcomes are less well understood. Maternal rejection appears to be related to the development of avoidant attachment in infants. Rejecting mothers are often described as angry and hostile, controlling, and irritable. They may consistently oppose the infant's wishes, pervasively scold the infant, or forcibly interfere with the infant's activities [Ainsworth et al. 1978; Lyons–Ruth 1987]. Avoidant behavior by these infants is theorized to be a defensive and protective strategy. The determinants of resistant/ambivalent attachment are thought to include inconsistency and unpredictability in maternal behavior; that is, sensitive and responsive at times, and insensitive and unresponsive at others [Isabella 1993]. Maternal depression, hostility, and the presence of psychosocial problems appear to also increase the risk of disorganized–disoriented attachment [Lyons–Ruth et al. 1993].

In summary, the research suggests that maternal behavior is a potentially strong determinant of the nature of attachment in infants and children, but it is clearly not the only factor. However, the strong association between sensitive and reciprocal caregiving and healthy attachment would suggest that child welfare workers should promote the development of healthy attachment as often as possible. And, the high correlation of maladaptive attachment in samples of abused and neglected children would also suggest that we regularly intervene to help maltreating parents learn to relate in more sensitive and responsive ways with their children.

Application

ASSESSING AND PROMOTING SECURE ATTACHMENT

Child welfare workers should observe parents with their infants and young children to assess the quality of their caregiving behaviors, and should involve parents in learning more effective ways of meeting their children's needs.

The parental behaviors that promote secure attachment can be categorized as follows:

- The parent accurately recognizes the child's cues of distress and need, and quickly intervenes to provide comfort and remove stress.

- The parent provides the child with stimulation and initiates playful social interaction.

- The parent provides the child with contact comfort and closeness.

Each of these will be discussed separately, and specific parental interventions that promote secure attachment will be reviewed. While many of these activities will seem to be "common sense" to caseworkers who are parents themselves, it must be remembered that parents of maltreated children may need help in recognizing the importance of nurturant caregiving and in learning how to provide it.

1) The parent accurately recognizes the child's cues of distress and need, and quickly intervenes to provide comfort and remove stress.

Most parents quickly learn and respond to their children's expressions of need. Parents who have not experienced close attachments, or who lack parenting ability may need to be trained to recognize their children's cues, and to respond to them properly.

Crying usually indicates distress. Crying can have multiple meanings, and parents must learn how to differentiate them. According to Bowlby;

> Crying from hunger builds up slowly. When first heard it is of low intensity and arrhythmical; as time passes it becomes louder and rhythmical, an expiratory cry alternating with an inspiratory whistle. Crying from pain, on the other hand, is loud from the start. A sudden long and strong initial cry is followed by a long period of absolute silence, due to apnoea [lack of oxygen]; ultimately this gives way, and short gasping inhalations alternate with expiratory coughs [Bowlby 1969].

Fussiness is generally characterized by whimpering, wailing, and intermittent short cries. Eventually, this may progress to loud and constant crying. Fussiness can indicate early stages of hunger; discomfort because the baby has a wet or dirty diaper; indication that the baby is too cold or too hot; sleepiness (particularly if the baby has been awake for a while and rubs his eyes and face with fists);

or because the baby desires attention. The caregiver should respond to crying or fussiness in the following manner:

1) Check for the source of discomfort, including a wet or dirty diaper, or skin that is hot or cold to the touch. Parents should understand that for the first several weeks, newborns often cry when they are unclothed, and will stop crying as soon as they are dressed or wrapped in a blanket. The infant may, therefore, cry when being bathed or diapered. This is eventually outgrown.

2) Determine whether the infant is likely to be hungry, based on the length of time since the last feeding and the amount of food taken. (Some parents mistakenly believe that every time their infant cries, this indicates hunger.) If attempts to feed the infant do not quickly resolve the fussiness, the infant is likely not hungry. Spitting food out or turning the head away from the bottle or spoon also suggests the child is not hungry. It is important to help parents understand that an infant's refusal to take food does not indicate rebelliousness or stubbornness. Force feeding can result in unproductive struggles between the parent and infant.

3) Pick up the infant and hold him upright on the shoulder. If the crying stops immediately, the infant may have simply wanted a change of scenery, stimulation, or physical comfort. To stimulate a bored infant, moving to a different room, changing position, providing new toys or visual stimulation, playing music, or talking may settle him.

4) Bowlby [1969] suggests that when the infant is not hungry, cold, or in pain, the most effective terminators of crying are: a) the sound of the mother's voice; b) nonnutritive sucking (a pacifier, a nipple, or sometimes water or juice in a bottle); and c) walking or rocking the baby. When infants are rocked, crying often ceases. Bowlby also describes research that suggested that infants who are rocked before they become distressed are often content longer, and that periodic rocking can prevent later crying.

5) Parents must be taught to recognize signs of illness in the infant, including fever, congestion, and difficulty breathing.

Healthy infants also provide signals that they desire attention and personal interaction. For example, smiling signals an interest and a desire for social contact, and requires a reciprocal smile from the caregiver. Babbling also signals an interest in social contact, and requires that the caregiver talk to the infant or involve him in face to face interaction.

A loud vocalization to attract attention in a not–yet–verbal child, or calling "Maaaa"or "Daaaa," is a signal that the child wants attention, and desires a response from the caregiver. The parent can respond verbally by saying "What?" or "I'm right here." Sometimes moving into the child's field of vision, establishing eye contact, and talking briefly may placate the infant. Additional calling might require more focused attention, as well as some stroking of the child, talking for a minute, patting him, or playing briefly.

If the child raises her arms as the parent walks by, or after the child has locomoted toward the parent, this almost universally means "pick me up." After a brief period of cuddling and holding, the child can often be put back down and redirected.

2) *The parent provides the infant with stimulation and opportunities for playful social interaction.*

Interaction with the caregiver provides the infant with experiences that stimulate learning and strengthen attachment. Many activities can also be taught to older siblings. These activities include:

- The parent should place the infant in an infant seat or play pen, or on the floor on a blanket, so the infant can see and interact with family members. Generally, infants should be isolated only when sleeping or resting, or when they need quiet time or a reprieve from overstimulation.

- The parent should give the infant safe objects to explore, both visually and tactiley, including rattles, balls, colorful objects that the infant can transfer from hand to hand, blocks, crib toys and mobiles, bright and colorful pictures on the walls near the infant's bed, or other objects with interesting colors and shapes. Objects can have varying textures, such as sponge balls, fuzzy toys and blankets; and smooth, satiny cloths.

- The parent should initiate conversation with the infant and respond when he babbles. After the age of about three months, infants can be engaged in reciprocal vocalizing. The infant should be placed on his back, and the parent should make eye contact with him. The parent should smile and talk to the infant, then wait. The parent should keep prompting by talking to the infant. Eventually the infant will coo, babble, gurgle, or make some other vocalization when the parent's vocalizations stop. The parent then reinforces the infant's vocalizations by smiling, nodding, and saying things like, "Is that so?" "Tell me more," "Uh huh," "So what do you think?" or anything that comes to mind. Eventually, the infant will learn this reciprocal game and will find great pleasure in these "conversations."

- The parent should encourage play during regular caregiving activities, such as bathing, diaper changes, and dressing the infant. The parent can provide rubber toys in the bath; tickle the infant with the washcloth; or pour water from a cup onto the infant's tummy. Parents should use a face-to-face position, and talk with the infant while bathing and dressing her.

- The parent should address the infant with animation in the voice, and should avoid a monotone or harsh tones. The parent should vary the tone of voice and inflection to communicate interest and positive response. The caseworker can help the parent model and practice how to talk to an infant. It matters less what is said than how it is said. The worker can point out how infants will orient and attend to variations in expressiveness of the parent's voice.

- The parent should smile and encourage reciprocal smiling and laughing. Teach parents to play simple games, such as "patty cake" and "peek a boo," or to dance a toy or doll in front of the infant. After the infant is age six months, the parent can place a handkerchief or a light cloth over the infant's head for a few seconds, and then pull it off, and laugh. Older infants will learn to pull the cloth off themselves and laugh.

- Once the child has become mobile and can stand unassisted, the parent can encourage her to "dance" to music. The parent can model "dancing" by clapping hands, snapping fingers, swaying, moving, and taking the child's arms and moving them rhythmically. The parent can also dance, holding the child, being cautious not to overstimulate or bounce the child too heavily.

- After the child is nine months to one year old, learning words and names of objects is a game that can promote language development. The common "Where's your eyes? Here they are!" can be applied to almost all easily identifiable body parts (nose, mouth, ears, hands, feet, belly button). As the child begins to learn the names of objects, the game can be expanded to, "Where's the ball? Where's your bear?" A parent can also look at a magazine or book during quiet time with the child in her lap or sitting next to her, and can point out and name objects in the pictures. The parent can also help children develop language by commenting on the child's activities. For example, "You're sitting so quietly. Are you a happy baby?" "What a nice ball you have there." "Are you looking at the kitty? That's a nice kitty."

3) The parent provides the infant with contact comfort and closeness.

Parents should provide the infant with physical closeness and comfort in a manner that is consistent with the family's culture. Cultures differ in the degree of physical closeness that is appropriate. In many ways, western culture promotes more physical distance between parents and infants than do many other cultures. Consider the many societies in which infants are carried on their mother's backs (or fronts) in slings, or ride on her hip as the mother goes about her work. In many cultures, infants also sleep in the same bed with their mothers, both parents, or other siblings, until they are several years old.

Bowlby [1969] suggests that the need for physical proximity is innate. Infants universally approach their mothers, and follow them as soon as they are mobile. They often signal that they want to be picked up (the "arms up" behavior), or cry until they are held and cuddled.

Physical closeness can be promoted by the following:

- Keeping the infant in a playpen or infant seat in the same room with the mother, and frequently touching or gently patting.

- Laying the infant on the parent's lap while the parent is watching television, talking on the phone, reading, or sitting. The infant can also be placed next to the parent's lap on a couch or chair.

- Allowing a resting or sleepy infant to relax in the parent's arms; holding, cuddling, and rocking the infant. Or, bouncing the infant in the parent's lap, or holding the infant by the arms and standing her in the parent's lap.

- Holding the infant during feedings, or laying the infant on or next to the parent's lap. Feeding is an important time to promote attachment. Parents should not prop the infant's bottle in the crib and leave the room.

Parents may need help in recognizing the infant's cues regarding being held. Some infants, when busy or otherwise occupied, do not like the restriction of being held, and will protest, or wiggle or squirm to be put down. Some parents may experience this as rejection. The parent should be helped to learn to understand the infant's cues, and respond accordingly.

Caseworkers and other helpers can use several strategies to teach parents more effective caregiving skills, and to promote more secure attachment between parents and their infants and young children. These strategies include:

- While providing home-based services, caseworkers and homemakers can model more effective caregiving skills, and can provide guidance, coaching, support, and reassurance as parents try to learn and master these skills.

- Parents can be referred to infant stimulation programs, parent education programs, or parents-with-infants support groups offered through the child welfare agency or other local community agencies.

- Extended family members or volunteers (through church groups, community centers, etc.) can be engaged to work with parents and monitor the care of the child.

- If an infant or young child is in foster or kinship care placement, the foster or kinship caregiver can work directly with the parent in the placement setting. The substitute caregiver can model good caregiving, and can coach and support parents as they acquire these skills. Often, parents can eventually assume direct care of their infant in the placement setting. This is a valuable intervention to promote reunification.

- At times, parents' emotional problems may result in their ignoring or rejecting their infant. This is often the case in situations of failure to thrive. (See Section VI-B, "The Effects of Maltreatment on Infants and Toddlers," for a discussion of working with parents of failure to thrive infants.) The worker should assure that parents receive appropriate counseling in addition to training in parenting. At times, emotional problems may prevent parents from forming attachments to their children. Caseworkers should try to assure that these infants have regular access to a surrogate caregiver with whom they can form a strong attachment. This may be another family member who can assume primary care, active involvement of extended family members, or for children who cannot be protected at home, a foster, relative, or adoptive caregiver.

IDENTIFYING ATTACHMENT DISORDERS IN SCHOOL–AGE AND OLDER CHILDREN

With our recent acknowledgment of the relationship of maladaptive attachment to later behavioral and emotional disorders, there is a tendency to label any children with behavior problems that suggest failure to appropriately relate to others as having "attachment disorders." Zeanah [1993] suggests that professionals have oversimplified the construct of attachment, and have wrongly applied labels originally developed for infants (e.g., "insecure," "avoidant," and "ambivalent/resistant") to children of all ages, and in a wide variety of circumstances. Additionally, children may exhibit attachment difficulties to greater or lesser degrees, depending upon their early attachment history, the consistency of caregivers in their lives, their innate temperaments, and the extent of maltreatment or separation trauma they have experienced. Many of these children may exhibit ambivalence or insecurity in their relationships with caregiving adults, but not all of them have "attachment disorders."

There are, however, children with a particular complex of behaviors that suggest fundamental disorders in their social and emotional development. They appear unable to form and maintain emotionally close, reciprocal relationships with significant others. This pattern is often related to a history of severe maltreatment and/or separation. The Diagnostic and Statistical Manual of Mental Disorders, 4th Edition [American Psychiatric Association 1994] refers to this as Reactive Attachment Disorder of Infancy or Early Childhood. There are two typical manifestations of the disorder. Type I, the "Inhibited Type," appears to incorporate aspects of avoidant and ambivalent attachment. The children persistently fail to initiate or respond to social interactions in developmentally appropriate ways. These children are excessively inhibited, hypervigilant, and exhibit frozen watchfulness. They resist comfort or contact with others, or they show ambivalence, mixing approach and avoid responses. In Type II, the "Disinhibited Type," the primary characteristic is indiscriminate sociability, or a lack of selectivity in the choice of attachment figures. These children respond with apparently equal trust and affection to known caregivers or strangers, and are often overly familiar with strangers. Their affectionate overtures are often experienced as superficial, phony, or manipulative.

Both types have been associated with "grossly pathological care that may take the form of persistent disregard of the child's basic emotional needs for comfort, stimulation, and affection; persistent disregard of the child's basic physical needs; or repeated changes of primary caregiver that prevent formation of stable attachments" [American Psychiatric Association 1994].

Cline [1992] has done extensive therapeutic work with children and youth who have serious attachment problems. He describes many of the common characteristics of this disorder in school–age and adolescent children. Cline suggests these children are similar in many ways to character–disturbed adults, and without therapy, they often develop adult personality disorders. For example:

- They lack the ability to give and receive affection. They often do not allow themselves to be touched.

- They exhibit self–destructive behavior. They appear to "go out of their way to hurt themselves." Examples are: banging their heads repeatedly against a wall; burning themselves on objects they know to be hot; falling over on the pavement; or lighting matches and burning their own hands. They are often described as "fearless," and their behavior confounds their caregivers.

- They exhibit senseless cruelty toward others. They are mean and destructive. One attachment–disordered child tried to drown the family cat in the washing machine; another tried to set his younger sister's hair on fire.

- They are generally insincere and manipulative. The word "phony" is often used by both parents and professionals to describe this trait.

- They often steal toys, money, and objects, and gorge or hoard food and sweets.

- They may have speech difficulties. Speech may be frequently unclear, slurred, or mumbled. The content may be jumbled. Answers to questions may be particularly ambiguous.

- They have extreme control problems. This may, at times, be complicated by thought disorders. They may be demanding and obnoxious, willful, and unwilling to let others control their behavior. Major battles for control between these children and their caregivers often result.

- They have no long–term friends. Other children do not tolerate the willful lack of respect and cruelty that they receive from children with attachment disorders.

- They often demonstrate abnormalities in eye contact. Eye contact may be very intense or absent altogether.

- They are often preoccupied with blood, fire, and gore. They exhibit intense rage, often act as if they are "at war with the world." Many perceive themselves as inherently bad, and have been reported to identify themselves as evil.

- They exhibit superficial attractiveness and friendliness with strangers. They may appear attractive, winsome, bright, and loving; helpless, hopeless, and lost; or promising, creative, and intelligent; whichever front suits their needs at the time.

- They commonly lie in the face of absolute reality, often described as "bold–faced" lying. They lie even when they are caught in the middle of an act. One parent caught her son with his hands in her purse, taking money. She told him to leave her purse alone. He said emphatically, "I haven't touched your purse." Another mother told her son to let go of the dog's tail, and he said, "What dog?"

- They may exhibit various types of learning disorders. Some are thought to have underlying organic or neurological deficits, perhaps exacerbated by early deprivation [Cline 1992].

Cline also suggests that adults with reactive attachment disorders often retain the characteristics seen in children. The primary signs are lack of affectionate response to intimates; underlying rage and hate; a tendency to victimize others, while perceiving themselves to be the victim; chronic lying; superficiality of responses; an overlying charm; and destructiveness toward other adults. They lack conscience. They are frequently classified as having antisocial or borderline personality disorders.

THERAPEUTIC INTERVENTIONS FOR CHILDREN WITH ATTACHMENT PROBLEMS

From a therapeutic point of view, children with diagnosed attachment disorders, who have experienced consistently negative caregiving, and who have never experienced a positive attachment, are the most difficult to help. Treatment requires highly skilled, planful, intrusive, and consistent therapeutic interventions. Children whose attachments are insecure and ambivalent, but who have some prior experiences with positive attachment, are often easier to help. These children may benefit, in time, from permanence and consistently nurturant caregiving, although concurrent therapy may also be indicated.

Fahlberg [1991] suggests a variety of interventions that can strengthen children's attachments with their caregivers. Her strategies are referred to as the "arousal–relaxation cycle," the "positive interaction cycle," and "positive claiming." These strategies can be implemented by children's caregivers, or by therapists. While not always easy to implement, they have been shown to be successful in helping children with attachment problems.

The Arousal–Relaxation Cycle

This intervention is, simply, the parental response to a child in need, and relief of tension or stress for the child. This need–meeting behavior is one of the strong determinants of secure attachment in infants. The goal with the older child is the same. Caregivers are continually alert for signs that the child is experiencing distress. The child may communicate a need through cues such as crying, vocalization, and other expressions of unhappiness or discomfort. However, some children do not outwardly communicate their distress, and the caregivers must learn to read subtle cues that these children are in need. A child's need state is often accompanied by tension and anxiety. The relief of tension and anxiety that occurs when the need is met leads to contentment and comfort. Fahlberg suggests that the repeated, successful completion of this cycle promotes the development of trust, security, and attachment.

Lisa, age seven, provides a good example of a child who responded well to this intervention. Lisa had endured sexual abuse and several separations prior to her placement in a foster home. She exhibited charming superficiality in her attachments, combined with avoidant and pseudo–independent behavior. Typically, she did not signal her caregivers that she needed help. For example, Lisa would hurt herself playing, whimper quietly to herself, reject offers of help, then continue as if nothing had happened. Her foster mother understood how Lisa's background had contributed to her emotional distance, and she sought opportunities to nurture and care for Lisa. When Lisa hurt herself, the foster mother didn't ask permission to help her. She approached Lisa gently, refusing to be rejected or pushed away. She talked soothingly, wiped off Lisa's wounds, administered first aid when necessary, ignored Lisa's protests, and hugged her briefly before sending her off to play. Soon, Lisa's "injuries" became more frequent, and less serious, and she began to cue her foster mother when she was hurt, often by crying loudly and running into the house. The foster mother found herself tending to numerous miniscule injuries, but she recognized that Lisa had learned not to "fear the helper," and she continued to nurture her to reinforce this behavior. Eventually, the foster mother was able to help Lisa understand she could ask for hugs and attention without hurting herself first, and to trust that such contact was not the precursor of abusive behavior by a caregiver.

Fahlberg also suggests that intervening in a positive, soothing, and supportive way after a child has had an intense, emotional outburst, such a temper tantrum, or when the child is experiencing intense anxiety or depression, takes advantage of a brief period when the child is emotionally vulnerable and, therefore, more open to intervention. The adult's availability to provide emotional support, and to encourage the child to express feelings encourages the development of attachment.

Scott, age six, had been placed for adoption as an infant. The adoption was disrupted when Scott was five, and he was placed in foster care. The worker was able to ascertain that the adoptive family had never bonded to Scott, that they had frequently ignored him, and that he had often been locked in a room for hours at a time. When he began soiling, they decided to return him to the agency. Scott showed serious emotional and behavioral problems, and very disturbed attachment. He would approach the foster mother for affection, then change his mind and fight her; yet, he would scream in a panic if she left the house for even a short period of time. He would reject all attempts at affection. Scott had violent, raging tantrums, during which he would kick, scream, and roll on the floor. The foster mother learned that, when the worst of the tantrum was over, she could cradle Scott and rock him for 15 minutes or more while he settled, and he would not fight her. In this manner, she was able to begin to establish a more nurturant relationship with him. In time, when he was sleepy or distressed, he began to climb onto her lap on his own.

The Positive Interaction Cycle

When children with secure attachments meet new people, they often begin to establish a relationship through play and social interaction. In the positive interaction cycle, the caregiver promotes attachment by involving a child in pleasurable social interactions, such as playing, establishing eye contact, vocalization (singing, talking, cooing, reading), and other pleasurable contacts. Social attachment may be less threatening than physical affection or emotional intimacy. In time, the child may learn to trust the adult.

David, age two, had also been disrupted from adoptive placement as an infant. He appeared to have suffered severe emotional rejection. He avoided contact with people, and he rejected all overtures from his caregivers. He eventually developed a perfunctory relationship with his foster mother. He allowed her to feed, dress, and comfort him, but he did not reciprocate. He would have nothing to do with his new caseworker, and he ran and hid whenever she approached. The worker spent several weeks establishing a relationship with David by engaging him to play with her. She initially rewarded him with smiles for eye contact. She handed him interesting objects, which he took from her, and then quickly ran away. She talked to him, assuming he was listening, even though he did not respond. Eventually he was engaged to roll a ball with her and to play with other toys. After several weeks, the worker was able to take him into the yard, for a walk down the block, and then, for a ride in the car. David eventually developed sufficient trust to let the worker hold him, and to turn to the worker for support when he was frightened. Because of this trust, he was able to use the worker for support during his subsequent adoptive placement. His adoptive family used similar strategies during preplacement visits to strengthen his attachment to them before he was placed. The worker also made sure that he was firmly established in his adoptive home before she began to slowly reduce her contacts, and eventually terminate her relationship with him.

Claiming Behavior

Claiming behaviors are parental responses that communicate that a child is part of the family, belongs in a special relationship with family members, and is valued by other people. Claiming behaviors include: introducing the child to others as a member of the family; consciously including reference to the child in family histories; giving the child a special role or responsibility in family traditions; including the child in important family events; including the child's pictures in the family picture album; and other behaviors that clearly identify the child as belonging to the family.

Most healthy families engage in all three types of interactions as part of day-to-day life. Parents in abusing or neglecting families may need to be taught how to respond to their children in ways that promote attachment. The parents may, themselves, need to be helped to develop positive attachments with others. Often, the caseworker can help parents learn trust and confidence in other people through the casework relationship.

Professional help by therapists who are skilled in treating attachment disorders should be sought for children who demonstrate severe attachment problems, and for children who do not respond over time to attachment-strengthening interventions by their caregivers [See Cline 1992; Levy & Orlans 1995; Pinderhughes & Rosenberg 1990].

B. The Effects of Traumatic Separation on Children

Conceptual Framework

All of us have experienced separations during our lives, and we often remember these experiences as stressful, painful, and traumatic. Death, relocation, the emancipation of children, the dissolution of a close relationship, and other typical life experiences involve separation from persons, places, and things that are important to us. Most people experience similar feelings in response to separation: sadness, depression, or despair, often accompanied by anger, anxiety and fear, loneliness, and in some instances, a loss of self-esteem or direction. Some separations remain vivid in our memories, despite the passage of many years.

However, not all separations are equally distressing. By understanding the variables that contribute to traumatic separation, we can gain insight into why the separation of children from their families is potentially one of the most damaging and traumatic of all separation experiences.

One critical variable in determining the degree of trauma associated with separation is the significance of the lost person or persons. The stronger the relationship with the person(s) we have lost, the greater the likelihood of trauma. For this reason, the loss of a parent is the most traumatic separation a child can experience.

The extent of trauma is also affected by whether the separation is temporary or permanent. Temporary separations, while distressing, are rarely as painful as the permanent loss of a loved one. Many people are able to cope with even lengthy separations, if they are certain that the separation will not be permanent. While most separations in child placement are considered "temporary" by the placing agency, in the young child's mind, a few weeks is eons, and a few months is permanent. Children in lengthy substitute care may react to separation from their families as if it were final.

Third, if we perceive ourselves to be responsible for the separation through something we did or did not do, normal feelings of loss are exacerbated by feelings of guilt and self-recrimination. This increases emotional distress and trauma. Young children do not have the cognitive maturity to understand the reasons for placement, and complicated explanations about their parents' problems make no sense to them. Children often believe themselves to be at fault, and they often interpret separation as a punishment for some misdeed or wrongdoing. Many children firmly believe, and often express, that they were unwanted by their families and "sent away" because they were "bad."

The availability of other significant people to provide support and comfort during a separation experience can lessen its traumatic effects. Supportive relationships help an individual cope during a period of grieving, and can help temper feelings of loneliness and isolation. By contrast, the absence of such supports may exacerbate emotional distress and despair. When children are placed in agency foster homes, they are likely to be separated from many significant people, including extended family members, siblings, friends, and neighbors. Their usual sources of support and comfort are not available to them. This underscores the importance of placing children who must be removed from their families with relatives or other caregivers whom they know and trust, if we are to minimize separation trauma.

CHILDREN'S RESPONSES TO SEPARATION

Children often experience the separation associated with placement both as a loss, and as a physical and emotional threat to themselves and their families, and they respond to these threats and losses in typical ways. An understanding of this helps us put the child's experiences during placement into a relevant perspective.

Children in placement fear the unknown, and are anxious about potential personal harm. Initially, they worry whether they will be fed, clothed, sheltered, and protected. Some verbalize concern that they may die without their families to care for them. They can experience a type of "culture shock," similar to that experienced by adults who relocate to a foreign country. They must leave behind everything that is familiar and predictable, and must adapt to an entirely new environment and family culture, with many different rules and customs, and sometimes with a different language. They often feel out of place and fear being ridiculed or ignored. Children in placement often feel abandoned, angry at having been forced into a frightening situation, helpless, and hopeless.

The intensity of trauma experienced by young children in placement can be partially explained by considering their level of development. There are many things that adults have learned from experience and take for granted that children do not understand. Young children's cognition is egocentric and very concrete, and as a result they have a limited ability to understand the activities and events around them. Their limited perspective greatly increases their anxiety about even small changes. For example, in the car on the way to a preplacement visit, five-year-old Lisa anxiously asked her social worker whether the new family had a bathroom at their house. Her worker was surprised by the question at first, considered it from Lisa's point of view, and appreciated her concern.

Consider the confusion and anxiety experienced by a seven year old who was fed a pork chop and spinach for the first time in his foster home. For this child, eating spinach was like eating seaweed. When his foster mother told him he had to eat it, and assured him it was good for him, this only increased his anxiety.

A third child who was placed in a new home remembered that whenever he hurt his knee, his grandmother had some special medicine to make it better. He was worried because his grandmother, and the medicine, were not at the new home. He was concerned about what would happen the next time he hurt himself. Naturally, as a child, he did not understand that antibiotic ointment is common in most medicine cabinets.

When children go into a new home, the basic rules and expectations for behavior may be very different from those of their family. This is especially true if they are placed in a foster family of a different ethnicity, culture, or socioeconomic level. Differences in these behavioral expectations may confuse children. They may not understand what is appropriate behavior, nor why they are being disciplined. Concurrently, foster families may misinterpret the meaning and intent of children's behavior. This may increase the breach in their relationship, and can affect children's other social interactions and self-esteem.

Children in placement often wonder what will happen to their families while they are gone. They may imagine their families to be dead, moved away, or maybe that their families have forgotten them. They may worry that their families are looking for them, but don't know how or where to find them. They may despair of ever seeing their families again. This is accentuated when visits and other contacts with family members are infrequent.

Furthermore, children in placement are often frightened by their own anger. They believe they will be, and in fact often are, reprimanded for their angry behaviors. Many children learn that suppression of angry feelings is necessary, if they are to survive in the new home. The unexpressed anger may emerge in negative behaviors, or in subversive and passive aggressive ways.

In summary, the separation experience during placement is painful and potentially overwhelming for children. It is often difficult for adults to assume young children's perspective, but it is essential to do so to understand their perceptions of threat and loss. Caseworkers must be continually aware of the magnitude of the changes children experience when placed, the ways in which children's limited development can increase stress, and how these changes can contribute to the trauma experienced by these children.

CONCEPTS OF CRISIS INTERVENTION IN SEPARATION AND PLACEMENT

Traumatic separation and placement create a high risk of clinical crisis for children and their families. Caseworkers must understand and consider the dynamics of crisis when developing placement plans and strategies in order to prevent crisis and its potentially damaging consequences.

Crisis is the predictable emotional state that results when people are subjected to overwhelming and unmanageable stresses. Several theorists [Lindemann 1965; Parad 1965; Caplan 1965; Hill 1965; Rapoport 1965] have contributed to the development of crisis theory. Crisis theory suggests that much human behavior is directed toward maintaining physical and emotional equilibrium (homeostasis). When problems or events (stressors) occur which lead to an upset in this steady emotional state, people engage in a series of actions and behaviors (coping), to resolve the problem and to reestablish their psychological equilibrium. Crisis may result when coping strategies cannot resolve the stress, and equilibrium cannot be restored. Crisis theory also contends that not all events are universally stressful; the personal meaning of the event to the individual (perception) influences the degree to which the event is experienced as stressful. Each of these three contributors to crisis–stress, coping, and the perception of the event –will be examined individually.

Stress

Stress is usually precipitated by a change in life circumstances, including a change in the environment, in interpersonal relationships, in the family, or in individual health or development. Some events involving significant change are universally stressful and create a situation of potential crisis for most people.

These include death of a spouse, close family member, or close friend; marital separation or divorce; serious illness or personal injury; and environmental disasters. Normally, the extent of any stress is related to the magnitude of its associated change. For example, a tornado that uproots trees in the yard is considerably less stressful than one that destroys the house, and moving across the country is usually more stressful than moving across town.

Coping

Our most effective coping responses can be categorized as constructive problem solving. These responses include assessing and accurately judging the extent of the problem or situation, seeking and using appropriate problem–solving strategies, using resources and support systems, and engaging in activities that directly address and overcome the problem and restore equilibrium. When these strategies successfully mitigate the stressful situation, crisis is averted. When an individual lacks the coping responses to master and overcome a stressful situation, crisis often results.

Perception of the Event

The same or similar events may be perceived quite differently by different people, or by the same person at different times. The individual's perception of the event greatly affects the degree to which stress is experienced.

Crisis intervention theory has described three ways events may be interpreted, and the predictable emotional responses to each. If the event is perceived as a loss, or potential loss, the typical emotional response is depression; and, the greater the perceived loss, the greater the depression and stress. If the event is perceived or interpreted to be a threat, or a potential threat, the predictable emotional response is anxiety; and, the more significant the perceived threat, the greater the anxiety and stress. By contrast, if the event is perceived or interpreted as a challenge, and the individual believes himself or herself capable of avoiding a situation of significant loss or threat, the predictable emotional response is a mobilization of energy, and activity directed toward resolving the stressful situation.

Whether crisis develops in a potentially stressful situation depends upon the interrelationship of these three factors. Generally, low levels of stress, effective coping ability, and a realistic and accurate perception of the event tend to prevent the development of crisis. Conversely, high stress, poor or limited coping ability, and a distorted or inaccurate perception of the event increase the likelihood of crisis. People who have strong coping responses, and an accurate perception of the event, can often withstand significant stress without experiencing crisis. Other people, whose coping resources are limited, or who have grossly distorted perceptions of the event, can become prone to crisis in situations of little stress.

CHILD PLACEMENT: PROCLIVITY FOR CRISIS

When we assess child placement within the framework of crisis intervention, it is easy to understand why children are so prone to crisis as a result of traumatic separation. Children placed into substitute care are typically subjected to pervasive changes and high levels of stress. Concurrently, their cognitive and developmental immaturity not only reduces their internal coping abilities, but also contributes to an inaccurate and distorted interpretation of the placement experience.

Children experience many losses when they are placed. In addition to losing their parent(s), they may also lose siblings, grandparents and extended family members, teachers, neighbors, and friends. They are separated from meaningful places and objects including their house, toys, pets, beds, clothes, schools, churches, and neighborhoods. They are placed into new environments, which may be totally foreign to them, especially when different in culture, ethnicity, or socioeconomic level from their own families. Their sense of identity and belonging may be threatened. They often experience a complete and total life change.

Separation from known and trusted adults, especially parents, deprives children of their customary means of coping with stress. Children do not have well-developed internal problem–solving abilities. They depend on adults to meet their needs, and to solve problems for them. Without these supports, children experience severe anxiety and depression in situations of stress.

Children's developmental immaturity also affects their understanding of and emotional reaction to the stresses of placement. Children's immature perspectives of causality and time, their limited language ability, their egocentric thinking, and other developmentally determined cognitive limitations make it much more difficult for them to understand the complex realities of separation and placement. Children are very likely to have distorted perceptions regarding the reasons for separation and placement, the causes, who is to blame, and the expected outcomes.

Child welfare workers should become aware of emotional responses and behaviors that typically indicate that a child is experiencing stress related to separation and placement. The presence of these behaviors is an important diagnostic clue that can help the worker gauge the child's distress, and plan supportive interventions. Careful monitoring for "stress overload" is the most effective way to prevent crisis for children in placement.

THE STAGES OF GRIEVING

Clinicians have identified a series of stages, referred to as the grief or mourning process, which are commonly associated with loss, and which may be exhibited by children who have been separated from their families [Kubler–Ross 1972; Fahlberg 1979]. These are as follows:

Stage I: Shock/Denial

People in shock or denial appear compliant and disconnected from the event, as if the loss were of little significance. They often verbally deny the event ("No, it isn't true. I can't believe it. This isn't really happening.") Or, they may admit the event cognitively, but deny the feelings that accompany the event. Affect is muted and flat, and there may be little emotional expression. People in this stage may be described as "robot-like," "stunned," "shell shocked," or "dazed." The stage generally lasts from a few hours to several days.

Stage II: Anger/Protest

At this stage, the impact of the loss can no longer be denied, and the first emotional response is usually anger. Anger may be diffuse and directionless, or may be directed at the lost person or persons, at themselves, at God, fate, or at whomever or whatever is believed responsible for the loss. Guilt, blame, recriminations, protest, and other behaviors associated with anger are common.

Stage III: Bargaining

Typical behavior during this stage of grieving appears to be a final attempt to regain control and, if possible, to regain that which was lost. To the degree that people feel themselves responsible for the loss, they may resolve to change their behavior and to "do better from now on." They may try to bargain with whomever is thought to have power to change the situation. In child placement, this power may be attributed to the caseworker, the foster caregiver, or the agency.

The bargaining need not be this concrete, however. The process often has a magical quality. A person may come to feel and believe that a certain way of behaving or thinking will reverse the loss, regardless of its illogic. For example, a child may believe that by washing his face every day, or by being helpful to the foster mother, he can bring about a reunion with his family.

Stage IV: Depression

This stage is characterized by expressions of despair and futility, with or without episodes of fear and panic; listlessness; withdrawal; and a generalized lack of interest in people, surroundings, or activities. The despair is deep, and people in this stage often cannot be comforted. The loss is fully perceived as "real," and irrevocable, with devastating personal consequences.

Stage V: Resolution

Most people cannot tolerate intense psychic pain for extended periods of time. If previous relationships and attachments have been strong and positive, people at this stage will usually direct their behavior toward the development or strengthening of other relationships. They also begin to invest more emotional energy toward planning the future, and less in ruminating about the past. The final stage of grieving ends when they become actively involved in the present, and in new relationships. Adaptive energy is redirected toward compensation and reintegration.

CONSEQUENCES OF UNRESOLVED EMOTIONAL DISTRESS

It is evident that separating children from their parents can have multiple harmful effects upon their emotional well-being. The more traumatic or numerous the separations, the more likely there will be significant negative psychological consequences. Repeated traumatic separations can have long-term negative developmental consequences as well.

When child welfare caseworkers remove children from their families, the attachment of these children to their parents and to other significant persons is disrupted. These traumatic separations can interfere with the development of healthy attachments, and can affect children's ability and willingness to become involved in relationships in the future. Children who have suffered traumatic separations from their parents may also display low self-esteem and a general distrust of others. This is particularly true if they perceive themselves as having been abandoned, unwanted, or somehow responsible for the separation.

Children who have inadequate emotional support are often overwhelmed during the placement process. Littner [1956] contends that children who are emotionally overwhelmed during separation must psychologically repress their painful feelings, because they lack other ways of handling them. Littner states that the penalty of repression on a child's subsequent personality development may be severe.

> Repression bottles up the various impulses and prevents their full expression. It makes necessary the maintenance of unrealistic, childhood-derived behavior patterns. It freezes psychological energy that would otherwise be available for meeting and mastering new life situations. It reduces the child's emotional flexibility, and prevents him from functioning at his full physical, intellectual, and emotional capacities [Littner 1956].

When children remain in placement for extended periods of time, they remain in an emotional limbo. They cannot reverse the loss by returning home; nor can they fully grieve the loss and reestablish themselves in new families and communities. The unresolved nature of this situation can create emotional chaos for children, with chronic mood swings from hope to anger to despair, and back again. Most children in placement expend considerable emotional energy trying simply to manage their feelings.

Without frequent contact with family members, young children may grieve their loss and develop strong attachments to new caregivers. Infants and preschool children may do this within a few months, school-age children within a year. Unfortunately, many children remain in substitute care for longer than this. It is therefore likely that children in "temporary" care for long periods of time will suffer another painful separation from their substitute care families when they are returned to their own families, or to an adoptive family or other permanent home.

This does not imply that children should be frequently moved to different substitute care homes to prevent attachment! Some child welfare practitioners continue to adhere to the belief that if reattachment is prevented through frequent moves, children will not suffer the distress of separation. Unfortunately, this belief has persisted for many years in spite of its inherent disastrous consequences for children, and the repeated admonitions of child advocates that it be abandoned. This practice presumes that children are capable of comfortably suspending all meaningful involvement with adults for periods of time, depending only upon themselves, and then becoming reinvolved with adults "when the time is right." Children cannot turn attachment on and off like a water faucet, nor can they remain "emotionally suspended without human objects to love and depend upon—much as a trapeze artist might be expected to leave one hanging bar and remain in the air some time before grasping the next" [Gerard & Dukette 1953].

It is not surprising that children who have experienced repeated traumatic separations often become permanently damaged. Generalized cognitive and language delays, attachment disorders, sociomoral immaturity, and inadequate social skills are highly correlated with early traumatic separation. These children may be subject to chronic mood disorders such as depression and anxiety. Many adults with a clinical diagnosis of personality disorder experienced repeated traumatic separations in their early lives. Their behavior is often characterized by dependent or manipulative relationships, and an absence of social conscience, concern, empathy, or intimacy.

Once workers fully understand the potentially traumatic and harmful effects of separation and placement, they should find themselves with a renewed conviction that the best possible outcome of protective services would be for children to be protected and nurtured in their own homes. This belief is consistent with the values of family–centered practice, and also provides considerable impetus for the development and provision of intensive, in–home services to the family.

A commitment to family–centered practice would appear to make placement decisions much easier. In fact, many cases are more difficult because of our commitment to preserve families and protect children from the trauma of separation and placement. In many families, potential risk of harm is not easy to quantify. Workers will struggle with the difficult choice of leaving children at home with supportive services, and potentially subjecting them to increased risk of maltreatment; or, removing them and subjecting them to almost certain trauma from the separation in order to assure their safety. This is one of the most fundamental dilemmas of child welfare casework. There will always be children who cannot be protected at home, even with intensive services, and who must be placed to assure their protection. In addition, there are many children who have been subjected to repeated and traumatic separations from their families before coming to the attention of the agency, and do not have a family with whom to reunify.

To meet the needs of all these children, we must be committed to achieving permanence as quickly as possible. When appropriate, these children should be helped to maintain an attachment to their families and be reunified with them as quickly as possible. If reunification is not possible, then a carefully planned and executed separation and prompt placement into a permanent family environment should be achieved.

We must also be highly skilled in the technology of child placement to prevent crisis, and to help children manage and master the placement experience with the least amount of distress and pain. Placement strategies that prevent crisis and provide the maximum support to children are more fully discussed in Section VIII-C, "Placement Strategies to Prevent Trauma."

Application

A caseworker who fully understands the normal development of children will be able to devise appropriate placement strategies that can help to minimize the trauma inherent in separation and placement.

Listed below are important developmental characteristics of children at various ages, and the implications of these developmental variables for children during separation and placement. The characteristics listed here are typical for normally developing children. However, children who have been abused or neglected are often delayed in their cognitive, social, and emotional development. The caseworker should identify each child's developmental age and should plan interventions accordingly.

INFANCY: BIRTH TO TWO YEARS

Cognitive Development

- Infants have not developed object permanence; when things are out of sight they are gone! Even temporary losses of significant caregivers are experienced as total. Infants cannot comprehend that their caregiver "will be right back."

- Infants have a short attention span and poor memory.

- Infants do not understand change; they only feel its disconcerting effects. Without an understanding of events, they are easily frightened by environmental changes and unfamiliar sensory experiences, sights, noises, and people.

- Infants lack language ability and, therefore, have few means to communicate their needs or distress to others, except by crying. They also cannot be verbally reassured that they will be cared for.

Emotional Development

- Infants are fully dependent upon others for physical care and nurturance to meet their basic survival needs.

- Infants generally form strong and trusting emotional attachments to their primary caregiver and turn to that person when in need. Their scope of trusting relationships is very limited. After five to six months, infants can easily discriminate between people, display anxiety in the presence of unknown persons, and often cannot be comforted by others when distressed.

- Infants often experience anxiety in the face of even small changes. Emotional stability depends upon familiarity and continuity in the environment, and the continued presence of their primary caregiver.

Social Development

- Without language, infants have few ways to communicate their distress or needs. Most communications are nonverbal. If adults are not familiar with infants' cues, and do not recognize or understand the source of their distress, their needs may remain unmet.

- Social attachments are limited to infants' immediate caregivers and close family members. Infants do not easily engage in relationships with unfamiliar persons. Adults must generally initiate and reinforce interactions. Infants also vary in the speed with which they will interact and be comfortable with strangers. Many infants are temperamentally cautious, and need considerable time to become comfortable in the presence of new people, much less turn to them when distressed.

Implications for Separation and Placement

- Infants' cognitive limitations greatly increase their experience of stress. Without a well-developed cognitive perception of the event, any change is threatening. Infants will be extremely distressed simply by changes in the environment, and the absence of trusted caregivers.

- Infants have few internal coping skills. Adults must protect and provide for them by eliminating their distress, and meeting all of their needs. When deprived of the trusted, familiar adults upon whom they depend, they are more vulnerable to the effects of internal and external stresses.

- Infants experience the absence of caregivers as immediate, total and complete. Infants do not generally turn to others for help and support in the absence of their primary caregiver. Infants who have lost their primary caregiver often cannot be comforted by a caseworker, foster parent, or others.

- If traumatic separation occurs during the first year, it can interfere with the development of basic trust. This has serious implications for the infant's subsequent development of interpersonal attachments.

- Infants who are easily frightened by change and new people may react more strongly and exhibit more distress than a placid, more adaptable infant. This does not mean, however, that less temperamental infants do not experience severe distress during the placement process.

- Infants' distress during placement will be lessened if their environment is familiar or can be made very consistent with their old one. Caseworkers should also assess infants' attachments to adults, and should identify persons with whom infants have the strongest attachment. This is not always the parent; it may be an extended family member, a neighbor, or a babysitter. In the best situation, an infant's regular caregiver should visit frequently, preferably daily, and provide direct care in the placement setting.

- Seriously abused or neglected infants may appear to have no secure attachments with any caregiver. Infants who have not developed attachments, or who have insecure attachments, may not exhibit distress when placed. These infants will often be remote and withdrawn. Such attachment disorders should be of considerable concern to workers, as they indicate these children are at serious risk developmentally. Placement planning for children with attachment disorders should include the identification of primary caregivers, who can be a constant in the children's lives. Continuity in relationships with trusted caregivers will promote the development of basic trust.

- If the plan is to reunite infants with their families, parents should be included in all phases of placement and permanency planning, and the parent/child relationship should be maintained through regular visitation while the infant is in placement. Similarly, when infants are placed from foster care into adoptive families, the foster caregivers should remain actively involved until the infants are securely attached and fully integrated into their adoptive homes. This "transitional" approach to placement prevents the total disruption of critical attachments for infants, and can help to prevent the serious negative consequences of traumatic separation on development [Gerard & Dukette 1953]. The consistent involvement of a nurturing caregiver is essential to promote the development of healthy attachment. Once it has developed, separating an infant from his or her primary caregiver should be approached with extreme caution.

PRESCHOOL: TWO TO FIVE YEARS

Cognitive Development

- Preschool children use language to communicate, but they have a limited vocabulary, and do not understand complicated words or concepts. Many thoughts or feelings cannot be fully expressed. This makes it difficult for them to understand complex events or to fully communicate their concerns and distress.

- Preschool children do not have a well-developed understanding of time. They cannot discriminate between "next week," "next month," and "next year."

- They have difficulty understanding causality and are often unable to discern how events relate to one another, to explain why things happen, or to predict what may happen next.

- They are cognitively egocentric. They are not able to understand perspectives that are different from their own. The world is as they perceive it. Other people's explanations of events may make no sense to them, and they will stubbornly cling to their own perceptions and explanations. Their logic may be faulty by adult standards but seems rational to them.

- Preschool children may display magical thinking and fantasy to explain events, and may believe that their actions or thoughts have exaggerated effects on events in their environment.

- They may not generalize their experiences in one situation to another. They may be unable to draw logical, even obvious, conclusions from their experiences. For example, despite the fact that his house and all his friends' houses have kitchens, a child may still doubt the existence of a kitchen in the foster home until he sees it for himself.

Emotional Development

- Preschool children are still dependent on adults to meet their emotional and physical needs. The loss of adult support leaves them feeling alone, vulnerable, and anxious.

- Development of autonomy and a need for self-assertion and control make it extremely frustrating for children this age to have limits and restrictions imposed by others. When thwarted by adults, they are likely to create and engage in battles with adults to maintain some degree of control.

Social Development

- Preschool children are beginning to relate to peers in reciprocal, cooperative, and interactive play.

- They relate to adults in playful ways, and are capable of forming attachments with adults other than parents. They can turn to other adults to meet their needs.

- "Good" and "bad" acts are defined by their immediate, personal consequences. Children who are bad are punished; children who are good are rewarded. Self-esteem is often influenced by how "good" children believe they are.

Implications for Separation and Placement

- Preschool children are still essentially dependent and have limited coping abilities. They need dependable adults to help them manage day-to-day events. However, emotionally healthy children of this age can turn to substitute caregivers or to known and trusted caseworkers for help and support during the placement process. Having a relationship with an adult in the new home prior to placement also helps to reduce the stress of placement.

- Preschool children will display considerable anxiety about their new home. Because they are still unable to make logical inferences from much of their experience, preschool children may be unable to predict the seemingly obvious. Therefore, any change in environment can have exaggerated ambiguity, and be ominous and foreboding. They will be concerned about being cared for, but may not have adequate language to express the concerns in detail. Their insecurity may be expressed with questions such as, "Do they have bandages at their house? Does their dog bite?" They need reassurance that they will be fed, clothed, and that the new family will care for them when they are sick. While verbal reassurances are helpful, children will often not be comfortable until they actually experience the environment as safe and nurturing.

- Due to their immature conception of time, any placement of more than a few weeks is experienced by preschool children as permanent. Without frequent contact with their parents, these children may assume that their parents are gone and are not coming back. They may abandon hope relatively quickly, grieve the loss, and attempt to establish a permanent place for themselves in the substitute care home. This makes reunification at a later time, at best, another traumatic separation, and at worst, impossible.

- Preschool children are very likely to have an inaccurate and distorted perception of the placement experience and the reasons for their placement. They may feel personally responsible for the family disruption. Many children view separation and placement as a punishment for bad behavior. Egocentric thinking limits preschool children's ability to understand the reasons for placement. That they had to leave home because someone else (their parent) had a problem is beyond their conceptual capabilities. Children this age will cling to their own explanation for the placement, despite attempts by adults to explain otherwise. This self-blame threatens children's self-esteem and increases their anxiety.

- Forced placement without proper preparation may generate feelings of helplessness and loss of control. This may interfere with the development of self-directed, autonomous behavior. Children this age may learn that they cannot influence the environment, and may become placid and unassertive; or, they may become engaged in a power struggle with adults in an attempt to assert and assure their autonomy.

- Because preschool children do not fully understand the reasons for the placement, they often perceive the absence of their parents as abandonment, and they learn to expect abandonment in other relationships. They often express concern about the new family leaving them, or about having to move again; they are also anxious about whether the caseworker will return for them. Caseworkers are often these children's only perceived link to their family and prior life, and for this reason, the workers can take on extreme importance to them. The children's anxiety about abandonment is exacerbated if the caseworkers who conduct their placement "disappear" from their lives, which often occurs when the case is transferred after placement. The need to maintain continuity in all these children's relationships, including the casework relationship, cannot be stressed enough. A continuous parade of new faces in their lives is disruptive, and seriously damaging to their emotional development.

School–Age (Six to Nine Years)

Cognitive Development

- School-age children have developed cognitively to the stage of concrete operations. They understand cause and effect, and can often discern logical relationships between events. They will, however, have difficulty understanding abstract relationships. "Your mother placed you for adoption because she loved you and wanted the best for you," is a difficult concept for children to understand. In their concrete view of reality, people don't give away things they love.

- School-age children have developed some perspective–taking ability. They can, at times, understand other people's feelings and needs, and they are beginning to understand that things happen to them which are not their fault.

- School-age children usually experience the world in concrete terms. They are most comfortable if their environment is clearly structured, if they understand the rules about how things should be done, and if they have a clear definition of what is right and wrong. They are concerned with fairness, and often have difficulty accepting ambiguity, or changes in previously defined rules.

- School-age children have a better perspective regarding time than do younger children, and are able to differentiate between days and weeks, but still cannot fully comprehend longer time periods, such as months or years. A school year is often perceived as an eternity.

Emotional Development

- Children this age are performers. Their self–esteem is strongly affected by how well they do in their daily activities, in school, and when playing.

- They become very anxious and distressed when they are not provided with structure, or when they do not understand the "rules" of the situation. If expectations for their behavior are ambiguous or contradictory, they do not know what is right, and often feel helpless to respond properly. A significant change in expectations, such as occurs when children are placed in a home of a different socioeconomic class or culture, can create serious disruption and anxiety for them.

- The primary identification for school-age children is with their family. Their sense of self and their self-esteem are closely tied to their perception of their family's worth. If other people talk about their family in negative terms, it is an assault upon their self-worth.

Social Development

- School-age children can relate to many people, and can form significant attachments to adults outside the family and to peers.

- They derive considerable security from belonging to a same-sex social group. For many children this age, their friends are the focus of most activities and social interactions.

- They recognize that being a foster child is somehow "different" from other children at a time when it is very important that they be more like them and accepted by them. The tendency for school-age children to be critical of differences, and to ignore or tease children who do not "belong," exacerbates foster children's isolation and feelings of rejection.

- School-age children may be fiercely loyal and exclusive in their relationships, and may feel they must choose between relationships. They may not understand how they can care for old friends and new ones too, or love both mother and foster mother. They may feel they must choose between the old and new life, which creates emotional conflict and guilt. This is exacerbated when foster caregivers expect them to "become a part of their family," and subtly or openly expect children to lessen their attachments to their primary family.

- The value system of school-age children has developed to include "right" and "wrong," and they experience guilt when they have done something wrong.

Implications for Separation and Placement

- School-age children can develop new attachments and turn to adults to meet their needs. If previous relationships with unrelated adults have been positive, they will be likely to seek out help from adults, including a known and trusted caseworker, when they need it. This increases their ability to cope in stressful situations.

- Their perception of the reason for the separation may be distorted. They may verbalize that they are not at fault, particularly if this is reinforced by persons they trust, but they may not fully believe it. They will not want to accept that their parents are at fault either. Their self-esteem is closely tied with their parents' worth, and they need to view their parents positively. However, in the cognitively concrete world of school-age children, someone must be blamed; and often the caseworker, the agency, or the foster parents are faulted.

- School-age children will compare foster caregivers to their parents, and the caregivers will generally lose the competition. This may be expressed in a statement such as, "My mom's hot dogs are better than these old things." Caregivers must allow children to retain a positive attachment to their family without feeling threatened. They must also be able to talk with children in positive terms about their family, and reassure them that they can like the foster caregivers and care about their family, too.

- The loss of a stable peer group and trusted friends can be quite traumatic. Making new friends may be difficult. School-age children may be embarrassed and self-conscious about their status as foster children, and they may feel isolated. Maintaining contact with friends is helpful. Workers can also help these children by developing an explanatory story about the reasons for their placement to be used with peers.

- Children this age will be very confused if the rules or expectations in the substitute care home are different from those to which they are accustomed. They will be anxious and uncomfortable until they fully understand what is expected of them. They may also perceive differences in rules as unfair and protest the changes.

- School-age children have an improved conception of time. They can tolerate placements of a few months, if they understand they will eventually go home. Longer placements may be experienced as permanent. Because children this age need concreteness, if they cannot be told exactly when they are to return home, their anxiety increases.

- School-age children, who are placed after some perceived misbehavior, may feel responsible and guilty, and may be anxious about their parents accepting them back. Repeated placements are perceived as rejections, and threaten their self-esteem. Children who have been subjected to multiple placements often express a belief that they are not wanted by anyone.

PREADOLESCENCE (10 TO 12 YEARS)

Cognitive Development

- Most of preadolescent children's thinking is still concrete. However, some children begin to show an ability to think and reason abstractly, and to recognize complex causes of events.

- At the preadolescent stage, children develop the ability to better understand perspectives other than their own. Some children at this age have developed insight, and can recognize and respond to the needs and feelings of others. They may recognize that their parents have problems that contributed to the need for placement: "My Dad is nice until he gets drunk, and then he gets mean and hits us."

- Preadolescents also have a better and more realistic conception of time. They understand weeks and months, and they can recall events that occurred months and probably years earlier. They are also able to maintain a sense of continuity over time.

- Preadolescents can logically generalize from their experiences. For example, they will not question whether the foster family has a kitchen, even though they have never been to the foster home, because they understand that houses have kitchens.

- Children this age understand that rules often change depending upon the situation, and they can adjust their behavior to meet the expectations of different situations. This does not mean that changes are not stressful; however, the ability to adapt their behavior helps them cope with the changes.

Emotional Development

- Self–esteem and identity are still largely tied to the family. Adolescents often feel that negative comments regarding their family reflect upon them as well.

- Preadolescents have an increased ability to cope independently for short periods of time. They can feed, dress and care for themselves, and travel independently around the neighborhood. They can manage some problems and resolve them without assistance from adults. However, they still turn to significant adults for approval, support, and reassurance, and for help when things are difficult.

- They may be very embarrassed by their foster child status. They are self–conscious about their "differentness."

Social Development

- The social world of preadolescents has expanded to include many people outside the family. Peers are extremely important. Most peer relationships are same–sex. Both boys and girls may have best friends who form their social support network, as well as peer groups with whom they identify.

- Children this age still need trusted adults for leadership, support, nurturance, and approval.

- "Right" and "wrong" are complicated and evolving concepts. For most children this age, right and wrong are determined by principles which they believe apply to all people, including their parents. While children may not understand the sources or reasons for this moral code, they can begin to understand that their parents have the capacity to do wrong.

Implications for Separation and Placement

- Preadolescents have a better capacity to understand the reasons for the separation and placement. With help, these children may be able to identify the causes of the family disruption. They can be helped to realistically assess the degree to which their behavior contributed to the problems. With proper assistance, they can often develop a realistic and accurate perception of the situation, which can help prevent unnecessary and unreasonable self-blame.

- These children can benefit from supportive adult intervention, such as casework counseling, to help sort through their feelings about the situation. Some children this age are able to acknowledge their anger and ambivalent feelings, and talk about them. This helps them to cope.

- If given permission, preadolescents may be able to establish relation-ships with caregivers without feeling disloyal to their parents. If this is possible, placement in substitute care may not be as threatening.

- Preadolescents are often aware of the perceptions and opinions of other people. They may be embarrassed and self-conscious regarding their family's problems and inadequacies, and regarding their status as foster children. This may contribute to the development of low self-esteem.

- These children may be worried about their family as a unit, and may demonstrate considerable concern for siblings and parents. They will want reassurance that they are okay, and are getting the help they need.

- The loss of best friends and peers may be particularly difficult for chil-dren this age. It may be difficult to replace these relationships in the fos-ter care setting. They may be lonely and isolated.

EARLY ADOLESCENCE (13 TO 14 YEARS)

Cognitive Development

- Youths' emerging ability to think abstractly may make complicated explanations of reasons for placement more plausible. However, they still may be confused if the factors are too abstract. As with adults, the abil-ity to think abstractly may depend upon general intellectual potential and level of education.

- These youths may have an increased ability to identify their own feel-ings, and to communicate their concerns and distress verbally.

Emotional Development

- Early adolescence is a time of emotional lability. Early adolescents may experience daily (or hourly) mood swings and fluctuations. At its worst, this can be a chaotic time. At best, youths of this age are still unpre-dictable and emotionally volatile.

- Physical and hormonal changes, including significant and rapid body changes, generate a beginning awareness of sexuality. Early adolescents experience many new feelings, some of which are conflictual and con-tradictory. Emotional changes may be accompanied by solicitous and exaggerated behavior toward the opposite sex, or anxious withdrawal. Many youth display both behaviors at different times as they experiment with new feelings.

- Early adolescents begin to feel a desire to be independent. However, they are not emotionally ready for true independence. Independence is often expressed primarily through verbal rejection of parental values and rules, and adhering, instead, to the values of their peers.

- Despite a verbalized rejection of adult rules and values, youth this age experience considerable anxiety when deprived of structure, support, and clearly defined limits.

Social Development

- Early adolescents may be embarrassed to admit their need for adult approval, support, and nurturance. This makes it difficult for them to enter into relationships with adults, particularly when in an authority or parental role.

- Many early adolescents are conscious of their status or popularity, and their self-esteem is often derived from being accepted by the right peer group. These groups and their membership may change from day to day. Some youths may reject their childhood friends for acceptance into a more popular subgroup. Standards of acceptance are rigid, and many youth this age typically feel they do not adequately measure up.

- Many early adolescents may feel a need to keep up appearances, and may defend their family in public and to adults, even if they personally believe their parents to be at fault.

- At this stage, youths are beginning to become aware of social roles, and they experiment with different roles and behaviors. Consistent social role models are needed. Because sexual identity is becoming an issue, improper or atypical sexual behavior on the part of a youth's parents (sexual abuse, prostitution) may be of increasing concern.

- Although many youths will have developed a moral attitude with clearly defined "rights" and "wrongs," these values may take a back seat to their friends' opinions and attitudes regarding their thoughts and actions. The values of the peer group often supersede their own.

Implications for Separation and Placement

- Early adolescence is emotionally a chaotic period. Youth experience many stresses as a result of internal, biological changes, and changes in expectations for their behavior. Any additional stress has the potential of creating a "stress overload" situation, and may precipitate crisis.

- Early adolescents may resist relationships with adults, and may describe adults in uncomplimentary terms. In their minds, dependence upon adults threatens their independence. They may not be able to admit their need for support, nurturance, and structure from adults. Without these, however, they may flounder and experience considerable anxiety. By rejecting adults, they deprive themselves of a source of coping support. The peer group, to whom a youth may turn, cannot generally provide the stability and help needed.

- At this stage, youths may deny much of their discomfort and pain. This prevents them from constructively coping with these feelings, and they may be expressed through volatile, sometimes antisocial behavior. The general emotional upheaval of this developmental period may be exhibited in mood swings and erratic, temperamental behaviors.

- Separation from parents, especially because of family conflict and unruly behavior on the part of a youth, may generate guilt and anxiety.

- At a time when identity is an emerging issue, youths may have difficulty in realistically dealing with their parents' shortcomings. The parents may either be idealized, and their shortcomings may be denied; or, they may be discounted, verbally criticized, and rejected.

- The emotional and social nuances of emerging sexual relationships may be very frightening without the support of a consistent, understanding adult.

- Early adolescents have the capacity to participate in planning, and to make suggestions regarding their own life. This provides a sense of involvement, self-worth, and control. They will be less likely to resist or thwart a plan if they have been involved in developing it.

- Persistent, repeated attempts by caseworkers to engage youth can have very positive results. Even if they never acknowledge that their caseworkers are of help, early adolescents may greatly benefit from the workers' support and guidance.

MIDDLE ADOLESCENCE (15 TO 17 YEARS)

Cognitive Development

- By middle adolescence, youths have often developed the ability to understand complex reasons for separation, placement, and family behavior. They can understand that things happen for many reasons, that no one person may be at fault, and that their parents aren't perfect. They may not, however, be able to accept their situation emotionally.

- The ability to be self-aware and insightful may be of help in coping with difficult situations and their conflicting feelings about them.

- At this stage, adolescents have greater ability to think hypothetically. They can use this ability to plan for the future, and to consider potential outcomes of different strategies.

Emotional Development

- Middle adolescents are developing greater self-reliance. They are more capable of independent behavior, and can contribute to decisions about their life and activities. This helps them to retain some control of their situation, which helps reduce anxiety.

- Identity is being formulated by considering and weighing a number of influences, including family, peers, and their own values and behaviors. These adolescents are beginning to formulate many of their own beliefs and opinions. Many behaviors and ways of dealing with situations are tried, and adopted or discarded, in an attempt to determine what seems to be right for them.

- The development of positive self-esteem may depend as much on acceptance by peers of the opposite sex as by same-sex peers.

Social Development

- Considerable social behavior is centered around exploration of sexual relationships and concerns about intimacy. Much social behavior is centered around dating. Group identification is important, but less so. Individual relationships are becoming more important.

- Adolescents become very interested in adults or older youths as role models. They will be very responsive to people who are honest, and who will talk about their ideas without enforcing behavioral expectations or values. They are often willing to listen and to try new ways of thinking and behaving.

- Adolescents are beginning to focus on future planning and emancipation, and are experimenting with and developing self–reliance. But they still need the consistent support of their family.

- Toward the end of middle adolescence, many youth may begin to question previously held beliefs and ideas regarding "right" and "wrong," and they may be less influenced by peer attitudes. An emergence of independent ethical thinking may be evident.

Implications for Separation and Placement

- Adolescents will often reject a family's supporting, nurturing, and guiding efforts as they struggle to express their need for independence. This often results in conflicting, labile, and ambivalent emotions and feelings toward their family. Separation during this time further complicates an already complicated developmental dynamic. Youth in placement may need help and counseling to sort through their ambivalent feelings regarding their family.

- Adolescents' need for independence may affect their response to placement in a substitute family setting, especially if the caregiving family expects them to "become one of us." Adolescents' family identity may remain with their biological family, and they may be unwilling to accept the substitute family as more than a place to stay. This may be perceived as their failure to adjust to the placement, even though it is a healthy and reasonable response.

- Adolescents may not remain in a placement if it does not meet their needs. Some would rather find their own solutions and placements.

- Adolescents may constructively use casework counseling to deal with the conflicts of separation and placement in a way that meets their needs without threatening their self-esteem and independence. A strong relationship with a trusted caseworker or therapist can provide support, offer guidance and direction, and help them develop realistic, accurate perceptions of a situation and their role in it.

Recognizing Signs of Grief and Stress in Children

While the stages children experience in response to crisis and loss may be predictable, the behaviors exhibited by different children at each stage or at different ages may differ markedly. The common behavioral indicators of stress and loss at each stage in the grieving process are described below.

Stage I: Shock/Denial

After the initial distress of the move itself, children may appear to settle in and make an adjustment for a period of time. This period may last from several days to several weeks, and is sometimes referred to as the "honeymoon period." Children often appear placid, amenable, and easy to get along with. In truth, they are usually in emotional shock.

- Children experiencing shock or denial often seem indifferent in affect and behavior. They may not show any emotional reaction to the move; it appears to be "taken in stride;" for example, as when a child is observed to "wave good-bye at the door; she was all smiles, and went off to play with the children and all the new toys."

- Behavior may be robot-like. Children may go through the motions of normal daily activity, but there is a lack of investment or exuberance. They appear quiet, compliant, easy to please. This absence of emotion may indicate a defensive psychological withdrawal, denial of feelings, and emotional numbness. If workers have not observed children often prior to placement, it is sometimes difficult to determine if the present condition is typical, or a reaction to separation.

- Children often verbally deny a loss. They may say, "I'm not staying. My mommy will be back for me soon;" or, "The caseworker just left me here for a little while, and then I'm going home."

- Infants may exhibit physical symptoms, including respiratory or intestinal upsets or infections, and feeding or sleep disturbances.

One of the most common errors made by caseworkers, parents, and caregivers is to misinterpret children's compliant and unemotional behavior during this stage as indication that placement was easy, and that the children handled it well. If workers and caregivers do not recognize the grieving process, and anticipate its developmental progression from denial to anger, they may not recognize angry affect and behavior as part of the grieving process. Instead, they may mistake these for signs of more serious emotional or behavioral problems. The children may be punished for these behaviors, intensifying their distress and depriving them of support and help.

A few children who have not developed strong attachments to their caregivers may not react at all when they are moved. This lack of response may indicate that their ability to form relationships has been damaged. The absence of an emotional response by children in placement which extends beyond the initial shock stage of the grief process should be of considerable concern to caseworkers and foster parents.

Stage II: Anger/Protest

Children demonstrate anger in very different ways, depending upon their age and developmental level. They may be oppositional and hypersensitive. They may act out their feelings through angry outbursts, tantrums in response to minor events, by blaming others, and through verbal and physical aggression.

- In infants and preschool children, physical symptoms and emotional outbursts are common. Younger children may refuse to talk, eat, or sleep. In older children, anger may be directed into destructive and aggressive behaviors, such as tantrums in preschool–age children, and more complex behaviors such as lying and stealing in school–age or adolescent children.

- Tantrum behaviors and emotional, angry outbursts are common at all ages; these are often easily precipitated, and the intensity of a child's response often seems excessive for the situation.

- School–age children and adolescents may emotionally withdraw, sulk, or pout, and they may exhibit a sullen, self–imposed isolation. They may refuse to participate in activities or social interactions, and may be crabby, grouchy, and hard to satisfy.

- Children at this stage may also exhibit aggressive or rough behavior with other children, and may bully or physically hurt them. They may break toys or objects, lie, steal, and exhibit other antisocial behaviors. They may also refuse to comply with requests, may be both overtly and/or covertly rebellious and oppositional.

- Children may make comparisons between their own home and the one in which they are placed, and, in doing so, rarely find the new one as good. Older children may be very critical of new caregivers and the new environment.

It is difficult to live with children who are angry. Oppositional behavior may be disruptive to the caregiving family, and confrontations between caregivers and children may promote a struggle for control. Angry children may be diagnosed as severely behaviorally handicapped or emotionally disturbed, and may be punished for misbehavior. If their behavior is properly identified as an expression of normal grieving, caregivers are generally more able to provide support, and give them opportunities for appropriate expressions of angry feelings, while gently setting firm limits for their behavior.

Because these behaviors are also typical of children who have been abused and neglected, it may be difficult to distinguish such behaviors from placement–induced stress. However, caseworkers and foster caregivers should recognize that separation and placement of already emotionally damaged children can exacerbate their problems at the same time it potentially protects them from further maltreatment. We should always assume that these children are experiencing separation trauma, and respond accordingly in a supportive and helpful manner.

Stage III: Bargaining

This stage is more frequently exhibited by school-age and older children, who have developed more complex cognitive and social skills. They must have the cognitive ability to understand the potentials of cause and effect, and they must believe that their behavior can influence a change in their circumstances. Often these children's behavior will reflect their perceptions regarding the cause of the separation.

• They may become "good as gold," appear eager to please, and promise to do better. They may also try to undo what they feel they had done to precipitate the placement. For instance, a child who believes she was sent away because she didn't eat her dinner, will try hard to eat everything put in front of her.

• They may try to negotiate agreements with the foster caregiver or the caseworker, and will agree to do certain things in exchange for a promise that they will be allowed to return home; "I'll go to counseling and get better grades, and then I can go home." Some ritualized behaviors may be noted, reflecting both their obsession with returning home, and the emotional intensity of their compulsion to do whatever is necessary to achieve this goal.

• At times, they may appear moralistic in their beliefs and behavior. These behaviors and verbalizations are a form of self-reinforcement, and a defense against failure in upholding their end of the bargain.

The worker should remember that while many behaviors at this stage may be inherently desirable, they do not represent a positive change in character. At this point they represent a desperate attempt to control the environment, and to defend against feelings of loss and fear. In reality, there is little chance of children's behaviors producing the desired results of reunification. If workers are not fooled by the surface quality of the behaviors, they will be in a better position to provide the support needed when children realize the ineffectiveness of the bargaining strategy and begin to experience the full emotional impact of their loss.

Stage IV: Depression

During this stage children appear to have lost hope, and they experience the full emotional impact of the loss. There are several behavioral indicators of depression, which include social and emotional withdrawal, and failure to respond to other people.

• Infants or young children may cling to adults, but the clinging has an ambivalent, remote, forlorn, and detached quality. They may avoid contact or interaction, or be unresponsive when approached. Older children may isolate themselves and avoid interaction.

• Anxiety is often associated with this stage. Depressive anxiety is manifest by easily precipitated fear and panic within an overall listless and withdrawn demeanor. Children experiencing anxiety may be easily frightened, frustrated, and overwhelmed by minor events and stresses.

- Children may be listless, seeming to be without direction or energy. They may appear distracted and lost. They may play sporadically, but their actions may appear mechanical, and without emotional investment or interest. There is little goal–directed activity, and they may drift from one thing to another with a short attention span. They may be unable to concentrate. This may result in school problems or failure.

- These children may appear to be vulnerable to minor stresses and easily hurt. They may cry with little or no provocation. Generalized emotional distress is often seen in infants and younger children, including whimpering, crying, head banging, rocking, lack of interest in feeding, excessive sleeping, vomiting and other stomach upsets, and susceptibility to colds, flu, and illness. Preschool or school-age children may also demonstrate regressive behaviors, such as thumb sucking, toilet accidents, or baby talk. The signs of depression in adolescents are similar to those in adults and include: disturbances in eating and sleeping; depressed mood; inability to concentrate or attend to task; frequent crying jags; and feelings of futility and hopelessness.

There may be a considerable lapse of time between the original separation and the onset of depressive behavior in children. In spite of this, workers should recognize depressive behavior as a likely expression of the evolving grieving process.

Stage V: Resolution

The normal grieving process is an adaptive dynamic and is, therefore, time limited. Depressed feelings and behavior will eventually be replaced with constructive and adaptive attempts to reintegrate socially, and to reestablish emotional equilibrium. As children in placement give up hope of ever returning home, they will often begin to develop stronger attachments in the new home, and try to establish a place for themselves in the family structure.

- They may begin to identify with their new family and express this to others. They may want to assume the new family's name.

- General emotional distress will decrease, and emotional reactions to stressful situations will diminish over time, as they become more secure in their new environment.

- They begin to experience pleasure in normal childhood play and activities. Goal–directed activities resume.

- They reach out to engage others in positive social interactions and form new attachments.

When children's case plans include permanent placement with the current family, behaviors suggesting resolution are generally positive signs. However, if permanent separation is not the case plan, then resolution behavior seriously interferes with reunification. Furthermore, separation from their new family creates an additional, unnecessary stress for children. It is inappropriate for children to resolve the loss of their family, if their case plans include reunification.

Case Examples

Children experience separation distress in a variety of ways. The way distress is exhibited depends upon the child's age, personality, and previous experiences. The following case vignettes illustrate the reactions of several children to traumatic separations [Gerard & Dukette 1953]. All of these children were moved rapidly, without preparation, and without the benefit of preplacement visits.

- After having been removed from his family and placed in foster care by the caseworker, nine–month–old Todd became fearful and anxious when he had to ride in a car. For months he screamed and protested when taken near a car. Once in it, he settled, but again screamed when removed from it.

- Three–year–old Susan disintegrated emotionally when placed in her second foster home. For days she wandered around the new home calling "Mommy," looking for her mommy, refusing to eat, and refusing to interact with the new foster parents. She ignored toys and wandered aimlessly, intermittently breaking into tears, clutching herself and sobbing, and then stopping abruptly. She would not let anyone comfort her. When the foster parents tried to pick her up and hold her, she sat stiffly in their laps for several seconds and then squirmed away. She would not make eye contact with them.

- One–year–old Bobby clung to his hat and coat, and refused to give them up for several days after placement in an adoptive family. He rocked violently, clutching his hat and whimpering.

- Two–year–old Leon walked around his new home talking to himself, saying, "Now we go home. Leon go home now. Leon not go bye–bye. Go home to Mommy. No bye–bye." He had no interest in toys, and he ignored his new foster caregivers.

- Four–year–old Lucy, a plucky and self–directed child in her foster home, developed a severe anxiety reaction when moved to her adoptive family. She refused to go into dark rooms, was afraid of the "basement monster" despite repeated tours of the basement, and wouldn't go alone into the back yard. She locked herself in the bedroom when the service repair people came to fix the furnace. She had frequent night terrors, waking from a sound sleep screaming, sweating, and anxious. It took as long as an hour to calm her. During the day she tried valiantly to get along with the adoptive family, but she often dissolved into anxious tears at small provocation. Her behavior reflected a pervasive anxiety disorder over which she appeared to have little control. It persisted for months, despite her adoptive parents' consistent reassurances.

- Five-year-old Lester had protested violently when the caseworker came to move him from his home. He ran from her, hid in a closet, kicked and screamed, and refused to come out. He attacked the caseworker by trying to kick her. When she tried to reason with him and coax him out, he put his hands firmly over his ears and screamed "No, No." Finally, the much larger and stronger worker picked him up and carried him, screaming and crying, to her car and belted him in. He undid the seat belt and tried to open the door. The worker locked the doors from her side of the car and redid the seat belt. Lester then abruptly swallowed one last anguished sob, and looked out the window. At the new home he rejected the foster mother, and became totally focused on a toy truck in the new family's playroom.

- Eight-year-old Wendy moved from her foster home to another when her foster mother was suddenly hospitalized with a heart attack. She had suffered one previous separation from her family when she was five. Wendy appeared to take the move in stride. However, in her new home, she became uncharacteristically independent. She dressed herself, fed herself, and asked nothing of the foster mother. When she fell while playing, even though hurt, she whimpered to herself on the lawn, and rejected the foster mother's attempts to help her. She took food from the kitchen and began to hoard it in her bedroom closet. This behavior, often called "pseudo-independence" is typical of children who have learned that trusting and relying on adults only results in a painful separation.

- Chip, age 12, calmly told his caseworker that he wouldn't stay, wherever she placed him. He was not going to live with any more families. He wanted to live with his sister, a 17-year-old single parent living on her own. The worker questioned the adequacy of this environment for Chip, and tried to get him to agree to at least give the foster family a try, assuring Chip that they were very nice people. Chip was sullen and quiet during the ride to the foster home. Within 10 minutes after arrival, while the worker and the foster mother were talking quietly in the living room, Chip disappeared out the back door. A week later, despite several visits by the caseworker to the sister and Chip's extended family, Chip was still missing.

- Chris, age 13, had lived intermittently with a variety of caregivers for most of his life. The placements had been arranged by Chris' mother, who periodically moved away with boyfriends, returned to care for him for a few months, and then left again. She had been in and out of Chris' life since his birth. When Chris was placed in a foster home, he appeared nonplussed by the move, and shrugged it off as "no big deal." Within a few weeks of placement, his foster mother discovered he deliberately tore holes in his clothing and then hid them. He broke the other children's toys, took money from the parents' dresser, spent his allowance immediately on candy and toys for himself, and relentlessly tormented the family cat. He chose to play with much younger children, bossed them around, and often inflicted physical harm on them when they wouldn't do what he wanted. He was always pleasant and civil to the foster parents, but according to the foster mother, he seemed "remote," as if the "real Chris" were "peering at me through a glass wall, which he allowed no one to penetrate."

All these scenarios reflect a degree of emotional isolation and with-drawal by the children from interpersonal relationships. Some children, who are removed from their families abruptly and inappropriately, will not recover, even when adults are consistently warm and nurturing to them. Their willingness to risk in developing interpersonal relationships will be permanently damaged.

C. PLACEMENT STRATEGIES TO PREVENT TRAUMA

1. Conceptual Framework

2. Application

Conceptual Framework

In previous sections, the potentially serious consequences of separation and placement to children and their families have been identified. However, when a child cannot be protected at home, even with intensive in-home service interventions, out-of-home placement may become necessary.

When out-of-home placement cannot be avoided, placement should be structured to minimize trauma to children and their families, to decrease the likelihood of crisis, and to reduce the long-term negative effects of separation. Strategies include careful preplacement planning; selection of the most appropriate caregivers; adequate preparation of children, their families, and caregivers; conducting placement activities in steps that promote a gradual adjustment to the change; involving family members in all aspects of the placement process; and intensive follow-up supportive services to the children, the caregivers, and the families.

THE DECISION TO PLACE

There are two truisms in child placement. The first is that the only legitimate justification for out-of-home placement is that supportive family services and other interventions cannot assure protection of children in their own homes. The second is that children should *never* be left in a home when they cannot be protected from abuse or neglect. In practice, however, many children have been removed unnecessarily, or they have been left in high-risk situations without sufficient protective interventions.

The following are some inappropriate reasons for decisions to place:

- Workers may assume too quickly that a situation is an emergency, without first completing a thorough assessment of risk and determining whether a child can be protected at home with intensive family services.

- Other community agencies and professionals may exert pressure to remove and place children. These placement recommendations may be based on insufficient or incorrect information, or they may reflect the personal values of persons who lack expertise in risk assessment.

- Conversely, the recent national emphasis on family preservation has been improperly interpreted by some to mean that no children should ever be placed out of home.

- In some cases, workers view placement in foster care or with relatives as a simpler, better, or less time-consuming way to assure children's safety than providing intensive in-home services and monitoring. In short, once children are in substitute care, their safety and well-being can be assured, and busy staff can proceed with other activities. This practice is consistent with the attitude that "rescuing" children from "bad" environments, and placing them in better ones serves children's best interests.

- Agency and worker concerns about legal liability also can support a "better safe than sorry" attitude that promotes placement of children when the risk to them at home is equivocal.

- The rate of out-of-home placement is generally higher in communities that have few supportive service resources, such as homemakers, parent aides, protective day care, public health services, parenting classes, respite care, family support and counseling, or intensive in-home service programs. When foster care is the only resource available to protect children, it will be used. In these communities, a broad-based interagency and community effort must be undertaken to identify and strengthen family service resources.

- Research also suggests that the rate of out-of-home placements is disproportionately high for children of minority racial and cultural backgrounds [Stehno 1982; 1990]. This may be indicative of worker, agency, or community bias, and may also reflect our society's inability to provide many families with the resources necessary to assure basic survival and promote family integrity.

- When agencies lack standardized policies and procedures to guide risk assessment and placement decisions, and when workers and supervisors lack skill in risk and family assessment, placement practices are likely to be highly inconsistent. In some agencies, supervisors do not routinely review case decisions; workers may not receive regular consultative supervision; specialized training is not available; and staff make difficult and complex placement decisions without consultation and input from other professionals.

A broad-based agency approach is necessary to eliminate inappropriate placements. Placement decisions must always be based upon sound factual information about the child and family, gleaned from a thorough risk assessment. The effects of making placement decisions without first conducting a comprehensive risk assessment can be disastrous. Children not at high risk, as well as their families, may be unnecessarily subjected to placement trauma, while children at high risk of harm may be left unprotected in their homes. In addition, purported "emergencies" must be carefully assessed to determine the degree to which the child is truly endangered. Placement decisions are difficult and complex, and cases should generally be thoroughly discussed with other professionals before a plan to remove a child is formulated. Rarely should the decision to remove a child be made by any single individual.

Intake units must be staffed to permit thorough family assessments and a determination of risk before considering removal of children. When children are found to be at high risk, strategies to protect them in their own homes should be considered before a decision is made to remove them. Agencies that can provide crisis intervention and intensive in-home services will be better able to prevent placement. Even if a child must eventually be removed, intensive in-home intervention provides workers with an opportunity to fully assess the family's strengths and needs, and to develop a placement plan that minimizes trauma.

Agencies must also develop consistent policies regarding risk and family assessment, service delivery, and out–of–home placement, and assure that managers and staff correctly understand and interpret them. Caseworkers and supervisors must be well trained in risk assessment, family assessment, and strategies that support and strengthen families. The skills needed to conduct an accurate and comprehensive risk assessment are quite complex; the agency's most experienced and skilled staff should be assigned this responsibility. Unfortunately, openings in intake units are frequently filled by inexperienced caseworkers. This greatly increases the likelihood of faulty decision making, with often destructive consequences.

Finally, all agency staff must guard against the effects of personal and institutional racial and cultural bias in determining the need for the placement of children. A thorough knowledge of cultural differences, community standards, and personal values and biases can prevent subjective assessments of families, and the inappropriate removal and placement of children.

PLACEMENT STRATEGIES THAT DAMAGE CHILDREN

For more than 50 years, child development specialists have stressed the inherent dangers of abrupt removal and placement of children [Freud & Burlingham 1943; Littner 1956; Gerard & Dukette 1953; Bowlby 1973; Rycus, Hughes & Garrison 1989; Fahlberg 1979; 1991]. Yet, many child welfare agencies persist in abruptly taking children and their belongings from their homes and depositing them in new homes, often in the care of total strangers. The most common justifications for this practice are, "We don't have time to do any more," or "The child had to be moved immediately to protect him; it was an emergency."

While there is some truth in both statements, our time pressures cannot justify the serious harm we have inflicted on hundreds of thousands of children and their families over the years, while ostensibly serving their best interests. While we cannot always prevent maltreatment of children, nor fully undo the damage related to such maltreatment, we certainly can control how we place them! This is particularly true when children are moved between foster homes, or to adoptive or other permanent families. Children in these situations are generally at no risk of imminent harm, and the agency can plan and schedule placement activities that meet the children's needs and that prevent unnecessary stress. Even in emergency situations, there are multiple options available before, during, and after the placement that can ease the transition and can prevent serious and long–term harm to children or their families.

TRANSITIONING AS A PLACEMENT STRATEGY

The fundamental principle of effective placement practice is, while a move cannot always be avoided, separation trauma can be prevented or minimized. "Transitioning" as a placement strategy to prevent emotional trauma from separation was introduced as early as 1943 by Anna Freud and Dorothy Burlingham, who suggested:

> If separation happened slowly, if people who are meant to substitute for the mother were known to the child beforehand, tran-

> sition from one [caregiver] to the other would appear gradually...
> By the time the...child had [to] let go of the mother, the
> new...[caregiver] would be well known and ready at hand. There
> would be no empty period in which feelings are turned com-
> pletely inward...Regression occurs while the child is passing
> through the no–man's land of affection; i.e., during the time the
> old object has been given up before the new one has been found
> [Freud & Burlingham 1943].

The goal of the transition method of placement is to "place the child in a new home only after he has developed some familiarity with it and gives evidence of a beginning affection for and dependence upon the new parents." [Gerard & Dukette 1953].

The placement strategies described below operationalize the concept of tran-sitioning. They are designed to assure a sequence of activities that create a less stressful experience, and provide an emotionally supportive environment for children being placed, which helps prevent crisis and its debilitating effects. Specifically:

1) The degree of stress experienced by both children and their families dur-ing placement will be reduced. This is achieved by avoiding unnecessary changes, recognizing when children and families are experiencing exces-sive stress, and pacing the rate of placement to prevent children from becoming overwhelmed.

2) The children's and the families' ability to cope with placement will be strengthened by involving them in planning, preparing them for the placement, conducting placement activities in more easily managed steps, and by providing essential support before, during, and after the placement.

3) Families and children will be helped to achieve a realistic perception of the reasons for the placement, and will have opportunities to talk about their feelings and needs in a supportive environment.

4) The children's adjustment in the placement setting will be enhanced and supported by the caregiving families and caseworkers.

5) The substitute caregivers' ability to meet children's unique physical, emotional, and developmental needs will be strengthened.

6) When reunification is the case plan, families will be involved with their children in placement in a manner that reduces separation trauma, pre-serves and strengthens the parent–child relationship, and promotes prompt reunification.

Many workers believe they lack sufficient time to conduct placements in the manner described herein. However, we must seriously consider the negative consequences to children and families if we do not adhere to these principles, and we must prioritize our time to support as many of these placement practices as possible.

Finally, caseworkers cannot, by themselves, assure prudent child placement practices. A total agency commitment is necessary. Agency policies and procedures must be developed that support effective place- ment practices, and administrators and managers must facilitate such practice by providing flexible scheduling of case responsibility when a child needs to be placed; by mandating regular case review and consultation; by offering staff sufficient training in risk and family assessment; and by assuring opportunities for collaborative decision making.

Application

CHOOSING THE MOST APPROPRIATE PLACEMENT SETTING

The decision of where a child should be placed is as important as the decision to place. Placements that cannot meet a child's unique needs, or that subject the child to unnecessary stress, greatly increase both the trauma for the child and the likelihood of placement disruption.

A properly chosen placement will meet a child's physical, emotional and social needs, will strengthen and preserve the child's relationship with family members, and will minimize the changes to which the child must adapt. The following principles promote selection of the the most appropriate placement settings and caregivers.

- A child should be placed in the least restrictive, most home–like environment possible, and as close to the child's own home as possible. Relatives, family friends, and neighbors should be assessed to determine their willingness and ability to provide care and protection before considering a foster home placement. Family members can often participate in identifying potential placements for their child.

- The child's development, needs, and anticipated behavior problems should be carefully assessed prior to choosing a placement. A caregiving family should be chosen based upon its capacity to meet the child's special needs. Unfortunately, many placements are made solely on the basis of available bed space. Failure to properly match a child to the most appropriate caregiving family greatly increases the likelihood that the placement will disrupt, resulting in another unnecessary separation and rejection.

- The number of nontherapeutic changes in lifestyle and environment should be minimized. Whenever possible, a caregiving family selected for a child should be of similar ethnic, cultural, and socioeconomic level as the child's own family. This reduces the number of cultural changes to which the child must adjust, thereby reducing stress, and also helps to preserve the child's cultural identity. Continuity can also be maintained by allowing the child to remain in the same school, church, and community.

- A child should never be placed in a group home, receiving center, or other institutional setting because an appropriate family setting is not available. Identification and support of kinship caregivers, and the recruitment and training of appropriate foster family and treatment homes, should be considered an agency priority. (See Section X-A, "The Components of an Effective Foster Care System.")

The success of a placement is also greatly increased when a child's family and the foster or kinship caregiver are involved in the planning and implementation of all aspects of the placement. (This will be discussed at greater length in Sections IX-B, "Empowering Parents to Participate in Placement Activities," and IX-C, "Promoting Reunification.")

EMERGENCY PLACEMENTS

All high risk situations do not automatically require the emergency placement of children. In some cases, the risk assessment will suggest safety factors in the family environment that can be strengthened to help protect children in their own homes. Intensive in-home supportive services may effectively reduce imminent risk, while simultaneously strengthening the family. Protective day care, homemaker services, and other in-home supportive services can sometimes assure that children are not left in the sole care of an alleged perpetrator while a more complete family assessment and case plan are being completed.

An emergency exists when a child is determined to be at imminent high risk of harm, and the child cannot be protected at home, even with intensive, in-home and supportive services. In these cases, placement may be necessary to assure the child's protection while the family situation is fully assessed and a case plan is developed. When the child needs emergency care, the worker should attempt to maintain the child in familiar surroundings, preferably with extended family members or close family friends, while a more comprehensive family assessment can be completed, and the determination can be made of the best intervention plan for the family. This may include longer-term placement of the child in either a kinship or foster care setting. This also gives the caseworker time to become better acquainted with the child, to identify the most appropriate placement setting, and to move the child planfully, without subjecting the child to undue stress.

PREPARING THE CHILD, FAMILY, AND CAREGIVERS

Preparation for change helps people cope. Fear of the unknown and feelings of anticipatory loss, common in any significant change, increase anxiety, depression, and vulnerability to crisis [Parad & Caplan 1965]. Preparation for change helps to reduce ambiguity and fear of the unknown, and provides much-needed support and reassurance.

The success of any placement is, therefore, greatly enhanced if all participants are properly prepared. The child, the family, and the caregivers should all be given thorough information about the placement plans, and should have the opportunity to fully discuss the placement with the caseworker.

Preparing and Involving the Child's Family

Preparing the child's family and involving them in placement planning has several goals:

- Assuring that family members understand why placement is necessary, including the specific conditions in the family that created a situation of high risk for the children;

- Helping the family become engaged as a partner in the placement process, to reduce the stress experienced by their children, and to participate in developing and implementing the reunification plan; and

- Enabling the family's continued involvement with their children while in placement, thereby enhancing the likelihood of successful reunification.

The reasons for removal of the children must be thoroughly explained and discussed with the family. The worker should help the family recognize the conditions that contributed to high risk, and explain that the agency intends to reunite the family as soon as the home can be made safe for the children. The worker should also make the commitment to work in partnership with the family to make this possible. Finally, the worker should request that the family participate in the placement process to reduce stress for themselves and their children.

Once parents understand the reasons for placement, they can often help the caseworker explain this to the children. This helps reassure the children that their parents will work with the caseworker, and will visit with the children while in placement. If parents cannot or will not participate, another person important to the child, such as an extended family member, can play this role. This can be illustrated by a case example.

𝕏 Case Example: Alma Rogers

The child welfare agency responded to a neglect referral of two children, about ages seven and five, alone in their family's apartment. The neighbor who had made the referral had seen the children's mother leave the day before but had not seen her return. The neighbor said this wasn't the first time the children had been left alone, but this time the mother had been gone much longer than usual.

The worker called for law enforcement support, and together the worker and the officer entered the apartment. They found two little girls cowering in the bedroom. The house was in disarray, furniture had been overturned, and there were matches all over the kitchen floor. The seven year old tearfully said she had been trying to light the stove to make her younger sister some soup, because she had been crying that she was hungry.

The neighbor gave the caseworker the name of the mother's sister, Elaine. The worker contacted her. Elaine told the worker that her sister, Alma, age 29, had become a frequent user of cocaine. Elaine told the worker that Alma had a long history of mental health problems, and that she had repeatedly left her children alone. Elaine said she would come to stay with the children until Alma returned.

When Alma returned several hours later, the caseworker and Elaine confronted her with the risk at which she had placed her children, and strongly suggested she needed help. When Alma realized her children could have set the apartment on fire, she broke into tears, confirmed she was depressed and had often contemplated suicide, and was "too far gone on drugs to be any good to anyone." She refused mental health treatment, suggesting, "I've been through all that, more times than I can count, and you can see all the good it's done me." She also said she was obviously a failure as a parent and didn't see any hope of change.

The worker stressed that Alma could not continue to parent in her condition, and that a safety plan would have to be made for her children. The worker told Alma she could help make the plan, or the worker would have no choice but to make it for her. Alma agreed to allow temporary placement of her children, saying, "I guess it's time I give up," but she would not agree to any more treatment. The worker suggested the first step was to assure the children's safety, and that she needed Alma's help to keep the placement from traumatizing the children. Her children needed her help and support, even if they couldn't live with her right now. The worker encouraged Alma to tell the children about the placement, and to help move the children. The worker also obtained a commitment from Alma that she would set up, and keep, regular visits with the children. The worker prompted Alma regarding what she should tell the children, and she supported Alma while Alma told the girls that she had some drug problems, and she wanted them to stay with Aunt Elaine for a while. She would take them to Aunt Elaine's herself, she would visit them as often as she could, and she hoped they could come home again soon. The children were visibly upset, cried, and clung to her. Alma packed some of the children's clothes, and they all drove to Elaine's house. The children remained moody and sullen for several days, but their responses were more similar to those of children being left with a babysitter than children who had been traumatized by a forced separation and placement. They ultimately adjusted well, since they liked Aunt Elaine, and their mother had given them the necessary permission to stay with her. The children talked with their mother on the phone daily. The worker also made a commitment to the children that she would try to find the best help for their mom. She told Alma this, as well.

Whether a parent can be engaged to collaborate with the caseworker in planning and executing the placement is important diagnostic information. Parents who can support and reassure their children, and who will maintain contact with their children in placement, exhibit considerable strengths that work in favor of timely reunification. It is the caseworker's responsibility to encourage and empower the family to become involved in the placement, and to help eliminate barriers to such involvement. Providing transportation, asking parents to participate in preplacement visits, and preparing the foster caregiver to be supportive and receptive to the parent can increase the parent's comfort with the placement process.

When possible, parents should be asked to recommend family members or friends as potential caregivers for their child. These caregivers should be evaluated for the degree of safety they can give the child. Both parents and caregivers must understand that the parents cannot interfere with the placement. The worker's ability to engage a parent to make an appropriate substitute care plan for a child is an essential step in developing the collaboration needed to reunify a family. When such a collaboration exists, and the family is fully involved, they are much less likely to engage in activities that sabotage the placement, or to emotionally withdraw from the child.

Parents should be asked to provide detailed information about their children's schedule, routines, likes and dislikes, and needs. This will greatly help the caregivers maintain continuity for the children, and also supports the parents' importance as caregivers to their children, as well. It is very helpful if parents can communicate this information directly to the caregivers.

The caseworker should acknowledge parents' anger and grief in response to the loss of their children, and should expect them to be initially resistant to talking with the worker or becoming involved in the placement. The caseworker should continue to be supportive, while firm, and continue to encourage and support parental involvement in all aspects of the planning and placement process. In the long run, most parents are more resistive to working with the agency and more likely to sabotage the placement when their children have been "whisked away to the unknown" by agency staff, while the family remains isolated and uninvolved in the process.

Preparing the Relative or Foster Caregiver

Caregivers need complete and accurate information about the children coming into their home. To assure confidentiality, parents should sign a release of information. Again, the transfer of information is considerably easier if parents can talk directly with the foster or relative caregivers. If a parent will not consent to a release of information, considerable data can still be shared without breaching confidentiality. As an example, the worker could communicate to the caregiver that "John has been hit with a belt by a man, and is very cautious around men."

If the caregiver has detailed information about a child, it increases the caregiver's ability to maintain continuity in the child's life, and helps to reduce stress. Information should include:

- The child's sleeping, bathing, and eating habits and schedules; food preferences, including culturally specific dietary requirements and preferences; evidence of bed wetting, night terrors, or other sleep disturbances; whether the child sleeps with a light on, in a crib or bed, covered by a blanket or not covered, in pajamas or other apparel;

- The child's medical care needs, medications, special physical problems; the location of the child's medical records; the child's medical and inoculation history; the child's nontraditional medical experiences, and the family's expectations for medical care;

- How the child is accustomed to being comforted when upset;

- The child's interests, skills, and favorite activities;

- Behaviors and behavior problems that can be expected, and recommended methods of handling the child's problems; how the child has been disciplined in the past, and how the child should and should not be disciplined;

- The child's fears and anxieties, and how they are typically expressed;

- The child's school behavior, academic ability, extracurricular involvement, and special academic needs;

- The child's verbal ability and ability to communicate, and words that are important to the child that the caregivers may not understand;

- History of abuse, neglect, or sexual abuse, and how this may affect the child's development and response to the foster caregivers; and

- Culturally specific caregiving practices should be stressed if the child and caregivers are of different cultural backgrounds. This includes strategies to help children maintain their cultural identity and affiliations while in placement. Culturally specific caregiving and hygiene practices should also be communicated.

The relative or foster caregiver must be encouraged to tell the caseworker if, at any time during the preplacement planning or visiting process, they realize they do not want to proceed with the placement. The caseworker should respect the family's decision, and seek another home for the child. If the placement is pursued despite the caregiving family's concerns, the risk of later disruption is greatly increased.

Preparing the Child

Adequately preparing a child for placement serves several important purposes. First, the caseworker can alleviate many of the child's anxieties and fears by providing detailed information regarding the need for placement, and by familiarizing the child with all aspects of the new home. This is, of course, less critical if the child knows the caregiving family and has stayed with them before. However, the child must still be helped to understand why a move is necessary, and his anxieties and fears related to separation must be acknowledged and addressed. Knowing what to expect can greatly lessen a child's fear of the unknown.

The preparation period also provides caseworkers with an opportunity to fully assess a child's individual development and needs. This information can also be communicated to the caregivers to help them in easing the children's transition into placement. Caseworkers should also use preparation as a means of establishing a supportive and trusting relationship with the child, which enables the caseworker to be more helpful and supportive to the child, both during and after the move.

While it may seem illogical that a child would trust the caseworker who moved him, a caring, concerned worker who is willing to stand by a child during a distressing time can be an important source of comfort and strength to the child. Unfortunately, many well-meaning agencies or harried caseworkers send a case aide, a transportation aide, or other person to move children. The reasoning is that the caseworker will then be able to make a "fresh start" with children, once they are placed.

However, even if a person is angry with another person in a relationship, there is still a relationship, while an unfamiliar, "neutral" worker is still a stranger. If the caseworker properly and honestly prepares a child, the child's trust is likely to be greater, not less, even if the child is angry. A caseworker's relationship with the child can be strengthened by encouraging the child to express anger and fear, and validating those feelings. For example, the worker might say, "I know you're really mad at me for bringing you here, and upset about leaving Mom. It's okay to be mad, and I know you're scared too. Let's talk again about why I brought you here, and how I'm going to help Mom get better so you can go home." This will surface the child's fears and feelings about the placement, and the changes he is experiencing, ultimately easing the child's adjustment.

It is very important to most children that their caseworkers be a direct link to home and family. This assures them that they have not been set loose in the care of strangers who know nothing about their family or their past. Children are more likely to feel adrift, abandoned, and helpless without such a link. When distressed, children have been known to ask their caregivers to telephone their caseworker to find out what is happening, or how their family is doing.

The strategies used by the caseworker to prepare children for placement will vary, depending upon each child's age and level of developmental maturity.

INFANTS: BIRTH TO 24 MONTHS

Many preparation strategies commonly used with older children are less effective with infants and toddlers because of their developmental limitations. In addition, infants are highly vulnerable to the effects of change in caregivers and environment, and they typically experience high levels of stress during placement. The goal of placement preparation, therefore, is to minimize the number of changes to which infants must adjust. Preparation incorporates strategies that maintain continuity and stability in the caregiving environment, that prevent abrupt losses of primary attachment figures, and that use sensory input to familiarize infants with their new environment.

Workers must help new caregivers understand the importance of maintaining consistency and stability in their caregiving activities. Caregivers should initially learn and follow an infant's typical routine and daily schedule as much as possible, including feeding familiar foods, maintaining familiar light levels, sounds, and smells, and giving baths and naps at the same time of day, and in the same manner to which the infant is accustomed. If previous care was harmful or intrinsically disruptive, or changes are necessary for other reasons, these should be introduced slowly.

Photographs, audio tapes, or videotapes can be used to familiarize infants with the faces and voices of the new caregiver(s). For infants who have developed rudimentary language skills, pairing words such as "mommy" or "daddy" with visual images can help reduce their strangeness. Workers and caregivers can also talk in simple language to infants about what is going to happen. Even preverbal children understand some language, particularly related to familiar persons, events, and objects. A caregiver might talk to an infant during routine caregiving, such as: "Andy's going to have lunch with the new mommy. See Andy's new mommy?" (Show photo.) "New mommy will give Andy cereal." "New mommy loves Andy." "New mommy gives Andy a bath." "Andy go night night in Andy's new bed." "We go bye–bye in the car after Andy's nap to visit Andy's new mommy."

Infants should also be allowed to acclimate to new caregivers prior to making the final move. When possible, a new caregiver should initially visit the infant in the infant's home and should provide as much direct care as possible, in the presence of the parent or current caregiver. This reduces the infant's stress, maintains the infant's current attachments, and allows the caregiver to learn caregiving routines to which the infant is accustomed.

Subsequent preplacement visits should occur in the new home, and should be scheduled on consecutive days, at different periods of the day. The infant's familiar caregiver and strongest attachment figure should be present, if at all possible, during the entire preplacement process. After placement, visits or phone contact with the previous caregiver should occur three to five times a week, until the infant has formed an attachment to the new caregiver. Frequent visits will maintain the parent–child relationship, which is essential for successful reunification. If termination of the parent–child relationship is the case goal, this should occur over a period of time. Such transitioning of infants into new families is critical, since traumatic separation during infancy is believed to contribute to attachment disorders [Bowlby 1973] and the failure to establish basic trust [Erikson 1963].

PRESCHOOL (TWO TO FIVE YEARS)

Toddlers and young preschool children often have limited verbal ability, but they will probably be aware that something important is happening. They may become frightened and anxious when they perceive that their parent is upset, or sense that a separation is imminent. When preparing preschoolers for a move, caseworkers must explain each step of a move in simple, concrete language that the children can understand. This explanation may need to be repeated several times during the course of the placement, both by caseworkers, and wherever possible, by parents. The explanation should be simple and direct, and should focus on the immediate future. Some examples are: "Today we're going in my car, and we're going to visit the Jones family. Mrs. Jones will make you chicken soup for lunch. You can play with the children, Ben and Sally, and you'll take a nap in a new crib." "I'm going now, but I'll come back to get you after your nap, and you will go 'night night' in your own bed at Mommy's house." "Tomorrow after breakfast you'll go stay with Ben and Sally, and we'll help your mom so you can come home again." "I know you're very scared and maybe mad about leaving Mommy. But the Jones' will take very good care of you, and I'll be helping your mom while you're there. Your mommy will visit you lots of times, and you can talk to her on the phone."

Caseworkers can also use play techniques to communicate with toddlers and preschool children. This might include drawing pictures of the new family, the house, or the family dog; by telling stories; by acting out the move with dolls; and by showing photographs or videotapes of the new family members and their home.

During placement, many things are being done to children at an age when they need to be doing for themselves. Therefore, preschool children should be encouraged to make as many decisions for themselves as possible. These might include: what to take with them on visits; where they want to sit in the car; what they want the foster mother to make for lunch; where they want to take a nap, etc. They should also help pack their belongings and choose those items they want to take with them. Letting children leave important items at home can reassure them that they will be coming back.

Finally, during transitions, young children feel most secure when they can depend upon the people around them. Therefore, caseworkers should develop a strong relationship with children during the preparation period, which will enable them to be supportive and comforting throughout the placement process. This becomes less critical if children are to be cared for by people they know and trust, or if their primary caregiver participates in the placement, and can support and comfort them, both during and after the move.

SCHOOL-AGE (SIX TO NINE YEARS)

School-age children have well-developed language skills, and should be helped to talk about the placement and their experiences. Caseworkers can prepare children by describing the new home, the foster or caregiving family, and the neighborhood, and by answering children's questions. Children can also be debriefed after the move by being encouraged to talk about their experiences. Their responses can provide feedback regarding the degree of stress they are experiencing, and how well they are coping, which allows caseworkers to implement additional supportive measures as necessary.

Caseworkers should always explain to children why they must move. School-age children often believe placement is a punishment for something they did wrong. Caseworkers should reassure them and explain the reasons for placement in terms they can understand.

School-age children can also recognize and label some of their feelings, including being sad, scared, mad, lonesome, and worried. These feelings should be elicited and acknowledged by their caseworker and caregivers. Children should be encouraged to talk about their feelings, should be allowed to cry, and should be reassured that people know how hard it is and how badly they feel.

School-age children are less anxious if they clearly understand what is expected of them—that is, if they "know the rules." Caseworkers should insure that children are informed of the expectations in their new families, and help them understand that the caregiving family's rules might be different from those in their own families. Children should also be encouraged to talk with their caregivers, if they don't understand or like a rule. Caregivers should also learn each child's habits, likes and dislikes, and the rules to which they are accustomed. When feasible, some family rules can be modified to maintain continuity and consistency for the children.

When a child is placed in a family from a different cultural background, the caseworker should talk openly with the child about potentially feeling different, and the child's concerns about being accepted in the family and the new environment. The child should also be provided with opportunities to maintain culturally relevant activities and associations while in placement.

PREADOLESCENT (10-12 YEARS)

Many preadolescents have begun to develop abstract reasoning, and their ability to view events from multiple perspectives has improved. As a result, they may be able to correctly identify the family and parental problems that resulted in a need for placement, thereby avoiding unnecessary self–blame. Caseworkers should help children fully explore the reasons for the placement, and stress that their need for safe care is paramount. Children will also need reassurance that their family is receiving help. They should be given considerable opportunity to ask questions, and workers should provide as much information as the children can handle. It is important that caseworkers be straightforward and realistic.

Preadolescent children should be encouraged to participate in placement planning, and to make as many decisions as possible about the placement process. They need to retain an appropriate level of control of their life.

Caseworkers should fully describe the placement setting prior to initiating preplacement visits. Preplacement visits will allow children to become accustomed to their new environment in stages. A trusting relationship with their caseworker is invaluable support, as it allows children to express their impressions, fears, and concerns before, during, and after placement. This is preferable to having to manage their feelings alone, and can prevent emotional turmoil or behavioral acting–out.

Many preadolescent children have concerns about loyalty. They need a consistent message that they do not have to choose between their own families and their new caregivers. They must understand they can be loyal to and love their own families without risking censure from their caregivers. This will prevent them from having to reject their foster or caregiving family in order to reassure themselves of their own family identity, and will allow them to benefit from the placement without feeling disloyal.

When placed in a different cultural or socioeconomic environment, preadolescent children are often concerned about acceptance by peers and the community. They should be able to express these concerns with their caseworker and caregiving family. The caregiving family should intervene, when necessary, to protect a child from personal or community censure. Children should also have regular contact with their own community and cultural group. Placing children in homes in their own communities and cultural groups reduces this problem.

EARLY AND MIDDLE ADOLESCENCE (13-17 YEARS)

Abused or neglected adolescents are often developmentally immature. Each youth's developmental level should be carefully assessed, and placement preparation strategies should generally be chosen that match each youth's developmental, rather than chronological age.

Typically, preparation of adolescents should focus on discussing the reasons for the move, and providing a detailed description of the placement setting. They should be involved as much as possible in choosing and planning the placement. They must know what their caseworkers are planning, and why, and must be given opportunity for input.

Some adolescents retain considerable loyalty to their primary families, and may be threatened if the placement is viewed as a new family. For this reason, foster or relative care may be presented as "a safe place to stay" until the family problems can be resolved, or until the youth can emancipate to independent living. However, we should recognize that adolescents without close family associations may desire and welcome integration into a new family. Caseworkers should assess this with each youth individually and respond accordingly.

Adolescents may try to hide their anxiety and distress regarding a move. They may deny their concerns, and reject their caseworkers' attempts to provide support. Caseworkers should explain all aspects of placement anyway, "just in case any of this information might be of interest." Caseworkers should also prepare them for feelings of distress by saying, "Lots of kids in your situation are pretty angry about having to move," or, "Many kids don't like their new situation right away. If you don't, I'd like to hear about it. It's important that I help you feel comfortable."

If an adolescent must be placed in a culturally or racially different family or environment, the caregivers must understand the importance of maintaining cultural and ethnic identity while in placement. Adolescents are often very aware of personal, community, and institutional racism and bias. These need to be discussed, and they should be prepared with strategies to deal with them. They must be provided with opportunities for regular contact with their own community and cultural group. Again, as with younger children, developing placements for adolescents in their own communities and cultures greatly lessens this problem.

The preparation process is comparable when adolescents are to be placed in group or institutional care to meet special needs, or to provide opportunities for emancipation training. However, it becomes more important to identify a specific caregiver or caseworker who can establish a trusting relationship with a youth, and provide guidance and support during the adjustment period. This may be difficult when group homes or institutions are staffed on shifts. Without such a contact, however, adolescents are essentially left without situational support.

THE PLACEMENT PROCESS

Preplacement Visits and Activities

An effective strategy for reducing stress associated with change is to partialize the change into small, manageable increments, or steps. Smaller changes are less overwhelming, and can be more easily managed. Experiencing small successes also helps us feel in control, increases our confidence, and makes subsequent changes less threatening. Consider how often, in stressful and challenging situations, we say, "Well, I've gotten this far; I guess I can get through the rest." Preventing stress overload helps to prevent crisis and its resulting emotional turmoil and immobility.

Dividing placement activities among several preplacement visits allows children to become accustomed to their new caregivers and environment a little at a time. A sufficient number of steps should be planned to allow children to develop familiarity with and comfort in the new environment before they are placed there. In general, two or three preplacement visits in as many days can help ease the transition and remove some fear of the unknown. Some children will require additional time, and the placement plan should be individualized to meet each child's needs.

Preplacement visits should be a few hours in length, particularly for toddlers and preschool-age children. School-age children can tolerate visits of several hours. Visits should be scheduled to allow the child to experience the home at different times of day and under different circumstances, and to experience routine family activities. For younger children, visits should be scheduled to coincide with meals and nap times so they can experience these critical caregiving activities and feel more secure about them.

Early in the first visit, children should be given a tour of the home. Those areas which will be theirs (bed, closet, dresser drawers, toy box) should be pointed out, and they should be encouraged to use them by putting their sweater in their drawer, putting their toy bear on their bed, hanging their coat in the closet, and taking a nap in their bed. Caregivers should point out where the food is, where the bathroom is, and otherwise help make children feel secure and comfortable.

Only one member of the caregiving family, usually a parent, should be identified to initially develop a relationship with a child who has been placed. No more than one or two family members should be home during preplacement visits. Children should never be greeted at the door by parents, a group of children, grandparents, dogs, and curious neighbors. Children need a single, trusting relationship with someone in the home to provide them with support and comfort during the early adjustment period. The preplacement visits should focus on developing this relationship. Other relationships can be developed as a child is ready. Some children are more comfortable with other children and less so with parent figures. In this case, older siblings can initially bond with placed children and "show them the ropes."

During preplacement visits, caregivers should try to maintain as much continuity for children as possible. They can adhere to children's familiar schedules and routines, feed them familiar foods, let them choose and wear their own clothing, and use gentle and nonintrusive guidance and discipline to help them learn new rules. After several weeks, when children are more settled, caregivers can gradually revise their schedule to better conform to the family's.

Ideally, children should be given periods of respite away from the new home during the placement. These can be in their own home, or in familiar and comfortable surroundings, where they can reflect on what is happening and freely express their concerns and feelings. Even in emergency placements, where children cannot return home, a relative's home, a friend's home, or even the caseworker's car can serve as such a respite. These respite periods allow children to recoup their strength and receive support from known and trusted persons.

Determining the Rate of the Placement

The rate of placement is the total length of time between the decision to place and the final placement. The shortest placement is to transport children and their belongings from one home to another and leave them. A more extended placement may include several preplacement visits over a period of several weeks, as might occur when a child is being placed from a foster home to the home of a previously noncustodial parent in another community.

The rate of placement should be determined by two factors: the degree of risk to children in their home environment, and their coping abilities. The rate should be individualized to prevent undue stress and anxiety, and to help children comfortably transition from one home to another, without leaving them unprotected in a high risk situation.

In situations where children are not at risk, as when being placed for adoption, moving between foster homes, or being reunited with family or relatives, the rate of placement should always be determined by their needs and ability to cope with change. If potential risk to children in their current placement is sufficiently high to warrant an emergency removal, placement should proceed without extended preparation. In these circumstances, however, we can increase the rate of placement by protecting children in familiar surroundings with a relative, friend or neighbor while we identify the most appropriate placement setting, prepare the children, and conduct preplacement activities.

Interim placements in emergency foster homes are not, however, the same as interim placements with a relative or friend. Children are comfortable with a relative or family friend. Staying there is, therefore, less stressful. In emergency shelter care, we place children in one strange and unknown situation, and then move them to another, just as they are becoming accustomed to the first. Such multiple moves greatly increase their stress.

When there are no options but to place children immediately in an unfamiliar setting without preparation or preplacement visits, caseworkers must be prepared to do intensive and extensive postplacement supportive work with them to prevent or deal with crisis. If, despite attempts by workers to avoid it, a child does experience clinical crisis, intensive casework activities should be provided during the crisis period. Without supportive counseling at the time of the crisis, children may suffer long-term negative consequences.

To determine a child's coping ability, the caseworker must recognize normal signs of stress in children, and must be familiar with a child's individual responses to stress. The worker must carefully monitor the rate of the placement to prevent the child from experiencing crisis. When the child shows signs of excessive stress, the caseworker should slow down the placement process and provide the child with considerable support. This may mean increasing the number of visits, and/or shortening the length of individual preplacement visits.

A placement without proper preparation can cause overwhelming stress and emotional crisis. However, at times, providing too long a preparation and preplacement period can also increase the child's anxiety. It is easy to overextend the preplacement process in relatively low risk situations, such as adoption. Once the child is told about the move, preparation activities should begin immediately. Under most circumstances, preplacement visits can be completed and the child can be moved within a few weeks. The child can generally be placed comfortably in the new home when she is familiar with the environment, and when she has identified the caregiver as a source of support and help, particularly if she is allowed frequent contact with her parent or other trusted caregiver.

The following case examples illustrate differences in coping ability of several children of the same age, but with different temperaments and histories. They also illustrate how their caseworker structured placements to meet the children's individual needs.

⚘ Marie Sullivan, age two

Marie was a failure-to-thrive infant. She was placed in foster care for a month during infancy and returned to her mother. She was again placed in foster care at age one and a half due to severe neglect. When Marie was two years old, the agency was awarded permanent custody, and an adoptive family was identified.

Marie was an engaging redhead who was well into the "me do it" stage. She related to people surprisingly well, considering her history, and she showed considerable interest in people, toys, and activities. Her foster parents were elderly and had chronic health problems, which greatly limited their activities. Marie had received good basic care and affection from them, but very little stimulation. Their home was dark and quiet; television was the only activity. Marie did not appear to be particularly attached to either foster parent.

Within the first few minutes of the caseworker's first home visit, Marie invited the worker to "play dolls" on the floor with her. The worker took advantage of Marie's attachment to her dolls, and used play strategies to engage Marie, and eventually to prepare her for the impending move. In subsequent home visits, Marie and the worker took turns acting out the placement steps with Marie's dolls.

The adoptive family had four children between the ages of four and ten. On the first preplacement visit, the children greeted Marie at the door and immediately took her to the playroom, where they stayed for the three hours until the visit was over. On the second visit, Marie brought some of her clothes and left them at the new house, and she protested when the worker told her it was time to go back to the foster home. On the third visit, Marie got out of the worker's car unassisted, walked alone up to the front door, knocked loudly, and when the door was opened, walked straight into the house. Her first stop was her new bedroom, where she opened a dresser drawer, put her favorite teddy bear inside, and slammed the drawer shut. She then stopped in the kitchen, asked for a snack, and went off to find the kids. Essentially, Marie had moved herself in. The worker let her stay that night. Marie and the worker went back to the foster home the following day to say good-bye to the foster parents and to get the remainder of Marie's clothes.

The worker was initially concerned that Marie's behavior and apparent obliviousness to separation from her foster parents reflected an aloofness characteristic of attachment disorder, or reflected the "shock/denial" stage of grief. She prepared the adoptive parents for possible subsequent problems. However, Marie engaged quickly and appropriately with the parents and the children, and she never exhibited significant emotional distress or problems. She was doing very well six months later. The worker concluded that perhaps Marie had "gotten something good somewhere" in her chaotic early years, and had not lost her ability to engage in healthy relationships; or, that temperamentally, she was simply more resilient than other children.

⚘ David Vance, age two

David was a shy and retiring child. He was adopted during infancy, but was returned to the agency by the adoptive family at age one and a half, ostensibly because they "couldn't bond with him." He adjusted well to his foster home, but he exhibited excessive anxiety in response to new people and unfamiliar situations. He hid behind his foster mother and refused to look at the caseworker the first several times she visited. Eventually, the worker engaged him to play with her, but he began to cry each time the worker suggested they go for a ride in the car. It took many weeks of short walks in the yard and trips to the store in the worker's car, with the foster mother present, before David would go with the worker alone.

The adoptive family chosen for David was prepared for a lengthy preplacement process. The family initially met David at a park near his house. They talked with the worker while David played. David was curious, but unwilling to relate directly to them. The adoptive family visited the foster home several times. Eventually, David went for walks with them in the yard, and then allowed them to take him to the park. After the third park outing, they took David to their house for ice cream. Subsequent visits were held in the adoptive family's home, gradually extended in length to entire days. When David was finally moved, the foster caregivers helped, and they visited him twice weekly in the adoptive home for the first two weeks of the placement. A month after placement, the adoptive family took David back to the foster home to visit. All in all, the placement process spanned about six weeks, with another two months of follow-up support. In spite of the careful preparation and slowed pace, David exhibited considerable stress, including crying at night and symptoms of physical illness. However, he did not experience crisis, and he allowed his adoptive parents to comfort him. Regular contact with his foster caregivers also helped him feel more secure.

David and Marie represent two ends of the continuum of children's responses to placement-induced stress. Marie's placement went easily, largely because of her comfort with new people and new situations, and the absence of strong attachment to her foster parents. David, by contrast, was exceptionally vulnerable, probably due to his temperament and his previous separation experiences. The rate and length of each placement were determined by the child's needs and stress level. The worker was able to adjust placement activities to prevent crisis, while encouraging the child to form attachments to new caregivers, and a new home before the final move.

A third example demonstrates how a natural progression from one family to another resulted in a creative placement that met the child's needs. This case example also illustrates how a child's current caregivers can facilitate a move.

☥ Darren Thomas, age two

Darren was removed from his teenage mother when he was one year old. Considerable work had been done with the mother to help her keep Darren, but he continued to be subjected to serious neglect because of his mother's chronic use of drugs and alcohol. There were no relatives to care for him, and he was placed in foster care. The agency filed for permanent custody, and an adoptive family was identified.

Darren was two when adoptive planning began. The worker prepared Darren to move using dolls and photographs, and began preplacement visits with the adoptive family. Darren knew his caseworker well, and went willingly with her to the new home. However, upon entering the home and meeting the new family, he became uncharacteristically cautious, and clung to the worker. The family tried repeatedly to engage Darren and entice him away from the worker; the harder they tried, the more frightened Darren became, and the more he clung to the worker. The family suggested the worker leave so they could better focus Darren's attention on them. Despite her concern about leaving him, she complied. When she returned an hour later, Darren was distraught; he had cried continuously, and the adoptive family had decided this was not the "right child" for them. When the worker entered the house, Darren ran to her and promptly curled into her lap sobbing, and eventually fell asleep.

About a month later, adoption planning was resumed with a second adoptive family. This time the worker began placement activities on a Friday by having the adoptive family meet Darren in his foster home. They visited for three hours, talked with the foster parents, played with Darren, and expressed strong commitment to continue the adoption.

The caseworker had arranged to pick Darren up early Monday morning to transport him to visit in the adoptive home. When she arrived at the foster home on Monday, Darren wasn't there. The foster mother sheepishly explained that they had seen the adoptive family at their church on Sunday, and the adoptive family had invited the entire foster family to Sunday dinner. They had visited well into the evening. Darren had played with his new brother, and they both fell asleep in the bedroom they were to share. Rather than disturb Darren, the foster family let him sleep, and asked the adoptive family to call them if Darren awoke and was at all distressed. The foster mother acknowledged to the worker that she had wondered if this was permitted, but only after she had returned home. She had called and left a message at the agency early that morning, and apologized if she had erred in her judgment.

When the worker arrived at the adoptive home, Darren was contentedly having breakfast. The remaining placement steps went as planned, with Darren returning intermittently to the foster home to pack and move his belongings. The two families planned to visit often after church.

Darren was a friendly, adaptable child, who nonetheless reacted strongly to an unfamiliar and stressful situation. With the validation given to the adoptive family by his trusted foster family, he was able to easily engage and stay with them without distress. The ability to maintain contact with his foster parents after placement also helped to prevent a traumatic separation.

🚶 Rochelle Carter, age 10

Rochelle's case illustrates how a worker can prevent trauma when a child must be moved without preparation or preplacement visits.

Rochelle had lived with her grandmother intermittently for most of her life. Her mother was mentally ill and hospitalized periodically. Currently, the mother's whereabouts were unknown. Rochelle's biological father had died in a car accident shortly after her birth.

The child welfare agency became involved after a referral from a neighbor. Rochelle's grandmother had been taken to the hospital by the emergency squad, and it was believed she had suffered a heart attack. Rochelle was due home from school, and there was no one to care for her. The neighbor, also elderly and ill, knew of no other family or relatives in the area, and could not care for Rochelle herself. The intake worker arranged for the neighbor to meet Rochelle after school, and she began arranging an emergency foster placement for Rochelle.

The worker arrived at the home shortly after Rochelle returned from school. Rochelle was visibly upset, and very worried that her grandmother was going to die. She did not want to move; she wanted to stay alone in the house, or go to the hospital and stay with her grandmother. The worker explained how this was not possible, and began talking about going to a foster home. Rochelle protested strongly and said she would not go. The worker was very supportive and assured Rochelle that everything possible was being done to help her grandmother, but that it was important that an adult be there to care for Rochelle.

In spite of Rochelle's refusal to go, the worker began preparing Rochelle. She talked about the foster mother, Audrey, described her interests, told Rochelle that Audrey was very concerned about her grandmother and really wanted to help Rochelle. Audrey had a daughter who was grown, and she had lots of time to spend with Rochelle. The worker then asked Rochelle if she would be willing to talk to Audrey on the phone before they went to the house; Rochelle grudgingly agreed, and the worker placed the call. Audrey, who had been prepared by the worker, told Rochelle how much she wanted her to come stay for as long as she needed to, and that the first thing they would do when she got there was to call the hospital and check on Rochelle's grandmother. Rochelle agreed to stay with Audrey, but "just for now." She packed the bare essentials in an overnight bag, and the worker transported Rochelle to Audrey's.

The worker made daily follow-up visits to the foster home for the first week. Rochelle and Audrey called the hospital several times a day to check on Rochelle's grandmother, who remained in intensive care, but was stable. When Rochelle needed additional clothes, the worker transported her and Audrey to the grandmother's house, and together they decided what to take and what to leave. Eventually, most of Rochelle's belongings were moved to Audrey's.

Her grandmother's illness and the placement together precipitated an emotional crisis for Rochelle. She had long crying bouts, and she awoke most nights with nightmares. Audrey was up with her for many hours. They drank hot chocolate and just sat together until Rochelle fell asleep again. Rochelle could not concentrate in school and could not sit still in class. The caseworker talked with the teacher, who intervened gently and did not punish Rochelle. The worker and Audrey considered supportive counseling, but decided to wait a while longer to see if Rochelle settled in.

The grandmother was eventually discharged from the hospital to a nursing home. Audrey, who had lost her own mother recently, helped Rochelle deal with the loss, and took Rochelle to visit her grandmother frequently.

Eventually, Rochelle was placed for adoption with an aunt she didn't know she had—her biological father's sister. This time, the placement occurred only after extended preparation and preplacement visits. Audrey felt herself too old to adopt, but she remained close to Rochelle, and was accepted by the adoptive family as Aunt Audrey.

While Rochelle had to be placed with little preparation in a precipitous situation, the caseworker and the caregiver together provided sufficient situational and emotional support to prevent permanent negative outcomes from the crisis.

Providing Children with Opportunities to Talk about Placement and Their Feelings

Separation and placement are universally painful. Children typically experience feelings of loss, abandonment, fear, anxiety, confusion, isolation, anger, guilt, rejection, and depression as a result of separation. A child's expressions of emotional pain may elicit feelings of guilt from adults for having caused the pain, or feelings of helplessness at being unable to alleviate the pain. For these reasons, children are often not permitted by parents or other adults to express or dwell on painful feelings. Adults may subtly encourage a child to stop crying, or may try to redirect him to think about other things, or to become involved in distracting activities. However, as with any victim of trauma, the child needs to talk about his experiences, perhaps many times during a period of weeks or months, with a supportive and caring listener.

Unresolved painful feelings, and misunderstood experiences, will continue to cause fear and confusion for a child. The emotional energy expended in trying to cope with these feelings can reduce the child's ability to concentrate, interfere with school work, prevent him from dealing with fears about attachments, and keep him preoccupied with his own needs. The painful feelings may be manifested in unacceptable behaviors for which the child may be punished. This only increases the child's anxiety and depression, and may complicate his situation.

The caseworker should develop a supportive, nurturing relationship with the child that allows the child to communicate his painful feelings, either in words; through drawings, stories, or play; or through appropriate behaviors such as crying; by verbally and emotively discharging tension or anger; or choosing not to talk or play for a while. The caseworker should educate the caregivers to support the child in a similar manner. If the child can deal with negative feelings by expressing them in a supportive environment, these feelings are less likely to cause lasting harm. For less verbal children, the caseworker may need initially to label the child's feelings, such as, "You look like you're ready to cry. You probably feel really sad right now. You can cry if you like. I have lots of tissues;" or, "I know how mad you are about having to move. It's a hard time, and it's okay to be mad. You can tell me about it, if you like."

POSTPLACEMENT SERVICES TO CHILDREN

Once a child is moved, casework intervention can ease the child's adjustment, and help prevent subsequent trauma.

Assure that the Caregiver Receives Adequate Support

Postplacement support can greatly increase the likelihood of a successful adjustment by the child and the caregiving family, which helps to prevent placement disruption. Postplacement support can be provided in a number of ways. The caregiving family can be referred to appropriate community services that address the child's special needs. This may include medical services, special education programs, mental health counseling services, recreational opportunities, and developmental services. The caseworker, as a case manager, can help to arrange and access needed services. When a child is from a different cultural background than the caregiving family, the caregivers should be helped to locate culturally relevant service providers, particularly for developmental and recreational services.

Emotional support for caregivers is also important. The caseworker should be available to help the caregiving family identify and discuss issues and resolve problems. Respite services should be made available to caregivers who are caring for challenging children. Respite services are designed to offer short-term, out-of-home care for children to allow caregivers a reprieve from the stresses of foster care. This allows families to renew their strength, and to focus time exclusively on their own needs. Finally, invaluable support can be provided by the caseworker and by other caregiving families who have had similar experiences. The opportunity to talk with others allows caregivers to exchange ideas, vent their frustration, and receive encouragement and support.

(Strategies to support caregivers is more fully discussed in Section X-C, "Working with Foster and Other Caregivers.")

Help Children Develop a Story to Explain the Reasons for Placement

Many children have difficulty responding to questions from friends, neighbors, teachers, and other curious adults about why they are living in a foster home. Children are often embarrassed and self-conscious. They may fabricate reasons for their placement, or they may avoid discussing it.

The caseworker can help a child deal with this situation by helping her prepare and practice an honest, simple, but nonjudgmental explanation of why the child cannot live at home. Confidential information can remain confidential. Such a "cover story" can prevent embarrassment for the child. An example of an appropriate explanation might be: "I'm staying with my aunt till my mom feels better and can take care of me." "My mom is getting counseling, and she can't take care of me until she's better. When she is, I'll go back home." The foster family, including all children in the family, should be included in this activity, and all family members should use the same explanation when asked about the child. The foster family should offer the explanation to interested neighbors, other children, teachers, and others to reduce the number of persons who will ask the child directly about her status.

Help Children Maintain Continuity and Identity: The Lifebook and "A Story about You"

Children in placement are at a significant disadvantage. Each time they move to another home, a part of their past is lost. Most of us remember our pasts through photographs and anecdotes that we've heard from our families. Ironically, while fun for most people, these stories are not critical to identity development, since we learn who we are and understand our histories by growing up with our parents and extended families, and by sharing in their customs and traditions.

Many children in placement have neither memory nor knowledge of their early lives. Many children doubt they have a history. For example, a five year old solemnly told his caseworker that he had never been a baby; he had always looked just like he did now. If a child has correct information, supported by visual representations of his early life, he can be helped to construct a positive and realistic sense of self, along with a history. This helps children retain ties to their past, which is critical if a child is to be reunified with his family. It will also enable the child to integrate elements of his past and his future if placed into an adoptive or other permanent home.

Each child in lengthy out–of–home placement should have her own Lifebook to document her history. Lifebooks are scrapbooks that contain photographs, drawings, anecdotes, stories about the child, her family and her friends, and other memorabilia. The child can participate in developing the Lifebook, and in dictating or writing her own contributions to the history.

Lifebooks provides continuity, helps establish a positive identity, and allows the child to share her past life with others. Lifebooks are an excellent tool for caseworkers in helping children understand the reasons for placement. Lifebooks can also help children from ethnically and culturally diverse backgrounds maintain a positive cultural identity and self–esteem.

⚲ Lisa, age seven

Lisa's biological mother had left her with a neighbor in a laundromat "for a couple of hours" when Lisa was two. She never returned. Lisa lived with this woman and her husband, Jack, for several years. The woman subsequently divorced Jack, and left Lisa in his care. At age seven, Lisa was living with Jack, whom she called "Daddy," and his new girlfriend when, during an episode of domestic violence, a neighbor called the police. Lisa was placed into foster care to assure her safety. Further assessment revealed that Jack had been engaging Lisa in fondling and sexual play for many months.

The worker could find no historical information about Lisa, except for her mother's name on Lisa's birth certificate. The father was listed as "unknown." The mother could not be located, permanent custody was filed, and an adoptive home was sought for Lisa.

The worker began to prepare Lisa for adoption. Lisa was very confused about why she couldn't live with Jack, and didn't understand that he wasn't really her father. The worker developed a Lifebook with Lisa to help her better understand her situation and to reconstruct her early history.

The worker wrote, "A Story About Lisa," and read it to Lisa during visits. When the worker read parts that Lisa remembered, Lisa embellished the story from her own point of view, and her contributions were added to the story. The worker and foster mother also took pictures of Lisa for the Lifebook. The worker reconstructed what she could of Lisa's early life by photographing her old school, her teacher, and the home and neighborhood where she had lived prior to placement. A photograph of Jack was obtained and also put into the Lifebook. Lisa dictated what should be written about each picture.

One day, the worker brought Lisa a footprint and a picture taken immediately after she was born, obtained from hospital files. When presented with the photo, Lisa stared at it for long moments, then asked, "Are you sure this is really me?" Lisa pasted the picture on the first page of her Lifebook and told the worker to write, "This is Lisa when she was a very teeny, tiny, little baby."

There are many ways caseworkers can gather information for a Lifebook. Foster caregivers or relatives are often eager to help, and can assume most of the responsibility for gathering contents and compiling the scrapbook. There are many sources of valuable information:

- The worker can approach biological parents and other relatives and request pictures of the child. Families are often willing to provide pictures, if the purpose is explained, and if they are assured that the pictures will always be in the child's possession. If they have only original prints, photo shops can make copies, and the originals can then be returned to the family members.

- Family members can contribute pictures of themselves. This should include parents, siblings, extended family, family friends, and others who have been important to the child. This is particularly important if the child's biological parents are, or have been, absent.

- The worker can approach previous foster parents or caregivers; they may have many pictures of the child in their own family albums. They can provide negatives or extra photos, or copies can be made from prints or slides. Workers may find photos documenting a child's first tooth, first steps, birthday parties, and other family events. Photos of previous caregiving families should also be obtained.

- The worker can return with the child to her previous schools, neighborhoods, and communities, and together they can photograph people and places familiar to the child. The worker can also obtain class pictures from the school, and school pictures from the school photographer.

- The worker can call the hospital where the child was born, inquire whether infant photos were taken, and contact the photography department to obtain the negative or a reprint. Footprints and other documentation may also be available. The hospital building can be photographed, also.

- The worker can ask relatives and previous caregivers for examples of the child's drawings and artwork.

- The worker can ask key informants to tell their "cutest story" about the child, and then write these up into a narrative, identifying each storyteller and his or her relationship with the child.

- Workers can encourage current caregivers to document what appear to be unimportant daily events. These current events will one day be the child's history, and this documentation will be of particular importance if the child leaves their home.

Developing the Child's Story

Writing a story that presents the child's history and the reasons for placement requires both honesty and sensitivity. It is a difficult undertaking, since information about the child's early life may not be immediately available. However, workers can construct a history for most children that provides continuity and strengthens identity, and that can also help to explain the reasons for placement, even from limited information.

The story should begin with the child's birth information. Basic facts are essential, including the date of birth, the time, the child's weight and length, the place of birth, and the name of the hospital. If this information is not in the case record, it can be obtained by asking the parents or other family members, by checking the birth certificate, and by accessing the records at the hospital. A release of information may be necessary.

The child's history should include the ages at which he first sat up, cut teeth, crawled, walked, uttered his first words, started preschool, and other milestones. Information on developmental milestones can be gleaned from family members, or can be inferred from case dictation or photographs. For example, one worker found a family case dictation which noted that when the child was nine months old, he was "dressed inappropriately in only a wet diaper, and was crawling around on a filthy floor." It can be inferred that at nine months, the child had learned to crawl. Many developmental stages can be determined from this kind of description, and can be written in the child's story. For example, "When you were four you liked to ride your cousin's tricycle;" "Your grandma said even when you were very little, you loved chocolate ice cream;" "When you were two, you liked to play outside, and once you played in the mud and got it all over yourself;" "You were a quiet baby; you didn't cry very often;" "When you were three, you went to the zoo with your brother, and you really liked the elephants;" "By the time you were 15 months, you were toddling all over the house." While these do not state precisely when the events occurred, they do document the events. It is most important to provide the child with validation that he has a history; that he was once a tiny baby, then a young child, that he developed skills like all children, and that he did cute and unique things.

Factual and descriptive information about the child's parents and extended family are essential. This is made more difficult when biological parents have been absent and cannot be found. However, information can again be obtained from extended family members, and from the case record. Children will want to know not only what their parents looked like, but their interests, likes and dislikes, and accomplishments. This makes them real to the child. For example, a description of a child's parents could read as follows:

> Your mother had green eyes and dark blonde hair. She was of medium height and build. Her background was Irish, French, and Cherokee and Choctaw Indian. She was of the Protestant religion. She had a ninth grade education and worked as a waitress. Your mother was musical and artistic; she loved to draw, and she liked to play the piano. She also loved sports, especially swimming and softball. Your father had dark hair and eyes, and he was about six feet tall. He was a very skilled mechanic, who particu-

larly liked riding and working on motorcycles. He traveled all over the county on his bike with a group of other bikers. He met your mother on one of his trips.

It is important to present inherently negative information in a matter–of–fact and nonjudgmental way. We know that children need positive facts about themselves and their families to develop healthy self–esteem and identity. Yet, we cannot fabricate a story, nor hide important facts that will help a child better understand his history. Workers are confronted with the dilemma of how to tell a child that she didn't sit up until she was 11 months old because her mother never fed her; that a child was born prematurely because of her mother's drug addiction; or that her mother left her with a stranger at the laundromat and never returned. We must look for the strengths in the child's history, and interpret this information in a positive light.

An early case dictation by a child welfare caseworker describes Jenny, 11 months old, sitting on a filthy blanket in a ragged playpen, with a ball and two blocks. She had poor color and was very underweight for her age. Jenny was dirty, underfed, and wobbly, but she was sitting up by herself, and her mother provided her with a playpen and a few toys. The history might read:

> You lived with your mother in a small apartment until you were 12 months old. Your mother was very young when you were born, only 15, and she didn't understand how to feed and care for babies. Sometimes she forgot to feed you, or change your diaper. Still, she did what she could for you. She got a playpen and she put toys in it. When you were 11 months old you were sitting up all by yourself, and the first time the caseworker saw you, you were in your playpen batting around a pink rubber ball your mother had given to you.

Events like prematurity can be explained in general terms. Most children are not concerned with the medical reasons for their prematurity. A simple explanation will suffice, such as:

> Sometimes babies surprise everybody by being born sooner than expected! You were born two months early, and this is the reason you were so very tiny when you were born. Because you were so little, you got very special care in the hospital, sleeping in a bed that kept you warm and comfortable until you grew big enough to go home.

Stories from family members, albeit brief, can be embellished to create a picture of the child and her environment.

> Your grandma told me you were a pretty baby with white–blonde hair and blue eyes. She said your blue eyes were a family trait–your grandmother's eyes were blue, and so were your mother's. Your grandma called you "Sweet Pea" because when you crawled around on the floor in your flannel sleepers, you looked like Sweet Pea from the Popeye comic strips.

By describing parents' attempts to provide care, we can help dispel children's fears that they were blithely abandoned by selfish parents who didn't care whether or not they existed.

> You lived with your mom at your grandma's house for four years. Your mom tried very hard to take care of you and your brother. It was not easy, because two children, age four and six, can be quite a handful. Sometimes your mom wanted to be independent, and she and your grandma had fights. Sometimes the pressures got too great, and your mom took you and your brother to her girlfriend Sylvia's, and Sylvia cared for you while your mom tried to find a job. Some days there was nobody at home to take care of you. That was when you got your first case-worker, Sally, who wanted to be very sure that you and your brother were cared for. Sally moved you to a foster home, at least for a while, until she could find your mother and try to help her care for you herself.

In the story, the worker can acknowledge the child's feelings about loss and multiple placements. Children may have no memory of these feelings, or may believe negative feelings should not be expressed. Validating the child's negative feelings is an important part of the therapeutic process.

> During the summer, Mrs. McGraw learned she had to have a major operation. She didn't want to tell you, because she was afraid you would worry. It would take her many months in bed to recover, and she would have to go to the doctor often for treatments. She felt it would be better if you were in a family where the mom could be at home. So we moved you to the Andersons.
>
> This was your third foster home, and by this time, you were pretty confused, tired of moving around, and angry. You worried about how long you would stay with the Andersons, and whether you would move again. You wondered when you could go home, or when you would get a family you could stay with forever. It was really hard for you. Your caseworker kept working to help your mom solve her problems and take you home, or else find you a family of your very own to live with forever.
>
> After we moved you to the Andersons' house, you helped us to understand how very angry you were. You had lots of tantrums. You kicked and screamed, and sometimes you broke things. It was hard for the Andersons at first, and harder for you. But we talked about how bad you felt, how worried you were, and how mad you were that you had to move again, and the Andersons finally understood what you were feeling. They helped you learn to tell them when you were mad, so you did-n't hurt yourself or other people. Every day you and Mrs. Anderson would have 'mad story time' where you could tell her every single thing that you were feeling mad about that day."

Workers have little trouble describing well–meaning and sincere parents who just don't have the capacity to care for their children. Quoting or paraphrasing parents' reasons for allowing their children to be placed can help those children understand that their parents had their best interests at heart, and their parents didn't give them away because they were bad. While some children may believe their parents to have been weak or irresponsible, this is better than believing that their own inherent badness prompted their parents to abandon them.

> Your mom came to the agency and asked us to find you a permanent family where you would be loved and cared for. Your grandma had died, and your mom was alone. She had been on drugs for a long time, and she was struggling to get better. She knew that when she was on drugs she didn't give you very good care. She explained to me why she wanted us to find you a family to live with. She said, "I suppose this sounds very cold and unloving, but I've been doing a lot of thinking about this, and I cried most of last night. But I'm doing this for Danielle. I was raised on the streets, and not in the schools, and I don't want Danielle to have the sort of life I had. It's a hard life. Danielle deserves better than that. I'll always love her, but I want her to have a future, and I can't give it to her. If she stays with me, she'll always be hurt.

It is considerably more difficult to help children deal with serious parental problems or behaviors, such as drug addiction, criminal activity, abuse or neglect, sexual abuse, or violence. Older children may have some memory of these activities, and other family members may continue to reinforce their parents' "badness."

> Life was not very happy for your mother when she was growing up. When she was very little, your Grandpa Tom left your grandma alone with three little children. Your grandma had never worked before. She did laundry and cleaning to support her family. She didn't have much time to spend with her children. Your mother was always a strong–willed girl, and when she became a teenager, she became very rebellious. She dropped out of school, ran away from home, and lived with her friends. She took drugs from time to time. Most teenagers are rebellious, and it can be a hard time. But it was especially hard for your mother, because she was stubborn and wouldn't let anyone help her. She wanted to be independent, but she made some bad choices. Her relationship with your grandma was pretty stormy, and made things hard for both of them, even though your grandma always loved your mom. You were born while your mom was on the run, and your grandma took you to live with her, hoping that one day your mom would grow up enough to become a loving and responsible parent."

Helping children understand their history is much like providing sex education; we must give children enough information to answer their questions, but not more than they are ready for, or are able to comprehend. Adoption workers should consider writing each child's life story in two or three versions, covering the information at varying levels of depth for use at different stages of development. When children reach adolescence, they will need more in–depth information, and they will be more capable of understanding complex explanations. Information can be given to permanent families to be shared with children as they grow.

While young children may have difficulty understanding abstract reasons for behavior, older children may, in time, be able to understand that their parents were products of their own environments, and may be able to develop empathy for them, if not acceptance of their behavior. As Fahlberg [1991] states, an important goal of the life story is to eventually help adolescents and young adults understand the complex events that led to their placements, to perhaps understand, and possibly to forgive their parents for their actions.

IX. WORKING WITH FAMILIES OF CHILDREN IN PLACEMENT

A. The Emotional Impact of Placement on Family Members

B. Empowering Parents to Participate in Placement Activities

C. Promoting Reunification

A. THE EMOTIONAL IMPACT OF PLACEMENT ON FAMILY MEMBERS

1. Conceptual Framework

2. Application

Conceptual Framework

Families typically experience extreme psychological distress and, often, crisis when children are removed and placed. When out–of–home placement is the only way to assure a child's safety, caseworkers must understand the potentially traumatic outcomes to families, and must work to minimize the negative consequences, particularly if the case goal is reunification of the family.

Most families experience pervasive and painful feelings of loss when their children are removed. Parents may also experience psychological threats to their self–esteem, and to their identity as competent parents. They may lose their sense of purpose and direction, particularly if they have been full–time parents whose daily activities have revolved around their children. Separation usually threatens the family's identity, sense of belonging and togetherness, and feeling of security. Siblings also experience considerable distress. They may believe their sister or brother to be permanently gone, perhaps dead; and they may experience heightened anxiety that they, too, may have to leave their home.

Parents whose children are removed are often subjected to criticism and blame from extended family members, neighbors, and friends. They may lose an acceptable social identity, and the respect and esteem of important others. Strong cultural values about family unity and competent parenting may exacerbate this loss for many families, particularly if the child is placed with strangers outside of the immediate community.

Finally, removal of the children may reduce the family's income and financial security. When a family's primary source of income is public assistance, the removal of the children often results in a cut in their subsidy. They may have to move, and they may lose other supportive services, such as food stamps, medical care, and day care. A lengthy process of reapplication is often necessary to reinstate these services, and finding appropriate housing may involve long waiting lists. This may result in lengthy delays in reunification.

The multiple threats and losses inherent in child placement often precipitate a clinical crisis for families. When in crisis, family members are often immobilized and emotionally disabled by overwhelming distress. They typically cannot engage in goal–directed or problem–solving activities. They may have difficulty just getting by, much less have the stamina to make the changes necessary to have their children returned. Unresolved crisis can increase families' vulnerability to stress, and can sometimes result in a generally lower level of functioning than the family had prior to the crisis [Parad & Caplan 1965].

Many families served by child welfare agencies have a history of marginal adaptive behavior. They may have psychological and emotional problems, may be in dire poverty, may have substance abuse problems, and may have limited coping ability. Some parents have had consistently painful experiences in their interpersonal relationships, and in contacts with social institutions, and they may not trust the agency or the caseworker. They may have limited sources of emotional support. Negative life experiences may also contribute to a general perception of futility and helplessness, and some families may be without hope that their children will ever be returned. This is exacerbated by the serious, sometimes permanent damage that separation inflicts on the parent–child relationship. Families may give up, withdraw from agency contact, grieve their loss, and resign themselves to life without their children. This seriously compromises the likelihood of successful reunification.

The outcomes of placement for the family may depend largely upon the case-worker's success in engaging and empowering them before and throughout the placement. The degree of loss and threat experienced by family members can be minimized through appropriate casework interventions. By involving parents in planning for their children, and by empowering them during all parts of the placement process, we achieve several objectives: we can maintain and strengthen the relationship between the parents and the child; we can develop and strengthen the parents' parenting skills; we can help the parents work to create a safe home environment for their children; and, in doing the above, we can reduce the traumatic effects of placement for families and children. This can promote reunification, or can provide the worker with essential information with which to conclude the child cannot go home, thus enabling workers to direct their efforts toward placing the child in an alternative permanent family.

Application

BEHAVIORAL EXPRESSIONS OF GRIEF AND LOSS IN PARENTS

Certain behaviors typify family members' responses to the losses and threats experienced during placement. If a worker does not properly interpret the meaning of these behaviors, and fails to recognize them as symptoms of grief and stress, the worker may respond in nonproductive ways. For example, the stunned immobilization of a parent in shock could be misinterpreted as a lack of motivation, or as agreement with the placement. Depressive withdrawal could be misinterpreted as a lack of desire to work with the agency toward reunification, or disinterest in the child. Rather than responding with understanding and support, the caseworker might respond in an authoritarian or demanding manner, or may withdraw from contact with family members.

There are many differences in peoples' expressions of loss and grief. However, many behavioral responses to the placement of children are predictable, and can be interpreted as normal manifestations of the stages of grieving [Kubler–Ross 1972; Fahlberg 1979]. The following lists the behaviors typically seen in family members in response to placement of their children, and the stages in the grieving process with which they are correlated.

Shock/Denial Stage

- Parents may exhibit a robot–like, stunned response at the move. They may be immobilized. A characteristic response of people in emotional shock is, "This can't be really happening!"

- Parents may be very compliant, and may express little emotion or affect. They may appear bland, uncaring, or uninvolved.

- Parents may deny that there is a problem, or deny that the agency can remove the children. They may insist the children will be home in a day or so, or that, "No court will ever give you custody."

- Parents may avoid the caseworker and deny the need to be involved with the agency.

- Some parents who do not have close attachments to their children may not exhibit strong emotional reactions when their children are removed from them. These parents may have abandoned their children or left them in the care of others for long periods of time in the past. The caseworker should assess the parents' reactions over a period of time to differentiate the immobility typical of the shock stage from the emotional remoteness of parents who lack a strong attachment to their child. Parents in shock will move within a few hours or days to expressing anger and pain. Parents without close attachments often do not.

Anger/Protest Stage

- Parents may threaten court action or may directly threaten the caseworker. They may contact an attorney to fight the agency.

- Parents may behave in a contrary and oppositional manner by refusing to let the caseworker visit the home, or by refusing to talk with the worker.

- Parents may refuse to participate with the worker to develop a case plan or to make decisions about the child's welfare.

- Parents may become demanding, sometimes making irrational demands on the worker or the agency.

- Parents may blame the agency, the caseworker, the court, the system, the complainant, or others, for the existence of the problem. They may vehemently reject any need to change.

Bargaining Stage

- Parents may become semi-responsive to the caseworker and may behave more compliantly.

- Parents may make broad promises, such as, "It will never happen again," "I'll ask my boyfriend to leave," "If I go to all my parenting classes, will I get my children back?"

Depression Stage

- Parents may "forget" or miss appointments with caseworkers, or may fail to attend scheduled visits with the children.

- Parents may exhibit little initiative or follow-through in visitation, or in other activities designed to promote reunification.

- Parents may display futility and a loss of hope that their children will ever be returned home. Some parents even move away or disappear, and the agency loses contact with them.

Resolution Stage

- Parents may emotionally begin to restructure their lives without their children.

- Parents may move away without notifying the agency, may become involved in new relationships, may have other children, or otherwise "get on with life."

- Parents may not respond to their caseworker's attempts to work with them.

- Parents may stop visiting with their children.

- Parents may not protest court action for permanent custody, and may not attend permanent custody court hearings.

IX. A. The Emotional Impact of Placement on Family Members

Clearly, our goal is to support family members and employ strategies that maintain the family's integrity while the child is in placement. This reduces the losses and threats experienced by the family, and subsequently prevents the need to grieve. The extent to which family members experience placement as a loss depends largely on the caseworker's ability to keep them actively involved with their child, and involved in collaborative reunification planning while their child is in placement.

This also implies that we must actively engage families of children currently in placement as quickly as we are able. We will likely have to deal with anger and hostility, depression, and sorrow. However, this is preferable to allowing the grief to be fully resolved. Once parents have completed the grieving process, it becomes increasingly difficult to reengage them.

Strategies to engage and empower parents to remain actively involved with their children in placement are more fully discussed in Section IX–B, "Empowering Parents to Participate in Placement Activities."

B. EMPOWERING PARENTS TO PARTICIPATE IN PLACEMENT ACTIVITIES

1. Conceptual Framework

2. Application

3. Case Example

Conceptual Framework

Empowerment of parents and other family members is at the center of any effort to strengthen and preserve families. The word "empower" means to authorize, enable, or permit. When children are placed into substitute care, empowering their parents or caregivers means enabling them to retain as much parenting responsibility for their children as possible and assisting them in reunifying their family. Workers might question the validity of preserving parental responsibility when parents have demonstrated they cannot meet these responsibilities. However, preserving families requires a commitment not only to prevent placement, but to promote reunification of a family after a child has been placed. The active involvement of parents and other family members with children in placement is essential for successful reunification. (Refer to Section IX–C, "Promoting Reunification.")

Empowering family members, and particularly the parents of children in placement, can be a valuable therapeutic intervention for the entire family. There are several ways this may occur. First, by including parents in all placement activities, not only do we reduce the stress of separation for their children, but we also prevent the parents from becoming emotionally isolated and withdrawn from their children. This reduces the likelihood that parents will psychologically abandon their child in placement as a means of coping with loss and grief. Parents' continued emotional involvement with their children is essential for successful reunification.

Second, a properly executed placement can be a growth experience for families. Parents can learn a great deal by participating with the worker and foster caregivers in problem solving, case planning, and service delivery. The caseworker, and foster or kinship caregivers can also help parents learn and practice fundamental skills in parenting, child management, and home management by modeling, training, and coaching them in these skills.

Third, placement of children may be necessary before some families fully realize and understand the seriousness of their situation, particularly if they have previously denied or minimized it. Placement is an intrusive intervention, and it may create a crisis for the family. Placing the children can, therefore, motivate ambivalent or resistive parents to act, when they previously did not. This in no way suggests we should ever use placement as a punishment for parental non-compliance, or, as a worker was recently overheard suggesting, "to teach the father a lesson." The only valid utilization of placement is to protect a child from serious harm in his own home, when intensive in–home interventions cannot. When placement has the effect of mobilizing a family, however, we can take full advantage of the momentum by working to engage parents to collaborate toward making changes that will allow the return of their children.

Actively working to engage and involve parents while their children are in placement also constitutes reasonable efforts by the agency to promote timely reunification. If a child cannot safely be returned home in spite of these intensive efforts to involve and strengthen the family, there is legitimate justification to begin the process of placing the child in an alternative permanent home.

After placement, it is all too typical for busy caseworkers to reduce their involvement with family members and concentrate their efforts, instead, on supporting the placement and strengthening the child's relationship with foster or relative caregivers. Unfortunately, this usually represents the death knell for successful reunification. Until it is certain that the child and family cannot or should not be reunified, placement should be a powerful incentive for both caseworkers and foster caregivers to strengthen their involvement with the family, not to abandon them!

Application

The decision to place a child represents a critical point in the evolution of the casework relationship. Few parents fully agree with the decision to place their children. Many will not have acknowledged the serious risk to their children, nor will they fully understand their own inability to protect them. Placement usually occurs because a worker has had to exercise unilateral authority to remove children to protect them from harm. As a result, parents and other family members are often extremely upset and angry about the placement, may blame the worker, and will typically express their resentment and hostility openly. When confronted with such hostility, workers often become defensive, withdraw emotional support, or at worst, react in a punitive manner toward the family. These responses, while a natural reaction when verbally attacked, are unproductive, since they deprive families of emotional support and guidance at a time when they most need it. We must remember that hostility and anger are expected responses to the serious emotional trauma inherent in separation and placement. If workers are to promote continued growth and development by family members, they must work to minimize the loss and threats family members experience as a result of placement, and maintain constructive interaction with the family.

The first step is to prevent the placement from permanently damaging the casework relationship. The worker is less likely to react in nonconstructive ways if he can understand the family's untenable position, and can feel and demonstrate empathy for the family. The worker should encourage parents to verbally express their anger and resentment toward the worker and the agency, and the worker should acknowledge the validity of their feelings. Family members must also understand that their anger does not change the worker's commitment to working collaboratively to resolve the problems that led to placement. A worker's ability to "stick with the family," and remain supportive during the crisis of placement, is often the glue that cements the casework relationship.

The worker must also stress to family members that placement is intended to be temporary, and he should continue to engage the family to collaborate toward reunification. There are several steps in this process. The first is to address, in a straightforward manner, the reasons that placement is necessary. The worker should explain to the parents that the child is being removed only because the child's safety in the home cannot be assured. The worker must be able to provide the parent with specific, accurate, factual data to support this conclusion. The specific circumstances or parental behaviors that placed the children at risk should be clearly described. The worker must be certain that family members correctly understood and interpreted his communication. One strategy is to ask family members to repeat back what they have heard. At times, in spite of clear explanations, parents may continue to deny the allegations or may minimize or deny the risk to their children. The worker should stress that acknowledging and understanding the risks to their children is the first step toward having the children returned.

Second, the worker should reassert his intent to return the child home, as soon as the child's safety in the home can be assured. The worker should also stress the importance of the parents' involvement in the planning and development of services to make this possible, and should suggest some immediate activities that can initiate this collaboration. The worker should also explain the case assessment and planning process and define the parents' role in all aspects of case planning and service delivery.

The worker should then clarify that the parents have a choice. They can choose to contest or resist the agency's interventions, with potentially negative consequences; or, they can become involved and actively assist in planning and carrying out placement and reunification activities to the benefit of all. It must be stressed that this strategy is not intended to coerce parents, but rather, to engage them to work collaboratively toward a common goal of reunifying their family and closing the case, thereby assuring both protection of the children and the stability of the family.

INVOLVING PARENTS IN PLACING THEIR CHILDREN

There are several benefits to involving parents, or other primary caregivers, directly in the process of placing the child into substitute care. First, by asking parents to participate in the placement, the caseworker's actions are congruent with his previous verbal communications about the importance of parental involvement. This further facilitates the development of the casework relationship.

Second, by seeking parental involvement at the same time placement is made, the worker demonstrates both that he will do whatever is necessary to assure protection of the child, and, that he is still committed to a collaborative effort to enable the parent to reassume primary care responsibilities and authority.

In addition, active parental involvement with the child in placement greatly reduces separation trauma for the child and family members, and can also facilitate the child's adjustment in placement. The worker can help parents learn to be supportive and reassuring to the child by explaining that the child will be very frightened and needs the parents' continued help.

Finally, parents who are directly involved in planning and implementing the placement will be less likely to attempt to disrupt, sabotage, or otherwise interfere with the placement.

There are several ways that parents can be involved both in planning the placement and in moving a child into substitute care. For example:

- The worker should ask family members if there are any relatives or family friends who might be able to care for the child temporarily, and then should carefully consider the parents' suggestions. If a placement recommended by the family can assure the child's safety, and if parents agree not to interfere with the placement, the worker may be able to prevent placement with a stranger. The worker will, of course, have to meet and assess the relatives or caregivers, and determine their ability to protect the child, even if this means carefully regulating the parents' access to the child.

- If a physical examination is warranted because of physical abuse or sexual abuse, the parent should accompany the caseworker and the child to the hospital or doctor. The parent should be involved while the child is being examined, and should talk directly with the worker and the examining physician about the medical findings. This helps to reduce the parent's denial, and provides an opportunity for the worker to talk directly to the parent regarding the maltreatment and how it occurred.

- If a child is to be placed in an agency–operated foster home, the parent may be asked to provide information about the child's special needs. This can help the worker choose the best placement for the child. Involving the parent in the selection process can be reassuring, and can reduce the alienation and distress experienced by the parent.

- The worker should first discuss the plan for the move with the parent. Then the parent and worker should, together, tell the child. The worker should encourage the parent to help the child understand the need for a move, and give the child permission to be cared for by another family. This is easier, if the parent knows the caregiver, or if she perceives the caregiver as supportive and nonthreatening.

- The parent should help decide what clothing, toys, and belongings the child should take with her and should help the child pack. The parent should be asked to provide detailed information regarding the child's schedule, preferences in food, needs, and routines. If at all possible, the parent should communicate this information directly to the relative or foster caregiver.

- Finally, the parent should be encouraged to accompany the child during preplacement visits. This assures the child that the parent knows where he will be living, and reassures the parent that the home for the child is adequate. This also allows the foster or relative caregiver to learn important information about the child directly from the parent, and it enables the caregiver to begin to establish a relationship with the parent. Direct contact between parents and foster caregivers can be very reassuring to both the parent and the child, may reduce loyalty conflicts for the child, and helps to establish a positive relationship, which is particularly important if the foster caregiver is to be involved in family visits or work directly with the parent.

AFTER THE PLACEMENT

After a child has been moved, the caseworker should facilitate the parent's regular involvement with the child and the agency. The natural tendency after a placement is for the worker to provide everyone with a "cooling off" period, wherein the child can "adjust" without the stress of contact with the family or the worker. The worker might also reduce contact with the family. This is counterproductive in all respects.

Postplacement interventions are designed to keep parents involved with their child in placement. If the caseworker maintains regular telephone and face-to-face contact with parents, it is less likely that parents will withdraw, and the worker will be more successful in keeping parents involved with the child. Strategies should include the following:

- The caseworker should increase, not decrease, contacts with parents during and immediately after children are removed. This will reassure parents that they have not been abandoned, and that they remain an important part of the process.

- Parents should be involved in a case assessment and planning conference shortly after placement to begin development of the reunification plan. Parents should routinely be involved in agency staffings and conferences to review the case plan, or to discuss problems in case plan implementation.

- Regular and frequent visits between children and their parents is critical. The first visit should occur within 48 hours of placement. The worker should spend some time with parents prior to this visit to discuss their feelings, and to prepare them for the visit. The worker should assure that parents have transportation, and may himself transport and accompany them to the first visit. The worker should always discuss the visit with parents afterward. (Refer to Section IX–C, "Promoting Reunification," for a more detailed discussion of visits as a therapeutic intervention.)

- Relative or foster caregivers should be able to telephone parents with questions about a child's needs, routines, and schedule. The caregivers can use information provided by parents to help children adjust. This also promotes the parents' involvement and contribution, and gives children additional opportunities to talk with members of their family. Parents should also be involved in making major decisions about the child as much as possible.

- It is extremely important that the agency make appropriate services available to parents to enable them to implement the case plan. The parents generally may not have the capability to make the necessary changes without help; if they could, they likely would have done so. The case plan must be achievable, and casework services must support the plan.

In summary, if the agency does not involve parents from the earliest stages of placement, it often creates a sense of helplessness in parents that ultimately works against successful reunification. Caseworkers and foster caregivers should try to reinforce proper parenting, not take over all parenting responsibilities.

Despite a worker's best efforts, however, there are parents who will interfere with or sabotage the placement. In these circumstances, the caseworker's primary responsibility is to protect the child. With effective casework intervention, however, many parents can become responsible and valuable participants.

Case Example

⚊ Sheila Davis

The Davis Family had been an open case with the child welfare agency for approximately three months. The family had originally been referred by a neighbor, who reported that the three Davis children, ages two, six, and seven, were alone in their apartment. Their mother, Ms. Sheila Davis, had reportedly been gone for several hours. The neighbor had indicated that Ms. Davis repeatedly left the children unattended while she "went out partying all night." The agency had found the children to be at risk, and the case had been opened for in-home services. Don Harrison, a family services caseworker, was assigned to the case.

Don was able to maintain the children at home by working with Ms. Davis to develop a safety plan for the children. Ms. Davis arranged for friends to provide child care when she went out. She had also agreed to attend counseling sessions, and she and Don chose a counselor at a local community center. Don suspected that Ms. Davis had a drinking problem, but he could not determine its extent. Ms. Davis repeatedly denied heavy drinking, and claimed she was "just a social drinker."

During the ensuing weeks, Don monitored the family and provided ongoing support. Ms. Davis appeared to be trying to meet the agreed-upon terms of the case plan. She attended several counseling sessions, and was always home when Don called. She kept her appointments with Don, and the children were generally clean and seemed to be well cared for when Don visited. Don felt he had developed a good relationship with Ms. Davis; she often called him when she needed help or support.

Don had conducted a family assessment shortly after the case was opened. He had determined that Ms. Davis, age 22, had a long history of inconsistent child care. She often provided adequate care for weeks or months at a time, and then she would leave her children alone for long periods and neglect to meet even their basic needs. An aunt had confirmed that Ms. Davis had had a drinking problem since adolescence, and the aunt worried that recently her niece had also become involved with drugs. Ms. Davis reportedly had, on several occasions, left the children with the aunt and disappeared "for weeks at a time." The aunt said when Ms. Davis eventually returned, she always expressed her regret and apologized for her behavior, reclaimed her children, and worked to maintain a home for them "until the next time." Recently, the aunt's poor health made caring for the children impossible. The aunt said Ms. Davis had never been married, and she believed the children had different fathers. She had only briefly met one of them. She knew nothing about the others. The aunt said Ms. Davis's mother and brother lived in another state, but that Ms. Davis refused to talk with them. Ms. Davis's father had died when Ms. Davis was 10 years old.

Don had recently attempted to reach Ms. Davis to confirm an appointment. After several days of no response, he became concerned, and visited the home. When he knocked, seven-year-old Leanna, answered the door. Leanna told Don her mother wasn't home, that she had "gone out" and would be back "soon." Don questioned Leanna further, and based on her description of events, he determined Ms. Davis had probably put the children to bed the night before and left, telling the children she would be home "soon." Concerned about entering the home without Ms. Davis' permission, Don asked Leanna to bring her younger brother and sister to the door so Don could see if they were okay. Leanna said the baby was sick and had been crying all morning. She also said the baby was hungry. Don determined the situation to be an emergency. He went to his car and phoned for police support to enable him to enter the home.

When the officer and Don entered the apartment, they found pervasive disarray. Half-empty beer cans and dirty plates with rotting food littered the living room. The two year old was cranky, feverish, and was seriously congested. The temperature in the home was approximately 50 degrees, and there was a stiff breeze blowing through a hole in the window. Leanna said her mother had "busted it when she threw a shoe at Tommy." Tommy, Leanna explained, was Mommy's new boyfriend. Leanna said she didn't like him, that he "yelled a lot and was mean to Mommy." The children were icy cold to the touch. Leanna said she had turned on the stove "like Mommy does" to "keep the baby warm since she's sick." Don followed Leanna to the kitchen and noted she had pulled a chair to the stove and lighted two of the gas burners. The top of the stove and the floor around its base were littered with bent and used matches. Leanna said sheepishly that she "didn't know how to do it as good as Mommy did." Leanna said her baby sister was crying because she was hungry, but Leanna didn't know how to cook, and all the milk and cereal were gone. A quick look around the kitchen indicated there was little food in the house.

Don took the children into the bedroom, which was only slightly warmer. The beds were unmade and the room smelled of urine. There were dirty diapers and training pants strewn on the floor, and dried feces in one of the beds. He found some dirty, but warmer, clothing for the children in piles on the floor, and dressed all three children. He then called Ms. Davis's aunt, who said she hadn't talked with Ms. Davis in about a week and had no idea of her whereabouts. Don asked whether she could care for the children until Ms. Davis returned home. The aunt said she had just come home from the hospital and could hardly care for herself.

Don called the agency and requested an emergency foster home for the children. He then sat down to explain to the children that they would be going to a safe and warm foster home until he could find their mom and help her take better care of them. He was waiting with the children for the return call from the agency when Ms. Davis came home. She was coherent but disheveled, and the strong odor of alcohol confirmed she had been drinking. She was initially angry and belligerent, and told Don he had no right to come barging into her home unannounced. She then saw the police officer and began to cry. She said she was really sorry. She'd been doing really well, and she didn't know what had come over her, but she'd clean things up and feed her children, and she guaranteed it wouldn't happen again. Don pointed out that they had had a similar conversation three months earlier when the case was opened, and her care of the children was worse now than it had been then. Don said he was worried that Ms. Davis was having problems with her drinking. Ms. Davis continued to deny anything other than "social drinking." When Don asked why she had been out all night, she said she "ran out for a few minutes" to get some groceries, and then went with a friend to get some cigarettes. Their car had broken down and they were stranded. Don said firmly that her story did not explain why her children had been alone for 17 hours.

Don briefly considered involving a homemaker and protective day care and leaving the children with Ms. Davis, but realized that neither intervention could assure that Ms. Davis would provide proper care at night, which was when she generally left the children alone. He believed that until Ms. Davis acknowledged her drinking and its effects on her care of the children, the children were at significant risk in her sole care.

Don explained to Ms. Davis why the children were at risk of serious harm, and listed the cold temperature of the house; the youngest child's illness; the unsanitary conditions in the children's bedroom; the fact that there was no food for the children; and that Leanna had been lighting matches in the kitchen and could have seriously burned herself, or even set the apartment on fire. Don said he couldn't leave the children in Ms. Davis's care until they could find the best means of helping Ms. Davis break this pattern of neglect. Ms. Davis continued to cry, but said nothing. He asked if she had any recommendations of family members to care for the children for a while. She said she did not.

When Don outlined a plan to place the children in foster care, Ms. Davis began to protest. Don told Ms. Davis that the first priority was the safety of the children, and he wanted her help to make a safety plan. Then he would help Ms. Davis in any way he could so her children could be returned to her.

In Ms. Davis' presence, Don explained to the children where they were going, and prompted Ms. Davis to help him explain. When the children began to cry, Don explained that all children need to be fed, and warm, and safe. He explained that their mom couldn't do that right now, and that he would help her learn to take better care of them. He hoped they could come home again soon. Don also told Leanna she had done a good job taking care of her brother and sister, and that this was not her fault. He said she wasn't old enough to take care of little children, and she needed someone to look after her, too. He also told the children their mom would visit with them often at the foster home.

Don told Ms. Davis that if she could get cleaned up and act in a responsible manner, she could accompany them to the foster home. Don told her that the children would be less frightened if Ms. Davis could explain to them why they had to stay with another family for a while, and if Ms. Davis could go with them to meet the foster mother. He also indicated the foster mother would want Ms. Davis's help in learning about the children so she could also help them. Ms. Davis protested and said she couldn't, and wouldn't, help him. Don said it was her choice; but that she would be helping her children, not him. He also said that he and the children would be leaving, with or without Ms. Davis, but that he strongly encouraged her to come with them. Ms. Davis was quiet for a minute, and then said, angrily, "You're not taking my children anywhere without me." Don interpreted this as a strength, and commended Ms. Davis for her decision. She said nothing, and disappeared into the bathroom.

Don phoned the agency to confirm the placement, and then phoned Olivia McCarty, the foster mother, to prepare her for the placement. Don then asked Ms. Davis to help pack some of the children's belongings, and asked the children what they would like to take with them.

When they arrived at the McCarty foster home, Ms. McCarty invited them in, and showed Ms. Davis and the children around the house. Ms. McCarty made the children sandwiches and offered to feed the adults, also. Ms. Davis accepted a sandwich and tea. Ms. McCarty then told the children she "wanted to know all about how to care for them so they would be comfortable and feel safe." She asked Ms. Davis and the children numerous questions about their likes and dislikes, and their habits. The children told Ms. McCarty what they liked to eat. Leanna said her sister cried in the dark and was afraid. Ms. Davis answered the foster mother's questions, but offered little additional information. Ms. McCarty then exchanged phone numbers with Ms. Davis, and asked if she could call Ms. Davis if the children were lonely, or if she needed additional information. Ms. Davis agreed.

Ms. McCarty then told Ms. Davis that she understood how bad Ms. Davis must feel, and she wanted to help in any way she could. She reassured Ms. Davis that the children were in capable hands, and she hoped Ms. Davis wouldn't worry. Don then explained to Ms. Davis that she could visit in the foster home, provided she was not disruptive, behaved responsibly, and did not try to interfere with the placement. He also told Ms. Davis she could not visit without first making arrangements. Ms. McCarty told Ms. Davis she was welcome, and that they looked forward to having her. Don told the children he would visit them the next day. Ms. McCarty told Ms. Davis she would call later that evening to let the children talk with her. Don then left with Ms. Davis.

Don began driving toward Ms. Davis's apartment. Ms. Davis asked what she had to do to get her children back. Don said, "We need to talk realistically about your choices, but you need to be clear-headed and sober when we do." Ms. Davis said she was sober, she didn't drink, that she was just tired. Don said, "Ms. Davis, we've talked around this issue for three months. It's time to deal with it. I can smell the alcohol, and I recognize the symptoms of intoxication. If you like, we can start right now to work on getting your kids home. I can drive you to the detox unit at the hospital as easily as I can take you home." Ms. Davis insisted she wanted to go home. Don complied, reiterating that the ball was in her court, and he couldn't help her unless she let him. He told Ms. Davis to call if she changed her mind. He also said if he hadn't heard from her, he would be back in two days. Two days later, Don attempted a home visit. Ms. Davis was asleep when Don arrived, and she clearly had been drinking. He could not engage her to talk. He told her he would like to schedule a visit in the foster home soon, but reminded her that if she was drunk or disruptive, he would have to curtail the visit. Ms. Davis was neatly dressed and compliant when Don arrived to transport her to the visit two days later. He smelled alcohol, but Ms. Davis was coherent and amenable. The visit was uneventful. Ms. Davis was generally quiet, and spoke only minimally with the foster mother, but the children were happy to see her.

Don followed up immediately with a home visit to Ms. Davis, and continued to press her about the importance of sobriety to promote reunification. He was finally able to convince her to accompany him to the hospital to tour the alcoholism unit and talk with the staff. Three weeks later, after several more visits with her children in the foster home, and with the strong encouragement of Ms. McCarty, Ms. Davis called Don and said she was ready to talk about getting help for her alcoholism and getting her children back.

C. PROMOTING REUNIFICATION

1. Conceptual Framework

2. Application

Conceptual Framework

In previous sections we have focused on strategies to prevent out-of-home placement. Unfortunately, many children in foster or relative care are separated from their families for long periods of time before reunification planning is begun. Generally, the longer children are in placement, the more difficult it is to reunify them with their families.

Pine, Warsh, and Maluccio [1993] suggest several reasons for this. First, since young children cannot remain emotionally attached to persons without frequent contact, lengthy separation without regular visits can weaken the parent–child relationship. Children in long–term substitute care often develop strong attachments to their foster or relative caregivers, which may increase their ambivalence about reunification. Children's attachments to their substitute caregivers may also be threatening to parents, who may feel rejected or jealous of their children's affection and loyalty toward their caregivers. At times, parents feel they must "re-win" their children's affection. This is particularly difficult for parents who have experienced previous painful rejections, and who expect to be rejected.

Reuniting families often means integrating children back into a changed family system. Some parents may have remarried, had other children, or moved to other communities since their children were placed. The children have also grown and developed, and may be very different from what the parents remember. The parents and children may, at times, seem like strangers to each other. This can be very disconcerting to parents, and can make reestablishing the parent–child relationship more difficult.

Reunification can be threatening to parents for other reasons as well. Many parents whose children have been removed believe themselves to be failures as parents. Reinvolvement with their children reminds them of this, and they often reexperience the pain and anger that accompanied the initial separation. Reunification is likely to be viewed by some families as another potential failure, since there is no guarantee that their involvement with their child will be any different this time. Parents whose children have been removed often lack the confidence to attempt reunification.

It is not uncommon for children in placement to question why their parents didn't come to take them home sooner or work harder to get them back. Children who have been placed for long periods may be angry and hostile toward parents who, in their minds, have failed them. Angry children may display considerable ambivalence in relating to their parents because of their fear of being abandoned or rejected again. Parents must learn to deal with their child's anger and resentment before reunification is possible.

Some children who have developed strong and healthy attachments to their substitute care families may resist separation from them. Separation may, in fact, be seriously disruptive and emotionally traumatic. Some children may clearly express their desire to stay where they are rather than be reunited with their families. In these situations, children may even sabotage efforts at reunification.

Some parents may not want to be reunited with their children, but may not be able to acknowledge this. It may be expressed nonverbally by failure to participate in reunification activities, or failure to meet case plan objectives, in spite of intensive agency support and intervention. Other parents may want to maintain a relationship with their children, but may not want the responsibility of full-time parenting. While they may continue to visit, they will not take steps to provide a home for the children. This mixed message can be very confusing to the children.

ASSESSING FAMILY READINESS FOR REUNIFICATION

Reunification should be the goal for most families whose children have been placed. However, it is not the best outcome for all families. In some situations, reunification is not possible, either because the parents cannot be engaged to reassume care of their children, or because they have not been able to make the changes necessary to assure safety for their children at home.

There are several factors that can increase the likelihood of successful family reunification. They are:

- The risk factors that led to placement of the children were acute rather than chronic. If child abuse and neglect are untreated, they tend to become more severe over time. If intensive, in-home services are provided at the time of placement to families in acute stress or crisis, this can often resolve the problems that created risk for the child, which increases the likelihood of rapid reunification.

- When the parent is involved with the child throughout the placement, the likelihood of successful reunification is increased. With proper casework intervention, the parent-child relationship can be maintained and strengthened while the child is in substitute care. Many of the barriers to reunification that result from lengthy separation, including depression and grieving, and feelings of abandonment and/or failure can be reduced or avoided.

- Reunification success is increased if family members have nascent abilities and potentials that can be developed and strengthened by providing intensive support and counseling. As these interventions succeed, parents gain confidence and feelings of hope, which can increase parental motivation to regain custody of their children.

- Families who have strong support networks of extended family and friends, and who are willing to utilize community services and supports, have a higher likelihood of successful reunification.

- If parents are committed to the child and strongly express their desire to have their child returned home, despite the potential obstacles, this increases the likelihood of reunification success. However, workers must be careful not to mistake what appears to be ambivalence or a lack of interest as a lack of attachment or commitment. A parent's aloof or withdrawn behavior may, instead, represent the parent's fear about experiencing further hurt and feelings of failure. The worker must use the casework relationship to create a safe, nonpunitive, and nonthreatening environment in which parents can express their fears and anxieties about reunification, or can honestly communicate their desire not to be reunited with their children.

Parents who do not want to reassume full-time custody of their children, but who are ambivalent about permanently terminating their rights, can sometimes be encouraged to develop an alternative permanent plan for their children through custody or guardianship with relatives, or through adoption by the foster family or an adoptive family. Involving parents in permanent planning can sometimes help to alleviate their guilt. At times, some level of "openness" in the permanent plan may be warranted. This allows parents to maintain some level of contact with their child, while assuring the child permanence in a safe and nurturing family.

One final caution is warranted as we assess family potential for reunification. It is difficult to assess families who have never been provided with intensive, supportive, culturally relevant services regarding their ability or willingness to change, or their potential for successful reunification. This may be true even when the presenting risk conditions appear to be longstanding and entrenched. Families must be given the opportunity, with considerable agency encouragement and support, to jointly develop a case plan that identifies their needs. Services must be provided to help meet them.

Focusing on Strengths to Promote Reunification

Family-centered practice presumes that the vast majority of families have inherent strengths and capabilities, and that most families have the capacity to grow and change when given the proper enabling and supporting interventions. Family-centered practice, therefore, identifies and develops nascent strengths; enhances the potential of individual members and the family as a group; empowers families to identify and address their own needs; and helps them identify and implement constructive and relevant solutions to their problems. Family-centered child welfare asserts that properly delivered family services can strengthen many families sufficiently to enable them to care for and protect their own children.

This perspective is especially relevant in reunification work. Families who have had a child placed in care typically feel a sense of failure. They lack confidence that they can regain custody of their child; they feel disempowered and angry; and they often mistrust the system. Many believe they have "jumped through hoops" to regain custody, but to no avail. If workers also share the perception that reunification is likely to fail, this self-fulfilling prophesy will prevail. Zamosky and colleagues believe that examining and altering caseworkers' negative attitudes and beliefs is the necessary first step in successful family reunification [Zamosky, Sparks, Hatt, & Sharman 1993].

This is not to suggest that workers should minimize or ignore barriers and problems. Rather, a balanced approach that concurrently considers both deficits and potentials is the preferred intervention. Such an approach is most accurately called developmental. A deficit model often assumes that problematic traits and behaviors are permanent conditions that are immutable and unchangeable.

A developmental model acknowledges problems and limitations, but suggests that with the proper interventions and support, most people can learn different and more adaptive ways of thinking and behaving, and ultimately of rearing their children. A developmental model, therefore, identifies deficits but contends that they can be modified to varying degrees. Developmental casework interventions promote growth and productive change, and utilize strengths to help solve problems.

Part of the caseworker's job in reunification is to help family members assess and identify both the problems to be overcome, and the strengths and resources they have available to them. Zamosky and colleagues [1993] have identified strengths that are typical of many families attempting reunification. For example, many families retain a feeling of connectedness with their children, even though they are physically separated. Many families have demonstrated perseverance by remaining in their children's lives for years without having been the primary caregiver. Similarly, their willingness to pursue reunification, in spite of potentially ambivalent feelings, suggests a commitment that can only help them during difficult times to come.

A family's strengths may not be immediately evident to the caseworker or to the family members themselves. It is easy to lose sight of strengths and abilities when we are confronted with multiple, complicated, and challenging problems. In addition, many people take their strengths for granted, or fail to recognize them. Strengths may also be nascent, which means that precursor abilities or traits may be present, but they may not be fully developed. Developmental casework can help the parents identify traits, qualities, and attributes in themselves that can be considered elements of strength, and can help them learn to further develop and apply these abilities in productive ways.

THE ROLE OF VISITING IN PROMOTING REUNIFICATION

Regular and frequent parent–child visits are an essential component of reunification casework. We have already identified several ways that infrequent visits or long parental absences can potentially damage the parent–child relationship and increase barriers to successful reunification. Visitation, when properly planned and utilized, can also be a therapeutic intervention for the entire family, and can promote successful reunification.

Hess and Proch [1988] describe the important benefits of regular family visits:

- Frequent visiting reassures parents that the agency is not trying to keep their children from them, and that the agency is serious about maintaining family relationships.

- Children experience considerable anxiety and distress when separated from their parents for even short periods of time. Many children, particularly young ones, worry that their parents are dead, hurt, or otherwise permanently gone. Visiting reassures children that they have not been abandoned in substitute care, that their families are alive and well, and that their families still care about them. Frequent contact with parents can reduce children's anxiety associated with separation.

- Visits with parents help older children avoid self-blame for placement. Visitation reassures a child that his parent wants him, which can counteract the child's natural tendency to believe that he was abandoned by his family because he was somehow "bad."

- Visits present the caseworker with a valuable opportunity to help family members assess and identify their needs and strengths. By observing family members together, and using appropriate listening and interviewing techniques, the worker can elicit important information about the parent-child relationship, the parents' developmental needs, and the parents' motivation and capacity to reassume care of their children. The worker should discuss her observations with family members so they can be considered in reunification planning.

- Careful observation during visits can also help the caseworker identify when reunification may not be possible, or when termination of the parent-child relationship is in the child's best interests. Visits may also help ambivalent parents make a final decision regarding whether they want to pursue reunification or relinquish their children to an alternative permanent home.

- Visits help families prepare for reunification. Without frequent visits, parents and children are both likely to develop unrealistic expectations. Casework intervention during visits can help families develop realistic expectations for reunification, and help them identify problems that must be resolved before they can live together again.

- Family visits can be used as interventions to achieve specific objectives. For example, foster or relative caregivers might use visits to model parenting skills and train parents in home management, child care, and child management strategies. Parents can practice newly acquired parenting strategies during visits, and can receive immediate constructive feedback and coaching from the caseworker or foster caregiver.

- Regular and frequent family visits can greatly contribute to "reasonable efforts" to promote reunification. When these efforts do not result in reunification, the agency has adequate justification to pursue an alternative permanent family for the child.

Application

In general, reunification refers to reuniting children with parents who assume custody and permanent responsibility for their care. According to Pine, Warsh, and Maluccio [1993], lesser degrees of parent–child contact through phone calls, letters, or visits may be indicated in some situations. The maintenance of family and kinship bonds may be an important therapeutic intervention for some children who are permanently placed in relative or adoptive homes. An example might be an older child who has an enduring and affectionate bond with a parent with a chronic and severe mental illness, whose behaviors place the child at repeated risk of harm. Ongoing contact with their families can reduce separation trauma for children, can preserve continuity, can strengthen and support personal and cultural identity, and can assure children a sense of connectedness to their past. Children can also maintain important relationships with siblings and other extended family members through ongoing contact.

It is also necessary to determine with whom a child will be reunited. The parent who had custody of the child prior to placement is normally involved in reunification planning. However, for some children, this may not be the best plan. Continuing high risk in the family, parental abandonment of the child, or other family circumstances may prohibit placement of the child at home. However, reunification planning can still occur. It may be that the child can be reunited with a previously noncustodial parent now assuming custodial responsibilities. Some children will be reunified into their extended families, with grandparents or other relatives assuming custodial responsibility, and with biological parents maintaining a significant, but different, relationship with their child. Child welfare workers should obtain a family history and conduct a search to identify potential permanent caregivers, including a child's biological father and his extended family; grandparents; aunts and uncles; adult siblings; and other significant family members. The worker should contact these persons to determine their interest in providing a home for the child. If they indicate interest, the worker can conduct a homestudy to help the family assess their ability to care for the child permanently.

At times, it may be necessary to forego attempts at reunification and assure that the child has a permanent alternative placement. Family members may have failed to follow through with reunification activities, despite intensive efforts by the agency to support the plan. Some families will not have been able, even with agency assistance, to remove risk factors sufficiently to assure the child's safety at home. The worker must continually balance the benefits of reunification against the potential negative effects of continuing temporary placement. If permanence can likely be achieved with the child's own family in a reasonable period of time, the decision to continue to pursue reunification activities is warranted. However, if the likelihood of successful reunification in a reasonable period of time is remote, and reasonable efforts to reunite the family have not been successful, the worker should begin planning for placement in a permanent alternative family.

STRATEGIES TO PROMOTE REUNIFICATION

In most cases, reunification planning should begin as soon as the child is placed. However, even when family members are committed to reunification, it can be a difficult and time–consuming process. This is especially true when the child has been out of the home for an extended period of time.

The first step in reunification is to complete a thorough family assessment. The family assessment for reunification does not differ significantly from a protective services family assessment. The family's current situation and their strengths, needs, and problems must be fully assessed. The assessment of potential risk to the child in the home is a critical component of this family assessment. The worker must help the family assess whether the problems and conditions that led to the original need for placement have been addressed and resolved; and, what must be done to make the home safe for the child. (See Sections II–B, "Dynamics of Child Maltreatment;" II–C, "Risk Assessment;" and IV–C, "Conducting the Family Assessment.")

The nature of the parent–child relationship must also be fully explored. The worker must determine whether the family and child maintain strong emotional bonds, or have become emotionally distanced during the period of separation. The family's commitment to reunification must also be explored, and feelings of ambivalence must be identified and discussed. The worker and family must identify together the potential barriers to reunification to assure the proactive development of strategies to overcome them.

Once the family situation has been fully assessed, the worker and family should jointly develop a case plan with specific objectives and activities to achieve reunification. (See Section IV–D, "Developing the Case Plan.") The responsibilities of each family member, the caseworker, the foster or relative caregivers, and others, as appropriate, should be clearly outlined. The plan should also specify the services the agency will provide to support the family as the reunification plan is implemented. The child or children to be reunified, and any siblings currently with the parents, should be involved in case plan development, if they are old enough to participate and can benefit from participation. Otherwise, the caseworker should explain the goal and action steps in the case plan to the children in concepts and language that is appropriate for their level of development.

Once the case plan has been finalized, the worker must prepare the family and the child for reunification activities. The degree of preparation needed by families will vary, depending upon the extent of prior casework involvement, and the regularity of parent–child visits while the child has been in placement.

When a child and parents have not lived together for many months or years, preparation for reunification is in many ways similar to preparation for adoption. Both parents and child will need help in understanding what to expect. The worker should explain that they may feel uncomfortable at first, and that an initial period of getting to know one another is inevitable. Both parents and child may feel awkward, anxious, and ambivalent, and they may experience a recurrence of negative feelings from the past. The parents must be prepared to experience initial rejection and/or testing by the children. The caseworker must reassure the parents that this is normal and to be expected, and does not mean that reunification will not be successful. Children will also need opportunities to express their ambivalence and fears, their feelings of loss related to leaving their substitute caregivers, and their anxiety about another move.

VISITING AS A REUNIFICATION STRATEGY

A series of structured family visits is the best way to implement reunification. Each visit should have a clear purpose. This purpose should be discussed and agreed upon by the worker and family members prior to the visit. After each visit, the worker should debrief and discuss the visit with family members, both individually and as a group. The worker can then help identify and resolve problems, provide supportive feedback, and help family members plan for additional activities to work on identified problems or needs. The visits may continue for weeks to months, depending upon the family's progress toward readiness for reunification. Properly planned visits are both educational and therapeutic for family members, because they prepare family members to constructively deal with issues that are certain to arise as a result of reunification.

Several factors should be considered when making decisions about the location, frequency, and duration of visits, and whether the visits should be supervised. In general, the location of visits should be the least restrictive, most normal environment that can assure the safety of the child. Visits often occur in many child welfare agencies because they are more convenient for the supervising caseworker. Yet, the agency is the least normal, most institutionalized setting in which visits can occur, and the atmosphere may inhibit parents from interacting in a natural manner with their children. Visits should take place, in order of preference; l) in the home of the parent; 2) in the home of a relative; 3) in the foster home; or, 4) in a public community location, such as a park. Visits, should be held in the agency only if the protection of the child cannot otherwise be assured.

The frequency, location, and duration of visits should be individually planned with each family, and should enhance the objectives of the reunification case plan. For most children, reunification visits should be held weekly at a minimum; two or three contacts a week are preferred. Contacts may include telephone calls or parental attendance with the child at routine activities such as counseling sessions, medical appointments, or school events. For infants and preschool children, several visits a week will be necessary to maintain the parent–child relationship. In general, visits should increase in frequency over the course of reunification.

Objectives and activities for each visit should be negotiated and agreed upon by the family and the caseworker prior to the visit. Possible objectives for family visits might include: 1) establishing and/or strengthening the parent–child relationship; 2) instructing parents in child management or child care skills; 3) working together to solve a problem or develop a plan for reunification activities; 4) helping parents become involved in the child's school, church, or community activities; 5) helping parents gain confidence in meeting their child's needs; 6) helping siblings become comfortable with one another; 7) identifying and assessing potential stressful situations between parents and their children; and 8) giving parents an opportunity to decide whether they want to pursue full reunification.

While most visits should be held in the family's home, visiting in another setting can sometimes offer a therapeutic advantage. For instance, if the purpose of a visit is to help parents acquire more effective parenting or home management skills, this might be most easily accomplished if visits are held in the foster home in the context of the child's usual daily activities. The caseworker or caregiver can model the skills, instruct parents in their use, let the parents try them, and provide immediate feedback and reinforcement. If the family members attend a counseling session together, a visit could occur after the session in a nearby restaurant or a park. The visits should be of adequate duration to achieve the stated objectives. In general, two to four hours is an appropriate length of time. At least a portion of the visit should be allocated for family members to visit in private.

Several overnight and weekend visits should be held prior to final reunification. More lengthy visits at home can further prepare family members for the realities of full-time care. The worker should meet with the family after such visits to identify potential problems, and to help the family develop strategies to deal with them.

Under certain conditions, close supervision of visits by the caseworker or another responsible adult may be necessary. This will be more likely if the worker is using visits to assess whether reunification is possible, since observation of the parent–child interaction during visits can provide important information about several potential risk factors. Visits should always be closely supervised when there is concern that a parent might physically or emotionally abuse a child during the visit, or if a parent is known to often behave in inappropriate or unpredictable ways. Initial visits should always be monitored when the child is visiting with the perpetrator, or when the parent has been known to verbally abuse the child or make unrealistic and inappropriate promises to the child. Finally, supervision is in the child's best interests when the child is clearly afraid to be alone with the parent. In this situation, careful observation by the worker can help identify the reasons for the child's fear.

If the visit must be supervised, the caseworker, the foster caregiver, or the relative caregiver can provide the supervision. Foster and relative caregivers must be prepared by the worker. Supervision includes monitoring to assure that family members stay within the parameters established for the visit, and knowing when and how to terminate the visit, if it becomes necessary to protect the child. If the person supervising the visit is not directly involved in family counseling or coaching, he should maintain a low profile and intervene only if needed. Parents should be allowed privacy with their children, if the safety of the children can be assured. The supervisor can locate himself outside of the visitation room so he can see and hear what is going on without being easily visible.

Caseworkers must intervene when parents routinely fail to attend visits, make unrealistic promises to their children, or exhibit other destructive behaviors during visits. A parent's failure to attend a visit will be less disruptive to the child if the visit has been scheduled in the foster home or in the home of a relative. If the parent fails to visit, the child can participate in normal activities, or can visit with other people who are important to him. The caseworker should stress to parents the importance of visits, and should help eliminate barriers to visits. This might include transporting the children to the visit, or making transportation available to other family members. Reunification planning conferences involving family members, foster parents, the caseworker, and the casework supervisor should also address parents' failure to visit.

At times, children may become upset either prior to or after a visit. There are several possible reasons. Visiting is stressful. Visits often reactivate feelings of loss and insecurity for children, and their distress may be exhibited in emotional outbursts or acting–out behaviors. The child may appear to regress and reexhibit inappropriate behaviors which had been better controlled or eliminated prior to the visit. The child may also be anxious and fearful when with the parent. This is more likely if the parent and child have not seen each other for a long period of time, and are awkward and uncomfortable with each other. Children who have been previously mistreated by a parent may feel unsafe and anxious. Some children may experience loyalty conflicts after visits, and may feel a need to reject the foster or relative caregiver out of loyalty to the parent. Loyalty conflicts are exacerbated if the child has developed very strong relationships with members of the caregiving family, or if jealousy and competitiveness exist between the biological and caregiving parents.

The caseworker should use supervised visits to fully assess the reasons for a child's distress. Once the source of the problem has been determined, the caseworker should consider revising the visitation schedule or structure to lessen the child's discomfort. If a reactivation of feelings of separation and loss are determined to be the cause of the child's distress, the frequency of visits should be increased rather than decreased. The child may feel reassured and less anxious if she knows there will be another visit within a short period of time. If a child's anxiety results from discomfort and awkwardness with a parent, the caseworker's direct involvement to ease the discomfort and facilitate the visit is often helpful. If loyalty conflicts contribute to the child's distress, the caseworker can reassure the child that a choice does not have to be made between caregivers and biological family. It is useful if the worker explains this to both the parents and caregivers, so they too can reinforce this with the child. If the parents feel comfortable with the caregivers, and the caregivers are empathetic and supportive of the parents, loyalty conflicts are much less likely. Finally, if a parent threatens a child during the visit, or if a child does not feel safe being alone with a parent, the visits should be supervised.

The essential involvement of foster or relative caregivers in reunification planning and visiting requires that they, too, be well prepared. The child's behavior may change in response to the stress and uncertainty that accompanies reunification, and caregivers may interpret this to be "regression to all his old ways." At times, caregivers may feel their gains with the child have been eroded, which may result in resistance to the reunification plan. Caregivers may also believe the child has been harmed by the visit and that visitation should cease. Proper training and support of caregivers can help them be constructive and supportive to both the child and the family during reunification. (See Section X–C, "Working with Foster and Other Caregivers.")

When several children in a family are to be returned home, the worker should strongly consider reunifying one child at a time, with intervals of several weeks between placements. This may increase placement stability by giving parents sufficient time to adjust to the changes incrementally, thus reducing stress and preventing crisis. This practice also allows each child more intensive parental involvement during the early stages of placement back home. Parental visits with all the children should be continued throughout the reunification process.

DEVELOPMENTAL INTERVENTIONS THAT PROMOTE REUNIFICATION

There are several types of developmental interventions that are valuable in reunification casework. They build upon strengths, enhance motivation, and help family members acquire new skills. These include the following:

1) *The worker should identify and point out family members' strengths and abilities.* At times, family members may expect to be criticized by others for perceived shortcomings. Their strengths often are taken for granted, if they are recognized at all. During the family assessment, the worker should help the family become aware of their strengths and abilities. This can be done by pointing out behaviors and actions that reflect positive qualities and traits.

Any attribute or behavior that helps family members cope with daily events reflects an existing or potential strength. Many people view life as a process of "getting by," without recognizing the effort that goes into adapting to day-to-day demands. It is not unusual for family members and their caseworkers to underestimate the perseverance and skill needed to survive under challenging or adverse circumstances. These abilities must be recognized as valuable strengths. Examples might be the ability to meet the family's basic needs on a very limited income; maintaining a full-time job while being the single parent of several children; surviving a 24-hour day with four children under the age of five; providing a safe and secure home in a dangerous and difficult environment; providing care to a child with a serious disability or medical problem; or managing a home while experiencing medical problems.

There are several ways the worker can point out family strengths:

- In the context of observing and assessing the family, the worker can note the things they appear to do well and comment on them;

- When discussing problem situations, the worker can ask family members how they have approached problems in the past, and what they've done that has worked;

- Begin an interview by asking family members to talk about what has gone well or right since the last meeting;

- Ask family members to relate something they like or respect about each of the other family members;

- Ask family members to relate what they believe to be their best qualities;

- Ask family members to think about what they would like to do or become, if the world were perfect; and

- Prompt family members to help one another recognize and reinforce each others' strengths, and tell one another when they appreciate something that another family member has done.

2)   Adopt an optimistic outlook. At times, family members may have an unrealistically negative or pessimistic perspective, whereas realistic optimism is more likely to generate motivation to change. This can be illustrated by the classic adage, "Is your cup half empty or half full?" Someone with a "half empty" perspective typically focuses on a desired end point, and can only see how much more is needed to achieve the goal. The typical emotional response is pessimism, characterized by feelings of failure, "what's the use," and a loss of motivation to continue. By contrast, the "half full" perspective also focuses on a clearly stated goal, but success is measured in the gains made from the starting point. Recognizing success in getting this far increases motivation to continue.

Example #1

Worker:	"How did your interview go?"
Ms. Ott:	"Okay, I guess."
Worker:	"Tell me about it."
Ms. Ott:	I don't think I'll get the job. They didn't seem very interested in me.
Worker:	What did they say?
Ms. Ott:	That they'd call me. But I'm sure they won't. I forgot to tell them a lot of the things we talked about. And I'm sure they have a lot of people who are a lot more qualified. It was a waste of time.
Worker:	So you think it wasn't worth it to even go?
Ms. Ott:	I guess I don't.
Worker:	You know, I see it differently. A month ago you were afraid to even look for a job. You didn't think you could get through an interview. Yet today you got on the bus, went downtown, and talked to a perfect stranger about your qualifications. Don't you think that took guts?
Ms. Ott:	I guess.
Worker:	You know, very few people get the first job they apply for. In a tight job market, you might have to interview for ten jobs before someone hires you. But, each time you do it, you'll learn something new, and you'll do better each time. I think it sounds like you did well for your first time. What do you think you did right?
Ms. Ott:	Well, I did tell him about my other jobs, and gave him the names of my supervisors.
Worker:	Good, that was important. What else.
Ms. Ott:	I don't think I was too pushy; I tried to be polite. But I was friendly, too. I guess that's all.
Worker:	Well, I think those are all very important. Did you learn anything that will help you next time?

Ms. Ott:	I should make a list of everything I want to tell them before I go, and take the list with me so I don't forget anything.
Worker:	I agree. I don't think this job interview was useless at all! I think you've gained from it.
Ms. Ott:	I suppose you're right. I never looked at it that way.

Example #2

Worker:	How did those discipline strategies we talked about work out?
Father:	They don't work. Rodney is just as bad as he's always been. He's going to do his own thing, come hell or high water.
Worker:	How did you feel about trying time–out?
Father:	You want the truth?
Worker:	Sure, I always want the truth.
Father:	I felt pretty dumb. I'm standing there trying to keep this kid in a chair, and he keeps getting the better of me by running away. After a while I'm wondering, "Who's boss here anyway?"
Worker:	So you don't think it worked?
Father:	Not really.
Worker:	Did you ever get him to sit in the chair?
Father:	Yeah, after about the fifth time.
Worker:	Would it surprise you to know that's how it is with most kids? Three year olds will test you to the limit. But it sounds like you stuck with it and, in the end, got him to sit still. Did he finally settle down?
Father:	He squirmed a lot and sucked his thumb, and looked at me like he hated me.
Worker:	But he quit screaming?
Father:	Yeah. I guess he did. But it won't stop him from doing it again.
Worker:	No, you're right. Once in time–out won't stop the tantrums. But, if you keep at it, you'll be able to stop a tantrum from happening by warning him about time–out. Sounds to me like you did fine for a first time. Actually, I'm really pleased you stuck it out, even when you didn't like it! I give you credit for stamina!
Father:	Hard–headed is more like it.
Worker:	Well, hard–headed has its virtues now and then, don't you think?

3) The worker should help family members reinterpret negative self-assessments by identifying and discussing their positive attributes. Cognitive psychology suggests that negative self-assessments have a powerful influence on self-esteem, confidence, and motivation. In addition, poor self–esteem and lack of confidence predispose people to evaluate themselves in negative terms.

Cognitive restructuring is a term that means helping people rethink their beliefs and perceptions, and look at things in a different way. Workers can help family members reconsider their views, beliefs, and perceptions by offering alternative ways of thinking about them. This is particularly useful when family members have heard and internalized many "negative messages" about themselves. Many people have never identified certain attributes or traits as strengths, and do not know how to use them purposefully toward a positive end.

The caseworker can help family members reexamine and alter their behaviors, activities, and self-perceptions by reinterpreting their negative self-assessments in a more positive light. The worker's interpretations must always be realistic, however. False praise will generally be recognized as false.

Example #1

Mother:	I know I would have hurt Teddy eventually. I couldn't stand to have him around me. I know I could have killed him. How can anyone feel that about a six year old? But I would have hurt him. I had to send him away. He knows it too, and he hates me for it. As far as he's concerned, I've abandoned him. Who knows–maybe he's right, and it's too late to change it.
Worker:	I think it takes courage to admit that you feel violent toward a child, and to develop a safety plan to protect him. That's what you did, you know. You *didn't* abandon him, you *didn't* leave him in an unsafe place, and you *didn't* kill him. You found a good person to care for him. You were smart enough to do something before you hurt him. Let's work together to try to understand why you feel as you do. That's the first step in changing it. And, more than likely, it's not too late to change.

Example #2

Father:	It's all my own fault. I don't like to say so, but it is. I can't keep my temper, and I lost my kids because of it.
Worker:	Why do you say it's all your fault?
Father:	My wife says I'm the cause of my own problems–if I didn't shout and swear and tell people off, I'd be a whole lot better off. She's probably right. But I can't hold things inside. I get mad, and I blow. I tell people what I think. You should know; I've yelled at you enough times. My wife says it's why they fired me, too. But, I'm mad all the time. Seems about everything! But I shouldn't take it out on the family. I know I shouldn't show it.
Worker:	You know, this may sound strange to you, but for me, your yelling is a type of honesty. You don't hide things from me. You say what's on your mind, and you're not afraid to say what you mean. I can handle your yelling. With everything that's happened, you have a lot to be

angry about. And your anger won't put me off, as long as I understand why you're feeling angry. It's important that you keep letting me know how you feel. We can also work to help you find better ways to communicate your anger than by yelling.

4) The worker should help family members break complex and overwhelming tasks into their component parts, and then work on small steps one at a time. Many human behaviors appear, at first glance, to be deceptively simple. Yet, when we analyze the individual activities and steps that go into completion of a task, we are often surprised at the complexity of something we thought so basic.

Many complicated tasks are easy when we have mastered the prerequisite knowledge and skills. Yet, we often take the knowledge and skills we've developed for granted. We tend to forget the lifelong process of learning that helped us develop the many abilities we habitually use to solve problems and complete tasks.

Many of the skills family members must learn in order to provide safe and nurturant care for their children are very complex. In order to devise developmental case plans, the first step is to dissect complex activities into their component parts, and construct a step–by–step action plan. The worker should help family members master each step of the plan independently, which not only increases success, but provides an opportunity to learn problem solving and other skills by partializing and dealing with one thing at a time.

入 Emma

The home–based services worker wanted to help 17–year–old Emma learn to care for her two–month–old son sufficiently to permit reunification. The baby had been placed with Emma's mother shortly after birth because he had been seriously neglected while in Emma's sole care. The worker determined that, among other things, Emma had not been feeding the baby properly. Emma said the nurse had explained everything to her before she left the hospital, but she didn't remember it all. Emma and the worker together decided to use Emma's visits with the baby to learn better parenting methods. They would start by teaching Emma to properly feed her son.

The worker began by making a list with Emma of the steps in feeding her son, and then walking her through each one individually. Using modeling, coaching, and feedback, the worker was able to help Emma master bottle feeding. The list of steps the worker devised with Emma looked like this:

a) Talk to Emma about what the baby should be fed for healthy nutrition;

b) Help Emma learn what formula and baby food to buy, where to buy it, and how much she would have to budget each week for the baby's food;

c) Read through the instructions on the box or can with Emma so she understands how to prepare it;

d) Make sure Emma knows how to measure and mix liquids;

e) Make sure Emma has the proper equipment and knows how to use it (baby bottles, nipples, baby spoons, etc.)

f) Teach Emma to recognize the baby's behavioral cues of hunger, and to differentiate them from behavior cues indicating the baby is wet, cold, or tired;

g) Teach Emma to test the temperature of formula and food, and make sure she knows what temperature is best;

h) Show Emma how to hold the baby while giving the bottle, and how to sit the baby and use the spoon to feed the baby cereal;

i) Teach Emma how much food should be given at each feeding; and

j) Teach Emma how and when to burp the baby.

The list was valuable in several respects. First, it reaffirmed for Emma that feeding her new baby was, indeed, a complicated undertaking, and she felt less of a failure for not doing it right. Second, it helped the caseworker fully understand how complicated the task appeared from Emma's perspective. Finally, the worker taped the list to Emma's refrigerator, and when Emma completed an item on the list, she and the worker checked it off. When they had completed the whole list, Emma felt very proud at how much she had learned. She and the worker then prepared a second list to teach Emma to bathe the baby.

5) *Model New Behaviors.* Research suggests that people learn and remember a small percentage of what they hear, a little more of what they see, and quite a lot of what they do. This means that family members will better learn new skills when they can watch and participate in the learning process, rather than being told how and what to do.

Caseworkers can transmit new skills through a strategy called modeling. The worker demonstrates how something is done, one step at a time, and makes sure the learner can repeat the step before moving on to the next one. Once the learner has mastered the steps, the worker and learner go through it together several more times. First, the worker and learner do the task together. Second, the worker coaches the learner through an independent try. Third, the worker watches the learner, prompts only when necessary, and positively reinforces good performance. Finally, the learner performs the task independently, and asks the worker for assistance if needed.

Workers can help family members learn a variety of skills by modeling, including: basic child care skills; housekeeping and home management skills;

child management and discipline strategies; techniques to play with children, nurture them, and promote their development; and problem–solving skills.

POSTREUNIFICATION FAMILY SERVICES

There is no aspect of child welfare practice in which family systems theory is more relevant than reunification. The reunification of a child after a lengthy absence changes the family structure and functioning in significant ways. Even if the child and family have maintained contact during the separation, the child's reintegration into the family will still alter the family system and create stress for all family members. Reunified families often encounter problems and issues similar to those faced by stepfamilies or families created by remarriage. The absence of support for the family during the critical early stages after reunification can doom reunification efforts.

Intensive, in–home supportive services should be considered a valuable agency resource to help prevent placement disruption once a child has been returned home. The family should also be linked to community support networks and services. Parent support groups, respite care providers, mental health or family counselors, and other community service providers can help strengthen and sustain the family. Family services after reunification are not significantly different from in–home services designed to help families retain custody of their children. However, it is valuable if the family has access to counselors with special expertise in working with step and reconstituted families.

When the family has been stabilized, and a risk assessment has determined the children to be at little to no risk at home, the worker can consider closing the case. However, the worker should assure that the family has the knowledge and resources needed to access supportive services within its own family and community.

WHEN REUNIFICATION FAILS

Reunification case plans should specify an expected time frame for reunification to occur. As with any case plan, the reunification plan must be reviewed and revised as necessary. In most cases, this should occur every few weeks. If the family is working successfully toward reunification, but more slowly than expected, expanded time frames can be negotiated. However, if the agency has made reasonable efforts to support reunification, and the family does not comply with the reunification plan, the worker must consider termination of parental rights, and the formulation of a permanent plan for the child.

In these situations, it is important that the caseworker help the child understand the reasons for termination of contact with family members, and fully explain that a permanent family will be sought for the child. The child should be provided with a Lifebook and a "story about you," to explain the circumstances that led to placement, and the reasons reunification was not possible. Adoption or other permanency planning should be initiated. (See Section VIII–C, "Placement Strategies to Prevent Trauma," for information on developing and using Lifebooks, and stories for children in placement. See Section XI–C, "Preparing a Child for Adoption," for information on preparing a child for adoptive placement.)

X. WORKING WITH FOSTER AND OTHER CAREGIVERS

A. The Components of an Effective Foster Care System

B. Recruitment and Selection of Foster and Other Caregivers

C. Working with Foster and Other Caregivers

A. The Components of an Effective Foster Care System

1. Conceptual Framework

2. Application

Conceptual Framework

Child welfare professionals have recently identified serious problems within foster care systems. These include high rates of placement disruption; a lack of permanence for many children in foster care; the placement of children in institutions when they could be better served in family settings; an overrepresentation of children from minority cultures in out-of-home care; a chronic shortage of qualified caregiving families; an inability of many foster caregivers to address the special needs of the children in their care; and foster caregivers, overly stressed by the demands placed on them, often leaving the foster care system.

The evolution of family-centered services should have a significant impact on foster care programming. First and foremost, it should reduce the necessity of placement for many children. There are multiple decision-making points in a family-centered system at which children may be diverted from foster care placement. For example, accurate risk assessment at intake can prevent the inappropriate removal and placement of children who are not at high risk of harm. The utilization of intensive, in-home services can maintain some children safely in their own homes, while caseworkers help strengthen their families. If out-of-home placement becomes necessary to assure a child protection, we may be able to place the child with kinship caregivers. Such interventions can ultimately reduce the numbers of children who will need placement in agency foster homes. Conversely, it is possible that the thorough risk assessment required for family-centered interventions may better identify some children at high risk, who may not have been identified before. This has the potential for increasing the numbers of some types of placements.

Finally, family-centered interventions will change the types of children who are placed in agency foster care. Children coming into the foster care system will have been at higher risk at home. Their families may be more dysfunctional, and the children may, themselves, have more serious developmental, behavioral, and emotional problems. Reunification may be more difficult. This foster care population also includes adolescents, many of whom may require substitute care until emancipation. Foster caregivers in this changed foster care system will need specialized knowledge and skills. Therefore, to strengthen the foster care system, child welfare agencies must identify, prepare, support, and retain a cadre of professionalized foster caregivers, while simultaneously strengthening other family-centered services in order to divert children from placement into foster care.

DEFINING THE CONTINUUM OF CHILD WELFARE SERVICES

The "continuum of child welfare services" represents the broad range of community-based, family-centered services needed to assure that each child we serve has a safe, permanent family. To be effective, foster care must be seen as an integrated component on this continuum. It cannot be viewed as a separate and isolated program, a system of last resort that is involved only when other child welfare interventions have failed.

On this service continuum, interventions are hierarchically organized from least to most intrusive. The proper level of intervention for any child and family is the least intrusive intervention that can assure both protection of the child from maltreatment, and permanence for the child. We should never utilize a more intrusive service intervention when a less intrusive intervention will achieve our objective.

The chart below illustrates the continuum of child welfare services.

DEGREE OF INTRUSION

LESS .... > MORE

	A	B	C
	In–Home Family Support Services	**Temporary Out–of–Home Care**	**Permanent Care Alternatives**
	Referral to Services in Community	Respite Care/ Protective Day Care	Reunification with Own Family
	Supportive In–Home Services	Kinship Care Home	Guardianship/Custody by Relatives
	Intensive In–Home Services	Traditional Foster Home	Adoption by Relatives or Foster Caregivers
		Specialized Foster Home	Agency Adoption: Continuum of Openness
		Treatment Foster Home	Independent Living
		Community Group Home	
MORE		Residential Treatment	

(Left vertical axis label: DEGREE OF INTRUSION)

The services in Column A, "In–Home Family Support Services," are designed to assure permanence for children in their own homes. Utilization of these services can often sufficiently reduce risk to allow children to remain with their families. (See Section II–E, "Family–Centered Child Welfare Services.")

When in-home services cannot assure a child's protection, we must consider the services in Column B, "Temporary Out–of–Home Care." There is a wide range of out–of–home care options. Respite care, the least intrusive of these, provides out–of–home care for children for very limited periods of time. Respite care can be provided by kinship caregivers, by licensed family foster caregivers, and by day care providers and agencies. Respite care is principally a means of reducing stress for parents, and is an effective way to provide protective intervention for children without removing them from their families. Protective day care can also be provided by family day care homes, day care centers, or preschool facilities. Many day care providers can also provide developmental and therapeutic services for children.

Protective day care and respite services are less intrusive than full–time placement. One might consider respite interventions, for example, in a family where the children are at higher risk when in the care of one parent, but are at little or no risk when another adult caregiver is in the home. An example would be to place the preschool child of a mother with chronic mental illness into protective day care while the child's father is at work. For some families, access to respite care can reduce stress, thus reducing the likelihood of child maltreatment. Respite care, combined with intensive in–home supportive services, can also help to prevent the need for full–time placement.

When full–time substitute care is necessary, kinship care is often the least intrusive option. There can be many benefits to kinship care. For example, the child lives with people he already knows, which can prevent much of the separation trauma inherent when placed with strangers in an unfamiliar environment. Kinship caregivers are also likely to have a preexisting relationship with the child, and this emotional attachment may strengthen their commitment to caring for the child. Placement with extended family members also reinforces children's sense of belonging and identity, and it often allows them to remain in their own schools, churches, and communities.

However, kinship caregivers may be no more prepared than are agency foster families to meet the special needs of the children they are parenting. For this reason, many child welfare agencies do not differentiate between kinship caregivers and foster caregivers in homestudy and certification requirements. Kinship caregivers participate in a collaborative homestudy that helps them assess their capabilities in caring for a child. They must be approved by the agency, and sometimes licensed by the state. They are also expected to become involved in the development and implementation of case plans, and to support visits with the parents. And, they are expected to meet the developmental and safety needs of the child, even if this means directly confronting and controlling the behavior of the child's parents to assure the child's protection. It may also be difficult, at times, to maintain children in kinship placement unless the caregivers are provided with specialized training, in–home supportive services, linkage to appropriate community support services, and, when necessary, reasonable financial support. Without these supports, the kinship caregivers may not be able to withstand the stresses and challenges of caregiving.

While studies have suggested that the majority of children in kinship care fare well [Thorton 1987], placement in kinship care may not always meet children's needs for protection. The Child Welfare League of America North American Kinship Care Policy and Practice Committee [1994] suggests several factors that potentially increase risk to children in kinship care, including: the intergenerational nature of child abuse and neglect; intergenerational issues sometimes associated with substance abuse; and, the continued access that parents may have to their children living with relatives. By contrast, the Task Force on Permanency Planning found that the "majority of kinship care families…were poor but stable and hardworking families who cared about each other and could not understand the path that their children or siblings had chosen" [Task Force on Permanency Planning 1990]. Clearly, an individualized assessment of each potential kinship family is an essential first step in developing kinship care homes for children in need of placement.

When kinship caregivers are not available, or are unable to meet the safety and developmental needs of a child, other out–of–home care options, including agency–based family foster care, must be considered. Agency–operated foster homes can provide family placements for children with a wide range of problems and needs. However, the child welfare agency must have access to various types of foster home placements to meet the many different needs and behaviors exhibited by children in care. Foster care, therefore, forms a subset of services on the larger continuum. Foster care placement resources will range from typical home environments to very specialized and structured therapeutic settings. The type of home selected for any child should be chosen based upon the extent of the child's problems, and the complexity of the child's needs. In a comprehensive continuum of services, temporary placement for entire families is another valuable option, as it provides supervised care for the children without the trauma of separation from primary caregivers. Examples are foster or group homes for teen mothers and their infants; temporary group home placements for homeless families; protective residential placement for victims of domestic violence and their children; and, therapeutic residential or group care for families, wherein staff members both protect the children and provide on–site counseling and education to their parents.

Foster care is, by definition, a temporary intervention. A permanent plan must be made for all children in our care. The options in Column "C" on the continuum are designed to assure permanence for a child in a family setting, either in his own home, or in a permanent alternative home, unless or until the child can live independently. The least intrusive permanent option for a child who cannot be returned home is to finalize placement with relatives until emancipation, without terminating all parental rights and responsibilities. This can be achieved through legal guardianship or legal custody granted to a relative by court decree.

Adoption by relatives can also provide children with a permanent legal home while preventing traumatic separation. Adoption by relatives prevents children from having to sever past relationships and develop new ones with strangers who are to become their parents. Adoption by their foster caregivers can be a preferred option for children who need a permanent home, and whose strongest emotional bonds and identification are with their foster families.

Finally, formal agency adoption should be considered for children when other permanent placement options are not appropriate. Agency adoption often results in the severing of past attachments, and the reestablishment of the child in a new family milieu. While this is in the best interests of many children, it is also a more intrusive intervention than either guardianship or adoption by relatives or foster caregivers.

There is also a continuum of "openness" in formal agency adoptions. "Openness" refers to the degree to which there is an exchange of information or direct contact between the child and/or his adoptive family and members of the child's primary family. The level of contact may range from providing children with information about their primary families in the form of Lifebooks, letters, and narratives, to an arrangement wherein the child is legally a member of an adoptive family but maintains relationships with members of his primary family or previous foster families. This can include biological parents, siblings, extended family members, and foster parents. As an example, such an open adoption is often arranged when children have an enduring relationship with a parent who cannot provide them with safe care due to mental retardation or chronic mental illness, or when children cannot be adopted by foster parents with whom they have close emotional bonds.

All of the service interventions on the continuum promote permanence for the child in a family setting while removing risk of maltreatment, and can be utilized with strategies to minimize the traumatic effects of separation. They are, therefore, all valid family–centered service interventions for particular case situations and case objectives. The intervention of choice should be the least intrusive of these interventions that can still accomplish the case objective.

PRINCIPLES OF A FAMILY–CENTERED APPROACH TO FOSTER CARE

In a family–centered system, foster care services are considered one of many services that protect children and strengthen families. Foster caregivers provide developmental and remedial services to abused and neglected children in their care, and when appropriate, they also provide services to parents. In this capacity, foster caregivers are professional collaborators in a team approach to service planning and delivery. Their homes become a therapeutic milieu in which children can develop and grow, and where parents can learn to be better parents to their children.

Most primary families can, and should, remain actively involved with their children while in placement (See Section IX–B, "Empowering Parents to Participate in Placement Activities.") This prevents many of the negative consequences of separation, and can support successful reunification. Current foster care practice often promotes anonymity and secrecy when a child is placed into foster care. Such exclusion discourages primary families, exacerbates separation trauma, and ultimately works against successful reunification.

Children should always live in the least restrictive, most home–like environment that meets their needs. This requires the development of a variety of foster home and substitute care placement resources with increasing levels of therapeutic and protective structure. In practice, the lack of appropriate placement resources results in many placements that do not meet children's needs. The critical decision of where best to place a child is often made using the single criteria of "available bed space." Children and youth with developmental, emotional, or behavioral problems are often placed in group homes and residential institutions that are more restrictive than necessary, because the agency has been unable to develop and maintain family–based placements. A large percentage of children placed by child welfare agencies into residential care could be returned and successfully maintained in community–based, treatment-oriented foster homes, if such homes were available.

The inability of child welfare agencies to recruit and develop qualified foster care homes for challenging children is not, as is often believed, due to a lack of resources, but rather to a lack of vision, or a lack of technology and/or agency and community commitment. In many agencies, the annual budget to maintain children in residential treatment could easily finance family–based care in the community for most of these same children.

Child welfare agencies frequently assume, or are given, responsibility for children whose special needs could be better met by other service systems, including mental health, mental retardation/developmental disabilities, or juvenile justice. However, since child welfare's legal mandate is to serve maltreated children, and many children with other disorders are also maltreated, the child welfare system often becomes the primary case manager and caregiver for a wide variety of troubled children. Yet, the child welfare system is neither structured nor funded to provide this wide array of services. This underscores the necessity of integrating and coordinating child welfare services with those of other community agencies.

Development of the full range of services on the continuum makes family–centered practice possible, and also helps to more clearly define the scope and responsibility of foster care within that continuum. With a full range of services available, the following can occur:

1) The agency has numerous options available to protect children and strengthen families at home, thus preventing the need for out–of–home placement.

2) Children are not placed into agency foster care unless they cannot be protected in their own immediate or extended families through provision of family–based supportive services.

3) Children who need out–of–home care can be placed with families specifically selected for them, because the caregiving family has the skills to meet the children's individual developmental and treatment needs.

4) Whenever possible, children are placed with relatives or foster families in their own communities and cultural environments, close to their own homes. This allows them to maintain important relationships with family and friends, and it decreases the changes to which the child must adjust, thereby reducing the potential emotional trauma associated with separation and placement.

5) Qualified foster caregivers can provide a wide range of supportive and educational services to both children in care and their families. This utilizes currently untapped resources. Properly trained foster caregivers can serve as milieu therapists, family advocates, mentors, data gatherers, models, educators, service and transportation aides, respite providers, and home managers to support casework and other treatment interventions.

6) A community–based continuum of care involves the development of strong collaborative relationships between service providers in the community. Families can benefit from this comprehensive approach to services, not only while the child is in placement, but after the child returns home. A consistent support network is often the most important variable

in helping to support and maintain a family after reunification, thereby preventing recurrent need for foster placement.

7) Foster and kinship care families are often valuable resources as permanent placements for children who have been in their care. This helps assure placement stability and continuity for children who must be permanently removed from their primary families.

When child welfare agencies can develop services that span the continuum of care, we not only have the capacity to provide relevant and individualized services for maltreated children and their families; we also have the blueprint for foster care system reform. Foster care services must be strengthened to provide a range of services to a wide variety of children with exceptional needs, and to their families. However, by integrating foster care into the larger system of care, the other services on the continuum can also strengthen and support foster care programs.

Application

A well-integrated, agency-based foster care system has the capability to provide a hierarchy of services to children and their families along a continuum of increasing complexity of problems and needs. Homes in this expanded foster care system can be divided into four general types:

Respite Homes

The respite foster home provides short-term, hourly, or daily child care, including protective day care, which can prevent the need for 24-hour placement. In some cases, the use of respite care can sufficiently reduce parental stress and increase family support, so the children can be maintained at home at lessened risk while the family's problems are being addressed. If the children require emergency placement or longer-term care at a later time, they already know the foster family, which reduces placement trauma.

Respite homes can be a valuable resource to support an agency's home-based services efforts. Trained respite care providers can provide the agency with assessment information about a child's development, behavior, and needs. They can also involve the child in activities that promote the child's development. Respite caregivers can also assist primary parents to develop their parenting and child management skills. Properly trained foster caregivers can be engaged to work directly with primary families as educators, role models, and advocates to help resolve family problems in the areas of child care, child management, and home management.

Many families that would not consider becoming full-time foster caregivers might consider serving as respite caregivers. Respite caregiving very often involves regular work hours with scheduled evening and weekend time off the job.

Traditional Foster Care

The term "traditional" may be misleading, in that current practice in many agencies does not achieve the standards expected of a traditional caregiving family in this model. Traditional care refers to the placement of a child in substitute care on a 24-hour-a-day basis for a period of weeks to months. The case plan for the child can either be reunification with his own family, or placement in a permanent alternative family through guardianship or adoption.

In a family-centered service model, traditional foster care families are partners in planning and delivering services for the child in their care. They are well trained and are expected to contribute as a team member to the case assessment, the development of the case plan, and the delivery and evaluation of services. Traditional foster caregivers can also be trained to work with primary families to promote reunification. Traditional foster care families generally can provide care to children who have minimal to moderate physical, behavioral, or emotional problems.

Specialized Foster Care

Specialized foster care is designed for children who have unusual physical, cognitive, or developmental problems which require caregiving skills exceeding those needed for children in a traditional placement. A specialized foster caregiver, for example, might care for a child with AIDS, cerebral palsy, a physical disability, or mental retardation. Specialized caregivers are also better able to deal with the unique problems of adolescents. The specialized foster care home serves the child in a manner similar to the traditional foster care home, but caregivers must be trained in special caregiving and child management skills.

Specialized foster caregivers can train and coach primary families in the special skills needed to care for their child. They can also serve as respite caregivers to these families after the children are returned home. (Refer to Section VII-D, "Services for Children with Developmental Disabilities and Their Families.")

Treatment Foster Care

In a treatment foster home, the day-to-day home environment essentially becomes a treatment milieu for the child in a manner similar to that of a residential facility or group home. An important difference is that the environment in a family foster home is more typical of social reality than an institution or group home would be. This helps the child more easily generalize positive emotional and behavioral change from the treatment home to the larger social environment. The child also benefits from the presence of consistent caregivers, which is often not possible in a residential treatment facility that is staffed in shifts. The continuity of caregivers in a family foster home can promote the development of trust and attachment.

The children served in treatment foster care homes are generally school-age or adolescent children with long histories of maltreatment, and many resulting developmental, emotional, and behavioral problems. The foster caregivers must be highly skilled in using day-to-day activities as points of therapeutic intervention to help modify a child's attitudes and behaviors, to promote healthy emotional and social development, and to promote emancipation and independent living. A community-based treatment foster home is a better placement alternative for many children than the residential treatment or group home settings in which they are now often placed.

THE ROLE OF THE FOSTER CAREGIVER IN A TEAM APPROACH TO FOSTER CARE

Trained foster caregivers can contribute to the delivery of child welfare services in several ways. In a team approach to foster care, the caregivers are actively involved in the family assessment and the development of the case plan. After having lived with and observed the child, trained caregivers can provide valuable assessment information about the child's development, behaviors, needs, and strengths. Caregivers may also help determine the most appropriate service interventions to meet the child's needs, and they are integral to implementing the activities in the child's case plan.

X. A. The Components of an Effective Foster Care System

With proper training and support, foster caregivers can also provide valuable supportive and educational services directly to the families of children in their care. The goal of such intervention is to empower primary families, to keep them involved in their children's lives while in placement, and to increase their parenting capacity. (See Section IX–B, "Empowering Parents to Participate in Placement Activities.")

At a minimum, direct contact between the caregiver and the child's family should be considered at the time of placement to reduce placement stress and trauma. The foster caregiver and the child's family can be introduced during preplacement visits and can share information about the child. This provides valuable information to the caregiver to help maintain continuity and consistency for the child. Parents may also maintain regular telephone contact with the caregiver after the placement, and can receive frequent updates on the child, which also promotes their ongoing involvement with the child.

Foster caregivers can help strengthen and maintain the parent–child relationship by including parents in activities with the child. For example, a parent may accompany the foster caregiver and the child to the doctor, to counseling appointments, to school conferences, and to other community services arranged for the child. Parents may also be included in the child's school and recreational activities, and when appropriate, in foster family outings.

Involving parents and the caregiver in developing a plan for visits can greatly facilitate regular and successful visitation. If the child cannot visit in the parent's home, or if supervision of the visit is needed to assure the child's protection, visits can be held in the foster home.

Foster caregivers who are trained to work with parents can also provide an array of services not normally available through community service agencies. In the relaxed, informal, and natural setting of the foster home, parents can learn parenting and home management skills by modeling the activities of the foster caregiver. These skills can include: cooking, cleaning, and managing a household; budgeting on a limited income and shopping economically; providing physical care for an infant or young child; learning and using effective and safe strategies to discipline their child; playing with their children to stimulate cognitive and language development; nurturing behaviors to develop and strengthen attachment; establishing age–appropriate expectations for their children; developing behavior management strategies; accessing and using community resources and services; and developing social skills, including how to effectively communicate and work with others to resolve problems. The foster caregiver can be a teacher, a model, and a coach. If parents concurrently attend parenting classes, the foster home can provide a safe environment in which to practice skills learned in class.

This intervention model is most useful with parents who would benefit from a supportive relationship with a consistent and caring adult, and when a parent's lack of knowledge or skill contributes to inadequate care of children. The caseworker should carefully assess the needs of parents and the skills of foster caregivers prior to making a decision to pursue this intervention. Finally, foster caregivers who are being considered to work with families should receive special training to prepare them for this responsibility.

THE NETWORK CONCEPT

In order to develop and maintain a continuum of foster care services, the foster care system must be well organized and administered. The child welfare agency often serves as the primary developer and manager of the system. One very effective model of system organization and administration is the local foster care network.

A network consists of a group of homes and families, usually located within a circumscribed geographic community, and organized into a collaborative structure under the management of trained coordinators. The foster home network is a mini–organization, and foster caregivers have an important role in its maintenance and operation. In all respects, foster caregivers are members of the service delivery team. This promotes their identification with and commitment to the continuance of the system, in addition to providing caregiving families with an invaluable source of peer support.

Network functions can be used for many purposes, including providing ongoing training to caregiving families; sharing ideas and resources regarding available services for children; advocacy for the development of needed resources; and feedback to agency staff regarding program issues and problems. Network members can be organized into a formal "buddy system" to help orient and integrate new caregiving families into the system. The network is also an important resource in the recruitment and training of new families for the foster care system.

Since a network is located in a circumscribed geographic area, the agency can often place children within their own communities. This may also permit children in foster care to remain in their same school, go to their own church, and visit with friends and relatives with ease.

One network responsibility is to identify service resources in the community to meet the needs of children in care, and to advocate for the development of resources where none exist. This focus on community–based care requires the involvement of other service systems, such as mental health, mental retardation, education, and juvenile justice. The network members and network coordinator will generally develop formal contractual or compactual agreements with key service providers in these systems for collaborative service delivery. As an example, one foster care network was able to convince the public school system to develop its own services for children with severe behavior problems, utilizing the same money that was paying tuition for local children to attend special classes in another community.

In the most sophisticated network arrangement, community agencies in the different service systems jointly develop, fund, and maintain a network of treatment foster homes that serve children from all the participating service systems. This interagency approach to treatment enables children with multiple and complex service needs to access the comprehensive services they need, regardless of the service system that has case management responsibility for them.

THE LEAD ROLE OF THE LOCAL CHILD WELFARE AGENCY

While the technology to develop and maintain a continuum of foster care services is not extremely difficult, its implementation can be time consuming. However, the development of foster care resources is a logical next step in strategic planning for a more effective family–centered child welfare system. "Front–end" family–centered services must be available to divert children who can be protected in their own families from the foster care system. A plan for a comprehensive and effective foster care program must then be developed. This would include designing the foster care program; the revision of agency policies and procedures; appropriate staffing and management of the foster care program; identification or reallocation of resources; and the provision of training for staff and caregivers.

Unfortunately, many agencies believe it is easier to purchase care and case management from a residential facility, irrespective of high cost, than to develop and manage its own community-based system of care. In addition, many agencies have tried unsuccessfully to improve their foster care systems by implementing isolated interventions, such as launching a special public relations and recruitment campaign; raising per diem rates; conducting group home studies; or providing foster caregivers with extensive training. However, these singular and disconnected interventions often fall short of solving placement problems. Therefore, many local agencies seriously doubt their capability to care for challenging children within the community, or are loathe to commit what is perceived as the excessive time and resources needed to do so.

An agency's motivation to commit to the development of a new foster care system is highest when the program will serve its most challenging and troubled children, whose care consumes considerable agency dollar resources. Therefore, foster care reform can often be introduced into the system by developing networks of treatment foster homes. Once the agency has had a successful experience with its most difficult population, it can easily apply the newly acquired technology to other foster care program areas, with a high likelihood of success.

Systemic reform of foster care must occur at two levels simultaneously. At the state or provincial level, policies, procedures, rules, and resource allocations should be reviewed and modified to assure congruence with the community-based network philosophy and model. However, the most successful large–scale foster care intervention is initiated at the community level, and then linked into a larger state or provincial system, rather than being implemented from the "top down." For this reason, the primary point of intervention for foster care reform is in a community that is committed to providing effective services to its own children.

B. RECRUITMENT AND SELECTION OF FOSTER AND OTHER CAREGIVERS

1. Conceptual Framework

2. Application

Conceptual Framework

The evolution of child welfare has brought about significant changes in the roles and responsibilities of foster caregivers. Historically, foster families usually cared for children with few serious developmental or behavioral problems. The foster family's role was to provide a stable home environment for children and to promote healthy child development.

Recently, improved risk assessment, systemic pressure for timely case disposition, and the use of intensive in-home services have made it possible for many children, who would have previously been placed, to remain at home. Those children who are removed from their families are often more troubled and exhibit emotional disturbances, behavior problems, attachment disorders, and/or developmental delays. Many are older children and adolescents. Foster families whose experiences have been with younger neglected and abused children are generally not prepared for the challenges these children present.

What would motivate families to become foster caregivers for children with such extensive needs? In many respects, becoming and staying a foster parent is not unlike becoming and staying a child welfare worker. Some child welfare workers determine, after a short period of employment, that they are not suited for the job. The annual national turnover rate, estimated as high as 30%, attests to the difficulty of attracting and retaining qualified child welfare staff. Workers who choose to remain in the field usually view their work as a profession rather than a job, and they believe their work enhances the quality of life for children and families. This clear sense of purpose generates commitment, despite the inherent challenges of the profession, and this same sense of purpose often motivates successful foster caregivers.

Yet, there are many reasons qualified families might not become caregivers. Substitute caregiving requires a considerable commitment of time, and of physical and emotional energy. Foster care payments often do not meet even the basic needs of children in care, and in many cases, kinship caregivers receive no payment at all. The caregivers must be able to coordinate their activities with those of the caseworker, the child's parents, and other service providers. And caregiving families must readjust their family lifestyles to accommodate the children in their care. It is not an easy adjustment, and many families are ambivalent about such a challenging undertaking. Yet, in spite of the challenges, many families have made foster care their life's work.

Child welfare agencies have recently attempted to increase the availability of placements for children, while reducing placement trauma, by developing and supporting relative caregivers. Placement with relatives makes it possible for children to be protected within their extended families and communities, and relatives are often motivated by their personal commitment to a particular child or children. Yet, kinship caregivers may not have fully considered the implications of full-time caregiving, and they may be unprepared to cope with the children's multiple and challenging problems.

To assure that the best family placements are available for children who cannot be protected at home, child welfare agencies must develop programs that identify, prepare, support, and maintain a variety of foster and kinship care placement resources. The most effective programs provide prospective families with essential information needed to make well-informed choices about caregiving, and then prepare them to assume these responsibilities. These developmental activities can be categorized into four general program components: recruitment, screening, family assessment, and training. Each will be examined individually.

RECRUITMENT

In recent years, child welfare agencies have expended considerable effort to improve their foster care recruitment programs. With more sophisticated use of the media, community recruitment campaigns, and expertise in grass roots strategies, agencies have been better able to identify a larger pool of qualified foster families.

For many families, their first exposure to foster care is through the recruitment campaign. It is, therefore, important that we give families an accurate picture of the goals and expectations of foster care and the role of the caregiver. The most effective recruitment programs increase the prospective caregiving family's understanding of the scope of the job, enabling them to make informed decisions and choices. They must understand that caregiving is usually a short-term service that is part of a comprehensive family case plan. Prospective foster families must understand that reunification or permanence are the goals for most children in substitute care, and that the caregiver's responsibilities will often include helping the agency implement the plan to return the child home or to a permanent family. Families should be helped to understand the types of children who typically need care, and the challenges and rewards of caring for children with physical, emotional, behavioral, or developmental problems. Foster care recruitment is most effectively conducted by a recruitment team of caseworkers and experienced foster caregivers, which assures that prospective caregivers are informed about all aspects of caregiving early in the recruitment process.

SCREENING

Screening begins the process of gathering information from prospective foster families and educating them about foster caregiving. At the time of screening, the agency provides families with a general orientation that covers the roles, responsibilities, and agency expectations of foster caregivers; the rates of pay and benefits; and characteristics that typically enhance or hinder a family's ability to work with children with special needs. Prospective foster families provide the agency with basic information about themselves and the reasons they are interested in caregiving. The agency also uses screening to determine with a family whether they meet the basic qualifications, usually set in statute, to become licensed as foster caregivers. The agency also utilizes record checks to identify prospective caregivers whose backgrounds would preclude them from being approved.

Many families without the necessary ability or commitment will self–select out of the program after the exchange of information during the screening and orientation process. While the agency must screen out families who do not meet basic requirements, the goal is to encourage most interested families to continue to assess their suitability as care–giving families. Preservice training and a collaborative family assessment are designed to help them do this.

ASSESSING PROSPECTIVE CAREGIVING FAMILIES

During the family assessment, the agency and the prospective foster family jointly explore and assess the family's strengths, skills, needs, and areas of vulnerability, and determine the family's potential to work within the foster care program.

The family assessment serves several purposes. First, it is an educational process that helps the family refine their conception of foster care, and fully assess their own interests and commitment. Through discussion with agency staff and experienced caregivers, the family can develop realistic expectations for the caregiving experience, and can evaluate how their life experiences may have prepared them for the challenges and stresses they are likely to encounter as caregivers.

Second, the family is helped to identify their strengths and areas of potential vulnerability as caregivers. Certain personal and family attributes are often necessary when parenting foster children. Adjectives such as "adaptable," "flexible," "patient," and "consistent" have often been listed among the family characteristics associated with effective foster caregiving. These are often hard to quantify. There are, however, some attributes that can be quantified and should be evaluated during the family assessment process. The family assessment also helps families further consider the types of children they are best suited to parent, and the types of children for whom they should not provide care.

A third important purpose of the family assessment is to define, develop, and strengthen the collaborative relationship between the family and the agency. A positive relationship based on a team approach will promote honest communication between caregivers and caseworkers, and will provide the framework for collaborative case planning and service delivery. It is often a challenge for foster caregivers to develop attachments to the children in their care without feeling some conflict about sharing the child with his biological family, or sharing decision–making authority with agency staff. Caregivers must learn to view themselves as members of a professional team that provides coordinated services in the best interests of both the child and his family. Many prospective foster caregivers will not fully understand this role initially, but they can be helped during the family assessment to consider the many benefits of teamwork in assuring coordinated and effective services to children and families. Prospective families can also learn to view the agency as an important source of help and support. The expectation that the agency–family relationship will be based on trust and mutual respect should be developed from the time of the initial contact, but is strongly reinforced during the family assessment and preservice training process.

Some professionals strongly recommend a formal assessment and preparation process for kinship caregivers that is similar in many ways to the foster family assessment [Child Welfare League of America North American Kinship Care Policy and Practice Committee 1994]. The family assessment's strong focus on education and preparation can be equally valuable for kinship caregivers, as can the opportunity to participate in preservice and inservice training.

TRAINING

Ideally, preservice training should precede the family assessment. Preservice training gives prospective caregivers an overview of the child welfare system and its mission; the purpose of foster care services; roles, responsibilities, and expectations of caregivers, parents, and agency staff; and a beginning understanding of the types of children and families served by the agency. Formal preservice training also begins to prepare the family for foster care work by giving them opportunities to learn from agency staff and experienced caregivers. Attendance at preservice training also gives families sufficient information to make an informed decision whether they want to pursue foster parenting and proceed to family assessment.

Participation in a group also begins to develop supportive relationships among caregiving families. Concurrent individual assessment interviews help the worker further reinforce the caregiving family's role and responsibility, and the agency's expectations for their involvement within the program. Discussions during family assessment interviews can also address issues and concerns raised during preservice training.

Regularly scheduled job–related training must also be provided to foster and kinship caregivers to promote skill development. Core training [Hughes & Rycus 1989], or fundamental skills training, should routinely address such topics as the role and responsibilities of foster and kinship caregivers; the philosophy of permanency planning; implementing a team approach to foster care; working with children who have been abused, neglected, or sexually abused; the traumatic effects of separation and placement for children and their families; issues of culture and diversity; and behavior management strategies. Ongoing training can help caregivers learn to deal with special problems. Training should be scheduled at regular intervals. Each caregiving family should attend sessions that meet their individual training needs as jointly identified by the family and their caseworker [Hughes & Rycus 1989].

These program components are essential for the successful recruitment and selection of qualified foster and kinship caregivers. Even though many prospective families may be highly motivated and eager to provide foster or kinship care, if they are not properly prepared and trained, the demands of caring for children with special needs may prove to be overwhelming. The rate of placement disruption is much higher when inexperienced and untrained families are asked to care for children with serious emotional and behavior problems. And, the stress in kinship families is much higher when these families are unprepared and unsupported. Unfortunately, many potentially successful families withdraw from the program as a result, or experience disrupted placements.

Application

While the interventions described herein are largely applied to foster families, most of the concepts are equally valid for kinship caregivers. The term "caregiver" is used here to include any family providing substitute care for abused and neglected children under the agency's supervision. Where there are differences, they are noted. With some minor differences, these principles are also valid for adoptive families. (See Section XI-A, "Identifying and Preparing Adoptive Families for Children with Special Needs," for more detailed information on recruitment and selection of adoptive families.)

RECRUITMENT STRATEGIES

Identification of prospective caregivers can occur in several ways. Kinship caregivers are usually identified by the child's caseworker and the child's family. At times, foster families may be referred by experienced caregivers. However, foster families are usually recruited through large-scale, community-based recruitment efforts designed to generate interest from a targeted group of potential families. Many agencies conduct joint recruitment campaigns for both foster caregivers and adoptive parents, since many of the criteria for foster caregiving and adoption of children with special needs are the same.

There are several principles that greatly increase the likelihood of successful community-based recruitment [Horejsi 1979]:

- Recruitment of caregivers must be an ongoing process. It cannot occur once or twice a year as a "special event."

- Recruitment activities must target the proper audience. Unfortunately, recruitment often consists of sporadic "media blitz" campaigns that attract "inquiries, not prospective families." In other words, when recruitment is not targeted, it may generate interest among people who would not necessarily be good foster caregivers, or who aren't really interested in foster care once they understand the nature of the work.

- Recruitment is more effective if certain agency staff are designated as recruiters and are assigned permanent responsibility for recruitment activities. Recruiters can then develop the special skills necessary to conduct effective recruitment, and they can focus efforts on designing a variety of ongoing recruitment initiatives, without interference from unrelated and competing job responsibilities. The best recruitment programs use a team consisting of a caseworker and an experienced foster or kinship caregiver, or adoptive parent. Agency caregivers may also know of other families who might be good prospective caregivers, and can help the agency recruit by doing outreach, giving presentations, and orienting potential caregivers.

- The most effective recruitment occurs in one-to-one or small group personal contacts between the recruiters and potential foster families. Outreach activities, including presentations to small groups, visits with key community leaders, and involvement in child-related community activities, will help the recruiter identify potential families.

- The recruiter must know the community in which recruitment is to occur, and must understand the values and practices of the cultural groups within that community. Establishing preliminary contact with key community leaders can often help the recruitment team gain access to families they otherwise might not reach.

- Recruitment should be targeted to families most likely to be interested in foster care. These families may already do volunteer or church work to help others; they may provide day care, respite care, or baby sitting; their lifestyle most likely already centers around their homes and families; or they may have previously explored other types of professional child care. The recruiter should learn about the community in which recruitment is to occur, and locate community groups, clubs, and organizations whose members are already involved in community service projects to benefit families and children.

- The agency's image in the community can either attract or discourage families from applying to become caregivers. Therefore, the agency must conduct recruitment activities within the context of a total agency public relations program. The agency that is held in high regard in the community for the quality of its services and its responsiveness to community needs will be more likely to attract prospective caregivers.

- While a media campaign is not, in itself, sufficient to assure effective recruitment, it can create a general awareness of the need for caregiving families. A recruitment approach that "gets the message out" in several different ways will be more effective than any single form of communication. Many agencies use a variety of media events, including: 1) regular newspaper columns and special news releases or feature articles; 2) spot announcements on radio and television stations; 3) featured interviews on local talk shows on both radio and television; 4) distribution of printed literature at the local mall or at church-related activities; 5) buying advertising space in community service bulletins or other community publications; 6) attending job fair activities; 7) doing presentations at meetings of local service organizations, such as Lions or Kiwanis clubs; 8) engaging local restaurants that are holding special events or campaigns to utilize placemats printed by the agency; and 9) agency events that benefit the local community, which also educate community members about the agency and its services, including foster care.

- Recruitment campaigns must communicate both the challenges and the rewards of foster caregiving. The difficulty of the job and the level of responsibility should not be glossed over and minimized. However, potential foster families should not be unnecessarily frightened about foster caregiving. The inherent satisfactions and rewards of caregiving must also be clearly communicated. The best communication is balanced, straightforward and matter–of–fact. This is one reason that current foster and adoptive families make such good recruiters. They can communicate from first–hand experience both the benefits and the inherent problems associated with foster, kinship, or adoptive caregiving. Photographs of infants and young children create an inaccurate perception of foster care. Photographs of families with school–age and older children are usually more reflective of the realities of foster care.

- Making the decision to become a caregiver is difficult, and many families may be ambivalent at first. The recruiter needs to give people sufficient time to think about the possibilities before making a decision to formally apply. If the recruiter is too pushy, prospective caregivers often become uncomfortable and terminate their involvement. However, if the recruiter does not follow up in a timely manner, families may interpret this as a lack of interest. This applies to phone inquiries as well. Quickly returning phone calls communicates the agency's interest in the family, and helps prevent the family from losing interest. In spite of this, it is not uncommon for families to consider foster care for many months after they have first learned about it, before contacting the agency.

SCREENING

While the primary goal of screening is to provide prospective foster families with sufficient information to make an informed decision about pursuing foster care, the screening process must also identify those families who, for a variety of reasons, should not be approved as caregivers. Foster care licensure is generally regulated by specific qualifications set in state or provincial law. Some of the criteria for disapproval at the screening stage include:

- The prospective caregiver has a history of alleged or substantiated child maltreatment or other crime involving children, or family violence.

- The prospective caregiver has a history of domestic violence for which no intervention was received; or a criminal record and/or felony conviction.

- The prospective caregiver has a serious physical disability that would significantly interfere with parenting; an untreated or uncontrolled mental illness; mental retardation; and/or a diagnosed characterological problem that would preclude the prospective caregiver from providing safe and nurturing care for children.

- The prospective caregiver is known or highly suspected of being currently involved in criminal activity or substance abuse.

- The prospective caregiver family's primary stated goals for the foster care experience are inappropriate, and would not be in the best interest of a placed child. Examples of inappropriate motivating factors might be: to obtain a playmate for their own children; to see if they enjoy children before they decide to have their own; to save a poor child from his "undeserving" parents; to strengthen a faltering marriage; or to replace a child they have lost.

While the above–listed factors would, in general, indicate a prospective caregiver's lack of suitability to foster parenting, the final determination must be based on an individualized assessment that considers all factors, including the prospective caregiver's history of rehabilitation. When a family should not be approved, the caseworker should fully explain the reasons, help families understand why they would not be suited for foster caregiving, and help them to self–select out of the program.

THE FAMILY ASSESSMENT

The widely used term, "foster care homestudy," does not accurately communicate the intent or scope of this activity. Assessing the structure and safety of the home is only a small part of the assessment. Rather, prospective caregiving families must be involved in a comprehensive and collaborative process with three distinct purposes: 1) to help the prospective caregiving family determine whether they should become foster or kinship parents; 2) to identify the types of children the family should and should not care for; and, 3) to begin educating and preparing the family to perform this role.

The process used to conduct a foster family assessment is essentially the same process we use with any family. (See Chapter IV, Case Planning and Family-Centered Casework.) The foster or kinship family assessment is conducted within a framework of mutuality and collaboration. The assessment worker does not conduct an assessment *of* the family, but rather, *with* the family. The skilled assessment worker guides the family through an intensive process of self-examination that enables them to develop realistic expectations for themselves and the caregiving experience. Our goal is to help them arrive at well–informed conclusions about their own strengths, interests, and vulnerabilities, and to help them make sound decisions about the nature and scope of their involvement in foster or kinship caregiving.

Helping families understand the multiple purposes of the family assessment early in the process may relieve considerable anxiety about being evaluated, which helps family members participate more freely and comfortably. This is particularly important for kinship caregivers, who may rightfully resent having to be "evaluated and approved" to care for members of their own extended family. The mutual rapport that characterizes a good family assessment also promotes openness and honesty, which greatly enhances the quality of the assessment. Finally, defining the family assessment as a learning and preparation activity sets the expectation that challenges are normal and expected, and that the most skilled caregivers are skilled problem–solvers, not families without problems.

The family assessment should also set the tone for the family's ongoing relationship with the agency. This relationship is characterized as a partnership, in which caregivers and caseworkers must act as a team to achieve the goals for children in care and their families. If the worker establishes a trusting and collaborative relationship with the family at the time of the family assessment, the worker can better support and guide the family during their caregiving experiences. The worker also models a team approach to caregiving during the family assessment, thereby helping prepare the family to work collaboratively with agency staff and others.

Interviewing to Elicit and Assess Family Process

The family assessment is designed to help workers and potential caregivers understand key aspects of family process. While certain factual information is relevant, it is more important for caseworkers and family members to understand the structure and operation of the family system; typical family roles, relationships, and dynamics; the family members' culture, values, beliefs, perceptions, and feelings about critical issues; and the family members' linkages within their extended family and community.

The skilled assessment caseworker uses interviewing strategies that move the family from the content level to the process level in their communications. (Refer to discussion of content and process in Section IV-C, "Conducting the Family Assessment.") The worker must also use interviewing methods that promote the collection of comprehensive information; that assure the clarification of important issues; that guide the formulation of accurate conclusions; and that summarize the implications for the family. The caseworker will likely use open-ended and supportive questions early in the process to engage family members, to strengthen the worker–family relationship, and to encourage family members to share comprehensive information. In subsequent contacts, the worker will return to key issues, and help family members explore them in greater depth by using focused questions and clarifying responses. Periodically throughout the assessment, the worker will involve the family in summarizing what has been discussed, identifying prominent themes, and considering the relevance of the assessment conclusions to caregiving. All the fundamental principles of casework interviewing apply to the family assessment, including the scrupulous avoidance of leading questions. (See Section IV-F, "The Casework Interview: Implementing the Helping Process.")

The family assessment process itself should consist of several interviews with family members. In general, five or six meetings of one to one-and-a-half hours in length should be considered the average. Initially, the assessment worker should meet with the parents or caregiving adults together, and then with the family as a whole. Follow-up individual interviews should then occur with each adult, and if children are old enough, with each child. Additional sessions with the adults together should complete the assessment process, but one final meeting should be held with the entire family to summarize and share conclusions, and to develop "next steps."

The Assessment Criteria

Criteria are the standards, principles, or rules on which a judgment or decision can be based. The criteria for a foster family assessment are those personal and family characteristics that have been correlated with the successful temporary parenting of children with multiple problems and needs. The family assessment helps the worker and family determine whether, and to what degree, the family possesses these qualities, and what further development is needed to strengthen and enhance them.

Criteria for a foster or kinship family assessment can be divided into two broad categories: 1) the traits and characteristics that will enable the family to manage the caregiving experience without experiencing severe family stress; and, 2) the traits and characteristics necessary to meet the special needs and promote the healthy development of children in care.

Whenever we compile a list of highly desired characteristics and use these as criteria against which to evaluate families, we risk perpetuating the "superfamily" myth. That is, we may begin to view the criteria on our list as the expected standard rather than the ideal. Clearly, no family will ever have all the desired characteristics on our list to the ideal degree. Therefore, to be realistic in our assessments, we must define a "minimum standard," in addition to our "desired standard." Families who repeatedly cannot meet the minimum standards should not be approved as caregivers. However, many prospective caregiving families will meet minimum standards in most, if not all, categories. They will also exhibit qualities closer to the desired standard in other categories. These are, by definition, the family's areas of strength. In addition, education and training can help many families develop their skills in critical areas.

Prospective caregiving families must always be assessed within their own cultural context. Workers must be cautious not to view the family through an ethnocentric lens, in which anything "different" is interpreted as "deviant." In the absence of cultural knowledge, differences in family structure, organization, values, and coping abilities may be seen as dysfunctional, while valuable strengths go unrecognized. While many of the characteristics and traits described in the "ideal" criteria may be shared by many cultures, the ways these are expressed by people from different cultural backgrounds may differ. For example, in one family, "teamwork" by parents might be expressed as participating equally in all aspects of parenting, child care, and household management. In another family, roles of the parents may be more explicitly defined and separated, but the families feel their distribution of tasks is equitable and enables them to both make significant contributions to the family. The caseworker must create an environment in which the family's values and beliefs can be fully explored and considered throughout the assessment process. (Refer to Chapter V, Culture and Diversity in Child Welfare Practice.)

In all the descriptions below, the term "parent" or "parents" is used to refer to the adult caregiver or caregivers in the prospective caregiving family. This may be a single parent; a married couple; a single parent and an extended family member; or another combination of parenting adults. Each adult in the family should be assessed individually on each of the criteria, and their areas of agreement or disagreement should be determined. Areas where they can support and complement each other should also be identified. Finally, since one of the goals of the family assessment is to determine whether the adults in the family have the ability to act as a parenting team, the worker might ask them to first consider each issue individually, then identify where they disagree, and consider how they might need to revise or integrate their approaches to assure consistency for the child in care.

The intent of the following discussion is to help caseworkers recognize and understand the process-level issues to be examined during the family assessment process. The following criteria represent an attempt to identify and categorize the qualities and traits that have often been associated with successful substitute caregiving. Most of these traits and characteristics apply equally to adoptive families for children with special needs, even though there are some differences. (See Section XI-A, "Identifying and Preparing Adoptive Families for Children with Special Needs.")

This section also provides suggested interviewing strategies to obtain essential information about the family and to generate meaningful discussion. However, the caseworker should never simply ask the family the questions in the order they are written herein and dutifully record their answers. The effective family assessment is a conversation, a dialogue, that must ultimately address these topic areas. The list of interviewing questions can be used to assure that all relevant areas are covered at some point, and preferably at many points, during the family assessment process.

Finally, caseworkers must remember that prospective foster families will vary widely on their areas of strength and vulnerability. No family will exhibit strengths in all the areas listed below. Those few families with multiple strengths are often our strongest and most committed caregivers. However, families with more modest strengths are often excellent caregivers as well. It is the worker's job to identify their areas of vulnerability, and avoid placing children in their home who will overly challenge and stress the family.

INTRODUCTION–GETTING TO KNOW THE FAMILY

Open-ended questions are recommended early in the family assessment, particularly during the first family contact. The worker's genuine interest in the family will help to build a relationship, and will help family members feel more comfortable talking about themselves. By using open-ended questions, the caseworker can gain a general understanding of the family's history, structure, organization, and culture. Information gained during initial discussions can help guide the direction of the assessment interviews, and raise issues for further discussion. The caseworker might ask family members to write or prepare an oral "autobiography" and share it with the worker, either before or during the family assessment. The information in the autobiography can provide the topics for initial discussions. Finally, initiating discussion of cultural issues will help the caseworker avoid misjudging family members' behavior because the caseworker is unaware of, or insensitive to, cultural differences.

Assessment Questions

"What would you like me to call you?"
"Tell me about yourselves. Tell me whatever you think is important, whatever you think would help me get to know you."

"Where did you grow up? Tell me something about your own family. Who was in your family? Describe the members of your family and tell me about your relationships with them."

"Tell me about the things you feel are most important in life. What do you want for yourselves? For your children?"

"What is your ethnic or cultural background? What things about your family reflect your culture? What traditions do you retain from your own families? What have you changed? How do you see yourself as being different or similar to people from other cultures? Tell me what you think I need to know to better understand your culture."

CATEGORY I–THE FAMILY'S EXPECTATIONS FOR CAREGIVING

There are a variety of reasons families apply to become caregivers. Unfortunately, unrealistic expectations often result in dissatisfaction, disappointment, and placement disruption. All prospective caregivers have a vision of what the foster care experience will be like, and how they expect their families to benefit from the experience. The worker must explore this vision and help families consider the reality of their expectations.

This can be done by exploring the family's perceived "best and worst outcomes" for the foster care experience. The worker could directly ask prospective foster parents why they want to become caregivers, but this may prompt stereotypic responses such as, "I want to help children." People can help children in many ways, including volunteering at Head Start, teaching Sunday School, leading a scout troop, or giving money to children's charities. Families who want to become caregivers in some way find the idea of foster care appealing, even though it is considerably more challenging. It is important that we, and they, understand why, so their expectations can be tested against the realities of foster care.

It is very important that all family members, particularly the caregiving adults, be interested and committed to becoming caregivers. Successful caregiving requires consistent support, commitment, and direct involvement from all family members. Inconsistency in parenting, and a considerable lack of involvement by one of the parents often promotes attempts by the placed child to "divide and conquer," which greatly increases stress in the caregiving family.

Assessment Questions

"What are your reasons for wanting to become foster (kinship) parents?" [Prompt] "Can you tell me about that in more detail?" "How do you see it helping a child?" "How do you envision foster care benefitting you personally? How will it benefit your family?"

"Imagine the very best possible outcome for your becoming foster parents. Tell me about it."

"Describe the very worst possible outcome for you. In your view, what would "disaster" look like?"

"How do you imagine foster care changing you and your family?"

Strengths

The parents are motivated by factors that support the child's best interests, not by factors related to selfish personal or financial gain. Personal satisfaction is a byproduct of the experience; they are not seeking the experience primarily as a means of meeting their own needs. All family members have thought and talked about how caregiving will affect their family, and they have agreed as a family to pursue it. They seem to understand the complexity and stresses of caregiving. Examples of appropriate motivations might be:

- "I've worked with special needs children before, and I really like seeing them growing stronger and getting better. Every little step is a real victory."

- "I have always enjoyed a challenge, and this will certainly be a challenge! Plus, I can probably learn things that will make me a better parent."

- "I just really like kids. I'm happiest when I have a dozen of them around–all sizes and ages."

- "I know how much children need stability and closeness in a family. Our family has that, and I feel lucky. I'd like to be able to share that with children who have never experienced it, and give them a good base to grow from."

- "I was a foster child myself, and I'm grateful that my foster family stuck with me through all the hard times. They helped me to grow up and make something of myself. I'd like to be able to do the same for another child."

- "I've known Mickey since he was born. I know his mother has had drug problems and may never get it together, and I want to give Mickey a home and the love he needs."

- (In response to the "worst outcome" question): "That we don't have what it takes to help a child." "That it will be so stressful for us that I'd have to make a choice between helping a child or helping my family." "That it will hurt too much when the child goes back home, or is placed for adoption."

Minimum Standard

The parents' motivations appear generally positive, but they may not have fully considered all the ramifications of caregiving. Further training or discussion may help them expand their understanding of realistic outcomes. They may not understand how the experience will change them. Or, one parent is very interested, and the other will be supportive, but doesn't see himself or herself as being as involved. Examples of responses might be:

- "I like children and would like to help them."

- "I'm good at caring for children, and I think I could do this well."

- "I want my children to have the experience of giving of themselves to other people. They can learn many lessons from this experience. And we can help children at the same time."

- "Everyone in my church does community service. I believe it's very important to give back to the community."

- (In response to the "worst outcome" question.) "The foster child would be really messed up and hurt my kids, like pull a knife, or set the house on fire, or something like that." "That we'll lose him after he's become part of the family."

Caution!

The parents' motivation is largely selfish, or they have extremely inaccurate perceptions about caregiving. They perceive foster care as primarily benefitting themselves, and benefitting the foster children secondarily. Or, parents express attitudes about children and families that suggest they feel compelled to "rescue those children" from their "terrible situations." Or, one parent is very interested, and the other expects not to be involved. Possible examples are:

- "We've only been able to have one child, and a foster child could be company for my daughter. We have a lot to share with a child."

- "We lost a child two years ago to leukemia. I have all her things; toys, crib, everything. We haven't touched her room. The house has been so quiet since then. It seems to me another child should be able to benefit from it. It would be wonderful to have children around again, especially if we can help a child at the same time."

- "I can earn some extra money without ever having to leave home. I can still be with my kids." (While this individual might not be suitable for foster care, he or she should be helped to consider becoming a day care or respite provider.)

- "These children were dealt a raw deal in life, and their parents can't begin to give them what we can. They need a chance to learn what a good life can be like, to motivate them to better themselves."

- (In response to the "worst outcome" question). The caseworker should listen for accurate descriptions of some of the potential realities of foster care. For example, "We'd give a lot to a child and he wouldn't appreciate it," "We'd love the child, and the child would throw it back in our face by running away or something," or, "We'd get the child to begin doing really well, and they'd send him back to where he came from, and all our work would have been for nothing."

- "My wife wants to do this. I think it would be good for her. I don't have a lot of time to give—my job is pretty hectic, and I'm out of town a lot. But if she wants to, it's okay with me."

CATEGORY II–PERSONAL MATURITY

There are several personal characteristics that enable caregivers to withstand the challenges presented by caregiving without feeling personally threatened, or experiencing severe emotional stress. These include strong and positive self-esteem, the ability to care for themselves emotionally, and several qualities categorized as "ego strengths." People with these abilities are better able to cope with challenges without experiencing a threat to their competence, confidence, self-esteem, or identity. People whose self-esteem is easily threatened, or whose self-worth depends on their doing everything "well," or "right," may not admit problems to themselves or others. They may blame or emotionally reject the foster child in order to maintain their own self-esteem.

These traits are often best explored in individual interviews with the prospective foster parents. There is also value in asking family members to identify each other's personal strengths and areas of potential vulnerability.

Assessment Questions

"Can you describe your own personal strengths? Tell me about the strengths of other family members. Now think about your own and other family members' vulnerable areas or weak spots. Tell me what 'pushes your buttons.' How do you see a foster child possibly 'pushing your buttons?'"

"Have you ever really wanted something you couldn't have? How did you feel, and what did you do?"

"Have you ever had to stick with something for a long time before it paid off? What was it? Did you give up? At what point and why?"

"Have you ever felt rejected by someone you loved? What was it like? How did you handle it?"

"Do you ever feel unappreciated in this family? Under what circumstances?"

"What's it like for you when your children get angry at you, or don't want to be with you? How about when they challenge you?"

"How are anger and frustration handled in this family? How does each family member express it?"

Strengths

- Parents are able to delay gratification and to find satisfaction in small gains;

- Parents have good emotional control and the ability to discharge tension and negative feelings in nonharmful ways;

- Parents can continue to parent and nurture a child who does not show or return affection, nor demonstrate respect and appreciation;

- Parents can seek help and accept constructive criticism from other people;

- Parents can put other people's needs ahead of their own;

- Parents can critically and realistically assess their personal strengths and vulnerabilities; can articulate what situations or behaviors "push their buttons," and how they respond; parents have realistic expectations for their own behavior and performance;

- Parents can see humor in stressful situations, and use laughter appropriately to discharge and reduce tension; and

- Parents demonstrate the ability to make a commitment and stick with it.

Minimum Standard

- Parents experience strong feelings of anger in response to personal rejection and moderate levels of frustration, but have developed strategies to handle these feelings constructively;

- Parents may be able to describe some personal and family traits, but may have difficulty articulating areas of vulnerability, or describing situations that trigger strong emotional responses;

- Parents can delay gratification, but often feel let down or disappointed when things don't go as they would like;

- Parents experience moderate feelings of personal rejection when affection is not reciprocated and actions are not appreciated; parents are able to manage these feelings, but not without some struggle. Example: "Right off, it hurts. But I keep telling myself it's because of his background, not because of what I did. I have to keep reminding myself of that"; and

- Parents can make commitments, but may give up when things become too difficult. Or, parents have not had the experience of making long-term commitments to achieve long-range goals.

Caution!

- Parents' behaviors in response to stress and challenge suggest high levels of frustration when things don't go as they would like; parents have difficulty in delaying gratification; parents are dissatisfied with anything less than achieving their goals.

- Parents expect to see rewards or reciprocation when they give to others; are angry, disappointed, or feel unappreciated when their efforts are not acknowledged and appreciated to their satisfaction.

- Parents overestimate their own abilities. They cannot articulate their areas of vulnerability, nor predict how challenges from a foster child could "push their buttons." They respond defensively to constructive criticism. Example: "I've never had that happen, but I'm sure I could handle it without any problem."

- Parents have poor emotional control, exhibited by emotional outbursts or explosive temper; they are easily riled, or challenged by small frustrations.

- Parents have a history of "flight" when things become too tough. They cannot make long-range commitments and stick with them.

CATEGORY III—THE STABILITY AND QUALITY OF INTERPERSONAL RELATIONSHIPS

People who have a strong and dependable network of supportive and nurturing relationships are generally better able to cope with stress. When relationships within a family are unstable, or parents can't rely on each other for support, the emotional strain of adoption may be very threatening. Many foster children are very good at identifying areas of inconsistency, and playing one caregiver against the other.

Caregivers must feel secure and confident that their relationship is strong enough to withstand stress and challenges. In two–parent families, the quality and stability of the couple's marital and sexual relationship must be fully assessed. A high percentage of children in care have been sexually abused, and they may act out sexually. The parents must be comfortable talking about sexual issues with children; must set expectations for appropriate and inappropriate sexual behavior; and must be able to cope with a child's sexual behaviors without feeling threatened, jealous, or resentful.

More accurate information about the nature of the parents' relationship can often be gained during individual interviews with the parents. The same issues can be discussed in a joint interview at a later time, particularly if there are discrepancies in the information provided by the parents.

Assessment Questions

"Tell me about your relationship. Give me a history–how you met, how long you've been together, what your life together has been like."

"What do you see as your strengths as a couple. In what areas do you handle things as a team?"

"Are there areas in which you strongly disagree? How do you resolve disputes?"

"Have you ever had problems in your marriage? Can you describe them? How did you handle them?"

"Many children in care have been sexually abused, and will behave in overtly sexual ways. Have you ever been in a situation where someone has been inappropriately sexual toward you? How have you reacted? How has your spouse reacted?"

"How do you handle sexual issues with your children?"

"How satisfied are you both with your sexual relationship? Can you talk about times you have felt jealous, worried, or embarrassed?"

"How do your extended family members feel about your becoming foster caregivers?"

"How do you demonstrate affection in the family? How do you know that other family members care for you? How do they show it?"

"How do you make time for one another? How do you assure your privacy as a couple? How important is your privacy to you? How do you feel if you can't have private time?"

Strengths

- The family history reflects stability in the relationship between the parents. The parents have been together for at least a few years; they have the ability to disagree and to negotiate differences without feeling personally threatened; they have sought and constructively used help to resolve marital and family problems. (Note: the number of years the parents have been together cannot, by itself, determine the quality or stability of the relationship. Some parents who have been married for only a few years have extremely strong and stable relationships; others who have been together for 20 years may not.)

- When parents have a prior history of divorce, they appear to have learned and grown from the experience, and can identify how their current relationship is different from their previous relationships.

- Single-parent families have a strong support system of extended family and friends. They utilize this network regularly for emotional support, guidance, and direct assistance when needed.

- The parents, or adults in a multi-adult household, can describe how they operate as a team, particularly in parenting activities.

- The parents are comfortable with their sexual relationship. Parents are able to describe their own children's sexual behavior, and can discuss sexual issues comfortably within the family.

- Expressions of support, affection, and caring are overt, and are easily recognized by other family members. (Note: the particular ways that affection is expressed may vary among cultures.)

- Extended family members and close friends are generally encouraging, and they support the family's choice to become foster caregivers.

Minimum Standard

- The parents' relationship is moderately stable. They have not been together long enough to fully resolve issues of adjustment to the marriage; they have solved some problems, but have not had to deal with serious ones.

- The parents have had prior relationships or marriages, and are only partially aware of the factors that created the stress in the relationships; e.g., "It just didn't work out." They cannot articulate how their current relationship is better or different, even though they believe it is.

- There are some areas in which the parents disagree and cannot resolve their differences. They can tolerate some degree of dissension without feeling threatened.

- The parents exhibit mild discomfort discussing sexual issues with their children; they may be somewhat hesitant, embarrassed, or they may underestimate the importance of such discussion. However, they appear generally accepting of normal childhood sexual behavior, and they have given their children basic information when asked. Parents describe their own sexual relationship as "okay."

- Family has some support from extended family and friends, but are not certain they can count on them in a pinch. Some extended family members may express ambivalence or doubt about the family's decision to become caregivers.

Caution!

- The parents do not have a history of relationship stability. Their current relationship is unstable; The couple are only recently married and are still learning to adjust to one another; or, the parents' history demonstrates a pattern of past unstable relationships.

- The parents appear unable to negotiate differences. They become angry and are uncomfortable, or hostile toward one another, when they disagree. Or, emotionally charged issues are denied or minimized ("swept under the rug") to avoid a fight.

- The parents cannot articulate how they work as a team in parenting. Roles may be very rigidly defined as "her job, his job," and parents are not willing or able to help and support each other in their respective roles.

- The parents have limited support from persons outside their family. Extended family do not agree with the decision to foster parent. The parents have a limited support network.

- The parents appear to have rigid values and expectations regarding children's sexual behavior; they cannot tolerate inappropriate sexual expression. They may be indignant, moralistic, and demeaning toward an individual who expresses sexuality in a manner that is not consistent with the parents' own values. They may avoid discussing sex with their children; or, they may teach by "preaching" without listening to their children and understanding their children's feelings, concerns, and needs.

- The parents are not able to openly express affection to each other or to their children. (Again, appropriate expressions of affection will be culturally determined.)

CATEGORY IV—RESILIENCE, COPING SKILLS, AND HISTORY OF STRESS MANAGEMENT

The prospective foster family should have a variety of effective coping strategies. A family that has continued to function and remains productive in high stress situations usually has coping strengths that will help them adjust to the changes and stresses of caregiving. Conversely, families that have not dealt with instability or crisis often have less well–developed strengths and coping strategies.

We can determine a family's typical responses to stress by asking them to describe difficult or traumatic past life events, and relate how they dealt with them. We should look for responses that suggest capable problem–solving activities; effective use of interpersonal and community supports and resources; an attitude of having learned and grown from past stressful experiences; and indications of realistic confidence in their own strengths and coping abilities.

In addition, parents should be able to describe how their family unit has responded to changes brought about by the addition or loss of a family member. Past experiences with the birth of a child, the death of a family member, a divorce or separation, caring for someone else's children, or bringing an elderly parent to live with the family can provide insight into how flexible the family system is in reacting to structural changes. Parents should also demonstrate comfort with change and ambiguity, including an ability to "ride with the tide" until things get settled.

Finally, while all families should be expected to grow from the challenges of foster caregiving, overstressing an inexperienced family is certain to increase the likelihood of placement disruption, and may also result in the loss of a potentially good foster family. The worker and family should try to determine how much stress and change the family will tolerate without experiencing high levels of distress. This information will be important when matching a child to the family.

Assessment Questions

"Can you tell me about the worst thing you've ever had to deal with? What was it? What was it like? What did you do? How did it affect you? How did it affect your family?"

"Can you think of a time when you felt you just couldn't go on another day? Tell me about it. What brought it on? What did you do."

"What resources do you use to get you through bad times? Think about you own strengths. Who can you turn to, and how do they help?"

"Tell me about your hardest loss. How did you deal with it?"

"Tell me about a time when you felt really frightened or threatened. What did you do?"

"Who is your biggest source of support when you're upset or need help? (Some prospective caregivers may derive strength from strong religious faith. Prompt for sources of emotional support within the immediate or extended family as well.)

"Tell me about a time when nothing you planned worked…or, your plans changed at the last minute…or you couldn't plan, because everything around you was out of control."

Strengths

- Parents can describe how they have managed difficult situations or crises in the past, such as serious illness, chronic stress, moving, loss of a loved one, etc. Self-perceptions might include:

  "I hang in and tough it out. I'm a survivor. I've gotten through things you wouldn't believe."

"I think about it for a while, and pretty soon the right thing to do comes to me."

"I talk about it with my sister. She's really good at figuring things out."

"I dig in and go to work. That's my style. I don't just sit around and wait for it to go away."

"I don't know how I got through it...I was devastated when he died. I guess I wasn't as strong as I thought. But we got through it."

"Patience. I've learned things happen in their own way and in their own time, and sometimes you can't rush them. You can't fight all the time. Most things work out, but it often takes time. Sometimes you just have to wait it out."

- Parents have experienced changes in the family composition and can identify how such changes were stressful. The parents can describe how they "reorganized" as a family to accommodate a new member, or to regroup after the loss of a member.

"After Gram died, we were a mess for a while. We didn't real–ize how much she did for us! But we all took on her chores. It's a little harder on each of us, but we manage fine. Things just don't get done as *well* as she did them! None of us has the kind of time she did, or her ability. She will always be the best cook in the family."

- Parents demonstrate adaptability and flexibility in the face of change. They always have back–up plans, and they are able to go to plan two or three when the first one doesn't work. They are not threatened by a changed schedule. They appear to be effective at "continual planning."

Minimum Standard

- Parents have managed some stressful situations and have some con–structive coping ability. They may not have experienced seriously stress–ful situations.

- They express an absence of solid support from significant others, and describe often handling things by themselves.

- Parents may identify some ways the addition of a foster child to the fam–ily will be stressful, but appear not to fully realize the scope or impact of the change on their lives.

- Parents tolerate some change, but are annoyed and feel disrupted if things become too chaotic or unpredictable. They work to maintain order and a schedule.

Caution!

- Parents cannot describe a situation of high stress or crisis. They claim to have never had any serious problems. Their described losses and threats have been relatively minor.

- Parents' description of a high stress situation suggests turmoil, the absence of planning, poor strategies to manage, consistent "fight" or "flight" responses, and no resolution over time.

- Parents appear to consistently avoid facing up to problems; minimize their importance; ignore them; let someone else handle them; or believe themselves to be "victims," with little control over events that involve them.

- Parents describe themselves or other family members as "useless in a crisis"; "she just falls apart."

- Parents are very uncomfortable when things are ambiguous or do not go as planned. They resent when their plans are changed, and do not tolerate last minute changes. They have difficulty regrouping and trying something else when things don't work. They easily become angry and frustrated. (These persons are likely to show compulsive traits in other areas as well. They greatly prefer order, stability, and predictability.)

CATEGORY V–THE FAMILY IS AN OPEN SYSTEM

An "open system" refers to a family unit that is able to adapt and change in response to challenges from within and outside the family. The "open" family is also linked with a broader network of extended family, friends, and community groups. The boundaries of the family are flexible; people can come and go, and the family can comfortably readjust in response to these changes. (This should not be confused with a family in which the "comings and goings" of members reflects instability, a lack of emotional commitment in relationships, or superficial attachments.) Family roles are also flexible, when necessary, to help the family as a unit best adapt to changed circumstances.

A family's "openness" is also reflected by the family's willingness to allow persons from outside the family to help when under stress. There may, of course, be individual and cultural differences regarding where the family seeks help. For example, some families will not seek help from formal community agencies, but they maintain strong informal networks of kin and friends, or they turn to a minister or a church group for support. Finally, family members in an "open system" are able to acknowledge and appreciate differences. They enjoy contact with people of various ages and from other cultures, and they seek opportunities to be involved with a variety of people and situations. They accept people for who and what they are, and can see strengths and value in people who, by conventional standards, may be "less than perfect."

By contrast, a "closed" family system is insular, isolated, and rigid when confronted with change. Members may have fixed roles, which are rarely altered even in changed circumstances. Family members value independence and self-sufficiency, and do not often seek assistance from others. The epitome of a closed family system is, "It's just us against the world." Closed family systems are also often ethnocentric. Their members have difficulty understanding or respecting the values or perspectives of people who are different from themselves. They may also have more rigid standards for acceptable behavior.

Caregiving means being a member of a team. There may be several professionals working with the family and the child, and their efforts must be coordinated and integrated. Caregivers frequently need outside support to help cope with especially challenging children. They must be able to access respite care, emotional support, and concrete resources. The caregiving family must also be willing and comfortable working with others. They cannot feel that the involvement of outsiders is an unwarranted and insensitive intrusion into their family life.

In addition, the caregiving family system must comfortably incorporate not only the child in care, but the child's family as well. If the caregiving family resists contact with the child's parents, this increases distress for the child, and works against successful reunification. "Open" foster families acknowledge and accept the child's biological family as part of the child's "extended network," and they do not deny the child's relationship with them. They may also work directly with biological family members, when appropriate, and will collaborate during case planning conferences or during visits.

Assessment Questions

"Who do you include in your family?" "Can you draw me a picture that includes everyone who is important to you?" (Ecomaps can be used to help the family describe their position within their larger extended family network and in the community.)

"What responsibilities do family members have? Have your jobs ever changed? Under what circumstances? How did you all feel about it?" "How did you manage when your mom was in the hospital? Who cooked?"

"Who helps you when you are under stress or need help?"

"How have you used other people or community resources to help you solve a problem?"

"Have you ever been a member of a team? Tell me about it. What was it like? What did you like about it? Was there anything you didn't like?"

"How have you reacted to suggestions from other people about your life?"

"What kind of experiences have you had with people from other cultures and races? Have you ever been a "stranger in a strange land?" What was it like?

Strengths

- The parents have a strong and dependable support network through extended family, close family friends, or through organizational affiliations such as church or community group memberships.

- The parents' support networks are in agreement and supportive of the family's desire to become a foster caregiver.

- The parents' past behavior demonstrates a willingness and desire to "use all the help we can get," rather than expecting themselves to manage everything on their own.

- Family members demonstrate an ability to shift roles when necessary. "Who cooked when your mom was in the hospital?" "Sherry and Dad took turns." Or, "Well, we all did...if you can call microwave macaroni and cheese 'cooking.' We can't cook as well as Mom does, but we didn't starve."

- Parents can describe previous team affiliations (a sports team, a church committee, a community planning group), and can relate how they participated as team members and benefitted from the experience.

- Parents enjoy and appreciate differences, and are able to articulate ways that their lives have been enriched through cross–cultural contact. They describe relationships with people of different ages and social groups. They find differences interesting, and can describe how they have learned new things from people who were different from them. They are aware of how their own culture strengthens their lives, and can identify things about their own cultural backgrounds they do not like or have changed.

Minimum Standard

- Parents have some support systems, but they typically manage stress on their own. They seem to prefer to ask for help only when they cannot solve a problem themselves.

- Parents have clearly defined roles and responsibilities, and they exhibit some degree of discomfort or loss of direction if these must change. ("Who cooked when Mom was in the hospital?" "We ate out a lot, or got fast food.")

- Parents have limited experience working on teams, and do not appear to understand the nature of teamwork in complex situations.

- Parents express attitudes of acceptance of differences, and may have some experience in the workplace or community with people from different cultural, ethnic, or racial groups. However, their knowledge of other cultures and cross–cultural contacts are limited.

Caution!

- The parents' coping history suggests they do not seek help from outside the family, even when such help would have greatly benefitted them.

- The parents believe strongly in self–sufficiency and independence, and have not participated as part of a functioning team. Or, parents suggest that teams are "a waste of time–give it to one person and let them do it. It's faster and easier than all that talk."

- Roles and responsibilities are clearly assigned to individual family members and appear to be inflexible. Family members do not often perform tasks that are the responsibility of other family members. In two–parent families, if mothers are assigned the primary responsibility for home management, housekeeping, and child care, the additional responsibilities inherent in foster care will often overload them, unless all family members are willing to assume responsibility for some of these day to day tasks. ("Who cooked when Mom was in the hospital?" "Mom cooked as much as she could before she went in, and she left meals for us in the freezer." [Worker prompt:] "Is there a reason you didn't cook for yourselves?" "I'm too busy to have to think about cooking. I have enough responsibilities of my own." Or, "I don't know how to turn on the oven, much less make a dinner."

• Family members are uncomfortable with people who are culturally, ethnically, or racially different from themselves. They avoid contact when possible. They do not have strong relationships with people of different ages. Or, their attitudes reflect a reliance on stereotypes and misinformation. They display prejudicial attitudes toward others, and communicate stereotypes and misconceptions about other people.

CATEGORY VI–PARENTING SKILLS

Most prospective caregivers are parents whose children are at home, or are grown and living independently. Others have had considerable experience caring for nieces and nephews, or other people's children. Unless the family's history suggests significant problems in rearing their own children, most prospective caregivers will generally have appropriate parenting skills.

However, parenting a foster or relative child with special needs is quite different from parenting one's own children. The more relevant questions about parenting are, "Do the prospective caregivers have the skills needed to successfully parent children with special needs?" "How quickly can they develop these skills?" and, "What types of children are they best suited to parent?"

The following criteria should be assessed:

1) **The parents gain pleasure, gratification, and enjoyment from parenting activities.**

   Parenting, at its best, is hard work. It is harder when a child has special needs. Caregivers must be able to derive pleasure and satisfaction from the day–to–day activities of caregiving and nurturing, since the visible returns may be a long time coming and very small in scope.

   ### Assessment Questions
   "What do you enjoy most about parenting? What do you find to be the most fun? What do you dislike? Is there anything you'd give up forever and never miss?"

   "What kind of things do you like doing as a family? What do you like to do by yourself, or with other adults?"

   "How does parenting fit into your other activities? In what ways might it interfere with things you would rather be doing?"

   "What qualities do you think make a 'good' parent'? Can you identify your own, and each other's, parenting strengths? What do you feel you don't do as well as you would like?"

Strengths

- Parenting is important "life's work," and they take pride in doing it well. An important part of their identity is being a parent. (Note: this does not mean that the parents derive their self-worth from their children's accomplishments, or that their only source of gratification is their children's success. When parents depend upon their children's accomplishments to determine their personal worth, the child's perceived shortcomings are experienced as personal failures. Healthy children often cannot live up to such parental expectations, much less children with special needs.)

- The parents truly enjoy activities related to parenting. They enjoy participating in recreation activities, vacations, projects, and other activities with their children. They look for ways to spend time together as a family. The parents express feelings of satisfaction from helping their children learn; encouraging children to try new things; exposing children to new adventures; making children feel comfortable and content; and watching children grow and develop. They may be involved as volunteers with groups of children, such as coaching a sports team or leading a scout troop, "just for the fun of it."

- The parents can realistically assess their own and each other's parenting strengths and areas of vulnerability. "He's great at calming a frightened child. I do better getting a child motivated when he doesn't want to move."

Minimum Standard

- The parents view parenting as a lot of work, but with advantages. Their rewards may be expressed in terms of concrete outcomes, such as taking pride in their children's accomplishments, and progress toward specific goals. They may enjoy some developmental stages more than others.

- The parents enjoy their parenting time, but also greatly value their "adult only" or "quiet time," and may have successfully trained their own children not to bother them at these times.

- Parents may not have thought directly about their parenting strengths or vulnerabilities, or may not fully understand the importance of considering this. They may be able to identify some strengths and vulnerabilities.

Caution!

- The parents do what must be done to provide good care for their children, but they lack enthusiasm about the parenting process. Their satisfaction from parenting may depend on the circumstances.

- The parents may have many other interests or commitments outside the home, and caregiving demands may take time away from these activities. They may express resentment of unusual demands made on them by their children. ("I couldn't wait until he started school...I was trapped in the house until then. It about drove me crazy.")

- The parents display little insight regarding their own parenting strengths and vulnerabilities. Their responses may be simplistic or stereotypic: "I'm a good provider for my family." "I read to my children often." "I really support education."

2) ***The parents have the ability to individualize children and their needs, and to respond accordingly.***

Caregiving families must have the ability to individualize children's needs, and to use parenting and child management strategies best suited to each individual child. They must also understand how they might need to alter their parenting interventions to be responsive to a child's cultural differences.

Families who rely on the same parenting and discipline strategies for all their children, and who expect that these should work equally well for foster or relative children, will often have difficulty managing challenging or behavior-disordered children. They may blame the child rather than their intervention strategy for failure. The ability to assess each child's unique developmental needs and problems, and to modify parenting strategies accordingly are essential skills for a caregiver. If parents have this ability, they can be trained to recognize cultural differences as well, and modify their parenting strategies accordingly.

Assessment Questions

"Can you describe your own children for me? How are they alike? How are they different from one another? Be as detailed as you can."

"You said that Sandra is a more nervous child than Allan. Can you tell me what you mean?"

"If one of your children has a problem, how do you decide what to do? Give me some examples." [Prompt] "Would you handle it differently if Ann had the problem instead of Thomas? How?"

Strengths

- The parents can describe each child's unique personality, traits, and needs, and can explain why they approach the child differently because of this. (Example: "I can never yell at Tina…she's too sensitive. All I have to do is tell her once, and it's done. I also have to be careful to speak more softly with her. With Lisa, it's like talking to the wall. I have to make her look at me and make sure she's listening before I talk to her.")

- The parents appear to consider each child's viewpoint and perspective before making decisions that affect all of them. The parents understand that each child is an individual, with unique thoughts, opinions, and needs.

Minimum Standard

- The parents can describe fundamental differences in their children, but they do not always understand how their parenting interventions should change to address their children's differences. Some families actually do respond differently, and appropriately, to their children's differences, but they may not be able to verbalize how. The worker should observe them during their parenting interventions to identify similarities and differences in their treatment of their children. Training may help them further develop in this area.

Caution!

- The parents have a rigid conception of how children should behave, and they express their children's differences only superficially. They may say things like, "All children need love and discipline." "Depriving them of TV works every time." "My kids all know they'd better hop to it when I tell them to do something." "Sure Tom and Jon are different. (How?) Tom likes basketball, and Jon has no sports ability at all. But Jon does better in school."

- The parents appear to make most decisions for their children, including simple ones (what to wear, what to eat). They do not solicit their children's thoughts or opinions on decisions. They do not see their children as having different opinions or views on topics.

3) *The family has had prior experience parenting other people's children, including children who have had physical, emotional, or behavioral problems.*

If the family has had prior experience parenting children with problems, there are likely to be fewer surprises. If their only parenting experience has been with typical children, they may greatly underestimate the amount of stress associated with foster caregiving. Some parents may have never directly parented children with problems, but they may have worked with them as a teacher, nurse, classroom aid, or in another helping profession. This helps, but a few hours a day cannot be equated with full-time parenting. Parents should also have gained insight regarding their own strengths and vulnerabilities from these caregiving experiences.

Assessment Questions

"Have you ever had full-time responsibility for a child or children who had emotional or behavior problems? Tell me about your experiences."

"How were these children's needs different from the other children you have worked with? What did you have to do differently? Can you describe the most difficult child you have worked with?"

"What did you like or not like about caring for them? What was the best part? The worst part? What particularly challenged you? What part did you find the most rewarding?"

"What did you learn about yourself from these experiences?"

Strengths

- The parents have had prior experience parenting their own or other children with complex needs and problems, and can describe these experiences.

- The parents are aware of and will acknowledge how parenting children with problems is stressful.

- The parents can identify their own areas of vulnerability.

- The parents can articulate what they liked and did not like about the experience, and what they learned about themselves.

Minimum Standard

- The parents have had some direct contact with children with problems, but have not had full–time parenting responsibility for such children. Parents can accurately describe what would be necessary for a caregiver to effectively parent children with problems, even though they have not done it. (Note: this would suggest that if the family is approved, their first placement should be a relatively unchallenging child. They will need an opportunity to first acclimate to full–time parenting, and can then develop skills to manage more difficult problems.)

Caution!

- The parents have no experience parenting children other than their own, and they have had no prior contact with children who have problems. (Note: If the prospective caregivers have strengths in many other areas, they could be started as day care or respite care providers, and then be developed into full–time caregivers as they gain experience and training. If they are approved as caregivers, they may need a great deal of support.)

4) *The parents utilize discipline strategies that are appropriate for children who have experienced prior maltreatment and separation.*

Most child welfare agencies have strict policies regarding the discipline strategies that are allowable for children in care. Generally, these include: setting clear limits and using logical consequences for infractions; positive reinforcement for desired behavior; time out; restriction of privileges; redirection; and removal of the child from the problem situation. Physical discipline, strategies that shame or embarrass the child, segregation of the child for long periods, or withdrawal of affection are inherently less effective, and are potentially very harmful for children who have been subjected to maltreatment and separation.

Assessment Questions

"Can you describe how you normally discipline your own children? Why did you choose the strategies that you use?"

"When you have had to discipline someone else's children, what did you do the same or differently from disciplining your own children?"

"Please describe the last time one of your children did something that *really* upset you. Can you tell me how you handled it?"

"What discipline strategies do you find work best with your children?"

"What discipline strategies are you most comfortable with, and which do you find hard to implement?"

Strengths

• The parents already use the agency's recommended discipline and child management strategies, and can describe how these are used when disciplining or managing their own children.

Minimum Standard

• The parents use physical discipline and other strategies that are not appropriate for maltreated children, but clearly demonstrate a willingness to learn and use different strategies.

Caution!

• The parents adhere to child management practices that are not in the best interests of foster children, and staunchly support the validity of their own discipline practices. They cannot understand why their strategies may not work equally well with foster children.

5) ***Parents recognize the potential effects of foster care on their own children and have a plan to deal with them.***

It is important that parents recognize that fostering will not only alter their lives, but their children's lives as well. They should be able to predict what might be stressful for their own children and describe strategies to prevent unnecessary problems for them.

Assessment Questions

"How have you presented the idea of foster care to your children? What did you tell them? How did they respond?"

"What kinds of situations would create problems for your kids?"

"How do you handle fights, jealousy, competitiveness, privacy, sharing, allocating your time fairly, etc. with your children?"

"Have your children ever shared your attention with other children for an extended period of time? How did they react?"

Strengths

• The parents have already talked with their children about foster care, and have prepared them for the experience. The children understand and can tell the worker what things might change, and how they may feel about this.

• The parents have considered their children's feelings and needs in deciding what kind of child should be placed with them. ("I don't want a child the same age as Chloe. The child should either be younger, or much older, like a teenager. I don't want Chloe to feel like she's been displaced.")

• The parents have constructive strategies to deal with sibling issues. They can describe them and explain why they use them.

Minimum Standard

- The parents have never considered how foster care might affect their children, but they show interest and concern once this is brought to their attention.

Caution!

- The parents have limited insight into the effects of foster care on their children, and they minimize the importance of the changes their children will experience. ("My kids adjust to about anything. They're really good kids. They get along well with other kids, and they've been taught to share. I don't think it will be a problem.")

CATEGORY VII–EMPATHY AND PERSPECTIVE-TAKING ABILITY

Perspective taking is, simply, the ability to understand someone else's perspective or point of view. Empathy is the ability to relate to and understand another person's situation, feelings, and motives. Both are necessary prerequisites for effective caregiving. The following are relevant criteria to determine parental empathy:

1) *The parents are able to recognize and properly interpret each others' and their children's verbal, nonverbal, and behavioral cues, and can verbally articulate what other family members are feeling.*

   Parents must be able to recognize and properly interpret family members' needs and feelings in order to recognize potential stresses and problems early, and provide the necessary support. In addition, many children who have experienced maltreatment exhibit their distress behaviorally, and they often cannot articulate their feelings. Their visible emotional state is not always congruent with their feelings. For example, a healthy child who is feeling disappointed will usually cry. A child with emotional problems may react to disappointment by exhibiting rage, often in the form of a tantrum or other acting out behavior.

   If family members, including children, can identify each others' need states and feelings, they are more likely to understand what the foster children are trying to communicate through their often inappropriate behavior. This will permit them to respond to the child's needs, while concurrently limiting inappropriate behaviors. The ability to recognize and meet needs is also a critical factor in promoting the development of attachment. (See Section VIII-A, "Attachment and Attachment Disorders.")

   #### Assessment Questions
   "How can you tell when people in your family are upset? Mad? Sad? Can you sometimes tell what they're feeling from the way they act? Give me an example."

   "How do you help people in your family when they're feeling really upset? What do you want other people to do for you?"

   "Tell me about the last time you had a "tantrum"–what

happened, and what were you feeling?" (This can be asked of both adults and children.)

Strengths

- The parents can recognize and articulate how a child's behavior reflects a feeling or need state. Family members can recognize when other family members are distressed or need assistance. (Workers should be careful to consider cultural factors and communication styles when judging this criteria. The important factor is the accuracy of the parent's interpretation.) Examples:

    "Lee won't always tell me when she's upset, but I can usually tell. She gets quiet, won't look at me, and goes off to be by herself."

    "When Roy's mad, I've learned it's better to leave him alone for a while until he cools off. Then he'll talk to me and tell me what's happening. But if I ask him straight out, he'll storm out and yell, "I don't want to talk about it!""

    "Veronica will tell me straight out she's not afraid, and if you didn't know her, you'd have to believe her! She's such a good actress. But I know differently. When she doesn't think I'm looking, I can see how scared she really is."

Minimum Standard

- Family members rely on outward behavioral cues or direct communication to determine other family members' need states. They have some insight into other people's needs, but don't appear to fully understand how behavior is not always an accurate indication of a need state. "How do you know when he feels bad?" "He tells me." Or, "I can tell he's upset if he's been crying." "When he's mad, he stomps around here and shouts."

Caution

- Family members don't appear concerned about other people's need states, and lack insight into their importance. "Yeah, she gets mad, but she gets over it." "I don't care what he's feeling...he can just take himself off to his room until he's feeling better, then he can join the family again."

2) *Parents can articulate empathy for the child's biological family, and can understand the biological family's situation.*

The caregiving family must display an empathetic and supportive attitude about biological families that promotes positive self-esteem for the child and, when appropriate, that supports family reunification. Parents' attitudes about biological families and their ability to change must be explored during the family assessment process. The foster or relative caregivers may need to modify preexisting negative or stereotypic attitudes about abusive and neglectful parents, or in the case of kinship care, the parents of the children in their care.

The caregivers must also consider their ability to work directly with parents of children in care, including modeling and teaching parenting and home management skills, and providing direct emotional support to parents. All caregivers should be prepared to expect some degree of interaction with biological families, if only to reduce the stress for the child in placement.

Assessment Questions

"Why do you think parents maltreat their children? What would you guess they feel? What would you guess their children feel about them?"

"Have you ever known people before who have either abused or neglected their children? What were they like?"

"Have you ever had to explain a parent's negative behaviors to a child? Tell me about it. How did you explain it?"

"Have you ever done volunteer work? Tell me about the people you found hardest to work with. Why do you suppose they were the way they were?"

Strengths

- The parents express understanding of the problems faced by the child's biological parents. Parents express empathy regarding the pain the biological parents must be feeling related to separation from their child.

- The parents are sensitive to the child's feelings about his or her biological family, and can talk with the child in a supportive and nonjudgmental way.

- The parents express a desire that the child's biological family also receive help; parents are open to providing help where possible.

Minimum Standard

- The parents demonstrate empathy for the child's biological parents, but in a limited capacity. They understand that the child's parents may have problems or be under stress, but they are critical of abusive or neglectful caregiving. They have difficulty understanding how it could happen. They may "feel sorry" for the parent. However, they are not overtly hostile or punitive in their feelings. Training may help modify their attitudes.

- The parents are not certain that the child wants, or needs, to talk about his or her background. They may understand the importance of preserving a history or continuity, but may not fully understand the implications for the child's psychological development and self–esteem.

Caution!

- The parents express a desire to know as little as possible about the child's family, and resist any direct contact with family members. They appear to want to "protect" the child from the parent or other family members, even when the child is not at risk in their presence.

- The parents criticize the biological parents' behavior, and express attitudes such as, "Good parents don't hurt their kids. I don't care how bad things get. She could have gotten help." "I suppose she must not be a very strong person, if she left her baby." "He's in jail...that says about everything, doesn't it?"

- The parents don't understand why the child expresses love and loyalty to hurtful parents. Parents believe the child would "be better off if he let the past go and got on with it. Talking about it all the time only upsets him."

Adapting the Family Assessment for Kinship Caregivers

In many respects, kinship care families should be engaged to participate in a family assessment that is similar to that for foster caregivers. The Child Welfare League of America North American Kinship Care Policy and Practice Committee [1994] suggests that "an assessment of the willingness and ability of kin to provide a safe, stable, nurturing home, and meet the child's developmental and safety needs is essential in determining the appropriateness of the home for the child."

Quite often, kinship families assume full responsibility for one or several children with behavioral or emotional problems, and yet they are often unprepared for the experience, and they receive little to no support or remuneration. Despite their exhibited commitment to the children, this situation exacerbates stress, and increases the likelihood of distress and trauma for the caregiving family. The primary benefit of the family assessment for kinship care families is to help them understand and prepare for potential stresses, and to learn to utilize the agency and other caregivers as supportive resources. The family assessment can also help them learn to access and benefit from ongoing inservice training.

While many of the critical assessment factors for foster caregivers are equally relevant to kinship caregivers, there are additional criteria specific to kinship caregivers that should also be assessed [Child Welfare League of America North American Kinship Care Policy and Practice Committee 1994]. These are:

- The nature and quality of the relationship between the child and the kinship family should facilitate the child's adjustment. If the relationship is nurturing and strong, this can greatly reduce separation trauma for the child coming into care. However, if the relationship is negative and conflictual, or if the kinship caregiver has no preexisting personal relationship with the child, the degree of stress to the child may not be significantly less than if the child were placed in foster care.

- The kinship parent must be willing and able to work with the agency to protect the child from further maltreatment. This may involve confronting the child's parents, and regulating or restricting their access to the child. Concurrently, the kinship caregiver must also be willing and able to work collaboratively with the agency to empower the child's parents and support reunification, if that is the plan for the child.

- The home must assure the child's safety, and the kinship caregivers must be able to provide a nurturing environment for the child. One benefit of kinship care is that the kinship home may be similar to the child's own home, and the parenting practices may be similar. However, special parenting and caregiving skills may be necessary, if the child has special needs. Examples include a child who has been prenatally exposed to drugs or alcohol, has HIV or another physical illness, or has emotional or behavioral problems as a result of prior maltreatment. The caregiver must be willing to attend training, and utilize other developmental and therapeutic services to meet the child's needs.

- The nature and quality of the relationship between the biological parent and the kinship caregiver must be conducive to supporting the placement. As with any foster caregiver, if the caregiver is ambivalent about the placement, or clearly does not want to undertake care of the child, alternate placement should be pursued. The likelihood of disruption increases greatly if the caregiver's needs and feelings are not considered. In addition, a positive relationship between the child's parent and the kinship caregiver will greatly enhance the likelihood of successful reunification.

  It is also best if the biological parent understands that a kinship placement is in the child's best interests. However, at times, the kinship home may be the best placement for the child, even though the parent is not in agreement. In these situations, the needs of the child should generally take precedence over the wishes of the parent. However, the worker should continue to work with the parent and the kinship family to help them resolve conflicts and other family issues. Ultimately, family counseling can sometimes reestablish the kinship family as an ongoing source of support and nurturance for the parent, as well as the child in care.

- The worker must determine whether there are family dynamics in the kinship home that may condone or contribute to further abuse or neglect of the child. Child abuse and neglect are known to be, at times, intergenerational. It is not uncommon for maltreating parents to report personal histories of maltreatment as children. However, this is not always so. The worker should never make assumptions, but should conduct an objective and comprehensive assessment of each family's strengths and areas of vulnerability. This is best addressed by examining their current, demonstrated family dynamics, including their parenting styles and practices. While it is critical to note any past history of inappropriate parenting, we must also acknowledge the positive effects of maturity and subsequent personal development on people's parenting practices.

- When relevant, the worker must recognize the higher probability in kinship care placements that the caregiver may pressure the child to recant regarding disclosure of abuse or sexual abuse. This will be more likely if the kinship caregiver feels the biological parent has been unfairly accused of maltreatment, or that the situation is not sufficiently serious to warrant removal and placement of the child.

- The presence of alcohol or other drug involvement in the kinship home must be determined. This is especially important when alcohol or drug-related factors were significant contributors to maltreatment in the child's own home, and there may have been intergenerational alcoholism or drug abuse.

- The kinship family must be willing and able to collaborate with the caseworker and the agency. Because kinship care is a naturally occurring activity in many cultural groups, the kinship family may initially perceive agency involvement as intrusive and, perhaps, unwarranted. As with any family, the caseworker must engage family members, and develop collaborative relationships with them. This will enable the worker to provide services that can support and sustain the family, while concurrently assuring that the child is protected. Kinship caregivers should be helped to understand that they are partners with the child welfare agency, and whenever possible, with the child's parents, to create a permanent, safe, nurturing environment for the child.

PRESERVICE AND INSERVICE TRAINING

Regional or local implementation of training for foster and kinship caregivers is essential to meet individual needs and to insure efficient and cost effective delivery of training. Holding training in one centralized location often presents barriers for caregivers. Caregivers must allocate large blocks of time for travel and workshop attendance, must make arrangements for child care, and if they are employed outside the home, they may have difficulty obtaining release time during work hours. Training is best provided locally within the caregivers' home community, and scheduled at their convenience. This may require evening and weekend training sessions. Offering on-site child care will also encourage attendance. Training systems can also utilize videotape and library resources for self-study, or for use by foster care caseworkers in foster parent group meetings.

While direct training for foster caregivers is critical, the implementation of a successful foster and kinship care program requires that staff at all levels of the organization also be trained in essential concepts of foster and kinship care. Agency executives need to understand the systemic nature of comprehensive foster and kinship care, its benefits, and its implications for agency staffing and funding. Middle level managers need to be trained to develop program policies, procedures, and components that support professionalized foster care and the effective use of relative placements. Line supervisors and workers need to understand how to work collaboratively with foster caregivers and kinship caregivers in a team approach to service planning and delivery, as well as how to implement program components such as recruitment, family assessment, training, and supportive services to caregivers. And caregivers need training to enable them to participate as professional team members and provide high quality care to the children and families served by the system. Within this broad framework there will be a wide variety of individual training needs, based upon the individual skill level of the trainees, the size and scope of the foster care system, the types of children served, the cultural composition of the community, and the availability of special resources. These needs should be evaluated at least annually, using an individual training needs assessment format [Hughes & Rycus 1989].

The most effective recruitment and family assessment process will be of little value, if the agency cannot support and retain its caregivers. Continued access to high quality and relevant inservice training is a vital supportive service that can greatly increase both caregivers' skills, and their ability to withstand the stresses inherent in the caregiving experience. (Refer to Section X–C, "Working with Foster and Other Caregivers," for additional strategies to support and retain caregivers.)

C. WORKING WITH FOSTER AND OTHER CAREGIVERS

Conceptual Framework

Child welfare agencies utilize a variety of out–of–home placements for children at risk of maltreatment who cannot be protected at home. Most of these children live with relatives or in agency foster homes. A smaller percentage, generally adolescents, are placed in family group care, community group homes, or in residential treatment facilities. As discussed in an earlier section, in order to meet the needs of the children we serve, a spectrum of placement resources must be available to the child welfare agency. (See Section X–A, "The Components of an Effective Foster Care System.") Within this diversity of placement resources, the responsibilities of substitute caregivers and their needs for supportive services are very similar.

The success of any placement can be greatly enhanced if caseworkers properly support substitute caregivers, and assure they have the resources to perform their jobs. This section outlines casework interventions that will help substitute caregivers provide the best services possible to the children in their care. These interventions must be viewed as essential components of effective foster care practice. Without them, the likelihood of placement failure and disruption are greatly increased.

Throughout this discussion, the term "caregiver" is used to refer to agency foster parents, relative caregivers, and other substitute caregivers, including, at times, group home or residential treatment staff. Where there are differences, they will be noted.

Application

The caseworker should begin support of a placement even before the placement occurs. The first step in placement support is to assure that the caregiving family has the characteristics and abilities necessary to meet the special needs of the child to be placed.

The term "matching," originally used in infant adoption practice, commonly referred to selecting a family whose physical characteristics and ethnic background were the most similar to that of the child to be placed. While the criteria with which we match children to families have changed dramatically, matching remains an essential component of good placement practice. The selection of families that have the necessary skills and characteristics to meet a child's individual needs is critical for placement stability and success.

All families have strengths, skills, and vulnerabilities, and established patterns of family structure, organization, and intrafamily relationships. Before we select a placement for a child, we must assess whether a potential family can meet the child's individual needs, and whether the family has the ability to cope with the specific problems and behaviors the child is likely to present. Otherwise, placing the child can create undue stress and disruption for the caregiving family, ultimately undermining the placement.

While we cannot always predict placement outcomes, we generally can identify potential areas of incompatibility and problems. As an example, the Hudson family's strengths include unlimited patience and the ability to provide warm and consistent nurturing, but parents quickly become angry when faced with defiant children who challenge their authority. They might provide exceptional care to an affectionate child with a physical disability or developmental delay, but they would more likely have problems coping with a child who had severe behavior problems, or who continually tested limits. Conversely, the Baxter family has raised several autonomous, spirited, and independent children, and they are accustomed to an active lifestyle. They might better handle an overactive child with behavior problems than a child with excessive physical care needs requiring the commitment of many hours each day.

We also exacerbate stress, and potentially increase the risk of disruption if we place a child in a family that is vastly different from his own family in culture, values, communication styles, house rules, and expectations. Significant cultural differences can greatly complicate the adjustment process for both the child and the caregiving family. For this reason, matching the child to a family with a similar cultural background, in the child's home community, can minimize the effects of these differences.

The caregiving family should always be involved in assessing whether a particular child should be placed with them before a final decision is made. If the placement is pursued, this discussion begins the preparation process by helping the family anticipate both the child's needs and problems, and their own likely responses.

PREPARATION OF THE CAREGIVING FAMILY

The adage "forewarned is forearmed" is particularly valid in child placement. If caregiving families are properly prepared, they can anticipate a child's needs, and will be better prepared to respond in constructive and appropriate ways. Therefore, caregiving families should always be given complete and accurate information about the child prior to placement. When possible, caregivers should talk directly with the child's parent or other primary caregiver to obtain this information. This is equally true for kinship caregivers, unless they have routinely provided full-time care for the child in the past, and are already familiar with the child's needs and habits. Important information would include:

- Facts regarding the child's history, culture, and previous life experiences, including the factors that made removal and placement necessary;

- The child's medical and educational history, and any special medical or educational needs;

- The child's typical daily schedule, habits, likes, dislikes, food preferences, the type of discipline to which the child is accustomed, and other information to help caregivers plan and provide consistency in daily care. This may include culturally specific health and physical care needs and techniques;

- The child's expected emotional and behavioral responses to both routine and atypical situations, including expected behavior problems, fears, and emotional problems;

- The estimated length of time the child is expected to be in foster care, and the long-term plan for the child. Changes in these expectations should immediately be communicated; and

- The agency's expectations of the foster caregiver in caring for the child, including providing services for the child, expectations for involvement in family visitation, and direct contact with the primary family.

While issues of confidentiality may make communication of some types of information more difficult, the worker should try to give the caregiver a description of the problem or situation in general terms, avoiding identifying information if necessary. A better approach is to encourage the primary parent to communicate information directly to the caregiver, or to obtain a release of information from the parent, which gives the agency the authority to disclose important factual information about the child to the caregiver.

HELPING FOSTER CAREGIVERS MEET THE NEEDS OF CHILDREN IN CARE

Within a few weeks of placement the caseworker should convene a formal case planning conference to fully assess the family's and child's service needs, and to collaboratively develop the best plan to meet those needs. Case planning meetings should include the caseworker, the casework supervisor, the child's parent(s), other key family members, and the substitute caregivers. Other community professionals who are involved with the family should also participate.

Foster caregivers can be an excellent source of information about a child's development, needs, and problems. Caregivers should be trained to observe and document relevant information about the child and his primary family, and to contribute this to the case assessment and planning process. Foster caregivers who will be involved in providing direct services to the parent should also participate in the development of the service plan for the family. A comprehensive case plan guides caregivers' activities to assure they are goal-directed and congruent with the activities of other service providers.

An important component of postplacement support is to help caregivers understand and manage a child's behavior after placement. Caregivers should receive training to enable them to understand children's behavior, and to utilize appropriate behavior management and discipline strategies. Follow-up discussion and problem solving with the caseworker can further prepare caregivers to properly interpret and deal with a child's particular problems. Training in basic behavior management techniques is essential. This might include the use of "time out" or other restrictions; selective ignoring of misbehaviors; positive reinforcement for alternative behaviors; the use of logical consequences; and using behavioral charts to identify, assess, and record problem behaviors. Caseworkers can then assist the caregivers to develop and implement interventions that are appropriate for the individual child.

The caseworker can also help the caregiving family understand the profound impact for children of separation and placement, and how these feelings are often expressed in negative, oppositional, or other problem behaviors. The caregiving family should be trained to encourage the child to openly express painful, negative feelings in appropriate ways. This can help reduce some of the child's negative behaviors, and can also provide necessary support and reassurance to the child.

Supportive casework and referral to community service providers can also strengthen the caregiving family's ability to meet the child's needs. The caseworker and other agency support staff can assist caregivers by:

- Promoting arrangement of an appropriate educational placement for the child, including negotiating with school personnel to meet the special educational needs of children with learning problems or developmental disabilities;

- Providing a medical card or other medical financial assistance, and identifying resources for preventive health care, medical care, dental care, and other health related services;

- Arranging for appropriate mental health services when indicated, including an assessment of the child's emotional status, cognitive development, and social needs; and arranging counseling or therapy for the child;

- Arranging for counseling and supportive services, when indicated, for the caregiving family to help them adjust to the placement of a difficult child in the home, and to teach them to deal constructively with the child's problems;

- Offering regular casework support to help the foster caregiver deal with daily problems and stresses brought about by the placement;

- Assuring that foster caregivers receive reimbursement for expenses and adequate payment for their services;

- Providing caregivers with opportunities to participate in foster caregiver associations and support groups; this includes the development of "buddy systems," that pair new and experienced families for peer support and education;

- Making respite care available to foster caregivers; this will provide them with periods of time when they can be relieved of the stresses and responsibilities of direct child care; and

- Linking caregiving families to community providers who offer culturally specific services for children. These providers can also provide training to the caregiving family in culturally specific values and methods of care.

PREPARING CAREGIVERS WHEN CHILDREN LEAVE THEIR HOME

If foster caregivers are properly prepared to assist children leaving their care, either to return home or in a move to another placement, the separation trauma for the child can be greatly reduced. Normally, if caregivers have been involved in the ongoing case planning process, they will be aware of reunification plans. Caregivers can begin to prepare a child by talking about the move, and encouraging the child to talk about her feelings. It is important that the child understand what is happening as it occurs. If not told directly, even very young children will sense that "something is happening," and will be more frightened than they would be if the plan were fully explained to them. The caregiver should also be reminded to expect recurrences of acting–out behaviors, and to interpret this as an anxiety reaction to impending separation.

Children also need an opportunity to ask questions and express their fears and concerns. A prepared caregiver can respond by helping the child recognize and label feelings of sadness, anger, or fear. Foster caregivers should also express their own feelings of sadness about the move. This can prevent a child from feeling that he is being moved because of some personal fault or inappropriate behavior.

When the child has formed an attachment to the caregivers, some form of contact should be encouraged immediately following the move. Telephone calls, letters, and visits reassure the child that the caregiving family still cares about him and is thinking of him. This is important in helping retain continuity for the child, and also minimizes separation trauma and loss. When a relationship has been developed between the caregiver and the parent, ongoing contact after reunification can provide a source of support both to the child and the parent. In many instances, the caregiving family can provide occasional respite care for the child.

HELPING FOSTER CAREGIVERS WHEN A CHILD LEAVES

Caregivers, too, must be prepared and supported when a child leaves their home. Dealing with loss and grief is a recurrent part of the foster caregiver's job. Often, their grief is not discussed with others and may never be resolved. This may interfere with their ability to form attachments to children subsequently placed in their home. Unresolved grief from traumatic or repeated separations can also result in caregivers' withdrawal from the foster care program.

There are several factors that may inhibit the healthy expression of grief by foster caregivers. In some families, social or cultural expectations may prohibit outward expressions of grief and loss. Friends and family members may criticize caregivers, suggesting that they should not feel bad because they "knew from the beginning that the child would eventually leave the home." At times, unaware, busy, or insensitive caseworkers and other agency personnel may communicate this message to caregivers, depriving them of much needed emotional support.

⅄ The Walsh Family

The Walsh family provides a good example of one foster family's response to a traumatic separation from a child in their care. Melissa was placed with the Walshes at birth. Mr. and Mrs. Walsh, in their late 40s, and their two children, Laura, 14, and Theo, 12, immediately developed strong attachments to Melissa, who quickly became "one of the family." Legal entanglements precluded an early adoption for Melissa, and parental rights were not terminated until Melissa was two years old. The Walshes were offered the opportunity to adopt Melissa, but their age and Mr. Walsh's chronic health problems contributed to their decision to let Melissa go to a "younger, healthier family." Their decision was largely altruistic; they felt it to be in Melissa's best interests, despite their deep attachment to her.

The caseworker prepared Melissa for the adoption. Melissa attended several preplacement home visits, and was placed for adoption within a three–week period. A follow–up visit was scheduled in the Walshes' home two weeks after placement. The adoptive family felt further visits were counterproductive and requested they stop, because both Melissa and the Walshes were so emotional when they saw each other. The agency deferred to their wishes.

The Walshes, particularly Mrs. Walsh, experienced a profound and painful loss when Melissa was placed. The caseworker had brief follow–up contact with the family, but felt helpless to assist them, and uncomfortable with the scope of their distress. Another caseworker placed a toddler, Patty, in the home within a month of Melissa's removal, despite Mrs. Walsh's expressed lack of commitment or interest. The caseworker convinced her it would be helpful in "keeping her mind off Melissa." As could be expected, the placement failed within the first month. The Walshes had little emotional energy to respond to Patty's needs, and they formed little attachment to her. Mrs. Walsh continually compared Patty with Melissa, and Melissa's attributes became more and more idealized in comparison to Patty and her fairly typical two–year–old behavior problems. Patty was removed. The agency chose not to place another child with the Walshes because "they couldn't adjust to the loss of Melissa," and could not be counted on to provide good care to another child. Three months later, the family notified the caseworker that they would be withdrawing from the foster care program. Their 16-year-old daughter, Laura, had become pregnant, and Mrs. Walsh said they would need to focus their attention on preparing for the baby.

The family's response to Melissa's adoption probably resulted from many factors. However, the agency's failure to recognize the depth of the family's pain, the worker's naivete in thinking another child could be easily integrated into the family, and the absence of comprehensive supportive services to all members of the foster family clearly contributed to their crisis. The agency's quick termination of the relationship between Melissa and the Walshes after the adoption did not acknowledge the intensity of their attachment. This was emotionally disruptive for both Melissa and the Walsh family. The agency's mishandling of the adoption process resulted in the loss of an experienced and talented foster family after 12 years of service to the agency.

A supportive environment must be provided for foster caregivers to express their feelings after the removal of a child. The caseworker should offer support to foster caregivers for a time after children are moved. It can be very helpful if foster caregivers have an opportunity to share their feelings with other supportive foster caregivers, who have also experienced the loss of children. This can be promoted through neighborhood foster care networks or associations, or a "buddy system" for individual support.

The impact of separation, for both the child and the caregiving family, can be lessened when there is continued contact during a transition period. Phone calls, letters, cards, periodic updates by the caseworker regarding the child's progress, and visits can be reassuring and helpful both to the child and the caregivers. If the foster caregiver and the primary or adoptive family have developed a relationship during the period the child was in placement, visits may occur naturally within the context of their relationship. At times, caregivers can have periodic contact with children for years after they leave the caregiver's home. This promotes continuity for the child as well.

Timing the placement of another child in the home is critical. Placement of a new child with a grieving foster family can create serious problems for the placement. The caregivers may not be ready to establish a relationship with any new child, and the newly placed child may have to compete with the memory of the previous child for the foster caregiver's attention and affection. The child needs the full attention of a family that is capable of meeting his needs. Before deciding to place another child in the home, the caseworker and caregiver should jointly assess the family's degree of distress, and determine the family's readiness to accept another child in placement. The caseworker should never force a placement when the family indicates they are not ready. The worker should also discourage families from taking additional children because they think it will be "therapeutic" for them.

While we have focused on traumatic and painful feelings of loss, some foster caregivers may respond very differently when children are moved. Typically, the degree of attachment and the quality of the relationship varies with each child in their care, and there is a wide range of "normal feelings." Moreover, when a caregiver has had an ambivalent or negative relationship with a child, the caregiver may concurrently experience relief that the child has been moved, and guilt in response to negative feelings. This may create considerable emotional conflict. If this conflict is not addressed and dealt with openly, it may interfere with the caregiver's ability to objectively assess his or her ability to care for other children. Workers must help caregivers acknowledge when they were unable to form attachments with particular children and, together, assess the reasons for this. Some children, particularly those with attachment disorders, cannot tolerate emotional closeness, and forcefully reject their caregivers. (See Section VIII-A, "Attachment and Attachment Disorders.") Few families can provide unconditional acceptance and affection in these circumstances. At other times, the failure to form appropriate attachments with children in care may reflect characteristics of the caregiving family that would preclude their continuing as caregivers. This must be carefully assessed prior to deciding whether the family should be used for other children, and the types of children they are most capable of caring for.

FOSTER FAMILIES AS PERMANENT FAMILIES FOR CHILDREN WHO CANNOT RETURN HOME

There are several reasons why foster caregiving families should be considered as permanent families for children who cannot return home. If the child is adopted by his current caregivers, another painful separation is prevented, and the child does not have to reestablish trust and a sense of belonging with strangers. The caregiving family can also make an informed decision about adoption based on thorough and accurate information gained from months to years of living with the child.

If the caregiving family has had contact with the primary parent, the parent may be more willing to relinquish custody of the child to the caregiving family. This saves considerable time in legal action. It may also permit "open adoption," which allows children to maintain relationships with parents with whom they have strong emotional ties, but who do not have the capability to care for them.

The child's current caregiving family may not be the only available permanent placement resource for a child. Creative agency use of a child's previous foster family as a permanent placement resource is illustrated by the following case.

⚹ Linda Givens, age nine

Linda lived with her mother only intermittently from birth. She and her brother, Michael, had been placed in foster care several times due to their mother's drug abuse. After their mother completed drug treatment and had several months of stability, the children always went home; however, it was seldom longer than a year before the mother relapsed, and the children were returned to foster care.

When Linda was eight, her mother died of an overdose. Linda was in foster care at the time. Three months later, Linda's foster father was diagnosed with inoperable cancer. The foster mother asked that Linda be moved, and Linda endured her sixth foster placement in as many years. In spite of the many moves, Linda adjusted well to her new foster home. Surprisingly, her ability to respond to nurturing and caring adults appeared relatively intact, despite multiple previous placements. Even so, the worker was very concerned about subjecting her to yet another separation for adoption. Her current foster family cared for Linda but did not feel in a position to adopt her.

The worker began adoption planning by developing a Lifebook for Linda. The worker sorted through the extensive case record, located names and addresses of Linda's previous foster families, and wrote them letters requesting pictures of Linda while she was in their home. She also asked for anecdotal data about Linda's life and activities when she was with them. The worker received several positive responses and dozens of pictures, including photos of Linda at age one, taking her first steps.

One of the families, the Taylors, called the worker directly to express their interest in adopting Linda if she needed a home. The worker set up a home visit with them, at which time the Taylors explained they had cared for Linda and her brother intermittently when Linda was age three to six. Linda had not been replaced with them because their new home had not met the space and layout requirements for foster care licensure. Mrs. Taylor had appealed the decision, but Linda had been placed with another family. The Taylors then showed the worker photo albums and boxes of mementos from Linda's life with them, including drawings, art projects, and even some of Linda's favorite toys. The worker conducted a homestudy and determined the family to be a strong applicant to adopt Linda, largely because of their enduring emotional commitment to her.

The worker talked to Linda about the Taylors; she remembered very little about them. The worker prepared Linda to visit with them. Linda greeted the Taylors shyly at first, but when presented with the pictures and boxes of mementos, Linda began to remember and reminisce about things that had happened when she had lived with them. A series of visits began. Because of Linda's age and her history of separations, the worker involved her in the decision of where to live permanently. The Taylors told Linda that they wanted her to be their child forever, but only if she wanted to, and only when she felt ready. About a month into the visits, Linda announced that she thought she belonged there, since she had been there on and off for much of her life, but only if she could still see her current foster mother, who would then become her "aunt." With all in agreement, Linda legally became a Taylor.

"AT RISK" ADOPTION PROGRAMS

Many child protection agencies have developed successful programs of "risk" adoptive placements. A risk placement is placement of a child in a potential adoptive home before the child has been legally freed for adoption. The potential adoptive parent serves as a foster caregiver and works with the agency to implement the child's case plan until the child is legally freed for adoption. At that time, the adoption is legalized.

Permanent custody requires a permanent termination of parental rights by the legal system. To protect the rights of the parent, a juvenile court must hear the permanent custody action and determine whether the child should be freed for adoption. In situations where the custody action is contested or appealed by the parent, the child may not be freed. As a result, there are some concerns regarding risk placements.

There are also potential conflicts for foster caregivers in risk place-ments. Of most concern is the question whether a caregiver can effec-tively work with a child and her biological family to reunify the child if they hope to eventually adopt her. However, risk placements can be very beneficial for children in care for whom adoption is the desired goal. It prevents multiple separations and placements in different homes.

If the agency is considering a risk placement for a child, the foster parent must be involved in all aspects of the planning. There should be no surprises. Withholding important information can create unrealistic expectations for foster families. Many families can deal with change and uncertainty if they have full knowledge of what the potential outcomes of a situation might be, and they can prepare themselves psychologically for such outcomes. Finally, if the child even-tually does go home, the family must be supported throughout the grief process.

FOSTER CARE DISRUPTION

While many factors contribute to disruption of foster care placements, inade-quacies in the agency's foster care program are often contributors. Specifically, improper recruitment, screening, homestudy, and matching activities, and inap-propriate or absent case planning, can greatly increase the likelihood of place-ment disruption.

When shortages in available foster homes exist, placements are often made on a single criteria–available bed space. As a result, many children are placed with caregiving families who are not prepared to manage them. This practice greatly increases the risk of placement disruption.

A critical shortage of foster families is often the result of insufficient or inef-fective recruitment, training, and retention of foster caregivers. When recruit-ment billboards and advertisements depict attractive young children in need of families, applicants are given unrealistic expectations for the foster parenting experience. If the agency does not obtain sufficient or accurate information about a family during the homestudy process, serious misjudgments may be made about the family's abilities to care for particular types of children. The sub-sequent placement of a child in a family whose lack of skill or areas of vulnera-bility are not properly identified increases the risk of placement disruption and of turmoil within the foster family unit.

If a foster family is given insufficient information about a child prior to place-ment, the family cannot make an informed decision of whether to accept the child into placement. Without sufficient information, caregivers may feel that the agency "didn't tell us everything," or, "this is far worse than we expected." This creates anxiety and resentment on the part of foster caregivers, and a lack of trust of agency staff.

The risk of disruption also increases when caregiving families feel pressure from the agency to accept placement of a child, even when they have doubts about the child, or the timing is not right. Many families fear they will be con-sidered uncooperative, or that the agency will not consider them for future placements, if they choose not to accept a child into their home. Caregivers must be encouraged by the agency to say "no" to a placement without risk of censure or punishment.

The risk of disruption is increased when caregivers are inadequately supported by the caseworker and the agency. This includes insufficient contact by the caseworker during the early stages of the placement. Adequate support during the difficult initial adjustment period can ease the transition and may prevent later disruption.

If the agency does not clearly communicate the content of the case plan, including the long-term goals and the responsibilities of the foster caregiver in helping to achieve those goals, confusion and dissension may result. The caseworker should ensure that caregivers fully understand the expectations of them with each child, and the reasons for these expectations. Involving caregivers in all case review and staffing conferences can reduce or eliminate this problem.

The availability of support from other caregivers through a foster caregiver association, neighborhood network, or buddy system decreases stress and isolation for caregivers. Adequate support networks are an important component to reduce the stresses that can contribute to placement disruption.

Occasionally, emergency placements must be made, and a child may have to be placed in a home that is not appropriate to meet his needs. The caseworker should thoroughly discuss the options with the caregivers. If the family agrees to care for the child, intensive support and training must be provided to support the placement. At times, such experiences may stimulate growth and the development of new caregiver skills. Without proper support and training, however, the placement is likely to disrupt, and the overwhelmed family may withdraw from the program.

XI. ADOPTION*

A. Identifying and Preparing Adoptive Families for Children with Special Needs

B. Selecting and Matching Families and Children

C. Preparing a Child for Adoption

D. Services to Children and Families at the Time of Placement

E. Postplacement and Postlegalization Services to Adoptive Families

*Co–authored by Denise A. Goodman, Ph.D., M.S.W.

A. IDENTIFYING AND PREPARING ADOPTIVE FAMILIES FOR CHILDREN WITH SPECIAL NEEDS*

1. Conceptual Framework

2. Application

3. Case Examples

*Co–authored by Denise A. Goodman, Ph.D., M.S.W.

Conceptual Framework

For much of this century, adoption referred to the placement of healthy infants with childless families. Young, unmarried mothers, or women experiencing hardships, permanently surrendered custody of their newborns to public child-placing agencies, or placed their infants through independent adoption or within their extended families. At the time, adoption programs were established primarily to help infertile couples adopt infants. Children who were older, or who had developmental, emotional, or behavioral problems, were considered "hard to place," and were not often considered for adoption. They were typically cared for in foster homes or institutions.

Social trends in the past 25 years contributed to significant changes in the national adoption picture. The "sexual revolution" that began in the late 1960s and 1970s significantly changed sexual activity among youth and unmarried young adults. Birth control, and later, abortion, became more widely and easily available. Single parenthood was increasingly common, perhaps as a result of the increasing divorce rate, and it also became more socially acceptable for young and unmarried mothers to retain custody of their infants. Subsequently, the numbers of infants surrendered for adoption decreased, and the length of time prospective adoptive families had to wait before a healthy infant could be placed with them increased dramatically.

Concurrent studies of the national foster care system revealed that thousands of children were languishing in impermanent foster homes. A handful of progressive child welfare agencies began to develop adoption programs designed to place children with "special needs" in adoptive families. Initially, children with "special needs" could be as young as a year old, and few were older than school age. Most were healthy, although many had mild emotional problems and developmental delays as a result of prior maltreatment and separation. It was still widely believed that many children were "unadoptable," including children with serious or multiple physical, medical, behavioral, and emotional problems; children with mental retardation or other developmental disabilities; older children of minority or mixed racial/ethnic backgrounds; and children over the age of 12. "Permanent" plans for these children continued to include long-term foster care or institutional placement.

In 1980, the United States Congress passed P.L. 96–272, The Adoption Assistance and Child Welfare Act, to promote permanence for children in foster care. This legislation mandated that agencies make timely "reasonable efforts" to reunite children in foster care with their families. If reunification was not possible, the agency was to quickly pursue permanent termination of parental rights and placement of the child for adoption. Consequently, specialized programs and strategies were needed to successfully identify and prepare adoptive families for a wide variety of children and youth with complex problems and needs.

By the mid 1980s, toddlers and preschool children were not generally thought of as having "special needs," and they were quickly placed in adoptive families.

School-age and adolescent children with more serious developmental problems, including many who had previously been identified as "unadoptable," became the norm in adoption practice. The implementation of P.L. 96–272 profoundly impacted adoption services by shifting the focus of practice from "finding children for families" to "finding families for children." All areas of adoption practice, from recruitment to postlegalization services, were modified to reflect this changed perspective. And since so many children with multiple and complex needs had been successfully adopted, the description "unadoptable" was largely dropped from adoption vocabulary.

Despite the inherent difficulties of contemporary adoption practice, the child welfare field's ability to achieve permanence for so many children with exceptional problems and needs has been gratifying. We have not, however, fully met the challenge, as many thousands of children throughout North America, who cannot be returned to their families, remain in impermanent placements.

Who Are Children with Special Needs?

Children with "special needs" typically include a wide range of children with a variety of strengths and needs. They are generally described as meeting one or more of the following criteria: they may be school age or older; they may be part of a sibling group; they may be of minority or mixed ethnic or racial heritage; they may have mental or physical disabilities; or they may have serious emotional or behavioral disorders.

Many children with special needs have histories of physical abuse, sexual abuse, neglect, and/or repeated separations. These experiences can significantly impact their development. Some may have academic delays, emotional or behavioral problems, physical disabilities, an inability to trust others, or attachment problems. Multiple separations and placement instability may have affected their ability to trust others, and to form attachments with new caregivers. These experiences can create barriers to successful adoption in several ways:

- Some children can be very challenging to parent. This requires adoptive parents who are patient, resilient, creative, and self-assured. Traditional methods of adoptive family recruitment and family assessment have proven ineffective in identifying and preparing such families.

- Preparation for adoption is complicated, since many children are initially resistant to being adopted. They may maintain a strong identification with their biological families. Some children struggle with loyalty issues, and feel that a positive attitude toward adoption is essentially a betrayal of their own families. Adoption also threatens their fantasies of being reunited with their biological families. A few children may adamantly oppose, and diligently work to undermine, any adoption planning and preparation.

- Developing a relationship with the adoptive family may be a struggle for some children, particularly those with attachment problems. Both maltreatment and separation can contribute to the development of attachment disorders, a lack of trust in adults, and poor social skills. The development of attachments may be a lengthy process, and it may not result in the typical parent–child relationship the adoptive family expects. This can create high levels of frustration for many adoptive parents, who may give much affection and attention to the child, while often getting little reciprocated. Adoptive families of children with attachment problems must often learn special parenting skills. (Refer to Section VIII-A, "Attachment and Attachment Disorders.")

- Some children who are developmentally delayed or mentally retarded may lack the cognitive skill to understand and integrate the abstract concepts related to adoption. Consequently, they may be placed for adoption without fully understanding what is happening to them. When children do not understand the difference between adoption and foster care, adoption is often experienced as another impermanent home, increasing the child's anxiety and making it more difficult to fully integrate the child into the adoptive family.

STAGES IN THE IDENTIFICATION AND PREPARATION OF ADOPTIVE FAMILIES

Developmental activities to recruit and prepare potential adoptive families can be categorized into four general program components: recruitment, screening, family assessment, and training. Since these activities are essentially the same for both foster care and adoption, many agencies use a single program to recruit and develop both adoptive and foster families. (See related discussion in Section X-B, "Recruitment and Selection of Foster and Other Caregivers.")

For many families, their first exposure to adoption is through the recruitment campaign. It is, therefore, critical that we give families accurate information about adoption at this time. The recruitment campaign should educate prospective adoptive parents about the types of children who typically need families, and the challenges and rewards of adoption, including caring for children with physical, emotional, behavioral, or developmental problems. Recruitment is most effectively conducted by a team of caseworkers and experienced foster or adoptive families. This assures that prospective families are well–informed early in the recruitment process.

Screening begins to gather information from the prospective adoptive family, and orients them to adoption. During screening, the agency can determine with a family whether they meet the prerequisite qualifications to adopt, based on state or provincial law. Screening often includes a general orientation that gives potential families more in–depth information about the adoption program.

Many families without the necessary ability or commitment will self–select out of the program after the exchange of information during the screening and orientation process. While the agency must screen out families who do not meet basic requirements, the goal is to encourage most prospective families to continue to assess their suitability as adoptive families.

Preservice training and a collaborative family assessment are designed to help them do this. During both, the caseworker and the family together continue to evaluate the family's strengths, skills, needs, and areas of vulnerability, and determine the family's potential to be adoptive parents.

The family assessment serves several distinct purposes. First, it is an educational process that helps family members refine their conception of adoption and fully assess their own interest and commitment. Through discussion with agency staff and experienced adoptive parents, the prospective family can develop realistic expectations for adoption, and can evaluate how their life experiences may have prepared them for the challenges and stresses they are likely to encounter as adoptive parents.

Second, the family is helped to identify their strengths and areas of potential vulnerability. Certain personal and family attributes are helpful when parenting adopted children and dealing with adoption-specific issues. Adjectives such as "adaptable," "flexible," "patient," "open-minded," "committed," "tolerant," and "consistent," have often been listed among the desired family characteristics. These are often hard to quantify. There are, however, some attributes that can be quantified and should be evaluated by the family and their caseworker during the family assessment. The assessment process also helps families consider the types of children they are best suited to parent, and the types of children they should not adopt.

A third goal of the family assessment is to define, develop, and strengthen the relationship between the family and the agency. A collaborative relationship will promote honest communication between a family and their caseworker. It will also provide the framework for continued collaboration during and after a child is placed with the family. Through the family assessment, families learn to view the agency as an important source of help and support. An agency-family relationship based on trust and mutual respect is begun from the time of the initial contact, but is strongly reinforced during the family assessment and preservice training process.

The process we use to assess potential adoptive parents is essentially the same process we use with any family. The family assessment is collaborative. The assessment caseworker does not conduct an assessment *of* the prospective family, but rather, *with* the family. The skilled assessment worker guides the family through an intensive process of self-examination that enables them to develop realistic expectations for themselves and the adoption experience. Our goal is to help them arrive at well-informed conclusions about their own strengths, interests, and vulnerabilities, and to help them make sound decisions about the nature and scope of their involvement in adoption.

Helping families understand the multiple purposes of the family assessment early in the process may relieve considerable anxiety about being evaluated, which helps family members participate more freely and comfortably. This is important for all families, but particularly for foster families applying to adopt children already in their care, or kinship parents, who may rightfully resent having to be "evaluated and approved" to adopt members of their own extended family. The mutual rapport that characterizes a good family assessment also promotes openness and honesty, which greatly enhances the quality of the assessment. Finally, defining the family assessment as a learning and preparation activity sets the expectation that challenges are normal and expected, and that the most effective adoptive parents are skilled problem solvers, not people who have experienced no problems.

The initial educational phase of the family assessment is best conducted by combining in-home assessment interviews with preservice group training sessions. Preservice training gives participants an overview of the child welfare system and its mission; the purpose of foster care and adoption; and a beginning understanding of the children and families served by the agency. Formal preservice training begins to prepare families to consider the realities of adoption, raises critical issues, and gives families opportunities to learn from agency staff and experienced adoptive parents.

These program components are essential for the successful development of qualified adoptive families. Even though many families may be highly motivated and eager to parent children with special needs, if they are not properly prepared, trained, and supported, the demands of caring for these children may prove to be overwhelming. The rate of placement disruption is much higher when inexperienced and untrained families are asked to parent children with serious behavioral and emotional problems.

Interviewing to Elicit and Assess Family Process

The family assessment is designed to help caseworkers and prospective families understand key aspects of family process. While certain factual information is necessary, we are more interested in understanding, and helping family members understand, the structure and operation of their family system. This includes typical family roles, relationships, and dynamics; the family members' culture, values, and beliefs; their perceptions and feelings about critical issues; and family members' linkages within their extended family and community.

The skilled assessment caseworker uses interviewing strategies that move the family from the content level to the process level in their communications. (See Section IV-C, "Conducting the Family Assessment.") The caseworker must also use interviewing methods to generate discussion of critical information; to assure the clarification of important issues; to guide the family in coming to valid conclusions; and to summarize the implications of this information with the family. The caseworker will likely use open-ended and supportive questions early in the process to engage family members, to strengthen the caseworker-family relationship, and to encourage family members to share information. In subsequent contacts, the caseworker will guide discussion to key issues, and help family members explore them in greater depth by using focused questions and clarifying responses. Periodically throughout the assessment, the caseworker will involve the family in summarizing what has been discussed, identifying prominent themes, and considering the relevance of assessment conclusions. All the fundamental principles of casework interviewing apply to the family assessment, including the scrupulous avoidance of leading questions. (See Section IV-F, "The Casework Interview: Implementing the Helping Process.")

The family assessment itself should consist of several interviews with family members. Five or six meetings of one to one-and-a-half hours in length should be considered the average. The assessment caseworker should meet initially with the parents or caregiving adults together, and then with the family as a whole. Follow–up individual interviews should then occur with each adult, and the children individually, if they are old enough. Additional joint sessions with the parents should complete the assessment, but one final meeting should be held with the entire family to summarize and share conclusions, and to develop "next steps."

THE FAMILY ASSESSMENT CRITERIA

Criteria are the standards, principles, or rules on which a judgment or decision can be based. The criteria for an adoptive family assessment are those personal and family characteristics that have been correlated with the successful parenting of adopted children, particularly those with multiple needs and problems. The family assessment helps the caseworker and family determine whether, and to what degree, family members possess these qualities, and what further development is needed to strengthen and enhance them.

Historically, it was widely believed that adoptive parenting was not unlike biological parenting. In reality, they are quite different, particularly when adopting older children. It is conventional wisdom among adoption professionals that adopting an older child is more akin to an arranged marriage than to childbirth. Unless the child is adopted by relatives, the adoptive family and the child share no genetic heritage; they have no prior attachment and no shared identity; and their cultural and social backgrounds are often quite different. Yet, after only a brief and closely chaperoned "courtship," they are expected to become emotionally committed to each other and to function together as a family. The children's often traumatic histories can further complicate the process of becoming a family. That so many adoptions are successful, in spite of the odds, is testimony to the strength of the human drive to nurture and to form intimate bonds.

While issues related to the adoption of older children are well-known, professionals and families often fail to recognize adoption–related issues in children who were adopted as infants. Many children may not exhibit adoption–related problems until adolescence or early adulthood, when the primary developmental challenge is to formulate a positive and independent identity. Adoption issues can exacerbate this already–stressful developmental period. In some cases, the adoption can disrupt, either formally or informally.

After years of evaluation, the individual and family characteristics typically associated with adoption success have been delineated. Not surprisingly, the majority of these traits and characteristics are the same as those associated with successful foster caregiving. Adoptive and foster families are often the same people. Foster families frequently adopt children in their care, and some adoptive families continue to provide foster care after they have adopted. More important, the parenting strategies that work with children who have emotional and behavioral problems are often the same, regardless of whether the child is in a temporary or permanent placement. Many agencies recognize these similarities, and conduct joint recruitment and orientation for adoptive and foster families. They also use a common training and family assessment format, adapting them where needed to assure consideration of relevant differences.

XI.A. Preparing Adoptive Families for Children with Special Needs

The intent of the following discussion is to help adoption casework-ers recognize and understand the issues to be examined during the family assessment process. The specific traits and criteria delineated below apply equally to both adoptive and foster families for children with special needs. While the main points of this discussion are briefly presented here, the reader should refer directly to Section X–B, "Recruitment and Selection of Foster and Other Caregivers," for a comprehensive delineation of these characteristics, desired and minimal standards, areas that warrant caution, and interviewing strategies and questions that can generate discussion and elic-it information.

The criteria for an adoptive family assessment can be divided into two broad categories: 1) the traits and characteristics that will enable the family to parent a child with special needs, without experiencing severe family stress; and, 2) the traits and characteristics necessary to meet children's special needs, and promote their healthy development.

Whenever we compile a list of highly desirable characteristics and use these as criteria with which to assess families, we risk perpetuating the "superfamily" myth. That is, we may begin to view the criteria on our list as the expected stan-dard, rather than the ideal. Clearly, no family will ever have all the desired char-acteristics on our list to the ideal degree. Therefore, to be realistic, we must define a "minimum standard," in addition to our "desired standard." Families who repeatedly cannot meet the minimum standards should not be approved as adoptive parents. However, many prospective families will meet minimum stan-dards in most, if not all, categories. They will also exhibit qualities closer to the desired standard in other categories. These are, by definition, the family's areas of strength. In addition, education and training can help many families develop their skills in critical areas.

Prospective adoptive families must always be assessed within their own cul-tural context. Workers must be cautious not to view families through an ethno-centric lens, in which anything "different" is interpreted as "deviant." In the absence of cultural knowledge, differences in family structure, organization, val-ues, and coping abilities may be seen as dysfunctional, while valuable strengths may go unrecognized. While many of the characteristics and traits described in the "ideal" criteria may be shared by many cultures, the ways these are expressed by people from different cultural backgrounds may differ. For example, in one family, "teamwork" by parents might be expressed as participating equally in all aspects of parenting, child care, and household management. In another family, roles of the parents may be more rigidly defined and distinct, but family mem-bers perceive the distribution of responsibility as equitable, and they all make significant contributions to the family. The caseworker must create an environ-ment in which the family's values and beliefs can be fully explored and consid-ered throughout the assessment process. (See Chapter V, Culture and Diversity in Child Welfare Practice.)

In all the descriptions below, the terms "parent" or "parents" refer to the adult caregiver or caregivers in the prospective adoptive family. This may be a single parent, a married couple, a single parent and an extended family member, or another combination of parenting adults. Each adult in the prospective adoptive family should be assessed individually on each of the criteria, and areas of agreement or disagreement should be determined. Areas where parents can support and complement each other should also be identified. Finally, since one of the goals of the family assessment is to determine whether the adults in the family have the ability to act as a parenting team, the caseworker might ask them to first consider each issue individually, then identify where they disagree, and consider how they might need to revise or integrate their approaches to assure consistency in parenting strategies.

Caseworkers must also remember that prospective adoptive families will vary widely on their areas of strength and vulnerability. No family will exhibit strengths in all the areas listed below. Those families with multiple strengths are often our strongest and most committed families. However, families with more modest strengths are often excellent adoptive parents as well. It is the assessment caseworker's job to help families identify their areas of vulnerability, and avoid placing children in their home who will overly challenge and stress them.

Introduction: Getting to Know the Family

Open-ended questions are recommended early in the family assessment, particularly during the first family-caseworker contacts. The caseworker's genuine interest in the family will help build a relationship, and will help family members feel more comfortable talking about themselves. By using open-ended questions, the caseworker can gain a general understanding of the family's history, structure, organization, and culture. Information gained during initial discussions can help guide the direction of subsequent assessment interviews and raise issues for further discussion.

The caseworker might ask family members to write or prepare an oral "autobiography" and share it with the worker, either before or during the family assessment. The information in the autobiography can provide the topics for initial discussions. Finally, initiating discussion of cultural issues will help the caseworker avoid misjudging family members' behavior because the caseworker is unaware of, or insensitive to, cultural differences.

Category I: The Parents' Expectations for Adoption

There are a variety of reasons people decide to adopt. All prospective adoptive parents have a vision of what they want their families to be like, and how the adoption will help them achieve this vision. Unfortunately, unrealistic expectations often result in dissatisfaction, disappointment, and potentially, adoption disruption. The caseworker must help prospective adoptive parents explore their vision and assess the reality of their expectations. This is extremely important, as many lack even basic information about parenting a child with special needs.

Prospective adoptive parents should view adoption as an inherently good way to build a family. People who apply to adopt an older child only because they want children, cannot have biological children, and the likelihood of finding an infant to adopt is remote, may not be good candidates to adopt an older child or one with special needs. For these parents, adoption may be seen as an inherently less desirable option, and they are likely to be seriously disappointed.

It is also critical that all family members, particularly the parenting adults, be committed to adoption. Successful adoptive parenting requires consistent support, commitment, and direct involvement from all family members. A considerable lack of involvement by one of the parents can greatly increase stress on the involved parent. Inconsistency in parenting may also encourage the child to "divide and conquer," which further increases stress in the family.

Examples of motivations that are typically associated with adoption success are:

- The prospective adoptive parents enjoy children; they enjoy being around children; and they find parenting to be pleasurable and fulfilling;

- The parents enjoy and thrive on challenges; and

- The parents want to nurture and help a child to grow and progress, and want to make an investment of themselves, their time, and their emotional energy toward this end.

Examples of motivations which are likely to produce an unsatisfactory adoption experience are:

- The prospective adoptive parents view adoption as a means of providing company or a playmate for a biological child;

- The parents have lost a child and seek to "recreate" their family as it was prior to losing their child;

- The parents are receiving considerable pressure from immediate or extended family members to have children;

- The parents believe having a child will strengthen or save their relationship; and

- The parents want to help a "poor, unfortunate child."

People's motivation to adopt may be quite complex. When questioned directly about their motivation, some parents may not be able to answer easily. Issues around motivation and expectations must be discussed throughout the entire family assessment to help family members correctly identify their primary motivations, and to determine whether these will support or work against successful adoption.

Category II: Personal Maturity

There are several personal characteristics that enable adoptive parents to withstand the challenges presented by adoption without feeling personally threatened, or experiencing severe emotional distress. These include strong and positive self–esteem, the ability to care for themselves emotionally, and several qualities categorized as "ego strengths." People with these abilities are better able to cope with challenges without feeling that their competence, confidence, self-esteem, or identity are threatened. People whose self-esteem is easily threatened, or whose self-worth depends on their doing everything "well," or "right," may not admit problems to themselves or others. They may blame or emotionally reject the adopted child to maintain their own self-esteem.

These traits are often best explored in individual interviews with the prospective adoptive parents. There is also value in asking them to identify each other's personal strengths and areas of potential vulnerability. However, the caseworker must understand that these traits may be exhibited differently in different cultures.

Parents' strengths might include:

- The ability to delay gratification and to find satisfaction in small gains;

- Good emotional control, and the ability to discharge tension and negative feelings in nonharmful ways;

- The ability to continue to parent and nurture a child who cannot show or return affection, nor demonstrate respect and appreciation;

- The ability to seek help and accept constructive criticism from other people;

- The ability to put other people's needs ahead of their own;

- The ability to critically and realistically assess their personal strengths and vulnerabilities; the ability to articulate what situations or behaviors "push their buttons" and how they respond; the ability to set realistic expectations for their own behavior and performance;

- The ability to see humor in stressful situations, and use laughter appropriately to discharge and reduce tension; and

- The ability to make a commitment and stick with it.

Category III: The Stability and Quality of Interpersonal Relationships

People who have a strong and dependable network of supportive and nurturing relationships are better able to cope with stress. When relationships within a family are unstable, or family members can't rely on each other for support, the emotional strain of adoption may be very threatening. Many foster or adopted children are adept at identifying areas of inconsistency, and playing one adult against another.

Parents must feel secure and confident that their relationship is strong enough to withstand stress and challenges. In two-parent families, the quality and stability of the couple's personal and sexual relationship must be fully assessed. A high percentage of children in adoption or foster care have been sexually abused, and they may act out sexually. The parents must be comfortable talking about sexual issues with children; must set expectations for appropriate and inappropriate sexual behavior; and must be able to cope with children's sexual behaviors without feeling threatened, jealous, or resentful.

Family strengths include:

- The family's history reflects stability in the relationship between the parents or adult caregivers. Parents have the ability to disagree and to negotiate differences without feeling personally threatened; parents have sought and constructively used help to resolve marital and family problems. Single parents demonstrate similar qualities in their close personal relationships.

- When parents have a prior history of divorce or instability in relationships, they have learned and grown from these experiences, and can identify how their current relationship is different from their previous relationships.

- Both couples and single parents have a strong support system of extended family and friends. They utilize this network regularly for emotional support, guidance, and direct assistance when needed.

- Parenting adults can describe how they operate as a team, particularly in parenting activities.

- Parents are comfortable with their sexual relationship. Parents are able to describe their children's sexual behavior, and can discuss sexual issues comfortably and appropriately within the family.

- Expressions of support, affection, and caring are easily recognized by other family members. (The particular ways that affection and support are expressed may vary among cultures.)

- Extended family members and close friends are generally encouraging, and they support the family's choice to become adoptive parents.

Category IV: Resilience, Coping Skills, and History of Stress Management

The prospective adoptive family should have a variety of effective strategies to cope with change and stress. A family that has continued to function productively in high stress situations usually has coping strengths that will help them adjust to the many changes and stresses inherent in adoption. Conversely, families that have not dealt with instability or crisis often have less well-developed strengths and coping strategies.

We can determine a family's typical responses to stress by asking them to describe difficult or traumatic past life events and relate how they dealt with them. We should look for responses that suggest capable problem-solving activities; effective use of interpersonal and community supports and resources; an attitude of having learned and grown from past stressful experiences; and indication of realistic confidence in their own strengths and coping abilities.

In addition, family members should be able to describe how their family unit has responded to changes brought about by the addition or loss of a family member. Past experiences with the birth of a child, the death of a family member, a divorce or separation, caring for someone else's children, or bringing an elderly parent to live with the family can provide insight into how flexibly the family system reacts to structural changes. Family members should also demonstrate comfort with change and ambiguity, including an ability to "ride with the tide" when necessary.

Finally, while all families should be expected to grow from the challenges of adoptive parenting, overstressing an inexperienced family is certain to increase the likelihood of disruption, and may also result in the loss of a potentially good adoptive family. The caseworker and family should try to determine how much stress and change the family can tolerate without experiencing high levels of distress. This information will be important when matching a child to the family.

Family strengths include:

- Family members can describe how they have managed difficult situations or crises in the past, such as serious illness, chronic stress, moving, loss of a loved one, etc.

- Family members have experienced changes in the family composition, and can identify how such changes were stressful. The family can describe how they "reorganized" as a family to accommodate a new member, or to regroup after the loss of a member.

- Family members demonstrate adaptability and flexibility in the face of change. They always have back-up plans, and they are able to quickly go to plan two or three when the first plan doesn't work. They are not threatened by a changed schedule. They appear to effectively practice "continual planning."

Category V: The Family is an Open System

An "open system" refers to a family unit that is able to adapt and change in response to challenges from within and outside the family. The "open" family is also linked with a broader network of extended family, friends, and community groups. The boundaries of the family are flexible; people can come and go, and the family can comfortably readjust in response to these changes. (This should not be confused with a family in which the "comings and goings" of members reflect instability, a lack of emotional commitment in relationships, or superficial attachments.) Family roles are also flexible, when necessary, to help the family as a unit adapt to changed circumstances.

A family's "openness" is also reflected by the family's willingness to allow persons from outside the family to help in stressful situations. There may, however, be individual and cultural differences regarding where the family seeks help. For example, some families will not utilize formal community agencies, but they maintain strong informal networks of relatives and friends, or they turn to a minister or a church group for support.

Finally, family members in an "open system" are able to acknowledge and appreciate differences. They enjoy contact with people of various ages and from other cultures, and they seek opportunities to be involved with a variety of people and situations. They accept and value people for whom and what they are, and they can identify strengths and value in most people.

By contrast, a "closed" family system is insular, isolated, and rigid when confronted with change. Members may have fixed roles, which are rarely altered even in changed circumstances. Family members highly value independence and self-sufficiency, and they don't often seek assistance from others. The epitome of a closed family system is, "it's just us against the world." Closed family systems are also often ethnocentric. Their members have difficulty understanding or respecting the values or perspectives of people who are different from themselves. They may also have more rigid standards for acceptable behavior.

The adoptive family system must comfortably incorporate not only the adopted child, but the child's biological family, and at times, prior foster families as well. Whether or not a child ever has direct contact with members of her biological family, the child's family is an important part of her history and identity. At many developmental stages throughout the life cycle, the child is likely to need background information. "Open" adoptive families acknowledge and accept the child's biological family as part of the child's history or "extended network." They do not deny the child's relationship with important others, nor the child's need to know about them, or to locate members of her biological family when she reaches adulthood. Some adoptive parents may have direct contact with biological family members, and may collaborate during case planning conferences or during visits. Many adoptions of children by their foster parents remain "open," particularly when the foster family has had ongoing contact with members of the child's biological family while the child was in foster care.

Family strengths include:

- The family has a strong and dependable support network through extended family, close family friends, or through organizational affiliations such as church or community groups.

- The family's extended family and support networks are in agreement and supportive of the family's desire to adopt.

- The family's past behavior demonstrates a willingness and desire to "use all the help we can get," rather than expecting themselves to manage everything on their own.

- The family demonstrates adaptability and flexibility in family roles to meet changing circumstances.

- Family members can describe previous group affiliations (a sports team, a church committee, a community planning group), and can relate how they participated as a team member and benefitted from the experience.

- Family members enjoy and appreciate differences, and are able to articulate ways that their lives have been enriched through contact with people who are different from them. They have personal relationships with people of different ages and social groups. They find diversity stimulating, and can describe how they have learned new things from people from diverse backgrounds. They are aware of how their own cultural traditions strengthen their lives, and they can identify things about their own cultural backgrounds they do not like, or have changed.

Category VI: Parenting Skills

Some prospective adoptive families have biological children, foster children, or other adopted children, or have cared for other people's children. Others may never have parented, and may have had little experience with children with emotional or behavioral problems. In general, people with parenting experience will be better prepared to care for an adopted child, even though parenting a child with special needs may be quite different from their other parenting experiences.

The relevant questions about parenting are, "Do the parents have, or can they develop, the skills needed to successfully parent children with special needs?" and, "Just what types of children are they best suited to parent?"

Parenting strengths include:

- The parents gain considerable pleasure and personal gratification from parenting activities.

- Being a parent is important "life's work," and they take pride in doing it well. An important part of their personal identity is being a parent. (This does not mean that the parent's primary source of self–worth is derived from their children's accomplishments, nor that their children are their only source of gratification. When parents depend upon their children's accomplishments to determine their personal worth, a child's perceived shortcomings are experienced by the parents as personal failures. Few children can live up to such parental expectations, much less children with special needs.)

- The parents truly enjoy activities related to parenting. They enjoy participating in recreation activities, vacations, projects, and other activities with their children. They look for ways to spend time together as a family. The parents express feelings of satisfaction from helping children learn; encouraging children to try new things; exposing children to new adventures; making children feel comfortable and content; and watching children grow and develop. They may be involved as volunteers with groups of children, such as coaching a sports team or leading a scout troop, "just for the fun of it."

- The parents can realistically assess their own and each other's parenting strengths, and areas of vulnerability. For example, "He's great at calming a frightened child; I do better motivating a child who doesn't want to move."

- The parents have the ability to individualize children and their needs, and to respond accordingly. They are able to use parenting and child management strategies best suited to each individual child. They also understand how they might need to alter their parenting interventions to be responsive to a child's cultural background.

- Prospective adoptive parents who have no children of their own should have had prior experience parenting or working closely with other people's children, including children who have had physical, emotional, or behavioral problems. With some prior experience, there are likely to be fewer surprises. If their only experience has been with typical children, they may greatly underestimate the amount of stress associated with adoption, and they will need considerable coaching to develop effective parenting strategies.

- The parents use discipline strategies appropriate for children who have experienced prior maltreatment and separation; or, they clearly demonstrate a willingness to learn and use these strategies. Generally, these include: setting clear limits and using logical consequences for infractions; positive reinforcement for desired behavior; time out; restriction of privileges; redirection; and removal of the child from the problem situation. Conversely, harsh physical discipline, strategies that shame or embarrass the child, segregation of the child for extended periods, or withdrawal of affection are potentially very harmful for children who have been subjected to maltreatment and separation.

- The parents recognize the potential effects of adoption on their own children, and have a plan to deal with them. They have talked with their own children about adoption, and have prepared them for the experience. The children understand and can tell the caseworker what things might change, and how they feel about the changes. The parents have considered their children's feelings and needs in making adoption decisions.

Category VII: Empathy and Perspective–Taking Ability

Perspective taking is, simply, the ability to understand someone else's perspective or point of view. Empathy is the ability to relate to and understand another person's situation, feelings, and motives. Both are necessary prerequisites for effective adoptive parenting.

Parenting strengths include:

- The parents are able to recognize and properly interpret one another's, and their children's, verbal, nonverbal, and behavioral cues, and they can correctly describe what other family members are feeling or experiencing.

- The parents recognize that a child's misbehavior often reflects a feeling or need state. Family members can recognize when other family members are distressed or need assistance. (Workers should be careful to consider cultural factors and communication styles when judging this criteria. The important factor is whether the parents can accurately interpret the child's signals.)

- The parents express empathy for the child's biological family, and can understand the situation from the child's and family's perspective. (The parents' attitudes about biological families must be fully explored during the assessment process. The parents may need to modify pre-existing negative or stereotypic attitudes about biological families, and "abusive" or "neglectful" parents.)

- The parents understand the importance of providing accurate and complete background information to the adopted child. The parents can talk with the child about his biological family, and the child's positive and negative feelings about his history. The parents understand that the scope and depth of the information may need to change as the child develops.

UNIQUE CHARACTERISTICS OF ADOPTIVE FAMILIES

There are several traits that are less important when assessing foster caregivers, but which are very relevant when assessing prospective adoptive families. These qualities increase the likelihood of success when adopting children with special needs. They can be described as: 1) parental entitlement; 2) "hands on" parenting; and, 3) a lifelong commitment.

Category VIII: Entitlement

Entitlement is defined as the right to receive, demand, or to do something. In adoption, entitlement refers to the adoptive parents' belief in their inalienable right and responsibility to act in ways that promote the adopted child's best interests. People almost universally feel entitled to parent children who are born to them. The same cannot be said about caring for someone else's children. People are typically more hesitant to intervene, to discipline, or to make decisions for children who are not their own. They, appropriately, do not feel fully entitled to act as a parent. So, they say things like, "We'll have to ask your mother about that," or, "I'm going to have to tell your mother you did that, and she'll decide the consequences."

In adoption, it is not uncommon for adoptive parents to lack feelings of entitlement. The adopted child has been, by birth and by history, someone else's child. Other factors can also interfere with entitlement. The child may have had a traumatic history, or may have been hurt by adults in the past. The child often has emotional problems. Parents may believe that doing the wrong thing in these circumstances may do more harm than good. Parents who lack entitlement are often tentative in their parenting interventions. They fail to appropriately "take charge," make decisions, enforce these decisions, and discipline appropriately when the child does not comply. Lack of conviction or involvement may be perceived by adopted children as a lack of investment and commitment. The tentative and inconsistent nature of parental responses can also be confusing to these children, who may not fully understand expectations, nor be able to predict the consequences if they do not comply. A lack of parental entitlement often exacerbates parents' problems in managing their adopted child's behavior.

In the common vernacular, entitlement is expressed as, "treating him just like he was one of my own." This trait is essential for successful adoption. The adoptive parents must understand that adoption gives them both the right and the responsibility to be the child's primary and permanent parent, and to act "as if the child were my own." During the family assessment, the caseworker must help the family assess the degree to which they believe they are entitled to parent an adopted child, and to educate them about the importance of developing this belief.

Category IX: "Hands–on" Parenting

A characteristic of successful adoptive families is often referred to as a "hands–on" style of parenting. The term "hands–on" was likely derived from "hands–on experience," which means someone rolling up his sleeves and doing a task, rather than watching, hearing, or reading about it. A "hands–on" parent is one who does things *with* the child, rather than instructing the child to do them. In behavior management vernacular, "hands–on" parents primarily use behavioral approaches to parenting, including: modeling desired behaviors; providing immediate and concrete positive reinforcement for success; shaping desired behaviors; cheering, directing, and coaching; and disciplining quickly and appropriately when needed. They are not afraid to be directive and controlling when it is necessary, and they often participate with the child in activities.

Many parents use child management strategies of a cognitive nature. They provide instruction by talking things through with the child. They give verbal direction, or provide the child with options, and encourage the child to think for herself. These are excellent strategies to develop a child's capacity to reason, to predict consequences, to make decisions, and ultimately, to develop responsible self–reliance. As exclusive or primary strategies, these are less often effective with children who have emotional and behavioral problems. Children with special needs often respond better to more directive, concrete, consistent parental interventions, and they often need the parent's support and involvement in managing even commonplace daily activities. An exploration of the parent's typical parenting style is essential during the adoptive family assessment. In addition, adoptive families should participate in training to help them further develop "hands–on" parenting strategies.

Category X: A "Lifelong" Commitment

A unique feature of adoption is its long–term, permanent nature. This is quite different from the short–term focus of most foster care. Adoptive families must be helped to consider the challenges that are likely to occur throughout the child's development, and to address these challenges. This is equally true for families adopting infants. Preparation must include a discussion of topics such as: identity issues common to adopted children during adolescence and young adulthood; sexual issues for children who have been sexually abused; reasonable expectations for emancipation of a child with special needs; issues related to search and possible reunion with members of the child's biological family; and the potential need to provide guidance and support well into the child's adulthood. It is useful for prospective families to talk with veteran adoptive families who are at various stages in the adoption life cycle, to help prospective families recognize the lifelong commitment that adoption requires, and to determine whether they can make such a commitment.

When foster caregivers want to adopt children in their homes, the family assessment focuses less on issues of family process, child management, and direct caregiving, and more on long–term planning. Many of the questions we usually ask during a family assessment can be easily answered by talking with the family about their experiences while caring for the child, and by observing their family interactions. However, we must help them prepare for the future by considering the changes that will occur with adoption, and help them to plan for these changes.

FAMILIES WHO SHOULD NOT ADOPT

There are several individual or family characteristics and traits that place children at high risk of physical, sexual, or emotional abuse, or neglect. While this is not an exhaustive list of all such traits, the presence of these factors should serve as strong indicators that the family should not adopt. These factors include:

- A prospective adoptive parent has a documented or very strongly suspected history of sexual abuse against a child; or, has a sexual control or conduct disorder, such as pedophilia, voyeurism, or exhibitionism. These put children at high risk of further abuse. The motivation of these prospective adoptive parents might very well be sexual gratification.

- A prospective adoptive parent is currently abusing or addicted to alcohol or other drugs. Current substance abuse by either parent creates a chaotic and unpredictable home environment that places children at risk. The home environment may also be unsafe due to drug trafficking activities, or neglect or abuse when parents are "high."

- A prospective adoptive parent currently has a severe mental illness or emotional disorder, which would interfere with his or her ability to meet the child's needs. Severe individual pathologies such as schizophrenia, paranoia, or severe mood disorders; compulsive disorders, such as compulsive gambling, spending, or eating disorders; personality disorders; or severe emotional problems, such as a volatile and explosive temper, can place children at risk of harm.

Several other family and personal conditions can potentially affect an individual's ability to parent an adopted child. However, these conditions may exist on a continuum from very severe to less serious, and the circumstances surrounding them often vary. Therefore, workers cannot rely on rigid and overgeneralized standards. A thorough, individualized assessment must be made of each prospective adoptive family. Our goal is to protect children, without inappropriately rejecting potential adoptive families.

These conditions include:

- A prospective adoptive parent has a prior history, either substantiated or strongly indicated, as a perpetrator of physical abuse or neglect against a child. This information is generally obtained through a prior involvement with a child welfare agency, from police reports, and from references. These situations require a thorough individual assessment to determine: the circumstances surrounding the alleged abuse or neglect; its scope and duration (whether it was a single, acute, event, or a chronic condition); whether the family structure has changed since the maltreatment occurred; whether the family successfully completed treatment; whether they have demonstrated a long period of effective parenting since treatment; and the potential risk in the family of future abuse or neglect, particularly in highly stressful situations. Extreme caution is always necessary, as workers must assure that children are not placed at risk of future maltreatment. However, we must consider that some allegations of child maltreatment are unfounded, and that with proper treatment, some people can develop the skills to safely nurture and care for their children.

- A prospective adoptive parent has a history of arrest and/or felony conviction. The history should be fully explored with the individual to determine the nature and severity of the offense(s); the length of time elapsed since it (they) occurred; the circumstances surrounding each offense; and the history of rehabilitation, including the use of constructive coping techniques at present. Many states and provinces have strict guidelines prohibiting approval of persons who have felony convictions, regardless of when the felony was committed. Each individual must be assessed within state or provincial guidelines.

- A prospective adoptive parent has a history of domestic violence and spousal abuse, either as a victim or a perpetrator. This should be fully explored to determine the scope of abuse, when it occurred, the duration, and the history of rehabilitation. Single, isolated instances are generally of less concern than long-term patterns.

- A prospective parent has a history of previous substance abuse or addiction, but is in recovery. If sobriety has been maintained without relapse for an extended period of time, especially under stressful conditions, the individual may be an appropriate adoptive parent. However, workers should consider whether prospective parents, who no longer abuse alcohol or drugs, still maintain a chaotic and dysfunctional lifestyle that is often typical of persons who abuse these substances. The caseworker should also help these individuals understand how the stress inherent in adoptive parenting might exacerbate their conditions, and contribute a relapse.

- A prospective adoptive parent has significant personal issues related to childhood victimization from physical abuse, sexual abuse, or neglect that would make it more difficult to appropriately deal with an adopted child's needs. Or, a prospective adoptive parent was a victim of sexual abuse, physical abuse, neglect, rejection, or abandonment, but believes these have been effectively worked through and resolved. Some people who were maltreated as children, but who have been able to overcome the impact of these experiences, may have the special insight and empathy to successfully parent a child who has been maltreated. However, current interpersonal and family relationships should not have been negatively affected by the person's history. The person must also be helped to understand how the behaviors, emotions, and attitudes of children who have been maltreated may resurrect old feelings and behaviors, particularly in stressful situations. Unresolved issues can restrict a parent's ability to respond appropriately to a child's behavior and needs. This must be carefully and individually assessed. The parent's history must also be considered in matching. It is generally safer to place a child whose history of maltreatment does not closely parallel that of the prospective adoptive parent.

- Parents who have overly rigid and unrealistic expectations for children's behavior may lead to overly strict enforcement, with severe consequences for noncompliance. Children's behaviors that do not conform to the family's values may be identified as "deviant" or "disturbed." In such families, children are often expected to deny their past history and identity, and to behave in ways rigidly prescribed by the adoptive family. (The caseworker must be able to accurately differentiate between overly rigid and unrealistic expectations, and the parents' ability to provide clear structure and well-defined, but reasonable and age-appropriate, limits.)

- People who had significant problems parenting their biological children may also have difficulty parenting an adopted child. However, some people learn from previous parenting experiences, and can use this knowledge to guide them through difficult times with an adopted child. The caseworker must carefully assess the source of the earlier parenting problems, and make an individual determination regarding the parent's abilities.

- A prior history of mental health problems should be fully assessed by the prospective adoptive parent and the caseworker. Many mental health and emotional problems are treatable. An example is clinical depression, which often can be well managed with medication. In addition, many people with emotional problems respond well to therapy, and having learned to manage or resolve their issues is often a strength. The prospective adoptive parent and caseworker should assess the nature of the applicant's mental health condition; the family's ability to use supportive mental health services; and how the family has coped with the applicant's condition. However, we must help families understand that the added stress of parenting a child with special needs may exacerbate the applicant's condition, or contribute to a relapse. The caseworker and family must also determine what types of children might be too stressful for the family.

- Significant interpersonal problems, such as an unstable marital or couple relationship, chronic conflict, and significant differences in the parents' motivation to adopt, will likely be exacerbated by adoption, creating a greatly increased risk of disruption. The child may exacerbate family conflict; or, the child may be scapegoated and blamed for the couple's problems. There is also an increased risk of disruption should a divorce or separation occur. Consequently, couples who are currently experiencing serious interpersonal discord should be disapproved or deferred.

Caseworkers must be realistic, however, when assessing the extent of discord in the parents' relationship. Healthy couples have disagreements and arguments. More important is how the parents handle dis-agreements, and whether they can develop constructive solutions. A couple that airs differences openly and negotiates mutually agreeable solutions will usually learn to manage conflicts resulting from the adoption.

Many prospective adoptive parents will feel uncomfortable discussing these problem areas. The caseworker must first establish a positive relationship with the parents, and must then use good interviewing, observation, and listening skills to elicit information, and to help parents objectively consider these issues.

When a prospective parent has a history of substance abuse, mental illness, or emotional disorders, it is often useful to obtain another professional opinion. The caseworker might request a release of information to obtain past records, or may ask the parent to undergo a substance abuse screening, or a psychological exam. When this is necessary, the agency should help find service providers who are culturally sensitive and acceptable to the family. Many agencies also require fingerprinting or police checks of all prospective adoptive families. The caseworker should explain the necessity of this to protect all children from those few families who might place children at high risk of harm.

The caseworker should always try to help families recognize when adoption is not in their own, or an adopted child's, best interests, and encourage them to self-select out. However, the caseworker must also be prepared to disapprove or defer families, where necessary, to prevent placement of children into circumstances that are unsafe or potentially destructive.

CULTURAL ISSUES IN THE ADOPTIVE FAMILY ASSESSMENT

Caseworkers must understand the impact of cultural differences on the adoptive family assessment. The caseworker must be aware of cultural attitudes, values, and beliefs to prevent misinterpreting the meaning of family members' behaviors, traits, and communications. Likewise, the caseworker must recognize how his own words, behaviors, or actions may be misinterpreted by the applicant.

There are many ways that cultural differences can affect a family assessment. For example, during the interview the caseworker may observe that the prospective adoptive parent avoids eye contact. The caseworker might conclude that the individual is not being truthful, or is embarrassed by the worker's questions. However, in the family's culture, diverting one's eyes may communicate deference and respect. Similarly, caseworkers may expect prospective adoptive families to be readily forthcoming with highly personal information. When they are not, the caseworker might conclude that they are withholding information or hiding something. However, some cultures place high value on privacy, and people from these cultures may be particularly guarded when dealing with persons outside their families, particularly persons in authority. Similarly, direct eye contact, touching, or aggressive interviewing by the caseworker may be threatening to family members, as can using a person's first name in a culture that views the use of first names by unrelated persons as disrespectful. These miscommunications may create a barrier to the development of the caseworker–family relationship.

In addition, specific words or phrases may have different meanings in differ-ent cultures. For instance, when describing family relationships in some cultures, the terms "cousin," "aunt," or "uncle" will refer to family members who are genet-ically related. In other cultures, this title may be given to persons who have close relationships with family members, regardless of their biological relatedness. A second example is the term, "okay," which can mean that something is good, or that everything is "status quo," or "tolerable." Differences in the meaning of words and phrases can greatly confound verbal communication.

All cultures have values that describe "good parenting." However, the particu-lar parenting behaviors that are valued in the prospective adoptive family's cul-ture may be different from those in the caseworker's culture. The caseworker must develop an understanding of the accepted child rearing beliefs and prac-tices in the family's culture, when helping the family assess their parenting strengths and vulnerabilities. The caseworker can also help families recognize when additional training or coaching in parenting strategies for children with special needs would be helpful. Most families can benefit from such assistance, either through parent education programs, or coaching from veteran adoptive families.

In general, the caseworker should consider the following when beginning an assessment of a family whose cultural background is different from the worker's:

- Family members may have different communication and interaction styles;

- Nonverbal behaviors, such as eye contact, body posture, and physical touch may have different meaning, and be interpreted differently among cultures;

- There are cultural differences in the use and meaning of specific words and phrases;

- The family structure, the nature of family relationships, and the particu-lar characteristics of the home environment may be determined by cul-tural variables;

- To prevent misunderstandings, to help establish a positive casework relationship, and to promote an accurate assessment, the caseworker must understand her own cultural background and biases, and their effects on her behavior and communications; and

- If the caseworker does not recognize culture as an issue, there is a high risk of misassessment.

(Refer to Chapter V, Culture and Diversity in Child Welfare Practice, for a more comprehensive discussion of cultural issues.)

THE IMPORTANCE OF PREPARATION

Preparation to become an effective adoptive parent is an essential part of the family assessment and subsequent preplacement activities. Thorough prepara-tion of the family greatly increases the likelihood of placement success. There are several critical issues that must be discussed and dealt with during adoption preparation, including:

- Issues related to infertility must be discussed with prospective adoptive parents who are unable to have biological children. They must come to terms with their feelings about infertility, and the effects these feelings may have on their relationship with each other and with an adopted child. If adoption is perceived as an inherently less desirable option, it may result in unmet parental expectations and disappointment, which increases the chance of disruption.

- Issues related to the applicant's "fantasy family" must be discussed. Every parent has fantasies and expectations for the parenting experience. This includes how they will feel, what they will gain, what their child will be like, and the changes the child will bring to their family. Particularly with first children, these fantasies are quickly tempered by reality (when their "even-tempered and happy" infant cries all night for the third night in a row.) Adoptive parents often fail to consider the effects of children's history of abuse, neglect, sexual victimization and multiple separations on their behavior and ability to form attachments. Consequently, the realities of adoption are often far different than the image in the parents' minds. Adoptive parents must be prepared for the disappointment and "second thoughts" that are common in adoption.

- It will take time to develop a parent–child relationship. Many adoptive parents expect "love at first sight," or a rapid bonding experience, as is typical with childbirth. However, as discussed earlier, adoption is far more analogous to marriage than to childbirth. The family and child are essentially strangers who must learn each other's ways of thinking and behaving, their likes and dislikes, habits, feelings, and idiosyncrasies, and then must make mutual adjustments. As such, the parent–child relationship can initially be superficial and uncomfortable. Generally, bonds and reciprocity are forged over time. Adoptive families must be helped to develop realistic expectations for the development of attachment.

- It will also take time for the child to adjust to a new environment, and for the family system to accommodate its new member. The adjustment period is likely to be stressful and uncomfortable at best, and disruptive and chaotic at worst. All members of the family will be struggling to assimilate new roles and responsibilities, and to re-establish the family's equilibrium. During this time, the entire family (including the adoptee) is likely to individually (and, often, secretly) question the advisability of continuing the adoption. It is important that families be prepared for these feelings, and be encouraged to express them. The caseworker must be prepared to respond in a constructive, supportive manner.

- Prospective adoptive parents must be helped to understand that their traditional methods of child management and parenting may not be effective with their adopted child. The adopted child may be unique and challenging. Suggestions and advice from friends and family members may be of little use. Adoptive parents must often learn and use a repertoire of new parenting techniques. Linking the new family with veteran adoptive families is an essential part of preparation.

•   Adopted children will always be biologically and psychologically part of "another family." Adoptive parents must learn to recognize and validate the importance of the child's biological family. Successful adoptive parents are able to learn to constructively deal with their child's feelings or fantasies about the biological family. This is equally true when the child was adopted in infancy. At various points in the developmental cycle, adopted children revisit and reconsider issues related to their biological family and the adoption. Ongoing attention to adoption issues is critical, if adopted children are to develop a stable identity and healthy self-esteem. Adoptive parents must be prepared to help children deal with these issues, probably throughout life.

POTENTIAL CONSEQUENCES OF INSUFFICIENT PREPARATION

Despite the obvious need for in–depth preparation, some agencies still fail to adequately prepare adoptive families. There are several likely repercussions.

Unprepared adoptive parents will likely have high or unrealistic expectations for the adoption experience, will anticipate a smooth transition, and will expect themselves to be competent parents. They will continue to believe that the child will have minimal problems, or that they have the skills to deal with them easily. They expect attachments to form quickly, and they believe that the child will be readily integrated into their family.

When their expectations are not met, and if their parenting strategies cannot prevent or resolve problems, the adoptive parents may experience disappointment and frustration. They may misinterpret the child's misbehavior as ingratitude, or as personal rejection. They may scapegoat and blame the child, or they may blame themselves, and perceive themselves to be inadequate.

The frustration, emotional pain, and conflict that result from unrealistic expectations greatly increase the likelihood of disruption, displacement, or dissolution. When this happens, the child must deal with another rejection. Disruption can often be prevented if agencies assure that adoptive families are carefully and thoroughly prepared for the adoption experience.

Application

RECRUITMENT STRATEGIES

Many agencies use outdated and inadequate strategies to recruit and assess prospective adoptive families. While space prohibits a lengthy discussion of effective recruitment strategies, the following steps will aid in the development of a successful recruitment program. Agencies must first answer three critical questions:

1) For what types of children are families being sought? What types of children are currently awaiting placement? What are their needs?

2) What are the characteristics needed in families to successfully parent these children?

3) Where can people with the necessary qualifications be found in the local community? How can the agency access such families? Can they be accessed through adoption exchanges?

The answers to these questions can guide the development of an annual recruitment plan. If a group of waiting children have a common characteristic (a history of sexual abuse; attention deficit hyperactive disorder, or ADHD; mental retardation; physical disabilities; or are teenagers), recruitment strategies should highlight that need, and target persons who may have, or can develop, the skills to parent that type of child. Unfortunately, many excellent potential families are overlooked. They include teachers, pediatric nurses, physical and occupational therapists, child care workers, juvenile court employees, veteran foster and adoptive parents and their extended families, day care providers, sports coaches, Big Brothers or Big Sisters, members of children's advocacy groups, scout leaders, religious education teachers, youth group leaders, and support groups for parenting and children's issues.

The formation of a joint community–agency advisory board is an important prerequisite to effective recruitment. Advisory board members can educate agency staff about community values, norms, and important issues. They can provide guidance in designing culturally sensitive grass roots recruitment strategies, and can help staff gain access to key community members. The board can also help identify resources, such as local newspapers, newsletters, and radio stations, in which to publicize the need for adoptive families, and they can identify appropriate sites for special events.

Suggested members for an advisory board would include ordained and lay ministers; local day care, preschool, or school teachers; day care or teachers' aides; members of service organizations (such as Lions, Kiwanis, and neighborhood groups); small business owners; medical professionals and aides who serve children; city and local government personnel; human service professionals;

police and fire department personnel; radio, television, or newspaper reporters; veteran foster, adoptive, and kinship care parents; biological families; and adult adoptees. Adoption workers and other agency staff members should also participate, as every agency staff member is a potential recruiter of adoptive families. Representatives from minority communities can help access leaders and recruit families from those communities.

An annual strategic recruitment plan should be developed. Recruitment activities require considerable lead time for planning, preparation, and public relations. Agencies generally plan budget expenditures annually, and funds to support recruitment efforts must often be approved a year in advance.

Most child welfare agencies struggle continuously with budget constraints. Recruitment strategies should maximize the use of existing, low cost resources. This can be done in the following ways:

- *Use as many free media events as possible.* Most local radio and television stations and newspapers have a "community bulletin board," where public service announcements (PSAs) can be made at no cost. Newsletters of churches and other organizations (PTAs, labor unions, support groups, etc.) will often print information of interest to their members without cost. Newspapers will frequently print human interest stories regarding foster care and adoption in their Sunday editions. This is particularly likely during National Foster Care Month (May) and National Adoption Month (November). Libraries, churches, schools, and public buildings may have display cases or bulletin boards that can be reserved for up to a month.

- *Work with advisory board members to secure free or reduced cost goods and services.* Advisory board members may know people in the community who would donate or reduce the price on goods, such as paper products, novelties, or refreshments, or services, such as printing, public relations, space use, and entertainment.

- *Piggyback on existing events.* Holding a special event requires a large expenditure of time, money, and staff resources. Therefore, special recruitment events should occur no more than two to three times a year. Instead, staff should identify events or holidays that can be used to publicize the need for adoptive families. Mother's Day and Father's Day are excellent examples. Both holidays are well established and high profile in almost all communities. The agency could place a "Mother's Day Card" or "Father's Day Card" in the newspaper or on a billboard, thanking all foster and adoptive mothers or fathers. A human interest story could highlight several adoptive families and their experiences. During summer months, festivals and fairs provide an opportunity to generate direct contact with diverse groups of people. In the fall, fliers could be sent home with school children as part of a PTA newsletter. Of course, National Adoption Month, in November, is a great opportunity to highlight special needs adoption success stories.

One underutilized strategy is to involve foster and adoptive parents as recruiters. They are often excellent resources. They have firsthand knowledge of the system, and of caring for children with special needs, and they are a credible source of information to other parents. Veteran families could be asked to identify five potential adoptive families, and talk with them about the possibility of adopting. The adoption recruiter could follow up where indicated. Veteran families could also host a house party, where friends or neighbors could be introduced to the concept of adoption in a more personal and relaxed atmosphere. Veteran families can become very powerful spokespersons for adoption in newspaper articles, radio call–in shows or TV spots. They can also accompany agency staff to speaking engagements and provide information about adoptive family life.

The use of foster and adoptive parents as recruiters is also an effective strategy to recruit families from minority cultures. Successful adopters can not only help other minority families negotiate the formal system, but can help agency staff become more sensitive and responsive to the needs of families.

Agencies often fail to recognize the need to be culturally sensitive in the development and implementation of their recruitment plans. For example, the media used in recruitment campaigns may not be widely accessed by people in certain communities. The logos and slogans used may not be meaningful to certain groups of people. Agency practices and policies may present barriers to adoption for certain people, and agency practices may be discriminatory. Bureaucratic policies and procedures, application forms, and formal interviews may be barriers to many families. Or, people who have experienced racism and discrimination in the past may perceive agency practices as prejudiced or racist, whether accurate or not, particularly when the authority vested in the agency and its staff is considered. As a result, many agencies have difficulty recruiting and retaining families from minority cultural groups. To be effective, agencies must adopt proactive, culturally competent, and community–specific recruitment strategies. This includes both the utilization of outreach and community–based recruitment strategies, and eliminating barriers to adoption by families from minority cultures.

Recruiters should maintain a high profile in local neighborhoods in which recruitment is being conducted. Face-to-face contact is essential. Speaking engagements should be arranged with as many churches, community organizations, neighborhood centers, schools, clubs, and social service organizations as possible. Adoption staff may have limited time for such presentations. Therefore, adoptive parents, advisory board members, and other agency staff might be organized into a speaker's bureau. Every speaker should be well prepared with accurate information, answers to potential questions, and agency literature. Direct contact by people within their own communities also helps reduce some of the barriers to recruitment of families from minority cultures. The bureaucratic nature of many agencies, including rigidly scheduled appointments held at the agency, lengthy application forms, strict procedures and regulations, and formal interviews may be interpreted by many people, particularly persons from minority cultures, as distancing, impersonal, and insensitive. Outreach and informal discussions with prospective adoptive families can help reduce many of these barriers.

Each neighborhood or community should receive information about adoption in various print media two to three times per year. These can include posters or fliers in grocery stores, barber and beauty shops, restaurants, merchant shops, car washes, laundromats, schools, churches, neighborhood centers, at bus stops and on buses, at sporting events, and during school activities such as plays and music programs. Restaurants can be asked to use specially designed placemats, provided by the agency, for a two-week period. Fliers and notices can also be hung on doors or affixed to home-delivered foods, such as pizza.

Using the media effectively is essential. While some media coverage can be obtained at no cost, many agencies may have to contract for additional advertising. The use of TV, radio, and newspapers as a recruitment tool can be powerful, if used effectively. However, staff must always consider who the agency is trying to reach when planning a media campaign. Consequently, what newspaper to use, where to place the ad, and how to word it may vary greatly, depending on the intended audience. Likewise, the development and scheduling of television and radio public service announcements should consider the demographics of targeted populations. The use of media targeted to minority communities enhances success in reaching this audience.

Print media, including brochures, fliers and posters, should avoid communicating inappropriate messages. Too often, agencies use recruitment strategies that misrepresent reality, including depicting the waiting children as healthy infants or young children. Slogans such as, "Do you have a little extra love to share?" may mislead many people to believe that the adoption of a child with special needs is a simple task. Consequently, recruitment may create inquiries, but the families who make contact with the agency may not always be interested in children with special needs, and they may not be appropriate as adoptive families.

Photographs and text in brochures and other publicity fliers should reflect accurate images of children with special needs. Strategies might include highlighting the challenges and rewards of adoptive parenting ("In our family, one small step is a very big deal!"); stressing the importance of helping children achieve permanence; or joining a "community" of adoptive families who, together, advocate for children with special needs. Photographs should also represent a variety of children and families of different ages, composition, and from multiple cultural and racial backgrounds.

Every contact with the agency by a potential adoptive parent must be viewed as an opportunity to recruit. Recruitment campaigns generate inquiries. This is the point where many agencies fail to capitalize on their recruitment efforts. The staff person who handles inquiries must be well-informed about the adoption process, and must demonstrate a high degree of patience and sensitivity. The staff person must address each caller's questions and concerns in a warm and open manner, while informing the caller about basic requirements. Callers should be invited to attend an orientation session to obtain further information. At times, even if callers do not meet basic requirements, they may know other people who do. A caller's first impression of the agency is the first step towards the development of a collaborative relationship. If this contact is handled improperly, it is also the point at which potential families may be discouraged from continuing.

Application materials should never be mailed to prospective families in response to an inquiry. The paper work can be overwhelming, and may create a significant barrier for families. It also communicates that the agency is a bureaucratic institution, rather than an organization that is responsive to people. Typically, formal application forms should be given to prospective adoptive parents only after they have attended an orientation or preservice training session, during which time they receive more complete and accurate information about adoption. Prospective parents can then complete the forms after having made an informed decision to continue the process. This also enables them to be more realistic in their responses. The adoption caseworker should go over the forms with the parents in person, and be certain they understand how to complete them, or the forms should be completed together during a home visit.

The written application materials generally include: the application form; a financial form; health and medical information; a police check; reference forms; and questions to help the agency determine, in general terms, the type of child the family is seeking. The written materials may also contain questionnaires or homework assignments that help family members gain insight into the realities of adoption, while simultaneously initiating the family assessment. For example, application packets often ask prospective adoptive parents to prepare a written or oral autobiography or self-study. These can help the caseworker get to know the family; raise important issues; stimulate discussion; and provide insight into the applicant's attitudes, values, and past experiences.

ORIENTATION AND PRESERVICE TRAINING

Orientation and preservice training are the next steps in preparing adoptive families. The five primary goals of orientation and preservice training are:

1) To provide families with essential information about the adoption process and the realities of adoptive parenting;

2) To maintain the momentum of recruitment by motivating families to continue exploring and considering adoption;

3) To help families begin the self-assessment and self-selection process;

4) To allow caseworkers to begin to get to know and interact with families within a group setting; and

5) To strengthen participants' positive opinions of the agency and its services, thereby improving public relations and the ability of the agency to provide adoption services to the community.

Orientation and preservice training educate prospective families about child welfare and adoption. Sessions should educate families regarding the types and needs of children who are available for adoption; the dynamics of abuse and neglect in the children's histories; the potential challenges faced by most adoptive families; and the rewards of adoptive parenting. The key word in effective preservice training is "basic." Many agencies, particularly those that do not have ongoing training programs for adoptive families, feel compelled to teach prospective adoptive parents "everything they need to know" during the preservice program. Family members cannot assimilate such in-depth information during preservice, and they often become overwhelmed. It is more important that they get sufficient information to make an informed decision about pursuing the formal application and family assessment process.

Preservice training initiates the self-selection process. This goal should be clearly communicated to prospective families prior to beginning the training. Throughout the course of the training, participants should be reminded and encouraged to ask themselves, "Does this fit for me? Do I want to do this? Can I do this? What do I need to help me do this?" The content of the classes should raise critical issues, confront basic values, and explore participants' level of commitment to adoption. Consequently, class sessions should provide straightforward information, and generate open and candid discussion. By the final session, most participants will have sufficient information to make an informed decision to either proceed or withdraw.

It may appear that the goals of maintaining motivation to continue the adoption process, and also helping some families self-select out of the process, are at cross purposes. We must remember that recruitment and orientation activities work best when they simultaneously motivate most families to continue, while encouraging inappropriate families to self-select out of the program.

Preservice training also creates an opportunity to gather information to be discussed during the family assessment. An applicant's responses in large or small group activities can provide important insights, which can then be reviewed and further discussed during family assessment interviews. Some families may be more comfortable asking questions or sharing issues in a group setting, whereas a one-on-one "assessment" interview may promote a socially acceptable or expected response.

Preservice activities are also an important public relations event for the agency. Participation in preservice develops impressions of the agency, its staff, and its programs. These will be carried back to the participants' communities, schools, churches, neighborhoods, work places, friends, and families. Even if prospective families ultimately choose not to adopt, a positive word to extended family members or co-workers could motivate others to consider adopting.

Preservice training can be scheduled prior to beginning a family assessment, or it can be integrated as part of the assessment. For some agencies, it can be both. The "preservice first" format is usually 12 to 18 hours in length, generates large groups, and serves as a positive public relations event for the agency. The limitations of this approach are that it does not offer in-depth training, and families cannot immediately consider and apply this information to their own situation.

When preservice training incorporates the family assessment, there is an initial group orientation, after which more intensive training is combined with an individual or group family assessment. The length of the training increases to as many as 24 to 30 hours, and participants are given homework assignments to be discussed with their caseworker during assessment home visits. Participation in large and small group discussions also generates topics for discussion with the assessment caseworker. A coordinated and integrated educational and assessment process results. For some families, however, this format may be too intense, and may not provide sufficient room to weigh and consider their interest prior to committing to a formal family assessment. They may drop out.

XI.A. Preparing Adoptive Families for Children with Special Needs

Finally, some agencies offer training after the families have completed the individual family assessment. Training offered at this point can be in more depth, and the class size will generally be smaller, which promotes the transfer of knowledge and skills. Basic information will have been provided during the family assessment process by the caseworker. The length of postassessment training may be from 24 to 40 hours. However, in this model, since prospective adoptive families do not attend training until after the family assessment, they may participate in the assessment without having essential information to make an informed decision of whether or not to adopt.

Clearly, each of these models has its benefits and liabilities. Agencies should select the format that best suits their purposes, needs, and resources. For example, an agency that needs to "jump start" its recruitment and public relations efforts may plan a preservice program that orients and trains prospective adoptive families before the assessment process is begun. This allows the agency to be in contact with the largest number of individuals from the community in a single event. If an agency is focusing on the recruitment and preparation of a small group of targeted families, the agency might use a preservice program that is conducted simultaneously with the assessment process. Agencies might also consider a sequential training program that provides more general information to a large group during an orientation phase; targeted information during the family assessment to facilitate the assessment process; and finally, more in–depth skills training for approved families specific to issues of child management, stress management, and other topics to help families during the adjustment phase during and after placement.

Training sessions should be scheduled to be convenient for families. Sessions can be on consecutive weekdays, weeknights, or Saturdays. Larger urban agencies may offer more than one class at a time. To make preservice training more available to prospective adoptive families in smaller and rural communities, agencies should consider collaborating and combining preservice training sessions.

Preservice training should include basic content on the following areas:

- An overview of adoption, the adoption process, and the role and function of the child welfare agency

- How adoption affects the adoptive family

- Teamwork and using community resources

- The role and importance of the biological parent

- Attachment and separation issues

- Normal child development and the impact of abuse/neglect

- Parenting the sexually abused child

- Discipline and behavior management

- Talking with a child about adoption

- Adoptive parent/child issues

- Subsidy and legal issues

The training should be conducted using a variety of teaching modalities, including presentation, discussion, large and small group activities, videos, over-head transparencies, other visuals, role play, case examples, experiential exercises and guest speakers. Using panels of adoptees, biological parents and veteran adoptive and foster parents are an effective way to communicate important information and expose trainees to "real life" experiences. This helps to validate the training content for trainees.

The preservice trainers must be skilled in both the delivery of content and in group facilitation. Preservice sessions often trigger discussion of underlying personal issues. Some of the issues may reflect strongly held values, such as the belief that adoption success is enhanced by secrecy and denial of the child's prior life. The trainer must tactfully and skillfully handle these challenges. Trainers should receive formalized instruction in adult education, presentation and group management skills, curriculum development, and use of audio–visuals.

THE IN–DEPTH FAMILY ASSESSMENT

When conducted effectively, the family assessment is a mutual assessment by the family and their caseworker of the family's capability to parent an adopted child. The objectives of the family assessment are:

1. To determine the prospective adoptive family's individual and collective strengths and limitations;

2. To assess the family's level of understanding of the preservice training content and its impact on their attitudes, values, and beliefs;

3. To help the prospective parents identify past or current issues, personality characteristics, and behaviors which would significantly impact their ability to parent an adopted child;

4. To continue the family's education and orientation regarding the adoption of children with special needs;

5. To further develop the collaborative relationship between the family and the caseworker/agency;

6 To determine what types of children the family could most effectively adopt, and the types of children the family should not adopt;

7. To provide the family with continued opportunities for education and self–selection; and

8. To document that the family meets the agency's minimum requirements for adoptive parents.

There are several models by which the goals of the family assessment can be met. Many agencies use an individual approach, where the family assessment is conducted jointly by the caseworker and family members. This includes a series of personal interviews with family members, both as a group and in individual sessions.

The self-study, discussed earlier, provides an opportunity for prospective adoptive parents to evaluate and explore their own attitudes, values, beliefs, and goals. This can be accomplished through the use of questionnaires, surveys, or some form of autobiography. The questionnaires generally ask about the applicant's desire to adopt, their past experiences with parenting, their childhoods, and their current relationships with spouse, children, their own parents and siblings, and other extended family members. People who may be shy, or who lack verbal ability, often appreciate the opportunity to express their ideas and thoughts on paper. However, some may view the self-study as a "test," in which they must provide the right answers. If people are not comfortable writing, they could instead be asked to record their thoughts using a tape recorder. If a self-study format is used, the purpose of this activity must be clear, and prospective adoptive parents must understand that honesty can prevent serious problems later.

The following are examples of questions in an adoptive family self-study:

- What are your reasons for wanting to adopt a child?

- What do you consider your most important strengths as a person? As a parent?

- Briefly describe your own family and your development as a child. What experiences most influenced who you are today?

- How did your parents handle discipline problems? Do you feel that they did a good job? What do you do differently?

- All adopted children have a biological family. How might you feel about your child's request to make contact with them?

- How do you and your spouse manage disagreements? What types of things do you typically disagree about in the area of child rearing? How have you dealt with these issues?

- What type of child and what kinds of problems do you think you are best suited to handle? What do you think would be hard for you? What do you *know* you couldn't handle?

The self-study can stimulate dialogue among family members themselves, as well as with their assessment caseworker, and can raise issues for further discussion during assessment interviews.

Some agencies use group assessment meetings. In this format, families are convened in small groups to receive basic orientation and education about adoption, to receive answers to questions and concerns, to review agency policies and procedures, and to use this information in assessing their personal strengths and vulnerabilities. The participants are often given homework assignments from the group sessions.

Both the individual and group approaches have benefits and limitations. The individual family assessment supports the development of a collaborative relationship between the caseworker and the family. The interviews permit the caseworker to help families explore individual and family issues in greater depth. However, some families feel considerable pressure during these interviews, and may be inclined to provide "the right answer," rather than an honest response. This is more true if the caseworker has not first developed a relationship with the family and alleviated the family's anxiety about the assessment. When an individual family assessment is used exclusively, prospective adoptive families are often isolated, which denies them the opportunity to establish relationships with other adoptive parents and to benefit from their questions and experiences.

A group setting can be less threatening to some families, and may help them feel more relaxed and comfortable. Consequently, they may respond more honestly, which enhances the assessment process. Prospective adoptive parents can also develop relationships with each other, and can serve as an informal support system in the future. However, some people are shy in groups, and may not openly participate. And, the group approach does not permit the exploration of an individual family's concerns and issues to any depth.

Optimally, the integration of several strategies generates a holistic and comprehensive assessment, with the family actively participating in the entire process. For example, family members might attend an initial orientation meeting in a large group to learn basic information about adoption and the agency. Families who do not meet basic requirements, or who do not want to pursue adoption, can be helped to self-select out. Remaining families would then proceed to preservice training. Basic application forms would be distributed and reviewed during preservice training. Preservice training classes would help families begin the self-assessment process. At the midpoint of the training, prospective families would be assigned to an assessment caseworker, who would conduct the individual family assessment interviews while the families are completing their preservice training. This would permit the caseworker to assess family members' understanding and retention of information from the training. Homework assignments given in class would be forwarded to the caseworker to use in generating discussion with family members. The preservice training group could also be formalized into an adoptive family support group, which could continue to meet for additional training, and for mutual support after children have been placed in their homes. In some agencies, a support group is also formed for some of the children placed in these families. Meetings give them an opportunity to talk with others about their needs, feelings, and adjustment issues. In some cases, the families and the adoptees meet together to deal with postplacement issues. (Refer to Section XI-E, "Postplacement and Postlegalization Services to Adoptive Families.")

Home Visits and Assessment Interviews

The adoptive family assessment must include face-to-face contacts with all family members in accordance with these basic guidelines:

- There should be a minimum of four to six contacts with family members, in addition to group sessions. Several of the interviews should include all family members. At least one individual interview should be held with each parent or adult caregiver. The parents/adult caregivers should be interviewed together at least once. When single parents have a "significant other," it is important to involve this person in the family assessment, as he or she is likely to have a high degree of involvement with the child. The caseworker should also talk with others residing in the home, such as extended family members, children, room‑mates, and nonblood "relatives." The caseworker should talk with the children in the home individually to assess their under‑standing of adoption, and to identify any potential problems.

- Generally, the family interviews should take place in the family's home. However, when more convenient for family members, or to provide more privacy, individual or joint interviews could be scheduled at the worker's office. Some families may not be comfortable coming to the worker's office, and for some families, transportation and child care may be problem. Then, the caseworker might consider using a local commu‑nity center, an office at the church, or other community locations.

The family assessment should be structured to generate discussion that addresses the following:

- To help the prospective parents understand their motivation to adopt, and to explore how this decision evolved;

- Where appropriate, to determine the parents' attitudes and feelings about their infertility, and to understand their perceptions about child‑birth versus adoption;

- To understand the parents' attitudes, values, beliefs, and experiences related to children and parenting;

- To identify the feelings of extended family members and family friends regarding adoption;

- To help parents determine their strengths, and their areas of vulnerabil‑ity, and to explore how these would affect the types of children they should and should not adopt;

- To understand the nature of the family's social network, and their involvement in their community;

- To help family members gain knowledge and insight regarding the adoption of a child with special needs (behavioral dynamics, challenges, attachment process, needs, internal and external resources);

- To help family members assess their expectations of themselves, the adopted child, and the agency;

- To help families anticipate problems and consider potential solutions; and

- To help the caseworker identify conditions and behaviors that might preclude a prospective family from being approved.

Assessment Interviewing Strategies

Regardless of the strategies used to conduct the family assessment, expert inter‑viewing and assessment skills are essential for the assessment caseworker. A combination of open‑ended, supportive, and clarifying responses, as well as direct questions where needed, are most effective in generating information and helping both the caseworker and the family members develop relevant insights. Direct questioning of family members is the least effective method of interviewing for a family assessment, even if the questions themselves are relevant. The following case example illustrates the limitations of direct questions.

JENNY AND KEVIN PARSONS

Jenny and Kevin Parsons, ages 27 and 28, have applied to the Oak County child welfare agency adoption program. They have been married for six years, and have been unsuccessful in conceiving a child. Kevin is an activities director at a local neighborhood center, and Jenny works as a dental hygienist. Despite their two incomes, they are unable to afford the private adoption of an infant. They have come to the agency in hopes of adopting a preschool child. It is obvious to agency staff that the Parsons are very anxious about the adoption process. They have tried to be "the perfect applicants," demonstrated by their early arrival for preservice training classes, their typed (and quickly returned) autobiographies, and their frequent phone calls to the caseworker to make sure they have "met all of the agency's expectations."

During the first home visit and interview, their caseworker prepared and asked the following questions. The parents' answers are in italics.

Why do you want to adopt?

(*We love children and can't have any of our own. We want a family.*)

Do you think you could love an adopted child as much as your own child?

(*Yes, I'm sure we could.*)

Will you tell the child she is adopted?

(*Yes.*)

If your child wanted to meet his biological parents, would you help him?

(*Yes, when he reaches age 18.*)

Do you have a stable marriage?

(*Yes. We've been happily married for six years.*)

Do you believe that you have resolved your infertility issues?

(*Yes.*)

Are there any behavior problems you feel you may have
trouble handling?

(*No.*)

During a follow-up case conference, the caseworker related the results of the interview to the supervisor. The supervisor inquired about the couple's strengths and limitations, and what that meant about the types of children the Parsons could potentially parent. The caseworker was unable to respond to her supervisor's questions, and realized that her interview with the Parsons had been superficial and uninformative.

More accurate and comprehensive information can be obtained by more open-ended questions that assess family members' actual life experiences. For example, the caseworker could help the family assess the flexibility of their family roles by asking:

How were household responsibilities divided in your family of origin? Between your parents? Among the children?

How do you divide your household responsibilities now? How do you feel about this arrangement?

Has there ever been an occasion when you had to "fill in" for your spouse? Do someone else's job? How did you feel about that?

Case examples or vignettes can also be used to elicit attitudes, values, and beliefs. They can help the caseworker assess family members' understanding and retention of concepts and issues learned in preservice training. The "case study" strategy presents hypothetical situations, and asks family members to respond to them. If used correctly, these can be valuable assessment tools.

However, prospective adoptive families are often expected to provide information about situations with which they have no prior experience. This is particularly true if the prospective adoptive families are childless, or this is their first adoption experience. Their answers are then likely to be stereotyped, formulated to please the caseworker, or simply based on speculation. For example, questions like, "If your child sexually acted out, how would you handle it?" or, "If your child was caught stealing, how would you discipline him?" do not always elicit relevant, or accurate, information.

The Parsons' assessment caseworker, with the coaching of her supervisor, developed some case scenarios and relevant questions to promote discussion. She took these to the second interview with the family, and presented the following scenario to them:

Your child is six years old. She joined your family at age five.

Today, you were called by the school because your child stole another child's lunch money. When you come home after work, you confront your child. She gets angry and screams, "You can't yell at me, you're not my *real* mom (or dad)!!!. I wish I could go back to them. Leave me alone!!!" The child runs to her bedroom and slams the door.

The follow-up questions were designed to tap the family's past experiences with similar situations, rather than asking the family to hypothetically project what they might do in this situation at some time in the future. The questions included the following:

1. Why do children steal? Have you ever had to deal with stealing at work or home? How did you feel about it? How did you handle it?

2. What might have caused such an angry reaction in the child? How do you handle angry co-workers? Patients? Clients? How does their anger affect you?

3. What made the child bring up her adoption at this point? How would an adoptive parent feel being told, "You're not my real parent"? In the past, when you have had your feelings hurt, how did you react? How did you handle your feelings?

The caseworker was amazed at the discussion that was generated. She and the family were also aware of the amount of insight they had gained about Kevin and Jenny's strengths, limitations, attitudes, values, and beliefs.

Both had handled stealing problems with children. Kevin caught a boy trying to conceal sports equipment in a gym bag. Jenny discovered that a young child had taken her mirror from the dental tool tray. Both agreed that confronting the children and discovering their motives was critical. Kevin had discovered that the boy did not have any toys at home to play with, and that his family routinely "borrowed" things they needed. Jenny stated that the four year old thought that she could take the mirror for a "good girl" prize. The child was accustomed to picking a small prize from a basket for cooperating with the dental exam. Jenny said it was a misunderstanding, but the girl's mother took the time to explain to the child about stealing.

Jenny and Kevin had also dealt with their own and other peoples' anger. They related numerous anecdotes of confrontations they had been involved in. Jenny felt that the child in the case example had become angry because she had been caught and would be disciplined. Kevin remembered that the trainer told them that anger in adopted children was often colored by their past history of abuse, frustration, fear, or grief. He suggested that perhaps the child was afraid of being abused again for "being bad." Jenny agreed, said that it made sense to her, and then wondered if the child might also be afraid of being rejected.

The Parsons were initially unsure why the child in the example would bring up adoption at this time, but they both felt that any adoptive parent would be hurt and upset by the child's comment. When prompted, both described experiences of being hurt by friends and family. Kevin stated that he would forget about it and act as if nothing had happened. Jenny, on the other hand, stated that it sometimes took her a while to get over being hurt, and that her relationship with the person who had hurt her would be temporarily strained. She found that talking directly to the person helped her the most.

The caseworker decided to help the Parsons stretch their thinking and begin to relate their past experiences to adoption issues. Using strategies her supervisor had demonstrated, the caseworker asked Kevin and Jenny to think of times they might have said things they really didn't mean as a way of testing another person. Jenny blushed and giggled, and said that early in their marriage, in a fight about Kevin's long work hours, she had said to him, "If you feel that way, maybe you don't really want to be married any more." She related that Kevin had wisely told her, "Of course I want to be married. This has nothing to do with our marriage. It has to do with my career." Jenny realized that she had been feeling threatened by his commitment to his job, and had been asking him to reassure her of his love and commitment to her. Then she said, "I suppose that adopted children might feel that same sense of insecurity." The caseworker commended Jenny for her insight, and told her that understanding children's feelings would be a valuable strength in learning to manage their difficult behaviors.

The caseworker then asked, if that were the case with the child in the scenario, what would they say to the child? Kevin said he'd give the child a chance to cool off, then try to talk to her and make sure she understood that this was only about stealing, and not about whether she was going to stay in their family. He would reassure her that she was in their home to stay, and that he loved her and would not hurt her, but they had to work out a solution to the stealing problem. Jenny agreed that this would be a good strategy. The caseworker suggested they might also involve the child in working out a fair and nonharmful consequence for her behavior, and told them they would learn more about this in their preservice session on discipline.

After the home visit, the caseworker felt that she had a better understanding of Kevin and Jenny, and she felt that many of their life experiences were strengths that would assist them in adoption. The caseworker was impressed with their interactions with children, despite being a childless couple. The caseworker was also able to help them identify further training needs regarding the dynamics of adoption, and children's perceptions of being an adoptee.

ADOPTION APPROVAL

Because the family assessment is a collaborative process, the formal approval will evolve as part of the family assessment discussions. In most cases, there will be no surprises. Families with obvious limitations will have been helped to self-select or counseled out of the process. Discussions of the family's strengths and vulnerabilities will have resulted in a joint decision about the types of children they should and should not adopt. The final phase of the family assessment is to formalize the conclusions drawn from the family assessment, and to plan next steps. The caseworker must again review all of the applicant's information to identify inconsistencies, vague or unclear statements, or missing information. These should be explored and clarified with the family before proceeding with formal approval.

Formal approval is supported with documentation gathered during the assessment process. The findings and conclusions of the family assessment should be written into a formal family assessment report, which becomes a permanent part of the family's record. The caseworker should also record the age, sex, number, and types of children the family is best suited to parent, and those that the family should not parent. The family should receive notification of formal approval in writing.

In some cases, the caseworker will determine that despite the family's completion of the family assessment, they are not ready for adoption at this time. Reasons could include a serious illness in the family, an unexpected pregnancy, or other situation that involves high levels of stress. Or, it may be due to other conditions, which may or may not be resolvable. For example, if a family cannot realistically assess their potential to adopt because they have had no experience with children, the caseworker might recommend they defer their application and gain additional experience. They might volunteer at a children's recreation center, lead a scout troop or sports team, become a Big Brother or Big Sister, teach religious education classes, or volunteer as a classroom aide at a local school. The caseworker should discuss the relevant issues with each family being deferred, and explain that when their situation is more conducive to adoption, they can reactivate their application. The caseworker should provide the family with written documentation of this decision.

In some cases, the caseworker will have to formally reject a family that is not suitable to adopt. While it is hoped that the caseworker and family could reach this conclusion jointly during the family assessment, at times this does not occur, and the caseworker must deny the family's application. The caseworker should provide the family with written documentation of this decision, and clearly state the criteria for rejection. The family may need to be helped to understand the decision and deal with their disappointment.

Rejecting or deferring prospective families is a difficult task for most adoption workers, particularly when they have worked closely with the family for a significant period of time. They empathize with the family's disappointment and feelings of hopelessness. However, workers must recognize that their role is to recruit and prepare adoptive families who are capable of providing a stable and loving permanent home for a child. The following suggestions will assist the caseworker in rejecting or deferring prospective adoptive families:

- Raise concerns and issues early in the family assessment process, and continue to discuss them throughout.

- Help family members understand how these factors would be detrimental to children with special needs, and potentially detrimental to their family, if they adopted at this time.

- Give family members a very clear and honest explanation of why they are being rejected or deferred, and support these explanations with specific examples.

- Help them identify resources to resolve their issues and problems, such as marital or family counseling, or treatment for substance abuse. Help the family access these services.

The caseworker must remember that rejecting or deferring a prospective family will likely prevent an adoption disruption or dissolution for a child in the future, and may help some families develop into potential resources at a later time.

Case Examples

The following case examples depict three families who have applied to adopt children with special needs. They have all expressed interest in a school–age child. The first family, Robert and Elizabeth Clarke, appear to be excellent candidates for adoption, based upon preliminary information. However, a more thorough assessment suggests that they may need to make significant changes in their lifestyle to effectively parent a child with special needs. The second prospective adoptive parent is Marjorie Marks, a single parent, whose preliminary information suggests several potential problems. However, a more comprehensive assessment identifies numerous strengths that are not immediately evident. The third family, James and Betty Chambers, have both strengths and limitations that are apparent at the time of assessment, and that should be considered in determining the type of child who should be placed with them.

The information recorded below was gathered during the screening and orientation process, from written application materials, and from the initial in–home interviews with the parents. The families had attended several preservice training sessions as well. While the following information is not comprehensive, it provides relevant data to begin to help assess each family's suitability and readiness to adopt a child with special needs. Further discussion and assessment would be necessary to identify the types of children each family could best parent, and to begin to prepare them for the adoption experience.

🕺 Robert and Elizabeth Clarke

Robert and Elizabeth Clarke, an African American couple, have applied to adopt a child of either sex between the ages of five and nine. The Clarkes have been married for 12 years. Mr. Clarke is 33 years old. He has a master's degree in electrical engineering, and is currently employed by IBM in the research department. He enjoys stamp and coin collecting, and is an avid fan of old movies. Mrs. Clarke is 32 years old and has just completed her master's degree in nursing. She is Head Nurse in the neurology intensive care unit at the local medical center. She enjoys sewing, making pottery, and studying African art and classical music. The Clarkes are very stable financially, have a combined annual income of $127,000, and have planned well for their retirement. They enjoy travel, and have taken vacations to Europe, China, Japan, and Kenya. They are active in their church and family–both sets of in–laws reside within one hour's drive. Mr. Clarke was an only child, and Mrs. Clarke was the youngest child of two children. Her parents were in their middle forties when she was born. Her sister, who is 16 years older, lives in another state.

On their application the Clarkes indicate they are unable to conceive a child, and they waited to adopt until they were settled in their careers and financially secure. They feel they can offer a child an education, financial security, and "lots of love and attention."

The caseworker arranged a home visit with the Clarkes. The visit was scheduled during the evening to accommodate their work schedules. When the caseworker arrived at the home, Mr. Clarke apologized that Mrs. Clarke would be late due to an emergency in the intensive care unit. He stated that he was usually the one who was late coming home from work.

Mr. Clarke offered to show the caseworker their home while they waited for Mrs. Clarke. The home was spacious, immaculate, and had been carefully decorated with antique furniture and lovely oriental rugs. When the caseworker asked if they had hired a professional decorator, Mr. Clarke stated that Mrs. Clarke had done it all herself. He said she put a great deal of time and energy into the home, and was very proud of it. Mr. Clarke showed the caseworker his home office. It was a neatly organized with a computer, bookcases filled with books, filing cabinets, and a drafting table. Mr. Clarke said he often brought work home from the office when there was a tight deadline.

Mrs. Clarke arrived home shortly thereafter. She was a petite, well-dressed woman who looked younger than her 32 years. She apologized for being late, and stated that there had been a staff shortage and she had to fill in. She said it had been a tough day, filled with staff and patient problems, and that she was looking forward to putting her feet up.

The caseworker asked the Clarkes why they wanted to adopt. Mrs. Clarke quickly answered that she liked children and had always wanted a family. When asked about her "fantasy family," she said she wanted one or two children whom she could teach new things, and she would love to have a child to share her hobbies and interests. She said she liked helping people, and had a lot of patience, and she felt that would make her a good parent. The caseworker asked Mr. Clarke for his input. He stated that he had considered parenthood from time to time and hadn't been ready before now. But, he thought he was old enough and settled enough to give it a try. He believed he, too, had a lot to offer a child, and he supported Mrs. Clarke in her desire to have a family. Both the Clarkes felt that they could give a child a good education, as they lived in one of the best school districts in the state. Mrs. Clarke also stated that she would probably be more involved with the child, and would give the child lots of individual attention, since Mr. Clarke typically worked at home in the evenings, and was often away on business.

Mr. Clarke excused himself briefly, as he was expecting a message regarding a special project on his computer e-mail. Mrs. Clarke went on to say that while they would be happy with either a boy or a girl, she would prefer a girl who could become interested in sewing and pottery. They said they had agreed on a school-aged child, since both of them worked, and they did not want to worry about child care arrangements. After having attended preservice, she knew she didn't want a child with a lot of emotional or behavioral problems, but felt she could parent many of the other children that were described by the social caseworker. Mrs. Clarke said that with enough advanced notice, she had been able to attend the first two preservice training sessions. Her husband had been unable to attend, but she had told him what she had learned.

⚐ Marjorie Marks

Marjorie Marks has made an application to adopt a girl from birth to age 10. Ms. Marks is a 27-year-old African American single parent. Her daughter, Patrice, is 11. Ms. Marks' grandmother, Mrs. Bessie Stokes, age 68, also lives in the home. Ms. Marks has a high school education and works as a nurse's aide at a local nursing home. Her annual income is approximately $16,500 per year. Mrs. Stokes receives social security payments of approximately $450 per month. Ms. Marks noted on her application that her hobbies include singing in the church choir, and shopping with her daughter at garage sales and flea markets.

The home is owned by Mrs. Stokes. Ms. Marks does not pay rent, but she performs housekeeping and errands in exchange for housing. Ms. Marks comes from a large extended family of several brothers and sisters, many of whom live in the area. Her father is deceased, but her mother maintains the family home a few miles away, where two of Ms. Marks' younger siblings still live.

Ms. Marks stated that she wants to adopt because she enjoys parenting and she does not want Patrice to grow up as an only child. She believes that she is a good parent, that their family is very close and has a lot to give a child, and that any child would enjoy being part of her family.

The caseworker made a home visit in the late afternoon, as Ms. Marks had requested that Patrice be part of the entire process. The home was located in an older part of the city on a small lot, close to the street. There was a small yard with a swing set behind the house. The house, which was older, appeared to be in need of paint and minor repair. The inside was small and somewhat cluttered, but was clean and colorfully furnished. There was a stack of games, coloring books, and puzzles in one corner of the living room.

Ms. Marks introduced the caseworker to her grandmother, Mrs. Stokes, who appeared to be agile and in good health for her 68 years. Ms. Marks explained that she began living with her grandmother after her grandfather passed away suddenly 11 years earlier. It worked out well, as Mrs. Stokes had provided day care for Patrice, and Ms. Marks was able to finish high school. Ms. Marks offered her grandmother company, provided housekeeping assistance, and transported her to appointments, since Mrs. Stokes has never driven.

Patrice took the caseworker on a tour of the house. There were three bedrooms and a bathroom upstairs. The bedrooms were clean and comfortable. Ms. Marks had decorated with bright fabric curtains and spreads, and each room was decorated differently. In her room, Patrice proudly showed the caseworker her "mini gallery" of art work she had created while enrolled in an art program at a local neighborhood center. The first floor included a living room, dining room, foyer, and kitchen. A door off the kitchen led to an unfinished basement used for laundry, storage, and indoor play for Patrice on rainy days.

Mrs. Stokes invited the caseworker to sit with the family at the kitchen table during the interview. The caseworker asked Ms. Marks why she wanted to adopt. Ms. Marks replied that she had given birth to Patrice when she was in high school, and that she had never regretted it for a moment. She thoroughly enjoyed Patrice and being a parent. She stated that her family had been very supportive of her. She likes parenting and feels that she is ready for another child. She stated that she saw an advertisement for adoption on television and "the light bulb went on." She said that she, Patrice, and Mrs. Stokes had talked about it for weeks. They all realize that it will mean sacrifices on everyone's part, but they are ready to take on the challenge. The reason she requested a girl from birth to age 10 was that the child would have to share a room with Patrice, and she felt that Patrice should remain the oldest child. Ms. Marks said that before the child moved in, she would trade bedrooms with Patrice so the girls would have more space.

Patrice seemed excited about having a new sister. She said she knew there would be fights and jealousy, but she was used to that, since she has lots of cousins. She said she could help her sister get to know the neighborhood and school, and that she would take her to the public pool and library program next summer. Ms. Marks told the caseworker that Patrice has had problems in school, but she is doing better now. For a long time, the school did not believe that Ms. Marks was working with her daughter at home, since Patrice's performance was so poor. However, Ms. Marks insisted that the school arrange testing for Patrice, and she was found to be dyslexic. Now in special classes, and with the help of Mom and Grandma, Patrice is doing well in school. They also enrolled her in art and music classes at the local neighborhood center to help her find something she could do successfully.

Mrs. Stokes is a retired cook. She is very active in her church and several women's groups. She volunteers one day a week at the local hospital, and she fills in at the soup kitchen as a cook in emergencies. She is looking forward to a new addition to the family, and not so secretly would like an infant; but, she also said she knew an older child was more realistic, and that she "might be around long enough to see an older child grow up." She stated that "being around young people keeps me young." Mrs. Stokes said she had helped raise three of her sister's children years before. She said it had been hard at times, but seeing them grow up and be on their own was her best reward. She said at one time she had nine children in her home!

Ms. Marks, Mrs. Stokes, and Patrice are anxious for the next preservice training class. They have all attended the two sessions to date, and have reportedly learned a lot.

⚇ James and Betty Chambers

James and Betty Chambers are an African American couple who are 29 and 30 years old respectively. They have two boys, James Jr., age eight and Darnell, age six. Mr. Chambers is the minister of a local church, and has been with the congregation for three years. Mrs. Chambers is a secretary with a local insurance company. She works full time, but is very active in church and in the children's school activities. The Chambers report a combined annual income of $46,300.

The Chambers met in high school and married shortly after graduation. Rev. Chambers enlisted in the military for two years after high school, and enrolled in the seminary following his discharge. Mrs. Chambers stayed on base with her husband during his military duty and took night classes. She continued her education while her husband was in college, but she dropped out of school when she became pregnant with James, Jr., because she had a difficult pregnancy. The birth of her second child was also difficult, and resulted in a partial hysterectomy. She only recently returned to work outside of the home, since her youngest child now attends school full time.

The Chambers noted on their application that they wanted to adopt a girl, age eight to 12, as they were no longer able to conceive children. Since they already had two sons, they wanted "the chance to add a girl to our family." Rev. and Mrs. Chambers felt that God had blessed them with two sons, and that they would take this opportunity to give a home to an older child who might otherwise not be adopted.

The Chambers family live in a modest duplex in a suburban area of town. The home was warmly decorated, and family pictures were displayed everywhere. There were three bedrooms and a bath upstairs, and a large kitchen, dining room, and living room on the first floor. The basement had been partially renovated to provide Rev. Chambers a home office. The yard was fenced in, and had a well-used swing set and basketball hoop. At the present time, each of the boys has his own bedroom. However, following an adoption, the boys would share a bedroom, and the adopted child would have her own room.

The entire Chambers family was very active in church, school, and community affairs, and they enjoyed doing "family" things, such as camping, playing board games, and playing sports. This was evidenced by the toys, sporting equipment, and games that could be seen in and around the home. A large calendar which hung on the refrigerator was filled with appointments and activities. The family attended church Wednesday evenings and all day on Sundays. The whole family sang in the choir, which practiced on Thursday nights.

Rev. Chambers was friendly, outgoing, and well-spoken. He stated that while he enjoyed his boys immensely, he would like the chance to parent a daughter. He said he enjoyed working with the young girls in his congregation, as many of them had absent fathers. He believed his family could provide a moral atmosphere for a child, and he could teach a daughter how to grow up to be a respectable woman. Mrs. Chambers was quiet and reserved. She admitted to being initially shy, especially in strange situations. She appeared to be a well-organized and invested mother who took great pride in caring for her family. She stated that she came from a large family and had five sisters. She remains very close to all of them. She said large families are wonderful, and she would have liked to have had five or six children. However, her difficult pregnancies prevented that.

Both children were reported to be excellent students in school, and well-liked by peers and adults. During the home visit they were polite, well-behaved, and affectionate toward their parents. They appeared to get along well with each other, and played at the dining room table during much of the interview. When the caseworker asked the boys about the adoption plans, Darnell was very shy and hid behind his mother. Mrs. Chambers told the caseworker that Darnell did not talk much around strangers due to a speech problem, but that he will talk once he is familiar with a person. Darnell attends speech therapy twice a week at school. When asked, James, Jr. indicated that he wouldn't mind having a sister around, but that he wasn't very happy about having to share his room with his brother. He also thought it would be better to have another brother so they could "shoot hoops." His father told the caseworker that James is very active in sports, and is currently playing in a basketball league on Tuesday evenings and Saturday mornings.

The Chambers are anxious to begin the adoption process, but are concerned about the scheduling of the preservice training due to their active schedule. They were able to attend the first session, but the second session conflicted with a church activity they were committed to attend.

SYNOPSIS

This early in the family assessment, we have only preliminary impressions of these three families. There has been little in-depth discussion of family members' values, attitudes, beliefs, child-rearing practices, or of adoption-specific issues. With the information to date, the caseworker has begun to formulate perceptions of each family's strengths, possible areas of vulnerability, and how these might affect the type of child each family could best parent. The following are the worker's thoughts on each family. These would be shared with the families during further interviews to generate additional discussion.

⚐ The Clarke Family

At first glance, the Clarke family would appear to be potentially excellent adoptive parents. Both parents have stable careers; they are financially secure; they live in a well-furnished home in an excellent school district; and they could provide a child with many opportunities for development. Mrs. Clarke exhibits skill and patience in caring for persons with serious medical problems, and both Mr. and Mrs. Clarke demonstrate commitment and perseverance, evidenced by their active involvement in their respective careers. However, there were also several issues that would need further assessment and discussion. The Clarkes have no parenting, and limited child caring, experience. Both said that Mrs. Clarke would be the more involved parent, due to Mr. Clarke's often lengthy absences from home, and his involvement in his job. They appear to have limited understanding of the changes in their lifestyle that will occur if they become parents, and especially adoptive parents. They currently have little time to devote to a child. They live far from extended family, and their schedules lack flexibility, which would make attendance at appointments, such as school conferences and counseling, more difficult. Their expressed motivation to adopt lacks insight into the needs and problems of the types of children available for adoption. It appears that Mr. Clarke may be ambivalent about parenthood, and he appears less committed to adoption than is his wife.

Based on the information to date, it would be hard to determine whether the Clarkes should adopt a child with special needs. The Clarkes do not yet know enough about adoption to effectively self-assess. In the next family assessment interview, the caseworker should begin to help them better understand the realities of parenting a child with special needs. Their history in managing change and stress should be further explored. The caseworker should arrange for them to meet with adoptive parents of children with special needs to help them better understand the long-term realities of adoption, and the range of emotional and behavioral problems typical of children who have been abused or neglected. The caseworker should prompt the Clarkes to consider lifestyle changes, such as the possibility of Mrs. Clarke working part time, and Mr. Clarke altering his work activities to make time for parenting. Whether they can negotiate changes in their work schedules so Mr. Clarke can participate in preservice training and adoption preparation should, itself, be educational for them.

It is possible that the Clarkes might choose not to adopt, after they better understand the adoption process. However, it is also possible they could develop or demonstrate more interest and commitment than are immediately apparent. The completed assessment might determine that they could potentially be good adoptive parents for certain types of children. For example, they might be good parents for a child with a chronic or correctable medical condition, particularly because of Mrs. Clarke's medical background. They might also be able to parent a child who exhibits few emotional or behavioral problems, but who needs a permanent and secure family, provided the Clarkes can make sufficient adjustments in their lifestyle to accommodate any child. In any case, extensive preservice training and education would be necessary to help prepare them for adoption.

The Marks Family

At first, Ms. Marks seems to have more responsibilities than she can handle. She is a young, single parent who works full time, and cares for both a daughter and an elderly grandmother. Her income is limited, and she lives in a small home. Mrs. Stokes, while currently healthy and agile, is almost 70, and the caseworker would have to question how Ms. Marks might respond if Mrs. Stokes were to become ill. This is of particular importance, since Mrs. Stokes is also Ms. Marks' primary support and, in many respects, her co-parent.

The family has many strengths as well. Ms. Marks has creatively dealt with and overcome difficulties in the past. The family is very involved in the community, and is part of a large extended family that, historically, has been very supportive. Ms. Marks has shown she can, and will, advocate for her child. Ms. Marks, Mrs. Stokes, and Patrice have thoughtfully made the decision to adopt together, and have planned ahead for expected changes.

The Marks family, at this point, appears to have much to offer a child with special needs. However, they will need to fully consider financial issues and the long-range needs of a child with behavioral and emotional problems. They should be helped to identify sources of long-term emotional and financial support, including subsidy. These issues will be important in determining the type of child and scope of problems the family can handle. Their expectations that a child would be close to Patrice, and would become an integral part of this close-knit family would suggest they might not be comfortable with a child with a serious attachment disorder. In addition, a child who would require regular and potentially long-term medical services, intensive counseling, or other complicated treatment interventions might create high levels of stress in the family, since Ms. Marks' job schedule does not appear to be flexible, and Mrs. Stokes does not drive.

⚐ The Chambers Family

The Chambers family possesses both strengths and limitations. They are financially secure, and they are well connected and supported by their community and family. They have successfully dealt with the challenges of military life, difficult pregnancies, and Darnell's speech problems. Their marriage has remained strong in the face of these changes and problems. They demonstrate perseverance and the ability to delay gratification; they continued school despite interruptions, and Mrs. Chambers deferred career achievement when they became parents. The Chambers are very involved with their children, and demonstrate a high degree of pleasure in parenting. Rev. Chambers has had some experience working with youth through the church, and feels positive about these experiences.

Their limitations include their exceptionally active lifestyle and very limited free time. This may affect the type of child they should adopt, since parenting a child with special needs is likely to require a significant time investment. The family's expectations for themselves and for an adopted child may be unrealistic. Their request to adopt a child who is older than their boys suggests limited insight into how adoption could affect their own children, particularly James, who would be displaced as the oldest child. The family should be helped to fully assess their expectations for a child, and consider the types of behaviors exhibited by children who have been abused or neglected. For example, based on Rev. Chambers' statement regarding helping a young girl become a "respectable woman," it would be important to help the family explore their level of comfort with sexual and behavioral acting out before considering placement of a child with severe behavior problems, or one who had been sexually abused. Preservice training and follow-up discussions with the caseworker, and with other adoptive families, would be helpful in further educating the family regarding the realities of adoption. The caseworker should help the family fully explore their areas of strength and vulnerability, and work with them to select a child whose needs best matched the family's strengths. The potential success of this family will be enhanced with adequate preparation, further education and development; careful matching and selection; and postplacement supportive services.

B. SELECTING AND MATCHING FAMILIES AND CHILDREN*

1. Conceptual Framework

2. Application

3. Case Example

*Co–authored by Denise A. Goodman, Ph.D., M.S.W.

Conceptual Framework

The matching of children to adoptive families has changed dramatically in the past two decades. In the years that preceded special needs adoption, infants and families were normally matched on criteria that included ethnicity, physical characteristics, and traits of the infant's biological parents, such as level of education, interests, and skills. Matching decisions were usually made by adoption caseworkers and supervisors to assure that the adopted child would resemble, as much as possible, a child that could have been born to the family. This was not simply to assure compatibility; it was also intended to help adoptive families maintain the secrecy of the adoption.

At other times, matching decisions were made solely by adoptive families. During the late 1800s and early 1900s, "orphan trains" transported orphaned and dependent children from east coast inner cities to be adopted by families in the midwest and far west. The children were dressed in their best clothing and displayed on the train platform. Prospective parents selected a child who, they believed, would best fit into their families. Often, their choices were based on pragmatic and immediately visible criteria. Farming families might select a strong, healthy boy to help with the farm work. Or, a family with all boys might select a girl to help the mother with household chores or to provide her with companionship. Personality traits, other personal attributes, and the child's needs were not generally considered.

As adoption professionals began to understand the critical relationship between a "poor match" and the increased likelihood of disruption, matching strategies became more selective and planful. Physical attributes were often found to be of less importance than personality traits, strengths, lifestyles, special needs of the child, family expectations, and the extent of a child's developmental problems. The importance of placing children in families who could meet both their short–term and long–term needs was also recognized. Consequently, selecting an adoptive family for a child evolved into a thoughtful decision-making process, requiring considerable insight and foresight by both professionals and adoptive families.

WHO SHOULD BE RESPONSIBLE FOR MATCHING?

Successful matching depends upon a thorough and accurate assessment of the adopted child's needs, and of an applicant family's ability to address them. Many people contribute to this assessment. During the home study, the applicant family and their assessment worker will have identified the family's strengths and vulnerabilities, and will have determined the types of children the family is best suited to parent. The child's caseworker, the child's current caregivers, members of the child's immediate or extended biological family, and other professionals who have worked closely with the child, such as teachers or mental health counselors, provide essential information about the child's history, needs, and strengths. Collaboration by these persons greatly enhances the depth and accuracy of the information on which the matching decision will be based. In most cases, the final selection will be made collaboratively by the child's caseworker, the family's assessment caseworker, and the applicant family. At times, the child's biological family or current caregivers may also be directly involved in the selection process, particularly in open adoption.

In order to identify potential families who can best meet a child's individual needs, the caseworker must gather and assess comprehensive information about the child. This information can be obtained from the child's current and past caregivers, including members of the child's biological family; from the child's case record; from the child's teachers and others who know or work with the child; and from the caseworker's own experiences with the child. There are several areas that must be addressed in the assessment:

- The child's current level of functioning and special needs must be fully assessed. This includes the child's present cognitive, social, emotional and physical development; the child's prominent personality traits; the child's typical behaviors; and the child's immediate and long–term academic, mental health, medical, social, and parenting needs.

- The long–term impact of abuse, neglect, sexual victimization, and/or separation on the child's development and behavior must be understood. Based upon the child's history and past behaviors, the worker must be able to predict, with some degree of accuracy, expected problems and needs throughout the course of the child's development. Adoptive parents must be chosen who are able to make a commitment to meeting the child's needs at least until, and sometimes after, the child emancipates.

- The child's particular strengths and limitations must be assessed. The worker must identify those attributes that could facilitate the child's adjustment in a new family, as well as traits that may present barriers to successful adoption. For example, an ability to enter into close, affectionate relationships with adults would be a strength, whereas fear of attachment could represent a potential barrier.

The worker must use information about the child's history, development, and immediate and long–term needs to identify the family structure and parental characteristics that would most likely promote adoption success. The worker must also identify the family structures and characteristics that would not be recommended for the child. Ultimately, the worker must identify potential families whose structure, lifestyle, traits, expectations, and strengths are well suited to meet the child's individual needs.

However, while a careful consideration of the needs and strengths of applicant families and children is necessary, it is not always sufficient to assure a successful adoption. Intangible emotional factors play a critical role in determining whether close interpersonal relationships and commitments will develop in a newly formed adoptive family. Therefore, only the adoptive family can ultimately determine whether a particular child is "right" for them. For this reason, the final matching decision must be made by the adoptive family in collaboration with a skilled adoption professional. If an applicant family expresses ambivalence, or chooses not to pursue placement of a particular child, the agency must respect their decision, whether or not the agency agrees. If a placement is made in spite of a family's ambivalence about the "right-ness" of the child for them, this greatly increases the risk of disruption.

At times, the agency may elect not to pursue placement of a particular child with an applicant family, even though the family would like to continue. Such decisions should be based on evidence that the child is likely to be at risk of short- or long-term physical or emotional harm in the family. However, while the agency must retain final matching responsibility, caution is warranted. Caseworkers must be vigilant to prevent ungrounded subjective biases from affecting matching decisions. For example, if workers overidentify with either a child or an applicant family, it can limit their objectivity. An adoptive family's worker may have difficulty selecting a child for "her" family that she, herself, finds unappealing and would not want to parent. Similarly, a worker who has a strong investment in a child might resist placing the child in a family in which she, herself, would not want to be raised. Such biases may also prevent workers from objectively considering potential adoptive families suggested by the child's biological family. While a worker's emotional responses to a family or a child can, at times, provide clues about important diagnostic information, these "gut feelings" should always be translated into concrete issues or concerns so their accuracy can be tested. The worker must not allow inappropriate personal biases and preferences to drive matching decisions.

CRITERIA ON WHICH TO MATCH CHILDREN TO FAMILIES

While there are no definitive "rules" in matching, understanding the importance of several factors can help families and workers assess the compatibility of a particular child and family. The list below presents some of the more critical factors to be considered in a match. However, the list is by no means comprehensive, and it should be used *only* to raise appropriate questions and to generate discussion. Each family and child must be assessed individually. Children in the adoptive family, extended family members, and the community in which the family lives should also be considered in matching decisions.

It must also be remembered that the family characteristics represented in the "good match" and "poor match" categories below represent the ends of a continuum. In practice, most families' traits will fall somewhere between the two polarities. Further, the parents or caregivers in an adoptive family will usually not be equivalent in their strengths and limitations. Each parent must be assessed individually. The matching process becomes further complicated when placing sibling groups, in which the children's needs and personalities may be very different, requiring different parenting skills. Ultimately, a family must be identified whose primary strengths best match the children's most critical needs, while minimizing the impact of areas of incompatibility.

In all the descriptions below, the terms "parent" or "parents" refer to the adult caregiver or caregivers in the prospective adoptive family. This may be a single parent, a married couple, a single parent and an extended family member, or another combination of parenting adults.

Child's Trait	"Good" Match	"Poor" Match
Child's physical appearance; gender, size, weight, skin color, features.	Parents find child to be appealing; describe child's traits in positive terms; are comfortable with child; or, see child's appearance as irrelevant.	Parents find child unattractive; are bothered by certain traits; don't feel that the child "fits" into their family or meets their expectations, or have reservations that cannot be put into words.

A child's physical appearance, more than any other factor, relates to the elusive and subtle influence of intangible emotional factors on the development of human relationships. For people to develop close emotional bonds, they must, at a very fundamental level, find each other appealing. It must be remembered, however, that "attractiveness" must be evaluated through the eyes of the beholder. For some parents, physical traits may be of significant importance. For other parents, they may be of no importance at all. Similarly, characteristics or traits that would appear, to an objective observer, to be minor or even irrelevant may be very important to an adoptive family. Parents must be encouraged to communicate those characteristics and traits they find to be unattractive in other people. These might include body shape and size; weight; skin color; body odors; specific features; or general demeanor. It is always in the child's best interests to be adopted by a family whose members describe the child in positive and complimentary terms. Conversely, the presence of certain visible traits in a child, no matter how subtle, that "push the parents' buttons," can significantly interfere with the development of attachment.

Child's Trait	"Good" Match	"Poor" Match
Child lacks trust; has attachment problems. Is emotionally remote and unresponsive.	Parents can meet own emotional needs; they do not interpret the child's detachment as a rejection of them.	Parents derive self-esteem from their children's affection; have difficulty tolerating rejection. Are put off by child's distance.

All healthy parents derive satisfaction from emotional closeness to their children. The issue is whether the parents can tolerate emotional distance, and continue to promote the development of attachment, without expecting the child to reciprocate in kind. Parents who have already raised children, who have had positive nurturing experiences, and who have strong self-esteem as parents may be better able to work with children who lack strong attachments. A child with attachment problems should never be placed in a family that has strong needs for emotional reciprocity. Neither the child nor the family will benefit.

Child's Trait	"Good" Match	"Poor" Match
Child's behaviors are likely to create high levels of family stress.	Parents have dealt well with stress and crisis in the past; they can articulate what they can and cannot handle.	Parents did not deal well with stress or crisis; they have not had to deal with crises; they do not know what they would find stressful.

All adoptions of older children or children with special needs create some level of stress for families, particularly during the initial adjustment phase. However, some children are significantly more challenging than others. It is important to determine which of the child's behaviors and attributes the *parents perceive* to be stressful, and whether they have the strengths and emotional resilience to handle these challenges. If the parent does not perceive a child's behaviors to be stressful, the level of emotional distress they experience is lessened.

Child's Trait	"Good" Match	"Poor" Match
Child is dependent; needs constant care, attention, nurturance, and reassurance.	Parents are comfortable in a nurturing role; enjoy nurturing and caregiving.	Parents prefer children to be independent and self-sufficient; parents have little extra time to spare.
Child is independent, self-sufficient; does not often turn to parents for help; is emotionally remote at times.	Parents can accept child's "distance" and do not interpret this as rejection.	Parents "need to be needed," thrive on emotional closeness, and expect to nurture children.

Parents should consider the types of children with whom they are the most and least comfortable. While some parents enjoy all stages of their children's development equally, most have their "most and least favorite" stages. Parents who loved the infancy and preschool periods may be more comfortable in a nurturing role with a dependent child. They are often better able to comfort a crying child; to physically hug, cuddle, and rock a child; to respond positively when a child is clingy, whiny, or needy; and to initiate nurturing interpersonal exchanges. The parent who didn't mind changing diapers might also be more tolerant of an eneuretic or encopretic child. Conversely, parents who were thrilled when their children were toilet trained, went to school, and began extracurricular activities, which freed the parents to do other things, may resent a whiny, demanding, or needy child. A parent who had difficulty with a three-year-old's stubbornness, autonomy, and tantrums, or an adolescent's push for independence may do better with a child who will need long-term nurturance, such as a child with a moderate to severe disability who will always need some degree of parental support.

Child's Trait	"Good" Match	"Poor" Match
Child is confrontational and oppositional.	Parents are not bothered by confrontation; can be appropriately directive and controlling with child; will not be engaged in power struggle.	Parents expect children to be appropriately respectful and compliant. Cannot tolerate "mouthy kids." Or, parents are afraid of confrontation, and avoid struggles by abdicating control.

The primary issue is how much direct conflict and confrontation the parents can tolerate without feeling personally threatened. Parents of children with special needs must often be strong and appropriately directive and confrontive. Such confrontation needs to be constructive for the child, however, not simply an attempt to reassert the parent's own authority or power. The worker should avoid matching a child with a family that is likely to become engaged in a power struggle with the child.

Child's Trait	*"Good" Match*	*"Poor" Match*
Child has particular interests and skills.	Family's interests and activities are similar to those of the child.	Family and child have few, if any, common interests.

Common interests are not essential to a successful adoption. Families and children will always have to adapt to one another's interests, and, hopefully, will share them, as well as develop new ones together. However, common interests can help facilitate the initial bonding process. If an applicant family is greatly interested in sports, placing a child who loves soccer can provide the family and the child with many hours of pleasure. Examples of other common interests might be: a love of animals; enjoyment of music; playing, hiking, or camping outdoors; large family gatherings; church related activities; family group activities; abilities in arts or crafts; interest in cooking; or a love of books and reading.

Child's Trait	*"Good" Match*	*"Poor" Match*
Child has mental retardation and/or a developmental disability.	Academic achievement and intelligence are not as important as other factors in determining a person's worth. Parents can "love the child for what he or she is." They have prior experience parenting a child with retardation.	Parents value high levels of academic achievement and take great pride in their children's performance. Child with retardation would be viewed as significantly "different" from other family members.
	Parents can be satisfied with small gains in ability. They are able to commit to assuring supportive services for the child, perhaps for the child's lifetime.	Parents have rigid expectations for children's growth and performance; would be frustrated by slow progress. Parents cannot commit large amounts of time to direct caregiving and providing necessary services.

Many prospective adoptive parents can communicate whether they can manage a child with mental retardation or other developmental disabilities. However, it is important to determine whether their preconceptions about the child's characteristics, needs, and prognosis are accurate, and not derived from myths and stereotypes. Parents who have had previous experience with children with disabilities are often more able to make appropriate decisions. While such prior experience is helpful, it is not essential. If parents are adamant about not wanting a child with a developmental problem, the worker should respect this wish. However, if parents are ambivalent, further knowledge and experience, including meeting and talking with parents of children with disabilities, can help them make an informed decision. The caseworker should help such families consider new parenting challenges without making them feel guilty, if they ultimately choose not to parent a child with a disability.

Child's Trait	*"Good" Match*	*"Poor" Match*
The child behaves in ways that are socially inappropriate; steals, lies, sexually acts out, or hurts others.	Parents view child's behavior as symptoms of underlying problems; are not offended or seriously distressed by child's behaviors. See themselves as contributing to the child's treatment in the family context. Are comfortable with therapy to deal with these problems.	Parents have personal values or religious beliefs that strongly condemn child's behaviors; child is likely to be perceived as deviant, sinful, or in an otherwise negative light. Not tolerant of psychological problems; unconvinced of the legitimacy of therapeutic interventions. Expect child to "right the wrong" because "it's the right thing to do."

No family is immune to a child's negative behaviors, particularly when they involve intrusion on other people's rights and safety, or when they involve inappropriate sexual behavior. The issue is the family's level of tolerance for behaviors that deviate from their expectations of normalcy, and their ability to intervene in constructive ways. Parents with rigid or moralistic expectations may be threatened and embarrassed by a child's acting out behaviors. They may respond by blaming and condemning the child, and exerting more rigid control. However, overly negative parental reactions may serve to increase the frequency of these behaviors. Parents who see the behaviors as signs of emotional distress, rather than moral failure, are sometimes better able to tolerate them, and to help the child develop alternative ways of responding to stressful situations. However, research suggests that the presence of certain behaviors significantly increases the likelihood of placement disruption. These behaviors include: wetting or soiling bedclothes; stealing; serious eating disorders; physically injuring others; threatening or attempting suicide; sexually promiscuous behavior; vandalizing property; and setting fires [Partridge et al. 1986]. Families who adopt children with these behavior problems should be provided with in-depth training, linkage to appropriate mental health services, and continuous emotional support.

Child's Trait	*"Good" Match*	*"Poor" Match*
The child is likely to need parental care, guidance, and perhaps financial support for many years past the age of majority.	Family is interdependent; continues to care for family members even after they are of adult age. Adult family members share	Children are expected to emancipate to independence. Parents of grown children engage in activities that do not generally involve their

housing, income, and other resources. Leisure activities revolve around the extended family. children. Continued support of adult children is viewed as a failure of the parent or the child; or, potentially a burden.

Children with special needs may require parental supervision and support for many years. They may develop the skills to live independently very late; some may always need supervision and assistance from others. Families in which there is no defined age that delineates emancipation, or families in which members remain interdependent even after emancipation, will often be more tolerant of adult children living at home with parents, or grown children who need long–term parental support.

Child's Trait	*"Good" Match*	*"Poor" Match*
Child has strong cultural identity and background that is different from adoptive family's culture.	Family members respect and appreciate cultural differences; will integrate traditions and practices from child's background into family traditions; adopted child is given opportunities to preserve cultural identity.	Family members disregard the importance of maintaining cultural identity; expect child to adapt to family's culture; do not see need for child's ongoing contact with members of his or her own culture. Or, family members view all people as "the same," regardless of culture or ethnicity.
	Family is already "multicultural," intercultural, or the marriage is interracial. Other adopted children in the home are from diverse cultural and racial backgrounds. Family lives in diverse ethnic, cultural, and racial community.	Family, extended family, and community in which family lives are culturally and racially different from that of the adopted child. Community is not racially and ethnically diverse.

In situations where children are placed in families of different racial, ethnic, or cultural backgrounds, it is important that they be given opportunities to preserve elements of their own culture, even as they adopt some of the cultural values and traits of their adoptive families. The cultural sharing should be reciprocal. The most effective adoptive families are as interested in adopting aspects of their child's culture as in transmitting their own cultural traits to the child. They tend to live in multicultural communities and neighborhoods, have a diverse circle of friends and acquaintances, and will encourage activities that help an adopted child develop and be comfortable with an identity that incorporates more than one culture. Families whose members already represent different races or cultures may also be valuable placement resources. In these families, where diversity is "the norm," children of a different background are less likely to be self-conscious about their "differentness" [Bourguignon & Watson 1990]. (See more in-depth discussion of transracial and transcultural adoption later in this section.)

ISSUES RELATED TO FAMILY STRUCTURE

The structure of a family is an important criteria in making matching decisions. Relevant family characteristics related to structure include: 1) the size of the family; 2) the number of parent figures and their relationship; for example, a married couple, a single parent, two unrelated adults, or a single parent and an extended family member; and 3) the family's stage of development, including the age of their children.

No generalizations can be made regarding the types of children who can best be placed in families with different structures. A statements such as, "Don't ever place a challenging child in a family that has no children," is a generalization that may be inaccurate and misleading, and may inappropriately rule out families who could be developed for a particular child. Assessing family structure can, however, give us clues to important information about family process, and resulting family strengths and vulnerabilities.

Large vs. Small Families

Both large and small families have their benefits and their liabilities for an adopted child. In a family with many children, it is less likely that the parents will have the time and energy to provide each child with intensive, individualized attention. This may be a liability for children who need consistent and intensive parental involvement to promote healthy development. Large families may also be traumatic for children who are shy, introverted, who lack assertiveness, and who cannot compete for attention. These children may become lost in the fray, and their less obvious needs may go unnoticed and, therefore, remain unmet. An exception might be a large family in which the older children typically assume a nurturing role with younger children, or where extended family members also live in the home. In this case, the child might benefit from the consistent involvement and support of several caregivers. A large family may also be a problem for a child who lacks the ability to relate to other children, and is more comfortable and responsive with adults. Placement with a large number of siblings may result in continuous discord, fighting, and jealousy, which can be avoided if the child is an only child, or has one or two siblings who are not close to the child in age.

By contrast, large families may be the best placement for a child who is uncomfortable with intense relationships with adults. This may be true for older children with strong loyalties to their biological families, children with attachment problems, and adolescents striving for independence and emancipation. The large family can provide these children with affection, structure, and consistency without expecting them to engage in intensive, reciprocal interpersonal intimacy [Bourguignon & Watson 1990]. In large families, the parents may also be less dependent upon the adopted child for their own parenting gratification.

Large families also tend to be, by necessity, flexible and adaptable. They may tend to ignore minor or less important infractions; may be more comfortable with differences; and may be more tolerant of unexpected events. Their expectations for an adopted child may, therefore, be less rigid, and they may have less need for the child to conform or perform.

Single Parents vs. Married Couples

A married couple is a system. When assessing a married couple, the worker must not only evaluate each parent individually, but how they operate as a team. The dynamics of a marriage can either contribute to, or interfere with, a successful adoption. There are many benefits to adoption by two-parent families. The collaborative involvement of a two-person team provides a built-in support system for the parents, which can sustain them during rough times. They can divide up parenting responsibilities, making it easier to provide additional time and attention to the adopted child. Living in a two-parent family also provides a child with opportunities to interact with and model the behavior of adults of both sexes. Finally, growing up in a healthy two-parent family can teach a child a great deal about healthy marital and adult interpersonal relationships.

There are issues in two-parent families that do not exist with single parents. For example, it is not uncommon for one of the parents to be somewhat more involved in and committed to adoption than the other. Large discrepancies in the parents' level of commitment to the adopted child may increase the likelihood of disruption. Some authors have suggested that single adoptive parents "usually bring a strong commitment and sense of responsibility to the parenting role" [Bourguignon & Watson 1990]. This same parent in a two-parent family may be just as committed to the child and strongly motivated to maintain the adoption, but may not be able to, if the spouse exerts a strong influence to disrupt. Also, the adopted child can create marital discord by identifying the parents' vulnerabilities, and learning to play one parent against the other. The anxiety and tension created in the marriage may bring on a crisis for the family, and it is more likely the couple will choose to preserve their marriage than the adoption.

In families where two or more unmarried adults will participate in parenting the adopted child, these adults must be assessed in a manner similar to a married couple. Examples might be a single parent who lives with an extended family member (sister, uncle, grandmother), or two unrelated adults in a permanent family relationship, as in gay or lesbian couples. The adults' strengths and limitations must be assessed both individually and as a team. Both adults must be equally committed to the adoption, even if only one of the adults will have legal custody of the child.

The greatest potential liability in single-parent adoptive families is whether the parent can tolerate the stresses associated with adoption. These parents' issues are not unlike the issues faced by any single parent who has sole responsibility for the family's economic, social, and emotional stability. But, they must also deal with additional stresses brought about by an adopted child who has complex needs and problems. Dependable and available support systems through extended family members, friends, and community affiliations are essential for single adoptive parents. Single parents, particularly if they have experienced interpersonal rejection, may also be more empathetic to, and tolerant of, the adopted child's feelings of emotional isolation and fear of closeness.

Young vs. Veteran Families

Young families with limited or no parenting experience may have unrealistic views regarding parenting, particularly parenting an adopted child with special needs. Their life experiences may be limited as well. They may not have had to sustain themselves during very difficult or crisis situations. Young families are often struggling to stabilize themselves economically, and they may be overwhelmed by the added stresses and financial demands of an adopted child. However, young families often have energy, stamina, enthusiasm, and an expectation that they will parent far into the future.

Veteran families, by contrast, are generally older, have both parenting and life experience, will probably have dealt with stress and crisis, and are more likely to be financially stable. Some families will have enjoyed rearing and emancipating their own children, and they may be highly motivated to continue the parenting experience. However, while veteran families bring experience, they also bring old habits and expectations derived from their previous parenting experience. What worked with their own children may not be appropriate for an adopted child, and they must be willing to adapt and learn new strategies.

SELECTING FAMILIES FOR SIBLINGS

Contemporary adoption practice strongly adheres to the practice of placing siblings together, whenever possible [Ward 1987]. The literature on children's attachment suggests that when deprived of their parents, sibling groups form a sub-family, in which sibling ties may become even stronger than ties to their biological parents [Jewett 1978]. Therefore, separation from siblings is often experienced as a painful and traumatic loss for these children.

There are generally two reasons why adoption caseworkers separate sibling groups. The first is that more families are willing to adopt a single child than a sibling group, and the children can be placed for adoption more quickly if they are separated. Matching is also less complicated, since a family must be assessed for only one child. The second reason is the presence of conflict, competition, or jealousy among siblings. When siblings have been separated from their families and placed together, the older children may assume a pseudo–adult role, and "parent" the younger children. This pseudo–maturity may make it more difficult for the older children to acknowledge and communicate their own needs for nurturance and comfort. The siblings may have also developed an "exclusive" relationship, wherein they turn to one another rather than members of an adoptive family. Workers may believe it would be in each child's best interests to have the undivided attention of an adoptive parent, and that this is best accomplished by disrupting the "unhealthy" dynamics among siblings.

However, the perceived gains made by separating siblings generally do not outweigh the trauma of another loss, nor the significant disruption in the children's relationships. Siblings who are separated often experience anxiety and depression, and, when placed at different times, may feel guilty about being placed, or jealous and resentful of having to remain in temporary care. These feelings can be divisive. Since the children may be together infrequently, there is little opportunity to deal with and resolve these feelings. Therefore, the physical separation of siblings often creates an emotional separation that is very difficult to bridge.

Jewett [1978] believes that in a secure, permanent adoptive home, where there is "enough love and attention to go around" and the parents have the ability to manage typical sibling dynamics, siblings can develop healthier and more appropriate ways of relating to each other and to other family members without having to experience the trauma of separation. However, the families for these children must be carefully chosen. Ward [1987] also suggests that in large families, the parents and children already have practice dealing with intersibling ties and conflicts, and may be more able to deal with these issues in the adopted sibling group.

Ward [1987] suggests that many of the desired characteristics of families for sibling groups are the same qualities needed for adoption of any child with special needs: flexibility and adaptability; the ability of the parents to support one another; and the availability of strong support systems within the extended family and the community. In addition, other qualities are important. These include:

- *Administrative ability.* Ward contends that "running a large family is like running a small business." Many diverse activities must be organized into a coherent whole to prevent chaos. Such administrative skills would include: setting schedules; delegating responsibility and assigning tasks to other family members; setting priorities; making decisions quickly and effectively; negotiating conflicts; and practicing 'continual planning' to adjust as the circumstances change.

- *Ability to cope with emergencies.* The larger the family, the greater the likelihood of emergencies and crises. Parents must have, or must develop, relative unflappability, and must be able to intervene quickly and decisively without becoming overly excited or panicked.

- *Ability to promote healthy family interaction.* Ward [1987] suggests this is critical in the placement of siblings for two reasons. First, sibling groups placed for adoption often have unhealthy interaction patterns among themselves. Second, at least initially, there is often competition and divisiveness between the adopted sibling group and the siblings already in the home. The parents must have the skills to referee disputes; negotiate solutions; help children work out their own resolutions to problems; and prevent disputes from escalating into wars. Parents can also help reduce rivalry among the children by organizing tasks and activities that benefit the entire group, and that allow children to work together toward a common goal. Finally, parents of large groups of children may need training in group dynamics and group management, similar to the training provided to a child care professional in a group home or residential treatment program. Strategies may include learning to use a group meeting format to resolve family problems and disputes between the children.

- *The ability to develop and enforce generational boundaries.* Ward [1987] also suggests that children in many sibling groups have developed inappropriate role relationships with each other. An older child may have assumed a parenting role with a younger child, and the younger child will turn to the older sibling, rather than to the adoptive parents, for nurturance and care. Adoptive parents must be able to enforce their own role as the "parents in the family," help the older children relinquish their parenting responsibility, and help all of the children learn to trust and turn to them for care and nurturance.

TRANSRACIAL AND TRANSCULTURAL ADOPTION

Historically, the terms "transracial" and "transcultural" have generally referred to the adoption of children from minority racial and ethnic backgrounds by Caucasian families. However, transracial or transcultural adoption is the adoption of a child by any family whose cultural or racial background is significantly different from the child's, including the adoption of children from foreign countries.

The validity of transracial and transcultural adoption has been debated for decades in child welfare literature. There are strong proponents and equally strong opponents on this topic, making it one of the most hotly debated issues in child welfare practice. The issues generally fall into several categories, which will be briefly explored below.

Issue #1: Whether there are sufficient numbers of families from children's own cultural and racial backgrounds to assure timely permanent placement for all children who are waiting to be adopted.

In most areas across North America, there are many more children awaiting adoption than there are approved adoptive families from these children's own cultural and racial backgrounds. Proponents of transracial and transcultural adoption contend that placing a child in a secure, stable, and permanent home with a family of a different race or culture is in the child's best interests, if the alternative is leaving the child in indefinite and impermanent substitute care, while a family of the same race or culture is sought. When children are school age or older, or have physical or medical conditions, developmental disabilities, or emotional or behavioral problems, there are even fewer families of any background with the inclination and abilities to adopt them. If permanent placement in a family that can meet a child's special needs is the primary goal, adoption by a family of a different race or culture can often achieve this goal more rapidly. Therefore, transracial or transcultural placement is believed to be preferable to long-term foster care or institutionalization [Simon 1993; The Metzenbaum Multiethnic Placement Act 1994; Howard, Royse, & Skerl 1977].

Opponents of transcultural and transracial placement contend that the unavailability of minority adoptive families is more a function of culturally incompetent agency practices and staff bias than any lack of qualified applicants [Rodriguez & Meyer 1990; Neilsen 1976; Washington 1987]. A variety of agency practices have been identified as obstacles to the recruitment and approval of minority adoptive families. These include: unnecessary and overly complicated bureaucratic procedures; cumbersome forms and paperwork, which families experience as distancing and impersonal; expecting families to travel to the agency for appointments during the regular workday, rather than meeting with families in their homes and communities at a time that is convenient for them; stringent licensing requirements related to family income and space requirements; and worker attitudes that reflect "insensitivity, superiority, and rigidity" [Rodriguez & Meyer 1990]. Neilsen [1976] also suggests that families currently caring informally for other peoples' children may be excellent potential adoptive families, but they are loathe to approach the agency to adopt, fearing that the children they are caring for will be taken from them. Finally, in some minority communities, there is a stigma about formal adoption that prevents their involvement with traditional child placing agencies, even though these families routinely care for dependent children on an informal basis.

> *Issue #2: Whether Caucasian families have the necessary attitudes and skills to help children of minority cultural and racial backgrounds develop a positive identity and learn to deal with prejudice, discrimination, and racism.*

Many practitioners see the greatest potential liability of rearing minority children in Caucasian families as the potential impact on the child's identity and ability to cope with racism and discrimination. Many contend that African American children reared in Caucasian families have difficulty developing a positive African American identity [Jones 1972; Morin 1977]. These practitioners stress that even Caucasian parents with the best of intentions cannot teach an African American child about being African American. They contend that African American children reared in Caucasian families can't relate to other African Americans, lack a congruent personal and racial identity, and have considerable difficulty when they encounter racism. Chimezie [1977] asserts that being reared in a Caucasian home is detrimental to the development of certain "indispensable characteristics," including ethnic awareness, identification with "blackness," and possession of survival strategies in a racially hostile environment. Williams [1987] suggests that African American children socialized in Caucasian families do not "fit" in the African American community, and that these children are not comfortable with other African Americans [Williams 1987].

Conversely, a 20-year study by Simon [1993] strongly indicates that most African American children reared in Caucasian families grow up "healthy and aware of their racial identity." Simon relates a typical comment from African American children reared in Caucasian families:

> Look, we were the kids nobody wanted. We know some people say we're Oreos–black on the outside, white on the inside– but that simply isn't true. We can speak 'white' English and dress as middle class people and still be black. We're comfortable with our identity [Simon 1993].

Jones and Else [1979] agree that racial identity is essential for healthy development, but they suggest that children can develop a positive racial identity in either a Caucasian or an African American home:

> [While] the child must learn the skills that minority persons learn to cope with racism, and must also learn the cultural and linguistic attributes of the minority community in order to

become an accepted member of it...many of these skills and attributes are derived from peers and contact with the minority community as much as, if not more than, in the home [Jones & Else 1979].

Proponents of transracial and transcultural placements do stress that if a Caucasian family is to rear a healthy minority child, it is essential that the adoptive parents provide the child with a bicultural socialization. If adoptive families have a simplistic view of race, lack experience with diversity, believe "all people are alike under the skin," or ignore racial and cultural differences, they will not recognize when their child's needs may be different from their own [Katz 1974]. By contrast, when adoptive families value diversity, have a broad multi-cultural network of friends and acquaintances, and nurture and support the child's relationships with peers and adults from the child's own race or culture, the child can develop a strong identity and positive self-esteem. For example, many of the Caucasian families in Simon's study had joined African American or multicultural churches, and were regularly involved with their children in criti-cal aspects of African American culture [Simon 1973].

Adoptive parents must also be able to prepare children from minority cultures to experience and deal with racism and discrimination. While adoptive parents may convey to their children that they, themselves, do not judge or relate to peo-ple based on race or culture, they must help the child understand that many people in society do, and they must teach their children skills to cope. Otherwise, the children are unprepared to understand and deal constructively with racism and discrimination [Jones & Else 1979].

Andujo [1988] compared the development of positive self-esteem and ethnic identity in Latino children raised in Caucasian versus Latino families. The find-ings suggested that most Caucasian adoptive families (80%) had de-emphasized ethnicity and had attempted to develop "strong and secure individuals, human beings," rather than ethnic individuals. By comparison, 87% of the Latino adop-tive parents had raised their children in a bicultural tradition that had empha-sized the development of ethnic identity. The Caucasian families generally used an educational approach to teach their children cultural awareness, whereas Latino families socialized their children through direct exposure and involve-ment in the Latino community. The Caucasian families helped their children deal with racism by providing them with support, or helping them learn to ignore racial incidents, whereas Latino families prepared their children by modeling coping skills that had developed out of their own experiences as minority indi-viduals. Despite differences in child rearing, the self-esteem ratings of all the chil-dren in both Caucasian and Latino families were comparable.

Andujo concludes that while placement in a child's own ethnic community is preferable, a transethnic placement is a better option than long-term foster care. She also suggests that specific selection criteria should be incorporated into the home study process to assure that transethnically placed children develop a strong ethnic and personal identity. Most important, the adoptive families must become part of the social and cultural milieu of their adopted child [Andujo 1988].

Issue #3: Children placed transculturally may experience a higher level of stress and trauma when placed in families whose cultural backgrounds are significantly different from their own.

By minimizing the number and scope of changes a child experiences during placement, we can significantly reduce placement–related stress, the propensity for crisis, and the long–term negative consequences of separation and placement.

Placement of a child in a family whose culture is different and unfamiliar creates a type of "culture shock" for the child. Like adults visiting in a foreign country for the first time, a transculturally placed child must adjust to a new environment with new sounds, sights, and smells, unfamiliar rules, different social norms, strange foods, and at times, a language the child cannot fully understand. All else being equal, transcultural and transracial placements can be inherently more stressful for children.

Kim [1980] studied three boys who had been adopted from a Korean orphanage by Caucasian families. The children were between 14 and 28 months of age when adopted, and they had been with their adoptive families for seven, eight, and 16 months respectively. Kim found an unusual pattern of disturbed behavior in all three children. Their symptoms included frequent and excessive crying; night terrors with mutterings in Korean; temper tantrums; avoidance of children of Korean descent; exacerbated symptoms after being exposed to Korean persons; hyperactivity; and excessive attachment to furry toys. While Kim acknowledged that separation experiences and previous institutional care likely contributed to the children's distress, he emphasized the probable role of "culture shock" for these infants. The children had to adjust to: significant differences in the facial features of their occidental parents; a new language, leaving them unable to either understand or communicate; sleeping alone in a strange room, rather than with other children; differences in the tastes, textures, and smells of food; and many other subtle, but significant, environmental differences. When we consider that infants' emotional security is dependent upon consistency and stability in their caregivers and environments, it is not surprising that a simultaneous change of caregiver and culture would result in heightened anxiety and emotional distress.

Few would disagree that placement in an adoptive family of the same ethnic and cultural background is normally in a child's best interests. However, in practice, other critical factors impact the choice of a family for a child. These include the need for a family with the particular traits and characteristics to meet a child's unique developmental needs; the potential emotional trauma to the child of being separated from foster parents of a different race or culture to whom the child is securely attached; and the fact that thousands of children throughout North America are currently waiting for permanent adoptive families.

In October, 1994, Congress passed P.L. 103–382, the Multiethnic Placement Act. The purpose of this act was to promote permanence for the tens of thousands of children in foster care waiting to be adopted. The provisions of this act were intended to do the following: 1) decrease the length of time children must wait before they are adopted; 2) prevent discrimination in child placement on the basis of race, color, or national origin; and, 3) facilitate identification and recruitment of foster and adoptive families that can meet the special needs of the children in care.

Specifically, the provisions of the act prohibit agencies or entities that receive federal assistance and that are involved in adoption or foster care from:

1) Categorically denying to any person the opportunity to become an adoptive or a foster parent solely on the basis of the race, color, or national origin of the adoptive or foster parent or the child involved; or,

2) Delay or deny the placement of a child for adoption or into foster care, or otherwise discriminate in making a placement decision, solely on the basis of the race, color, or national origin of the adoptive or foster parent, or the child, involved.

The agencies or entities may, however, consider the cultural, ethnic, or racial background of the child, and the capacity of the prospective foster or adoptive parents to meet the child's cultural needs, as one of a number of factors used to address the best interests of children. And, states and agencies should target recruitment efforts to identify adoptive families from the cultural backgrounds of the children who need homes.

The impetus for the act was the adherence, in some states and agencies, to policies that discouraged transracial placements, or that sanctioned lengthy searches for same-race families before authorizing transracial placements. In some cases, families were informally discouraged from applying to adopt children of a different race or ethnicity. These policies contributed to placement delays, and in some cases prevented adoption for many children, since the number of potential available families for the child was reduced [U.S. Department of Health and Human Services, Internet 1995].

The debate about transracial and transcultural adoption is as heated and as polarized today as it has ever been. The challenge for child welfare agencies is two-fold:

1) We must first design, implement, and maintain culturally competent recruitment, selection, and retention programs that develop adoptive, foster, and kinship families from a variety of racial, cultural, and ethnic backgrounds for children in need of permanent families. This will greatly increase the likelihood that children in need of adoption can be placed quickly within their own cultures; and,

2) To identify the traits and attributes necessary for foster and adoptive families to rear children from different cultures, and to assure the development of a healthy cultural identity and self-esteem for children in their care.

Strategies to strengthen adoption, foster care, and kinship care recruitment and retention, including focusing on families from minority cultural backgrounds, can be found in Section XI-A, "Identifying and Preparing Adoptive Families for Children with Special Needs."

Identifying and selecting families who have the prerequisite abilities to rear a child of another culture or race is another challenge. A second level of family assessment must occur with prospective adoptive and foster care applicants that specifically targets issues related to transracial or transcultural placement.

The applicant family should be engaged in a joint exploration of the family's cultural knowledge, experience, and attitudes in the context of the home study and/or the selection and matching process. In addition, training in cultural competence should be provided to all families who adopt transculturally to increase their sensitivity and skill. The following questions can generate discussion:

ASSESSMENT QUESTIONS

"What led you to consider transracial/transcultural adoption? How long have you considered this?"

"How much racial or cultural difference are you comfortable with? Describe the kind of child you would feel comfortable with. What physical attributes in a child would be comfortable for you? What would make you feel uncomfortable?"

"What experiences have you had where you have learned about other races and cultures? What do you know about the race or culture of the child you desire to parent?"

"What do you think is the difference between knowing culturally relevant information and stereotyping?"

"When did you first become aware of your own racial and cultural background? In what ways is your own cultural background important to you?"

"What are the most significant characteristics of your own racial or cultural background? How is your race or culture integrated into your everyday life?"

"Are people more alike or different? In what ways? Can you describe some similarities and differences across cultures from your own experience?"

"What is the best way for people of different cultures and races to learn about each other? What should people learn about each other, if they really want to understand cultural differences?"

"Have you ever experienced discrimination or prejudice? What were the circumstances? What was it like? How would you help a child cope with discrimination?"

"What are your own cultural biases, prejudices, and blind spots? What do you need to know more about? What things bother you about people from other races or cultures?"

"How much experience have you had with persons who are different from you? Childhood experiences? School? Church? Neighborhood? Do you socialize with people who are different from you? Do you have friends, neighbors, or work associates from different cultural backgrounds? Who within your network is of the same race or culture as the child you want to adopt?"

"How can you help a child from a different cultural or ethnic background establish a strong cultural identity? Do you understand what 'biculturalism' means?"

"Are you bilingual? Have you ever studied a foreign language? Are you willing to learn to speak a different language to better communicate with your child?"

"How can your family integrate aspects of your adopted child's culture into your family life? Have you ever done this before?"

"Is your immediate or extended family already multiracial or multicultural? How? How does your family feel about your decision to adopt transculturally or transracially? How about your friends and colleagues?"

"Is anyone in your extended family opposed to your plan to adopt transracially or transculturally? How might this affect your child? How would you handle it?"

"How is cultural diversity apparent in your home? Do you have books, videotapes, art work, music, magazines, and other things that reflect a multicultural perspective?"

"What is the composition of your current neighborhood? School system? Place of worship? Will the schools your child will be attending have both staff and students from the child's cultural background? What culturally specific recreational resources are there in your community? What clubs or organizations do you belong to?"

"What will you need to teach your child about discrimination, prejudice, and stereotyping? How would you do this? Who else in your network of family and friends might be a resource to help with this?"

"What will your child's cultural needs be as the child grows? What survival or coping skills will you and your child need as the child gets older?"

"What do you expect to be the most difficult issue you will face as a multicultural family in the future?"

STRENGTHS

- The prospective adoptive family is already multicultural or multiracial in its composition.

- The prospective adoptive parents have had prior experiences with children and/or adults from different races and cultures, and have established meaningful relationships with them. The parents view transcultural adoption as an inherently good way to add to their family.

- The parents have accurate knowledge about culture and diversity. They have lived in other cultures; they have participated in foreign exchange programs or served as host families for foreign students; they have close friends from different cultures; and their current lifestyle involves them regularly in cross-cultural contact.

- The parents demonstrate personal insight regarding their own and other family members' attitudes, perceptions, feelings, and biases regarding racial and cultural differences. They are honest about biases and areas of lack of cultural knowledge.

- The parents demonstrate an appreciation of diversity in actions and behaviors with people from different races or cultures. They accept and respect differences, and are continually open to new knowledge and experiences.

- The parents have had considerable exposure to persons who are culturally different in both work and social settings, and welcome future opportunities to interact with persons from different cultures.

- One or both parents are bilingual, or have studied foreign languages. The parents are interested in learning to speak a child's native language.

- The parents are interested in learning culturally specific child care and child rearing practices. They willingly attend training related to culture and diversity.

- The parents' friends and extended family members are encouraging and supportive of the parents' decision to adopt transracially or transculturally.

- The prospective adoptive family's home and neighborhood environment support and encourage a multicultural lifestyle. The family has art work, toys, books, magazines, and/or music that are representative of different cultures.

- The parents understand the importance of identifying and meeting the child's cultural needs on an ongoing basis, and can formulate a plan to do so. They understand the critical nature of a bicultural socialization for children adopted transculturally. They know or are eager to learn ways to help the child deal with racism and discrimination.

MINIMAL STANDARDS

- Adopting transracially or transculturally never occurred to the prospective adoptive parents, or they are unsure about this decision. They feel they need more information and experience to make an informed decision.

- The parents have limited cultural awareness or knowledge. However, they are open to considering cultural issues, and express a willingness to learn.

- The parents express empathy about the negative effects of racism and discrimination, but appear to have limited insight about their own behaviors, and how these may reflect personal bias or lack of cultural knowledge. The parents may use stereotypes, and believe these stereotypes to be based on accurate information.

- The parents do not actively seek cross-cultural experiences, but do not avoid them. The parents express attitudes that value diversity, but have not participated in many cross-cultural experiences. However, the parents are willing to become involved in cross-cultural experiences for self-growth.

- The parents lack understanding about the importance of culturally specific child care practices, but express willingness to learn.

- Friends and extended family members are ambivalent or uncertain about transcultural and transracial adoption, but the prospective adoptive parents are willing and able to educate family and friends, and confront inappropriate behavior toward the adopted child.

- The parents currently have little contact with multicultural community organizations or resources, but are willing to identify potential sources and become involved, including day care resources, schools, places of worship, clubs, and recreational groups.

- The parents acknowledge that the child will have ongoing cultural needs, but they do not fully understand these needs, nor do they know how to meet them. They express commitment to learning.

CAUTION!

- Prospective adoptive parents have applied to adopt transracially or transculturally primarily because they have been unsuccessful in adopting a child of their own race or culture, and they believe they will "get a child" faster by adopting transracially. Transracial/transcultural adoption is clearly a second, and inherently less desirable option.

- Parents have little or no meaningful cross–cultural experience. They lack knowledge of other cultures, or knowledge is limited to stereotypes, and largely inaccurate information.

- Parents lack personal insight, and are not motivated to examine their own attitudes, feelings, or perceptions regarding race or culture. They are not willing to explore their own areas of potential bias or ignorance.

- The parents' expressed attitudes and behaviors reflect ethnocentricity, prejudice, serious misconceptions about other people, a pattern of discriminating against others, and values that attribute superiority or inferiority based on culture, gender, age, or race.

- The parents have had no cross–cultural experience, do not desire such interactions, and are fearful and suspicious of people who are different.

- The parents lack understanding of the knowledge and skills needed to parent a child of a different culture, and they deny the need for training.

- Friends and extended family are strongly opposed to transcultural adoption, and are likely to withdraw support or discriminate against the adopted child. Parents seem incapable of dealing with these issues.

- Parents live, work, and socialize exclusively within their own cultural group. Parents deny the importance of raising a child in a multicultural environment.

- The family's neighborhood lacks diversity, and is indifferent or hostile to persons from different races or cultures.

- The parents are unable to consider the child's long-term cultural needs. They do not believe the child will have to learn strategies to deal with discrimination. The parents deny the importance of same-culture socialization to develop a positive identity, and do not see the value of a bicultural upbringing.

SELECTING FAMILIES FOR CHILDREN WITH DEVELOPMENTAL DISABILITIES

Developmental disabilities are physical, cognitive, or emotional conditions that have the potential to significantly interfere with the normal process of a child's growth and development. The most common developmental disabilities are mental retardation, cerebral palsy, epilepsy, autism, learning disabilities, speech and language disorders, spina bifida, hearing loss and deafness, visual disorders and blindness, orthopedic disorders, and congenital malformations. Many children served by the child welfare system have developmental disabilities, including a large number of children who are available for adoption. In a survey of approximately 800 child welfare agencies in 49 states, Coyne and Brown [1985] determined that 1,588 children with disabilities had been placed for adoption during a 12-month period.

Children with developmental disabilities have a variety of service needs, including medical care, physical support, special education, developmental services, financial support, and special recreation. When seeking adoptive families for children with developmental disabilities, workers must determine whether applicants have the particular traits and characteristics associated with successful adoption of children with disabilities. As part of the matching process, the caseworker may need to conduct a supplemental assessment of a potential family to fully assess their ability to meet a child's unique needs.

In addition to the family traits that are desirable for all adoptive families, the following traits should be assessed when evaluating families for children with disabilities [The National Resource Center for Special Needs Adoption, Spaulding for Children; undated]:

- The family demonstrates interest in, or has past experience with, individuals who have developmental disabilities.

- The family has prior experience with the child's disability, or is willing to learn about the disability, and is willing to incorporate special child-care strategies into their daily lives.

- The family is able to adapt their home environment to meet the child's special care needs. This may require making the home wheelchair accessible; arranging the home to accommodate special feeding, sleeping, toileting, and bathing equipment; modifying or removing physical structures that present safety hazards for the child; and providing special equipment for recreation.

- The family is able to develop and utilize support systems that are appropriate for persons with developmental disabilities. This may include specialized respite care, clinics, recreational programs, and other social services. The family is willing to meet with parents of children with disabilities, and are interested in participating in parent support groups.

- The family is willing to make long-range plans for the child after the child has reached adulthood. This includes identifying strategies for life-long support and care for children whose disabilities will prevent them from emancipating to independent living. The family will make necessary legal and financial arrangements to provide assisted or semi-assisted living after the parents' death, through assignment of guardianship, and utilization of wills and trusts.

- The family is willing and able to function as child advocates to identify and secure appropriate special educational services for the child.

- The family can access resources in their community to meet the child's special medical needs; or the family is willing and able to travel to secure these services.

- The family is aware of the possible changes in their financial situation after placement of a child with a disability, and can work with the caseworker to identify resources for financial assistance and support.

- The family has positive, constructive attitudes about the child's potential for healthy growth and development, while being able to develop realistic expectations for the child's performance.

Additional information related to children with developmental disabilities can be found in Chapter VII, Child Welfare Services for Children with Developmental Disabilities.

Application

ASSESSING THE CHILD

A concrete tool to help caseworkers organize critical information about a child is the Prediction Path, developed by Kay Donley Ziegler [Donley 1990]. This tool was designed to facilitate selection and matching by recording a child's past behaviors and needs, and using this information to predict problems and behaviors in both the immediate and distant future.

The completion of the Prediction Path requires that the worker carefully and thoroughly review the child's preplacement history; the child's genetic and medical history; the child's history of placements in substitute care; the findings of mental health evaluations and school reports; and descriptive information about the child from the child's caregivers.

Developing the Prediction Path is a three–step process. Part one is the "Placement Trail," wherein a child's history of substitute care placements is recorded and analyzed. The Placement Trail should list, in reverse chronological order, all of the child's substitute care placements, including: the dates of placement; reasons for the placement; reasons for disruption of placement; information about the substitute caregivers; and information about the child's adjustment.

The second part of the Prediction Path is the "Asset/Debit Sheet," which compiles information about the child's strengths and limitations. The Asset/Debit Sheet is compiled from information in the child's case file, information from current caregivers, and the worker's own impressions. The worker lists the child's strengths, abilities, skills, talents, and attributes likely to be viewed positively by an adoptive family. The worker then lists the child's limitations, deficits, problems, challenges, areas of need, and traits likely to be problematic for adoptive families. The worker must make concerted attempts to be balanced in the assessment. Frequently, caseworkers may overlook or take for granted obvious strengths and abilities, while dwelling on the child's shortcomings and needs.

The final section of the Prediction Path, called the "Prediction Narrative," is the synthesis of information derived from the Placement Trail, the Asset/Debit Sheet, information from current caregivers, and the child's case file. The Prediction Narrative attempts to predict the likely course of the child's short– and long–term adjustment in adoptive placement, including anticipated behaviors, problems, needs, and parenting challenges. While such prediction of a child's needs and behaviors is certainly not exact, the Prediction Narrative can draw reasonable conclusions, based on the child's past and current behaviors and needs, and can highlight the important issues the adoptive family may face in parenting the child.

The Prediction Narrative contains three basic elements: 1) the behaviors and needs that the child can be expected to exhibit; 2) when the behaviors or needs are likely to be exhibited; and, 3) parenting strategies to manage certain behaviors, or meet the child's needs. This prepares adoptive parents to expect problems, and gives them effective strategies to intervene. The Prediction Path helps adoptive parents anticipate and respond more effectively to the challenges of parenting the child, thereby reducing the likelihood of crisis.

This information can be invaluable in selecting an adoptive family that can meet the child's needs. Sharing the Prediction Path with potential adoptive families empowers them to make an informed choice about whether they have the ability to parent the identified child.

The use of the Prediction Path to select an adoptive family for a child, and to prepare them to parent the child is demonstrated in the following case example.

Case Example

⚊ Cindy, age eight

Cindy is an eight-year-old African American girl. She was separated from her biological family at age five, after substantiated and repeated sexual abuse by her mother's boyfriend. Cindy's mother, however, staunchly denied that the abuse had occurred, insisted that Cindy was lying, and continued to live with her boyfriend. Cindy's initial placement was with a maternal great aunt and uncle. Her aunt reported that Cindy denied the abuse occurred, but that Cindy had recurring nightmares for several months. Cindy's school adjustment was poor, and her aunt was often called to pick Cindy up at school because of violent tantrums. Additional attempts to work with Cindy's mother were not successful.

Cindy was moved to a foster home in December, 1992, when her uncle had a serious stroke and was bedridden. The aunt, feeling overwhelmed, requested Cindy be placed in a foster home where, "Cindy wouldn't be burdened with old people's problems." Cindy was moved to the Johnson foster home, and her worker filed for permanent custody. At the Johnson home, Cindy wet the bed for the first several weeks, and constantly talked of "going back with my mom." She was angry, and repeatedly told her worker that "she was bad, that's why no one wanted her." She also had a difficult time making friends in her new school due to her aggressive behavior. After the initial adjustment period of three months, she seemed to improve and settle in. However, her behavior deteriorated and reached crisis when the other foster children in the home were reunited with their biological family over the Thanksgiving holiday. The foster mother could not cope with Cindy's behavior, and requested that Cindy be removed.

Cindy was then moved to the Smith foster home, where she was the only foster child. Mrs. Smith stated that it took Cindy a few months to adapt to their home, and that she refused to unpack all of her belongings for three months. She also wet the bed for the first several months, but that stopped as Cindy became more comfortable in the family. Mrs. Smith stated that Cindy was an adorable child who liked to help and be praised by adults. Even though she liked school, Cindy had her share of behavior problems there as well. Her best classes were art and music, where she excelled.

The Smith's were a middle-aged African American couple. Most of their children were grown and emancipated. Only a 17-year-old son and a 16-year-old daughter remained at home. Cindy had her own bedroom at the Smiths, and Mrs. Smith indicated she kept it very neat and was proud of her belongings. However, she would often "borrow" her foster sister's things, and would only admit to taking them when directly confronted. While the Smiths felt considerable affection for Cindy, they did not desire to adopt her.

The following Prediction Path was developed to help find an appropriate adoptive family for Cindy, and to help prepare the family to care for her.

CINDY'S PLACEMENT TRAIL

Date of Placement	Caregiver Name	Reason for Placement	Adjustment Information
11/30/93	Smith Foster Family	Cindy's behavior too hard for Johnson foster family to handle.	• wet bed for two weeks • fought in school • would not unpack for three months
12/6/92	Johnson Foster Family	Uncle had serious illness. Aunt had to work and also care for her husband.	• bed wetting • school problems • insisted she was going back home • temper tantrums • tantrums at school
12/13/91	Maternal Aunt/Uncle	Removed from home due to sexual abuse by mother's boyfriend	• denied abuse had occurred • had repeated nightmares

Cindy's Placement Trail reveals several patterns. Cindy was moved three times in two years. At each placement, she had problems at night with bed wetting and/or nightmares. She did not wet the bed when placed with her aunt, but did so for several months after she was placed in each of the two foster homes. She consistently has acted out at school, and she often has violent temper tantrums. Cindy appears to use denial as a typical strategy to deal with stress and trauma. Finally, Cindy was moved each year at about the same time (around Thanksgiving and Christmas).

CINDY'S ASSET/DEBIT SHEET

Cindy's Assetts	Cindy's Debits
Physically attractive–cute.	Wets bed, has nightmares, anxiety reactions to stress.
Has sense of humor; is funny, can be very charming.	Gets into fights at school when left unsupervised.
Likes to be helpful; helps around the house; is eager to please.	Takes a long time to feel secure and to trust new people.
School work is generally at grade level.	Has violent temper tantrums if frustrated, and is easily frustrated. Is stubborn.
Is neat and clean; takes care of her belongings.	"Borrows" other people's things; can be sneaky.
Enjoys art and music; appears to be talented in these areas.	Swears loudly when angry.

Appears to enjoy many aspects of school. Likes her teachers.

Has difficulty making friends with peers.

Has a positive cultural identity.

Is bossy and argumentative. Has low self–esteem; blames self for being moved.

Exhibits ability to be affectionate with persons she knows and trusts.

Has strong tendency to deny pain and avoid dealing with traumatic experiences.

The worker then used the information she had gathered to develop a Prediction Narrative for Cindy. This would be used to help choose a prospective family and to prepare them to parent Cindy.

PREDICTION NARRATIVE

Child's Name:
CINDY MARTIN
Date Compiled: July 14, 1994

Expected Behaviors	When Expected	How To Handle It
Bed wetting Fear of dark Nightmares	At placement, for up to three to four months.	1. Buy plastic bedsheets. 2. Limit fluids after dinner. 3. Take to bathroom two hours after bedtime. 4. Put night light in bathroom and in Cindy's bedroom. 5. Show Cindy how to change and help launder sheets. 6. Reward and praise Cindy for dry bed. 7. Provide reassurance and comfort after nightmares. Use this time to build attachment. 8. Help Cindy understand that bed wetting and nightmares will go away when she feels better.
Fights at school	At placement, maybe ongoing, until Cindy develops better skills relating to peers.	1. Prepare Cindy for new school placement. 2. Meet with teachers; plan intervention strategies together. 3. Do contract with Cindy, reward often for good school conduct, as

reported by teacher.
4. Coach Cindy to relate better to peers.
5. Provide positive peer experiences.
6. Be accessible to talk with teacher when needed.

Expected Behaviors	When Expected	How To Handle It
Cindy lacks trust, has difficulty in forming new attachments.	At placement, and for several months after placement.	1. Follow through on all promises. Be consistent in doing what you say you will do, including discipline. 2. Plan "special time" with Cindy each day. 3. Develop a daily schedule and follow it. 4. Provide reassurance of love and commitment to her.
Tantrums. Testing behaviors.	In two to six months.	1. Intervene using "time out" during escalation. 2. Withdraw attention until tantrum subsides. 3. Be patient, calm, use low voice. 4. Give Cindy alternatives when frustrated, such as talking about it, or punching a pillow or bean bag. Use positive reward for no tantrums. 5. Help Cindy reduce frustration. Select low–frustration activities.
Threatened at anticipated move.	At one year.	1. Plan a celebration to mark the one year anniversary. 2. Talk about differences between foster care and adoption. 3. Put her fear into words and reassure her of permanence in the family.
Denial of problems and feelings	At placement, ongoing.	1. Give Cindy permission to talk about "bad things"

and "bad feelings" in a supportive environment.

2. Talk openly about family and personal problems, and include Cindy in discussions.

3. Acknowledge any disclosure by Cindy of problems or feelings; offer support and assistance.

Conflicted loyalty. Attachment to biological mother	At legalization, adolescence.	1. Review Lifebook with Cindy. 2. Talk openly about her biological mother.
Identity issues	Adolescence.	3. Reassure her that she can love her adoptive family and still care about her biological mother. 4. Participate with Cindy in an adoptive family support group. 5. Seek professional help, if needed. 6. Gather further information about Cindy's family; share with Cindy.
Possible sexual acting out resulting from sexual abuse	Any time.	1. Set clear boundaries for appropriate/inappropriate behavior in the home. 2. Gently confront inappropriate behavior. Provide alternatives. 3. Model appropriate behaviors. 4. Respect privacy in family. 5. Talk openly with her about sexual issues. 6. Encourage her to talk about sexual abuse, when she is ready. Listen well.

7. Participate in "survivors" group with Cindy.
8. Attend parent training for special interventions with sexually abused children.
9. Seek professional counseling when needed.

The Prediction Narrative helps the caseworker identify the type of parent the child will need, both currently and in the future. By reviewing Cindy's Prediction Narrative, Cindy's caseworker was able to delineate the following desirable characteristics for a family for Cindy:

- Must be able to make a commitment to permanence for Cindy and communicate this to her in both words and actions.

- Must demonstrate entitlement, and must be able to consistently follow through with planned activities and interventions.

- Must be an involved, "hands–on" parent, who actively and directly intervenes when necessary.

- Must be willing to listen to Cindy's problems and issues; must be able to provide consistent support, reassurance; should be able to model different ways of solving problems.

- Must be able to devote considerable time to Cindy, and be available to attend school meetings, mental health appointments and/or group sessions, as well as provide ample individual attention.

- Must be tolerant of Cindy's tantrums, bed wetting, sexual behaviors, and school problems. Must understand these result from prior trauma; must be empathetic rather than punitive; and must be patient and realistic in expectations for their improvement.

- Must not feel threatened by Cindy's divided loyalty and her strongly voiced (if unrealistic) estimations of her biological mother's positive attributes. Must be able to talk objectively with Cindy about her mother, and help Cindy develop a realistic understanding of her mother's strengths, as well her problems.

- Must be patient in developing a relationship with Cindy. It is unlikely that Cindy will be able to reciprocate parental love and affection early in the placement. Parent must tolerate ambivalence from Cindy.

- Must be an advocate for Cindy with the school, neighborhood, and with other professionals to insure that Cindy's needs are met.

Desirable, but not essential, characteristics in a family for Cindy would include the following:

- Family members who are, themselves, interested in art or music, or who are willing to support the development of these skills in Cindy.

- Cindy would probably benefit from being the youngest child, or one of a few, rather than many children. It is important that she receive individual attention.

- Cindy is at grade level in school. Her potential is not known. A family that advocates for her educational development, without expecting her to be a high academic performer, would be preferred.

In summary, the Prediction Path provides a concrete tool to assist the caseworker in highlighting the child's critical issues, while developing a profile of the family who can best meet the child's needs. This tool will also be utilized by the worker when presenting the child to the prospective family, as well as at placement and during postplacement meetings and home visits.

Once the child's needs are clearly identified, potential adoptive families should be re-assessed to determine their appropriateness for the child. Families may be eliminated from consideration if they strongly desire a child of a different age or sex, or if their strengths and vulnerabilities do not "fit" with the needs of the child to be adopted. After identifying the families that could potentially adopt the child, the worker should list their strengths and limitations in a manner that is similar to the Asset/Debit sheet developed for the child. The worker should try to list the family's skills and attributes that would contribute to effective parenting of the child, and family characteristics that might create potential barriers to successful adoption. With this information, the caseworker can select families that might best parent the child. Whenever possible, more than one family should be selected for consideration.

The following lists document the second step in the assessment of three potential adoptive families for Cindy: Robert and Elizabeth Clarke, James and Betty Chambers, and Marjorie Marks. (Initial assessment information about these families was presented in Section XI–A, "Identifying and Preparing Adoptive Families for Children with Special Needs.")

ROBERT AND ELIZABETH CLARKE

Strengths	Possible Limitations
Two–parent family	Work long hours
Stable income	No parenting experience
Can meet child's cultural needs	Unrealistic expectations for adoption
In a good school system	Little flexibility in work schedules
Room for child in home	Limited free time
Family can provide good education	Little support from outside family
Mother has nursing background	Dad may not be strongly motivated to adopt
Mother very interested in art	Crisis resilience not tested
No children in home to compete	Have not considered impact of adoption

JAMES AND BETTY CHAMBERS

Strengths	Possible Limitations
Two–parent family	Hectic family schedule
Stable income	Limited free or uncommitted time
Can meet child's cultural needs	Not knowledgeable about adoption
Successful parenting experiences	Adopted child older than oldest biological child
Advocates for children's needs	Possible unrealistic expectations for child
Have faced adversity in past	Limited experience with special needs child
Strong links in community	

MARJORIE MARKS

Strengths	Possible Limitations
Parenting experience	Limited income, small living space
Established support systems in extended family	Single parent with responsibility for another child and grandmother
Has advocated for child in school	Close age between girls, may lead to competitiveness
"Hands–on" parent	Risk of being overwhelmed financially and emotionally
Uses community resources	
All family members highly motivated to adopt	
Strong parent figure in Mrs. Stokes; extensive parenting experience	
Family has planned and is well prepared for adoption	
Parent's need for nurturance met by other child	
Mother enjoys activities with Patrice, including crafts	
Can meet child's cultural needs	

Based on the limited information we have about these three families, Marjorie Marks appears better suited to adopt Cindy than either the Clarke family or the Chambers family. The Clarkes' hectic, career-focused lifestyle currently leaves little room to parent an eight year old with special needs. They would need to make significant changes in their lifestyle to accommodate Cindy. The Chambers family could potentially be developed to provide a home for Cindy, with continued self-assessment, training, and preparation. They might do better, however, with a younger child who had fewer special needs, and who would be a middle or younger child to their biological children. While Ms. Marks has many strengths, she and the worker should further consider Cindy's specific problems and needs before making a final decision about placement.

THE "PRESENTATION" MEETING

Once a prospective family has been selected for a child, the worker must begin to share information about the child with the applicant family. A formal "presentation meeting" should be scheduled. The participants should include the adoptive applicant family, their assessment worker, the child's caseworker, the child's current caregiver, and where appropriate, members of the child's biological or extended family. This initial "presentation meeting" serves several purposes, including:

- The family is provided with extensive background information about the child, and is helped to consider the implications for the child's future behavior and needs.

- The family is familiarized with the child's needs by reviewing the Placement Trail, the Asset/Debit Sheet, and the Prediction Narrative.

- The family views photographs, and whenever possible, videotapes of the child.

- The prospective family is given the opportunity to talk directly with the child's current caseworker and foster or kinship caregivers, and is encouraged to ask questions.

- The family is guided in assessing their own strengths and areas of vulnerability as they relate to the prospective adoptive child.

- The family is asked to consider both the short-term and long-term implications of placement of this child with their family, and to begin to think about the changes that this will bring about in their family.

The prospective parents should never be expected to make an "on the spot" decision about adopting the child. In fact, many agencies do not permit prospective parents to indicate their interest at the presentation meeting. The parents should be encouraged to take notes during the meeting, and they should be given copies of the Prediction Path materials. They should be asked to review the materials and continue their discussion at home. The parents should be contacted by the caseworker a few days after the meeting to determine if they want to proceed. If the prospective parents believe that they can successfully adopt the child, a preplacement visitation plan should be developed. If, however, the family declines to adopt the child, this process is repeated with the other potential families that have been identified for the child.

C. PREPARING A CHILD FOR ADOPTION*

1. Conceptual Framework

2. Application

3. Case Examples

*Co–authored by Denise A. Goodman, Ph.D., M.S.W.

Conceptual Framework

Adequate preparation of both adoptive families and children can mean the difference between a successful adoption and disruption. The adage "forewarned is forearmed" is the watchword of adoption practice. Helping adoptive families learn exactly what to expect, and helping them develop strategies to manage potential problems, greatly increase their capacity to manage the stresses associated with adoption. Similarly, constructive preparation can help children resolve emotional issues and better manage change.

Conversely, failure to fully address a child's concerns can contribute to placement instability and, potentially, disruption, dissolution, or displacement of the child. There are several issues that are likely to interfere with the adoption if they are not dealt with early in the process.

First, most children have unrealistic expectations for adoption. Their fantasies about adoptive families range from Daddy Warbucks to Ebenezer Scrooge. They are likely to be disappointed and disillusioned if not helped to develop realistic expectations for adoption early in the process.

Second, moving a child into an adoptive family without sufficient preparation will almost certainly precipitate a crisis for the child. This can exacerbate emotional and behavioral problems, and can greatly complicate the adjustment process. Many children do not understand the difference between adoption and their earlier placements. They may perceive adoption as just another in a series of temporary placements. This can resurrect painful feelings of loss, rage, rejection, helplessness, abandonment, and grief from earlier separation experiences.

Third, unresolved concerns and issues can interfere with these children's ability to form attachments with an adoptive family. They may experience loyalty conflicts because of strong attachments to their biological family, extended family, or foster caregivers. They may have developmental and emotional problems resulting from previous abuse, neglect, or sexual abuse. They may feel anxious and threatened, particularly if they have a history of disrupted foster or adoptive placements. All these can significantly affect their behavioral and emotional responses to adoption.

Many of the strategies used to prepare children for adoptive placement are the same as those to prepare children for placement in foster care. (Please refer to Section VIII-B, "The Effects of Traumatic Separation on Children," and VIII-C, "Placement Strategies to Prevent Trauma," for extensive discussion of relevant issues and effective placement strategies.) In addition, several strategies that deal directly with adoption issues are discussed in the following section.

Application

STRATEGIES TO PREPARE CHILDREN FOR ADOPTION

The preparation of a child for adoption should begin as soon as the decision is made to pursue permanent termination of the biological parents' rights. The emphasis of work with a child should then shift from reunification to securing a permanent home.

Certain skills are necessary for a caseworker to prepare a child for adoption. They include:

- The caseworker must have a thorough knowledge of normal child development, and the impact of abuse and neglect on development. This is essential, if the worker is to develop a preparation program that is appropriate for the child's age and developmental level. (Refer to Chapter VI, The Effects of Abuse and Neglect on Child Development.)

- The caseworker must have a thorough understanding of the impact of separation on children of various ages. This will help in assessing the impact of past losses on the child's current behavior; in predicting the child's potential reaction to the impending move into adoption; and in designing placement strategies that minimize the traumatic effects of separation. (Please refer to Sections VIII–B, "The Effects of Traumatic Separation on Children" and VIII–C, "Placement Strategies to Prevent Trauma.")

- The caseworker must have skills to engage children into a trusting and supportive casework relationship, despite the difficulty some children have in establishing trust. The continuous presence of a trusted caseworker during the adoption process can provide the child with considerable support, can help the child maintain continuity, and can help the child deal constructively with problems and issues as they arise.

- The caseworker must recognize the potential impact of cultural variables on the child's and the family's adjustment, and must be able to help prepare the adoptive family to respond constructively to cultural differences.

TECHNIQUES AND METHODS OF PREPARATION

Caseworkers can work with children individually or in groups to prepare them for adoption. Many adoption programs use a combination of both. Individual preparation allows the caseworker to identify and address each child's particular needs and concerns. Participation in a group helps children understand that their fears and concerns are quite normal, and are shared by others. Children can also be reassured through direct contact with children who have been successfully adopted.

While the child's caseworker generally has responsibility for preparing the child, many agencies also involve mental health professionals. Some children may need professional counseling to deal with issues related to prior maltreatment and separation. These mental health professionals must be proficient in the treatment of children, well-versed in issues related to separation and grief, and must fully understand the dynamics of adoption. Ideally, the caseworker, the foster parent and the mental health professional should work as a team to prepare and support the child throughout the adoption. Foster caregivers should be trained to assess the child's needs, and to support the child by providing regular opportunities for the child to ask questions or express concerns and fears.

Casework with any child begins with the development of a trusting relationship. For some children, this is easier said than done. They may be frightened, suspicious, angry, or generally mistrustful of adults. The caseworker can facilitate relationship development with any child by doing the following:

1) *Be honest.* Dealing with difficult feelings or topics with unwavering support helps the child to develop trust in the caseworker.

2) *Follow up and follow through.* Trust and credibility must be earned. Children will trust adults who are consistent, reliable, and dependable. Even activities that may seem unimportant to the caseworker, such as phone calls or home visits, are often very important to the child.

3) *Learn to listen.* Children feel important and "heard" when adults listen carefully to what they say and respond honestly. The caseworker must learn to remain quiet and give the child sufficient time to talk. This often means resisting the temptation to give untimely advice. (Strategies to communicate with children can be found in Section IV-F, "The Casework Interview: Implementing the Helping Process.")

4) *Be patient.* Building a positive relationship with a child may take time. Some children may test the worker's commitment and perseverance by refusing to talk, avoiding contact, or becoming defiant and argumentative. The caseworker must continue to be positive and encouraging, yet persistent.

Since establishing new relationships is difficult and time consuming for many children, the caseworker or therapist who has the strongest relationship with the child should generally do the adoption preparation. The child's emotional energies should be reserved for development of relationships with the adoptive parents, not with a new caseworker. If the adoptive family's assessment caseworker will work with the adoptive family during and after placement, the child can eventually develop a relationship with this caseworker. However, maintaining relationships with known sources of support is critical, until the child has settled into placement and has begun to transfer attachments to the new family. (See Section VIII-C, "Placement Strategies to Prevent Trauma," for a discussion of the transitional model of placement.)

The caseworker can help the child develop a positive attitude about adoption by using language that is free of negative connotations, and by avoiding terms that subtly communicate inappropriate or destructive messages. The following are some examples of both positive and negative adoption–related terminology:

Negative: Terms like "real mother," "natural father," and "primary parent," when referring to the child's biological parents, subtly infer that the adoptive parent is somehow not "natural," not a real parent, and not the child's primary, or most important parent. This greatly interferes with the development of entitlement—the understanding by the adoptive parent and child that the adoptive parent has the right and the responsibility to be that child's parent.

Positive: The child's parents should be referred to as "biological parents," or by their names ("Janice and Ted.") If the child was cared for by persons other than biological parents, they should be also referred to by the name the child is accustomed to calling them, such as "Aunt Helen," "Grandma," or "the Morrisons."

Negative: "Your parents gave you up for adoption," "You were put up for adoption," or, "You were put out for adoption." These imply a calculated act of rejection.

Positive: "An adoption plan was made for you." "You came to live with your permanent (forever) family." "You joined the Webb family."

Negative: "Their real kids" and "their adopted child." This creates a strong perception that the adopted child is substantially different from children born to the family, and perhaps less a member of the family.

Positive: "My brothers and sisters." "All of you Webb kids."

Workers and caregivers should choose language that communicates that adoption is a carefully planned event, one that completely integrates a child into a permanent family. This can help differentiate adoption from other temporary placements, can help reduce the child's fear of rejection, and can strengthen the child's self–esteem.

COMMUNICATION STRATEGIES WITH CHILDREN

Several tools can be used during individual sessions with children to help elicit and talk about important issues. Workers should receive additional training in the use of these and other therapeutic strategies to prepare children for adoptive placement. These strategies include:

- **The Life Map.** The life map is an art therapy technique. The child is asked to draw a "map" that depicts his placement history. The map can communicate where the child has lived, how long he lived there, the people who were important to him, why he had to move, and how he felt about it. The child should be allowed to draw his map in any way he likes. The primary purpose is to open discussion about the child's history, and give the caseworker the opportunity to discuss and clarify the child's misconceptions (particularly self–blame), to provide support for painful feelings, and to provide reassurance about the present move. The completion of the map may take several weeks. As the preparation process continues, the child can include the adoptive family in the map, and can add information about the family as he acquires it.

- **The Lifebook.** Lifebooks are scrapbooks, diaries, or logs that describe the child's life. The Lifebook should be begun as soon as a child enters placement, but it becomes essential when adoption planning is initiated. The caseworker should help the child record the following: 1) information about the child's biological family and extended family; 2) the reasons the child needed placement; 3) the child's history in substitute care; 4) the child's educational and developmental background; 5) the child's medical information; and 6) information about the child's recreational and social activities.

Photographs should be included of biological and extended family members; siblings; prior foster or kinship caregivers; the child's friends; past homes; the child participating in favorite activities; pets; and schools, teachers, and classmates. Photos can be provided by relatives, and by previous and present caregivers.

The information in the Lifebook must be honest and accurate, yet tactful. Written descriptions of the biological parents should include their positive attributes, as well as their limitations. As with the life map, the Lifebook gives caseworkers the opportunity to involve the child in discussions about critical issues and concerns that, if not addressed, can interfere with the adoption. The Lifebook also provides a detailed and continuous personal history that the child can refer to throughout her life. This will be very important during certain developmental periods, such as identity formation during adolescence and young adulthood. (Refer to Section VIII-C, "Placement Strategies to Prevent Trauma," for a more detailed discussion of Lifebooks, including "A Story About You.")

- **The "Family Tree."** This modification of the more common "family tree" (genogram) can help children organize all the people who have been an important part of their lives. The caseworker should help the child draw a tree and all its parts. The biological family members can be identified as the roots of the tree. These "roots" (the biological family) cannot be seen, but they anchor the tree, just as the biological family provided the child with a genetic heritage, and will always be part of her. The child's foster or kinship families can be represented on the trunk of the tree, as they have helped the child grow. The adoptive family may be represented on the upper trunk, branches, leaves, fruit, and flowers. Through this activity, the child learns she does not have to choose between families, and she can come to understand how each family played an important role in her growth and development.

- **Collages.** A collage is a collection of pictures that are glued together, either in sequence, or overlapping one another, on a large piece of poster board or cardboard. In adoption work, the pictures can be glued to a cutout of a body outline of a child. Collages are used to represent past, present, and future events. They serve a similar purpose as a Lifebook or life map. It is a fun and nonthreatening means of interaction with the child. The child is instructed to cut out pictures from magazines, or to draw pictures that, to him, represent important people or events, and that represent his wishes for the future. The child describes the pictures, and explains why he chose them. This can elicit discussion that helps the child develop realistic expectations for adoption, clears up misconceptions, or strengthens identity.

- **The "Goodbye" Visit or Letter.** The "goodbye" visit or letter allows children to reach closure regarding their past. When feasible, the caseworker arranges for the parent or a member of the child's extended family to write the child a goodbye letter, make an audio or videotape, or to participate in a goodbye visit. According to Kay Donley Ziegler [Donley 1990], the critical messages to be conveyed by the family are: "You are loved;" "You are wished well;" "You will be remembered;" "You may love another parent." While not all parents will be able to participate in this activity, some parents who recognize their limitations and are in agreement with the adoption plan can be helped to do so. When a goodbye visit or letter are not possible, the child can be encouraged to write a letter to his biological parents. There are no right or wrong words. The child may express grief, loyalty, anger, guilt, or hopelessness. The child may or may not mail the letter. The process of writing the letter may, itself, be cathartic for the child. Receiving validation for his feelings from his caseworker or foster caregivers is also therapeutic. The caseworker should note that if the child sends the letter, the biological parents may need support.

Many of these tools are also useful for group preparation. One benefit of group preparation is that the children are all awaiting adoptive placement, and they can validate and support each other by sharing their artwork and feelings. Peer validation often carries a high credibility among children.

Adoption preparation groups should include six to eight participants of similar ages. There should generally be at least two leaders. The groups may last between six to eight weeks, and each weekly session should be an hour and a half to two hours in length. During the initial session, the leaders should help the children understand the purpose of the group, and establish ground rules. In the following weeks, the art therapy techniques described above can be used as large or small group activities to generate discussion. The children should be encouraged to share their individual projects with the group. Guest speakers, including older children who have been adopted, adoptive parents, and a biological parent whose child was adopted in the past, create stimulating discussion and provide the children with examples of actual adoption experiences. The children might also visit the court and talk with the judge, which helps to reduce the fear and mystery surrounding the legal aspects of adoption. The caseworker may also use stories, videotaped movies, or television programs about adoption to stimulate discussion by the children.

In selecting members for a group, the leaders should carefully consider the children's developmental level, their behavior, and their individual needs. Some diversity of backgrounds and experiences is valuable, as children can learn that despite apparent differences in their experiences, they often share the same fears and feelings. However, children with more severe emotional or behavioral problems can often divert the leaders' attention from adoption preparation to group management and control. Group leaders should be very experienced in adoption issues, knowledgeable about child development, skilled at group process, and able to constructively help children confront their misconceptions and fears.

WHEN ARE CHILDREN READY?

For most children, the following characteristics indicate that they are ready to pursue adoptive placement:

- *The child understands and accepts the reasons for separation from his biological family, and the child knows that reunification is not possible.* The child's level of understanding will be consistent with his age and developmental level. For example, a two-year-old child may understand only that his mother couldn't take care of him and keep him safe, while a 12 year old may be able to understand the impact his mother's crack addiction had on her ability to care for the family. The child should understand, and be able to verbalize, that the separation was not his fault.

- *The child has psychologically disengaged from the biological family.* This does not mean the child has forgotten her family, nor that they are unimportant to her. It does mean she knows the separation is permanent, she has begun to deal with feelings of loss, and she is willing to accept new parents. While the child may express a desire that things were different, she realizes that it is impossible, and has accepted that she will not be reunited with her family. In situations where an open adoption is planned, this may be less of an issue, since the child is not expected to sever these emotional ties. However, she must understand that the nature of her relationship with members of her biological family may change.

- *The child is motivated to accept an adoptive family.* This is critical for older children, who are capable of sabotaging an unwanted placement. Children may demonstrate this by expressing their desire for an adoptive family, fantasizing about what the new family may be like, expressing curiosity about a new family, or agreeing to meet them.

Many children continue to exhibit ambivalence about adoption even after extensive preparation work. This is normal and to be expected, and the child's feelings should be accepted and validated. Children may be appropriately skeptical that this family will be different from previous families; they may still feel some blame and responsibility for past separations; they may be threatened by intimacy and attachment; or they may simply feel threatened about another move to a strange environment. For a well-prepared child, however, these feelings are more manageable, and the child has outlets to discuss and deal with them. The child's concerns are, therefore, less likely to interfere with the child's willingness to pursue adoption.

Similarly, while children may appear ready for adoption, it is not uncommon for them to regress after placement. Adoptive placement is itself stressful, particularly once the family is beyond the "honeymoon" period, and it can resurrect powerful feelings and concerns related to separation and attachment. For many children, past issues and concerns about permanence, security, attachment, and identity will not be fully confronted and resolved until they can test and deal with them within the adoptive family setting. Consequently, the child's caseworker and therapist will often need to continue the work begun during the preparation period throughout the postplacement adjustment period, and often, well into postlegalization.

The following describes two very different processes of preparing a child for adoption. The first example demonstrates the problems that occur when children are not properly prepared. The second example illustrates the use of both individual and group methods to effectively prepare the child.

Case Examples

⚐ Ricky, age seven

Ricky had lived with his foster family, the Espositos, for three years. He had been placed with them after he had been severely neglected. His mother was addicted to crack, and despite several attempts by her caseworker to involve her in drug treatment, she was unable to provide a stable home for Ricky. Ricky's caseworker, Rachel Dunn, had pursued permanent custody and began adoption planning. She told the foster parents about the plan, but asked them not to discuss it within earshot of Ricky, since it could take many months before Ricky was legally freed for adoption, even if there was no appeal; and she felt knowing about it would heighten Ricky's anxiety.

The Espositos were experienced foster parents. They had two other foster children, ages 12 and nine, in the home. Two of their five biological children, both teenagers, also lived at home. While they were very attached to Ricky, they had repeatedly told the caseworker that they could not consider "starting a new family." Mr. Esposito was a few years from retirement, and the Espositos planned to travel, and enjoy their children and grandchildren.

Several months later, Rachel phoned the Espositos to inform them that the judge had awarded permanent custody of Ricky to the agency, and that Ricky was legally free for adoption. She asked, again, if the Espositos would be interested in adopting Ricky. Mrs. Esposito stated that she and her husband had talked it over, and that they did not feel they could make a commitment to adopt Ricky. Mrs. Esposito affirmed that they would help in any way they could, however, and would be happy to keep in contact with Ricky after his adoption, if he so desired.

Rachel told Mrs. Esposito that she would talk with the adoption department and locate a family for Ricky. She asked Mrs. Esposito to keep this information a secret from Ricky until something was more definite. "No sense getting him all upset for nothing," she said.

Two weeks later, Rachel phoned the Espositos to say that she believed a family had been identified for Ricky. Rachel said that she would come by on her way home from work to tell Ricky about his new family, since the first preplacement visit with the adoptive family had been scheduled for the following day.

Rachel came to the Esposito home about 4 p.m. and called Ricky out of the bedroom. She asked him to come and talk with her at the picnic table out in the yard. Rachel told Ricky that she had some great news, "You'll be going to live with a new family that will be yours forever!!!!" Ricky was shocked. He said that he wanted to go live with his "real mom," or stay with the Espositos. Rachel told him that neither of those options was possible, and that he would meet his new forever family tomorrow.

Ricky screamed, "NO, NO, NO!" and ran from the table into the woods behind the house. Rachel went into the house and told the Espositos what had happened. She told them not to worry because, "Kids are more resilient than adults realize, and can bounce back quickly. He'll adjust fine."

⚐ Jack, age seven

Jack was placed in foster care as a result of physical abuse and neglect. Both of his parents were substance abusers. The agency had developed a case plan for reunification, and had provided the family with extensive services. However, the parents never complied with the case plan, and the caseworker filed for permanent custody after Jack had been in foster care for a year and a half.

Jack's parents had visited him sporadically in the foster home, and each time they visited, they promised Jack that he could soon come home. Jack would become hopeful about reunification, only to be disappointed when his parents did not follow through. As happens with many children this age, Jack blamed both himself and the agency, rather than understanding that his parents' drug abuse made it impossible for them to care for him.

Jack had lived with the same foster family since he was removed from his family. The Wilsons were an older couple who lived on a sprawling farm. They had been foster parents for 17 years. They were the biological parents of four children, and had adopted three others. All the Wilson children were adults, and were living independently. In addition, several foster children had been emancipated from their home, but still considered the Wilsons to be "Mom" and "Dad."

Carl Maldonado, Jack's caseworker, phoned Mrs. Wilson to inform her that he was filing for permanent custody of Jack. The agency had worked to reunite Jack's family, but it was clear they could not care for him, and Jack needed a permanent home. Carl asked Mrs. Wilson about the possibility of their adopting Jack. Mrs. Wilson said that she and her husband loved Jack, but were too old to make such a commitment. The Wilsons expressed strong interest in maintaining contact with Jack and his adoptive family.

Carl told the Wilsons he wanted to meet with them to develop a plan to prepare Jack, and to enlist their support and cooperation. Carl met with the Wilsons the following day while Jack was at school. Carl outlined his plan to work with Jack, and asked the Wilsons if they could help by putting together Jack's Lifebook. Carl also suggested they write a letter to Jack highlighting important events during his two years with them. The Wilsons discussed how hard it would be to tell Jack that he couldn't go back to his biological family, and that he was to be adopted. They anticipated his probable reactions, and together they developed possible supportive responses. They all agreed to tell Jack together, and the Wilsons would explain to Jack why they could not adopt him.

Carl scheduled an appointment for early the following week. Carl and the Wilsons sat with Jack at the kitchen table. Carl began by telling Jack that they had a lot of important things to talk about, that Jack could ask questions about anything he wanted, and he could say how he felt, no matter what. Carl then said that the agency had made a very hard decision. Carl told Jack that his parents had not followed the case plan, and that their home was still an unsafe place for Jack to live. It didn't mean that his parents were bad, and it didn't mean they didn't love him. Carl told Jack that being a parent is a hard job, and parents have to make good decisions, or their children won't be safe. Carl reminded Jack of their previous discussions, when he had explained why Jack had to live in a foster home, and explained that his parents still could not make good, safe decisions for Jack. Carl explained to Jack that his parents hadn't learned to care for him, and still had many problems. Carl then told Jack he deserved a family where he would be safe and cared for, and where he wouldn't have to worry about being hurt. Carl said most children he knew felt sad and scared about this, and that Jack might too.

Jack began to cry. Mrs. Wilson asked him to come sit on her lap. She reassured him that she wanted him to have a forever family, and that he had done nothing wrong. In fact, he had done things just right, he was a wonderful boy, and his new family would love him a lot. Jack turned to her, and asked if he could stay with her. She hugged him, and gently told him that she and Mr. Wilson could still be his "grandma and grandpa," but they were too old to be his mom and dad. Carl then explained to Jack what would be happening in the next few months. He said Jack would be asked to help make lots of decisions. He asked Jack if he had any questions at this time. Jack said, "No." Carl told him to call the office, or talk with the Wilsons if he thought of anything later.

Carl called the following day to see how Jack was doing. Mrs. Wilson said that he had been quiet and withdrawn, and was following Mr. Wilson everywhere. Carl said he would visit again the beginning of the following week to begin work on Jack's Lifebook. He asked Mrs. Wilson to gather anything that would be appropriate for the Lifebook before the home visit.

Carl spent the next several visits helping Jack and the Wilsons update Jack's Lifebook. During some of the visits, when they looked at old pictures, report cards or mementos, they all laughed and joked. At other times, when they discussed why Jack had to leave his family and how it felt, Jack would become upset and sometimes would cry, but he could explain, when asked, why he had to leave.

Carl was able to secure copies of photos of Jack's biological parents from the local high school yearbook. Jack told Carl how much he missed his family, and Carl said that most children who are adopted feel the same way, and that was okay. They spent a lot of time talking about Jack's biological parents, and wrote down information about them into Jack's Lifebook. Carl told Jack that the Lifebook could help him remember all about his biological family when he was older.

The Wilsons contributed many photographs, copies of Jack's school work, and other mementos for the Lifebook. Mr. Wilson took Jack on a photo expedition around town, taking pictures of all of Jack's favorite places and people.

One day Carl stopped by to invite Jack to a series of group meetings for children who were going to be adopted. He told Jack that the first meeting would be a get acquainted party, but that the second meeting would be "show and tell," using everyone's Lifebooks. Jack attended the meeting every Wednesday after school for eight weeks. Mrs. Wilson would pick him up and ask him what happened at the meeting. On some days he told her about events in the group; on other days, he didn't talk much, because, "All we talked about were sad things."

During the sixth week, Jack said that he had met a girl his age who had already been adopted. He said, "She was scared and mad at first, but she got used to her new family. Now she loves them a lot!" Jack said he had met her adoptive parents, and they seemed nice, and everyone was happy about the adoption. He said her new family let her talk about her biological family anytime she wanted. Jack also told Mrs. Wilson the next week he was going on a field trip to the courthouse, and was going to meet the judge.

During the final week of the group sessions, Jack invited the Wilsons to the meeting. There was going to be a pizza party, and all the kids were going to share their artwork, and what they had learned about adoption. On the way home after the last meeting, Jack told the Wilsons that maybe being adopted wasn't so bad, but that he would still rather stay with them. The Wilsons reassured him that they would always love Jack, and that they would be happy to have him visit them often.

SYNOPSIS

In the first scenario, Ricky was not given any information until the last possible moment, and therefore, was deprived of the support and nurturance of his foster family and caseworker while he dealt with the reality of the adoption plans. His foster parents were asked to keep the adoption a secret, and were not able to participate in preparing Ricky, or themselves, for his separation from their family. Ricky's caseworker lacked insight into his emotional needs, and failed to provide either an adequate explanation, or sufficient support to Ricky during this difficult transition. Unfortunately, many workers believe that children will adapt to new situations with little help. This type of preparation frequently leads to crisis and, potentially, disruption in adoptive placement.

By contrast, Carl began the preparation process prior to the permanent custody hearing, thus giving Jack adequate time to understand and adjust to the upcoming changes in his life. Carl used face-to-face contact effectively to assist in building a relationship with Jack. In addition, Carl fully engaged the foster parents in this process, as they had been the most trusted individuals in Jack's life. Together, Carl and the Wilsons used Jack's Lifebook as a tool to organize his life history, and to provide him a safe means to express his feelings. The adoption group further oriented Jack to the adoption process and validated his feelings. With supportive help from the adults he trusted, he acquired a positive, if still tentative, view of his impending adoption.

D. SERVICES TO CHILDREN AND FAMILIES AT THE TIME OF PLACEMENT*

1. Conceptual Framework

2. Application

3. Case Examples

*Co-authored by Denise A. Goodman, Ph.D., M.S.W.

Conceptual Framework

Successful placement of a child with an adoptive family requires careful planning and preparation. Proper services at the time of placement can help prevent crisis for the child, and can minimize stress for all involved. An in-depth discussion of placement strategies to prevent trauma can be found in Section VIII-C, "Placement Strategies to Prevent Trauma." Some of the major points are summarized briefly below.

Services at the time of placement are designed to achieve several objectives:

- **To help the child, the adoptive family, and the foster family cope with stress related to the move**. Anxiety about change, and depression and sadness due to separation, create a time of emotional vulnerability for everyone, but particularly for the child. Careful placement planning can help everyone cope with the move, thereby reducing its traumatic effects and preventing crisis.

- **To provide the child a sense of control.** Children in care often feel, legitimately, that they have no control over their lives. Many children react by behaving in ways to gain and assert control, including acting out and challenging persons in authority. Other children may become emotionally withdrawn. Most children react to this loss of control with high levels of anxiety. The caseworker can minimize this by involving the child in all aspects of planning and preparing for the adoption.

- **To help the child understand what is happening**. Many children do not understand the difference between foster care and adoption. Moving to an adoptive family often resurrects old issues, concerns, and separation feelings. The caseworker can help the child understand the ways in which adoption is different, and the roles that previous families have played, and thus, can help the child develop realistic expectations toward the new family.

- **To ease the child's adjustment to a new environment.** Using a "transition" method of placement makes it possible for the child to develop a degree of comfort in the new environment before having to move. This reduces stress, and increases the child's ability to cope with change. During preplacement visits, the child can become familiar with the norms and rules in the new family, can acquaint himself with a new school, church and neighborhood, and can begin to develop a place for himself within the family. The caseworker can minimize the child's feelings of confusion and bewilderment by arranging and implementing activities that specifically familiarize the child with the new environment. Reducing the unknown greatly minimizes the child's anxiety.

- **To facilitate the development of new attachments**. Attachments take time. Histories of abuse, neglect, sexual victimization, and multiple separations make it more difficult for many children to trust. If children can begin to form an attachment with the adoptive parents before the move, the parents will be more able to provide comfort and support to the child during stressful times. During the preplacement period, the caseworker should help the adoptive family begin the attachment–building process.

The caseworker has a pivotal role in providing services at the time of placement. Consequently, the caseworker must have considerable knowledge and well–developed skills in the following:

- The caseworker must recognize and understand the impact of separation on children, and the behavioral and emotional expressions of stress and grief in children of varying ages. Recognizing and acknowledging the child's feelings of loss and anxiety can help the caseworker gauge placement activities to prevent overwhelming the child, and to assure that the child receives much–needed emotional support.

- The caseworker must be able to select and implement a variety of casework techniques to help children make the move successfully. These include the use of communication tools such as dolls, toys, puppets, and other play activities; interviewing techniques; and the use of adoption-specific tools, such as Lifebooks, life maps, family trees, and collages, to help the child understand what is happening to him.

- The caseworker must have expert assessment skills to determine the level of stress experienced by all parties, and to determine an appropriate rate of placement to minimize stress. The caseworker must also be able to help the adoptive family assess the child's behavior, and identify appropriate interventions to help the child during the move.

- The caseworker must be able to plan and coordinate placement activities, serve as a liaison between the foster and adoptive families, and provide crisis intervention services as needed.

Application

The phrase "at the time of placement" refers to the period that begins with an adoptive family's commitment to seriously consider adopting a particular child. It continues through preplacement activities, and, by definition, ends during the first week after the child is moved into the adoptive family. At that time, a post-placement service plan is developed and implemented.

PREPARING THE ADOPTIVE FAMILY

Many caseworkers mistakenly believe that preservice training is sufficient to prepare families for the placement of a child. Although preplacement training can prepare adoptive families for general dynamics associated with adoption, the caseworker must help each family individually prepare for the adoption of a particular child.

The adoptive family must first learn as much as possible about their intended child, initially through discussions with the caseworker, and second through direct contact with the child's current caregivers. Prior to the beginning of preplacement visits, the caseworker should schedule a formal meeting between the child's caregivers and the potential adoptive parents. Members of the child's biological or extended family may also be included, when appropriate. The agenda for the meeting should include the following:

- Establishing a cooperative relationship between all parties that will facilitate the transition for the child to the adoptive home.

- Sharing information about the child's history, daily habits and routines, school behaviors, likes and dislikes, fears and anxieties, diet needs and preferences, discipline issues and strategies, religious practices, culture, rituals and traditions, and culturally specific caregiving practices.

- Developing a preplacement visitation plan that specifies when and where visits will take place and their duration; finalizing transportation arrangements; identifying possible activities to engage the child during visits; deciding when overnight visits will begin; and, using the child's Placement Path, identifying potential problems and strategies to deal with them.

- Identifying a projected date for the final placement.

The caseworker should record the information discussed during this meeting, and should provide written copies to all participants. In some instances, a second meeting may be necessary to complete the agenda.

During the week preceding the adoptive placement, the adoptive family should meet with the caseworker to fully review the child's Prediction Path. Particular attention should be given to the placement narrative section, which highlights the child's adjustment to previous moves. Contingency plans should be developed to manage potential problems. Changes should be formally incorporated into the Prediction Path, and updated copies should be given to the family.

It is not uncommon for some adoptive parents to consider stopping the adoption process at this point. The caseworker must help them determine whether this reflects normal ambivalence, whether the family is no longer sure they want to adopt, or whether they are uncertain that this is the "right child" for them. If the family remains committed to the child, but is anxious about what is to come, the caseworker should reassure them that their feelings are to be expected. The caseworker can suggest additional reading materials, connect the family to an adoptive parent support group, or link them with a "buddy" adoptive family. The child's foster family or current caregivers can also provide reassurance. However, if the family expresses concerns about the child, indicating uncertainty about the "rightness" of this particular child for their family, the caseworker should delay placement activities until this issue is fully resolved. It is much better for families to back out before the placement is made, rather than to disrupt several weeks or months after the child is placed.

PREPARING THE CHILD

When the adoptive family has made the commitment to meet the child, the caseworker should visit the child to begin preparing for preplacement activities. (The child will have been previously prepared for adoption. At this time, the child can become familiar with the prospective adoptive family.) During this home visit, the following agenda items are discussed:

- **The caseworker helps the child learn about the prospective adoptive family.** This can be done using a videotape of the adoptive family, or the "Family Book," a scrapbook about the adoptive family that is similar to the child's Lifebook. These should present pictures, stories, and other information that will help the child learn about the adoptive family. Pictures should be included of all immediate and important extended family members; the family's home, inside and out; the yard and the neighborhood; the family's pets; the school and church the child will attend; family activities in and around the home, such as hobbies, picnics, or decorating for holidays; vacations; activities outside the home; and possible playmates and neighborhood children. All pictures should be described as well. Family members can write short descriptive stories about themselves. The discussion about the adoptive family must be appropriate for the child's developmental level. The child should be encouraged to ask questions and voice concerns, and must be given ample time to do so. The child's current caregiver should be present to offer the child support, to demonstrate approval of the plan for adoption, and to minimize loyalty conflicts.

- **The caseworker reviews the placement plan with the child.** It is essential that the caseworker review, step-by-step, what will be happening. This can be done using charts, calendars, pictures, diagrams, or other visual aids to assist the child in understanding adoption events. The caseworker should elicit the child's input to plan the details of the particular visits, which enhances the child's feelings of control.

- **The caseworker must reassess the child's readiness for adoption** and plan additional services, if necessary. The caseworker evaluates the child's understanding of adoption, the level of disengagement from the biological family, and the child's feelings about the adoption. At this time, many children will say that they do not want to be adopted. The caseworker should not confuse a child's fear of the unknown, or a desire to not separate from current caregivers as unwillingness to be adopted. The child who has been well-prepared and has agreed to adoption, but who changes his mind when preplacement visits are scheduled, is more likely anxious and ambivalent than resistive. The caseworker must reassure the child that no final placement will be made until he and the adoptive family have had time to get to know each other better.

- **The caseworker helps the child begin to disengage from the foster family or other caregiver.** Most children who are adopted have experienced painful separations in the past. The caseworker can use the adoption planning process to help the child experience a nontraumatic and easier transition, rather than an abrupt, forced separation. The caseworker can help the child begin to separate from the foster family by reviewing the child's placement history and relationship with them. The child should be encouraged to identify persons she will miss, to plan ways to say "goodbye," and to identify ways that contact can be maintained with people who are important to her after the adoption. This process is continued during subsequent contacts with the child.

PREPLACEMENT VISITS

As previously noted, the noncrisis nature of adoption provides the caseworker an opportunity to use preplacement visits as a means of transitioning the child to a new environment.

The adoptive family should generally first meet the child in her current home. This gives the child a sense of control in a familiar setting, and affords the child the continued support of the foster parents or other caregivers. The caseworker begins the visit by introducing the adoptive family to the child, but is generally minimally involved in activities. The adoptive parents may bring a small toy or activity to engage in with the child. No more than two or three members of the adoptive family, and preferably the parents only, should attend the first visit. Instead, the adoptive parents may use their Family Book or a videotape to acquaint the child with other members of the adoptive family.

The first visit should last approximately one to three hours, based on the child's age and needs. It is important to consider the child's normal routine when scheduling visits. Visits should not be planned when the child would normally be napping, or at times when the child is typically tired or cranky.

The second visit may be planned in the child's home, or in a neutral setting such as a park, playground, roller rink, bowling alley, or restaurant. The foster parents do not typically participate in this visit. A neutral setting is less threatening to the child than the adoptive home, yet provides the adoptive family some private time with the child, and provides a "built in" activity. The caseworker may be present at the beginning and end of the visit, but the adoptive family is alone with the child for most of the visit. The visit may last from two to six hours, and can include one or two additional members of the immediate adoptive family, generally their children. Some children will need additional time before they are comfortable leaving the foster home with an adoptive family. If necessary, several visits can be held in the foster home before the family takes the child to another location.

The adoptive parents' home is generally the site for the third visit. The child is given a tour of the home. The child should be shown the location of the bathroom, the kitchen, the toys, and the television, and the family's "rules" should be explained. The child should also be shown her bedroom, bed, closet, and dresser drawers, and she should be encouraged to use them during subsequent preplacement visits. The child should also be encouraged to communicate her needs to the adoptive family.

During the visits, the adoptive parents should try to maintain continuity for the child. They should try to follow the child's daily schedule, maintain continuity in food, clothing, sleep schedules, and hygiene practices, and use familiar discipline strategies. Later on, the adoptive family can gradually alter the child's routine to more closely match the family's.

During the third and subsequent preplacement visits, the adoptive family can continue to acclimate the child to the family's home setting. This includes orienting and involving the child in the household chores, routines, rituals, traditions, guidelines, and rules.

When both the adoptive family and the child are comfortable together for six to eight hours at a time, an overnight visit can be scheduled. The child can begin to leave belongings at the new home to use in the future. The adoptive parents should begin to integrate the child into the family's routines and house rules. Two or more overnight or weekend visits are advisable to assist the child in making a smooth transition.

Once overnight visits have begun, the adoptive parents, foster parents, caseworker, and child (if appropriate) meet to choose a placement date, and make plans for moving day. The plan should include the day and time of the move, who will prepare the child, who will help the child pack, who will transport the child, goodbye activities at the foster home, and the nature of postplacement contact with the foster family. Any questions or concerns regarding the progress of the visits should also be addressed.

Since moving day can be an awkward and emotional event for both families, the caseworker should assume a leadership role, coordinating the activities. Cooperation and collaboration between the foster and adoptive parents will ensure a smooth transition for the child. Enough time should be scheduled to avoid rushing the child.

Prior to the move, the child's caregivers should help the child say goodbye to peers, teachers, neighbors, and relatives of the foster family. The child could host a party at school, and take pictures to add to his Lifebook. The foster parents should also plan a special dinner or activity. In addition, the foster parents should write a goodbye letter, and insure that the child's Lifebook is up to date.

Some foster caregivers believe it is important to "keep up a strong front," and not show their feelings. However, the foster parents should be encouraged to honestly express both their sadness about the separation, and their hope for the child's future, and the child should be encouraged to express happy and sad feelings as well.

Case Examples

The following case examples illustrate casework services at the time of placement. The first case study illustrates a placement made without the benefit of preparation and support. The second case demonstrates the application of effective casework practice methods with both families and children at the time of adoptive placement.

Danny, age eight

Danny, age eight, had lived in the Williams foster home for three years. His caseworker, Alice Miller, had filed for permanent custody, and had begun adoption planning for Danny as soon as it was granted. A videotape of Danny was aired on the morning television show, "Monday's Child." The next morning at 8:02 a.m., Mrs. Copeland, an adoptive applicant, phoned the agency to say that she and her husband were interested in adopting Danny. Mrs. Copeland said they had been studied and approved by the agency several months earlier, but they had not heard anything since. They had also attended the agency's orientation and preservice training. Alice made an appointment to meet with the family the following day.

Both Mr. and Mrs. Copeland were present at the meeting. Alice showed the Copelands several pictures of Danny, and gave them a brief history of his life. The Copelands were anxious to meet Danny, as they had been wanting to adopt for several years. Alice said she would arrange for them to meet Danny the following Saturday afternoon. She then called Mr. and Mrs. Williams and asked them to tell Danny that he would meet his new family that weekend. Alice told Mrs. Williams that she would pick Danny up at 1 p.m.

When Alice arrived to transport Danny to the visit, Danny was anxious and confused. Alice told him that there was a big surprise for him at the agency. When they arrived, the Copelands were waiting in their car in the parking lot. When Alice parked, the Copelands approached the car, and smiled and waved at Danny. Danny asked Alice who those people were, and Alice replied, "They're your new mommy and daddy." Danny began to cry, and did not want to get out of the car. Alice calmed Danny, and told him that the Copelands had seen him on television and wanted to meet him. Danny held tightly to Alice while he was introduced to the Copelands.

The Copelands asked if they could take Danny to the park and for an ice cream cone. Alice agreed, and Danny went with the Copelands for four hours. When they returned, Danny had several bags of toys and a sticky face. He thanked the Copelands, and asked Alice to take him home so he could show his foster mom and dad his new toys.

The first phone call Alice received on Monday morning was from Mrs. Copeland. She stated that she and her husband could not stop talking about Danny since the visit. They wanted to have Danny placed with them as soon as possible. They had spent all day Sunday painting and decorating Danny's room. Alice told Mrs. Copeland that she was pleased the visit went well, and she would make arrangements for placement the following weekend.

Alice phoned to inform Mrs. Williams about the placement. Mrs. Williams was quite surprised, and said she had expected more notice. She said losing Danny would be very hard on their whole family, as Danny had lived with them for over three years. Alice thanked Mrs. Williams for her commitment to Danny, and said she appreciated how hard it must be for them. Alice said that was all the more reason not to drag things out…getting it over quickly was better for everyone. Alice said that she would pick Danny up at four o'clock on Friday, and take him to his adoptive family.

When Alice arrived on Friday afternoon, Danny was visibly upset, and stated that he didn't want to live with the Copelands. Mrs. Williams had tears in her eyes, and Mr. Williams went out into the yard. Alice tried to explain to Danny that the Copelands were his "forever" mommy and daddy, and that he could visit the Williamses soon. She put Danny's belongings in the car, and told Danny to say goodbye to the Williamses. Mrs. Williams cried as she gave Danny one last hug and kiss. Mr. Williams waved from the yard. Alice escorted Danny, who was crying quietly, to the car.

When they arrived at the Copeland home, Mr. and Mrs. Copeland greeted them in the driveway. They took Danny by the hand and told him that they had a surprise for him. The Copelands led Danny into the house, filled with friends and family, and showed him his new room. Alice carried in Danny's belongings, and found a subdued Danny quietly exploring the toys in his new room. She told Danny that she would visit him next week to see how things were going.

SYNOPSIS

There were many mistakes made in this case which greatly increased the stress for all involved, especially the child. The Copeland family was not given adequate information to help them make an informed decision about adopting Danny. Alice did give them background history, but the Copelands likely did not fully understand nor digest what was said, nor were they helped to consider the implications. No predictive information was given to help the Copelands ascertain what kind of child Danny would be in the future. Alice did not prepare the foster family for Danny's departure, and this was devastating to them as he had been a significant part of their family for over three years. This would likely affect the Williamses' ability to foster in the future.

The foster and adoptive families were not given an opportunity to collaborate to help Danny. The foster caregivers could not effectively prepare and support Danny, and they could not share essential information about Danny with his adoptive family. Furthermore, Danny was placed with his adoptive family after only one visit. He was not prepared to move, and he was placed into a totally foreign environment. In addition, Alice failed to help the adoptive parents prepare for Danny's placement. And finally, introducing Danny to many friends and family at the time of placement was overwhelming and frightening to him.

Not surprisingly, Danny experienced a crisis soon after placement. This could have been avoided, had the planning and implementation of the placement been better. The adoptive family was left with unrealistic expectations, and without dependable sources of support or guidance when they most needed it.

🚶 Jorge, age seven

Jorge, age seven, had resided with his foster mother, Mrs. Lucy Perez, for two years. A videotape of Jorge was featured on a local television program in an attempt to locate a family for him. The following morning, Mrs. Anna Quesada phoned the agency to state that she and her husband were interested in adopting Jorge. Mrs. Quesada said they had been studied and approved by the agency several months earlier, but they had not heard anything. They had also attended the agency's orientation and preservice training. She was very anxious, as she and her husband, a childless couple, had waited many years to adopt.

The call was forwarded to caseworker Tony DiMatteo. He told Mrs. Quesada that he would talk with the adoption coordinator and review the Quesadas' home study to see whether their strengths matched Jorge's needs. He explained that this was an important step, as the matching process was critical to assuring the success of a placement with a child of Jorge's age. He also told Mrs. Quesada he would call her back in a few days, and he thanked her sincerely for her interest and commitment in pursuing this.

Tony talked with the adoption coordinator who had studied the Quesada family. The coordinator had also conducted their preservice training classes. The coordinator said the Quesadas had originally requested a child under the age of five, but it was possible, with preparation and support, that they could successfully adopt a seven year old. Tony and the coordinator concurred that the Quesada family should be considered as an adoptive family for Jorge, but that there would need to be considerable preplacement work before a final decision could be made.

Tony scheduled a joint meeting with the Quesadas and the adoption coordinator. Together they reviewed Jorge's early history, his placement history, and his Prediction Path. They also discussed the Quesadas' initial interest in a younger child, and helped them understand that adopting a child of Jorge's age would likely be more challenging. The adoption coordinator talked about the importance of developing realistic expectations, and the probable long–term ramifications of adopting an older child with special needs. The Quesadas participated fully in the discussion, said that they understood, and indicated their continuing interest in adopting Jorge.

Tony told the Quesadas that before they decided whether to pursue this adoption, they should meet and talk with Jorge's foster mother, and learn more about Jorge. Tony arranged a joint meeting with the foster mother, Mrs. Perez, the adoption coordinator, the Quesadas, and himself for the following week. Tony introduced everyone, and asked them to tell a little about themselves. This helped establish rapport between the two families. Tony then asked Mrs. Perez to share as much information as she could about Jorge's strengths, problems, growth, needs, likes and dislikes, and the "ups and downs" since his placement. Mrs. Perez talked for approximately an hour. The Quesadas asked many questions. Mrs. Perez talked about Jorge's school problems because of dyslexia, and

Tony explained that this could require special education throughout Jorge's schooling. Mrs. Perez also talked about how she disciplined Jorge, and told the Quesadas that Jorge would probably test them, as he did every new teacher, coach, and babysitter.

Tony then asked the Quesadas to describe themselves, and to consider how their lives might have to change, if Jorge were placed with them. Tony felt it important that Mrs. Perez know as much as possible about the Quesadas, so she could help prepare Jorge, if the Quesadas were selected to adopt him.

At the end of the meeting, Tony told the Quesadas to go home and talk everything over. He said he would call them the following week. Mrs. Quesada said they already knew they wanted to continue. Tony said he truly appreciated their commitment, but he believed they should continue to think it over and make sure they had fully considered all the issues. Tony told the Quesadas to consider not just the immediate future, but the long–term issues, as well. Tony also offered to meet with them and help them, if they liked.

The following week, Mrs. Quesada notified Tony that they were definitely interested in continuing. Tony scheduled a visit for the Quesadas to meet Jorge two weeks later. He explained that this would give him enough time to prepare Jorge. In the meanwhile, Tony provided the Quesadas with additional readings about seven year olds and children with dyslexia. Tony called Mrs. Perez, who agreed to tell Jorge that Tony would be stopping by next week to talk with him about an adoptive family.

When Tony arrived at the Perez home, he brought the Quesadas' Family Book, with photographs of the Quesadas, their home, the neighborhood, their two dogs, and extended family and friends. Tony, Mrs. Perez, and Jorge sat at the kitchen table and talked about the new family. Mrs. Perez presented much of the information, and shared what she had learned from her meeting with them. Jorge was reassured that Mrs. Perez had met and liked them. Tony and Mrs. Perez also reminisced about how frightened Jorge had been when he had come to her home. Tony reminded Jorge that he could still talk to and visit with Mrs. Perez, even after he was adopted.

Tony explained the differences between foster care and adoption to Jorge, and told Jorge about the visits they had planned. Tony asked Jorge if he had any questions or suggestions for visits. Jorge wanted to know if the family watched TV or played outside. He thought they might play in the park across from the school. He also asked if the dogs were mean. Tony said he didn't think so, but that was a good question to ask the Quesadas when Jorge met them next week. Jorge didn't think he would want to move, but he agreed to let the Quesadas come to his house to meet him. Tony assured Jorge that he would be there to make sure everything went smoothly.

Tony and the Quesadas arrived at the foster home at 7 p.m. the following Wednesday. Mrs. Perez introduced Mr. and Mrs. Quesada to Jorge. Everyone sat at the kitchen table and looked at the Quesadas' Family Book. Mr. and Mrs. Quesada told Jorge about their home, the backyard, the neighborhood, the school, their church, and the rest of their family. Jorge sat close to Mrs. Perez, but he asked many questions and seemed comfortable with the Quesadas. He asked Mrs. Perez if he could show them his room and toys. When they returned, Jorge had brought one of his games and announced, "These people said they would play a game with me." For the next half hour, the Quesadas played the game with Jorge at the kitchen table, while Mrs. Perez and Tony chatted in the adjoining room. The Quesadas left the foster home at 8:30, as they knew it was Jorge's bedtime.

Tony phoned both families the following morning. The consensus was that the visit had gone well. Mrs. Perez said Jorge had told her, "Those people were nice." A second visit was planned for Saturday, when the Quesadas would take Jorge to a ball game. The Quesadas picked Jorge up at noon, and brought him back at 5 p.m. They commented that the visit had gone well, but that Jorge had a hard time sitting still through the game.

Mrs. Quesada phoned Tony the following Monday morning, asking how soon Jorge could move in. She said that she and her husband had wanted to keep him on Saturday. Tony reminded Mrs. Quesada that the placement procedures were developed to help children with the difficult transition to a new home, and that taking the placement slowly was best for Jorge. He also explained it would help avoid a major disruption for them later. Mrs. Quesada said she remembered that from preservice, but they were just anxious. Tony told her that a third visit could be scheduled for the following weekend, and that the Quesadas should take Jorge to their home for a while and let him become familiar with it. He would call back to confirm the arrangements.

Later that day, Tony stopped by to talk with Jorge. Jorge told him about the ball game. Tony asked Jorge how he felt about his new family. Jorge became quiet and told Tony that he liked them, but he wanted to stay with Mrs. Perez. Tony asked Jorge to get his Lifebook, and together they looked at the pictures and stories. Tony asked Jorge to tell him the story about coming to live with Mrs. Perez. Jorge described what he remembered, and Tony filled in the rest. Tony asked him how he felt back then. Jorge said he didn't remember. Tony reminded him that in the beginning, he didn't like Mrs. Perez very much. Jorge was surprised, and he didn't think that was true. Tony assured him it was, and said it was always scary and hard at first. He told Jorge that many kids who are adopted feel the same way, and that it was okay, because it took time to learn to care about new people. Tony told Jorge he didn't have to pretend everything was okay if he felt bad. In fact, Tony said he wanted to know exactly how Jorge was feeling, so he could help him during this change. He asked Jorge if he'd make a deal about that, and Jorge agreed.

The following Sunday, the Quesadas met Mrs. Perez at church, and took Jorge home for lunch. They took Jorge around the house, and showed him his room, closet, furniture, towel, drinking glass, and seat at the table. Jorge met the dogs, one at a time. The Quesadas told Jorge that on Sundays after church they watched a movie, played games, walked in the park, or visited with their cousins. It was a day to relax. They asked Jorge what he liked to do to relax, and together they wrote a list of ideas for Sundays, and put it on the refrigerator. They agreed to watch a movie for the afternoon, and Jorge was allowed to choose the movie. Afterward, Mrs. Quesada told Jorge that everyone in the family helped make dinner, and she asked Jorge how he wanted to help. Jorge said at home he set the table. She said, "Great!" and showed him where to find dishes and silverware. After dinner, they all helped to clean up. Jorge volunteered to wipe the table. He was returned to his foster home at 7 p.m. Mr. and Mrs. Quesada talked with Mrs. Perez, and told her about the day. They asked Mrs. Perez if they could call on Wednesday night to talk with Jorge.

For the next three weeks, Jorge visited with the Quesadas on Saturday or Sunday. He had begun "testing" his new parents. They seemed to handle his behavior well, and checked with Mrs. Perez each week for support and encouragement. Tony also met with the Quesadas, Mrs. Perez, and Jorge to evaluate progress. After the fourth visit, Tony felt everyone was ready for an overnight visit. Tony asked Mrs. Perez to help Jorge pack some of his belongings, and encourage him to leave them at the Quesadas.

By the second overnight, it was apparent that Jorge was ready to move. He had asked Mr. Quesada to call Mrs. Perez and see if he could stay a little longer so they could watch the ball game together. The next week, Tony, the Quesadas, Mrs. Perez, and Jorge met at the foster home to discuss moving day. They decided Mrs. Perez should help Jorge pack, and that she would drive with Jorge and Tony to the new home. "That way," Jorge said, "she will know where to visit me." They also agreed that Jorge would accompany Mrs. Perez to her granddaughter's birthday party the following month, as the two children were very close.

The night before Jorge's move, Mrs. Perez held a "Good Luck" party, and invited friends, family, and neighbors. Lots of pictures were taken, and Mrs. Perez asked each person to write a "memory" in a notebook for Jorge. She had also made cards with Jorge's new name, address, and phone number for Jorge to give each guest. He asked everyone to call and visit him in his new home.

The following morning, Mrs. Perez and Tony loaded Tony's car with the rest of Jorge's belongings, and drove him to the Quesadas. Jorge took Mrs. Perez by the hand and gave her a tour of the house. The truck was unloaded and everyone sat down for refreshments. Mrs. Quesada asked Jorge to get the surprise they had for Mrs. Perez. Jorge raced to the hall closet and presented his foster mom with a large, framed photo of him. When it was time for Mrs. Perez and Tony to leave, Jorge began to cry. Mrs. Perez hugged him, and told him she'd miss him too, but she would call him later that night. She reassured him that he was still special to her, but that she was really happy that he finally had a forever family. After they had left, Mrs. Quesada took Jorge's hand, dried his tears, and suggested they go feed the dogs, who had been waiting all day for Jorge to pay them some attention.

SYNOPSIS

In this case, a "transition" method was used to help both the child and the adoptive family through the placement. (Refer to Section VIII-C, "Placement Strategies to Prevent Trauma," for extensive discussion of the "transition" method of placement.) Tony encouraged the foster and adoptive families to collaborate to help Jorge. This also benefitted the adoptive family, and eased the foster mother's feelings of loss. Preplacement visits were scheduled to meet Jorge's needs. The placement was planned carefully and slowly, which allowed Jorge to retain as much control as possible. The child became acclimated to his new home and family a little at a time, which prevented his becoming overwhelmed and frightened. And

Jorge's attachment to his foster mother was transferred naturally to his new family without severing his former ties.

Tony scheduled the final placement only after Jorge seemed ready to move. The rites of passage planned by his foster mother helped Jorge with the difficult task of saying goodbye to many people. Moving day was less stressful because of planning and agreement among all parties. The child was given considerable input in planning the day's activities. Furthermore, the gift to the foster mother both acknowledged her importance to Jorge, and validated her continuing involvement in his life. And Jorge's distress at the final goodbye was minimized, because he had already developed a sense of comfort and belonging in his new family.

E. POSTPLACEMENT AND POSTLEGALIZATION SERVICES TO ADOPTIVE FAMILIES*

1. Conceptual Framework

2. Application

3. Case Examples

*Co–authored by Denise A. Goodman, Ph.D., M.S.W.

Conceptual Framework

The advent of special needs adoption practice has generated significant changes in postplacement and postlegalization services. Historically, few services were available to adoptive families after placement, and virtually none were available after legalization. It was widely, but erroneously, believed that there was little difference between adoptive parenting and biological parenting. Workers recommended that adoptive parents take the child home and parent as if the child were born to them. Such quick disengagement from the placing agency was desired by some families to maintain privacy and secrecy.

However, adoption professionals quickly recognized that many adoptive families need ongoing, and sometimes intensive, help. Many adopted children have experienced abuse, neglect, or sexual victimization, and multiple separations. Some have difficulty trusting adults, resist the development of attachments, and display a wide range of physical, emotional, cognitive, social, and behavioral problems. These factors create a higher risk of disruption in the months immediately following placement, as well as dissolution (legal termination of the adoption) or displacement (the termination of a parent–child relationship without a legal dissolution).

The lack of supportive services, both before and after adoption, has been widely identified as a critical contributor to adoptive placement disruption [Barth et al. 1986; Kagan & Reid 1986; Groze & Gruenwald 1991; Nelson 1985; Backhaus 1989; Goodman 1993]. Consequently, a wide range of services has emerged in the past decade, designed to promote the permanence of adoptive placements by strengthening and supporting adoptive families.

Adoption begins a process of change for the adopted child and the adoptive family that continues for many years. Therefore, families often need similar kinds of services and support before and after legalization. There are several objectives of such services:

- *Continue to address issues that were identified during the preparation period.* It is often necessary for family members to revisit issues discussed during the preadoption preparation period. Both families and children must continually address the negative influence of unrealistic expectations. The adoptive family may not be fully aware of the scope of the changes they are experiencing until weeks or months after the placement. The effects of the child's history on current behavior may not always be immediately apparent to family members. Further, the child's past experiences may have a more profound impact on some developmental stages (such as identity formation during adolescence) than on others. Parenting strategies may need to change as the child grows and develops. Families often need services that promote realistic expectations, that help families fully understand and deal with change, that increase the parents' understanding of the child's earlier experiences and their effects on current behavior, and that strengthen parenting strategies.

- *Help the child adjust to a new family and environment.* It is a significant challenge for an adopted child to establish a permanent and secure place in the adoptive family, and in the broader social environment. The child not only gains a new family, he may also attend a new school and church, will inherit a new extended family, and must make new friends. This often requires that the child establish new relationships, adjust to a different social culture, and learn new rules. For many children, the inability to trust others, low self-esteem, and feelings of insecurity may make this adjustment overwhelmingly stressful. Stress may be exhibited both emotionally and behaviorally. Providing the child with guidance and support in adjusting to change can be very helpful during the initial postplacement phase. The caseworker and adoptive family can also ease the child's adjustment by preventing unnecessary losses, and whenever possible, maintaining continuity in the child's attachments. This includes preserving the child's relationships with important persons from his past who can provide emotional support and reassurance.

- *Help the family adapt to changes in the family system, and facilitate the development of healthy family relationships.* Parents and children who are improperly prepared often assume that adoption will be "love at first sight," or they greatly underestimate the effort needed to integrate the child into the family. Even well-prepared families may be surprised by the scope and intensity of the changes brought about by the adoption. Because many adopted children have difficulty forming new attachments, the development of a reciprocal parent–child relationship can be quite difficult. The parents may become frustrated and disillusioned, and may even question the validity of their decision to adopt. Services must be provided to help families deal with the changes in the family system, and to develop realistically positive relationships.

- *Help the child maintain emotional ties with significant persons.* While some degree of separation is inherent in any adoption, we can unnecessarily exacerbate a child's loss by terminating his contacts with significant persons from his preadoption life. It is not only possible, but preferable, to help the child retain important relationships with siblings, previous foster caregivers, friends, teachers, and when appropriate, members of his immediate and extended biological family. The nature and degree of such contact may range from periodic cards, letters, or phone calls, to regular and frequent visits. This continuity serves several purposes. At a minimum, it reassures the child that these persons are alive, well, and still care about him. At best, it prevents the emotional trauma inherent in multiple losses. Some of these contacts may be transitional, lessening naturally over time as the child grows and becomes more invested in a new family and social community. At other times, we would encourage the child to maintain and strengthen these relationships throughout life. At times, important persons from the child's preadoption life can become permanent members of the adoptive family's extended network. Caseworkers may have to help adoptive families understand the importance of maintaining or reestablishing the child's ties to earlier attachment figures. Such contacts can help prevent emotional harm, and may also help counteract some of the traumatic effects of previous losses from separation.

- *Help the child deal with issues of separation and loss.* For most children, the move to an adoptive home is experienced as another dis–ruptive separation. This is likely to resurrect feelings of anxiety and loss associated with previous separations. Older children who have disrupt–ed from previous placements may be very skeptical about the stability of the placement, despite an understanding that adoption is intended to be permanent. Young children may not be able to differentiate adoption from foster care, and may experience adoption as temporary. Resulting feelings of anxiety and depression can generate crisis for the child, par–ticularly if intensive emotional support is not available. Many children regress behaviorally in response to the stresses of placement. Supportive interventions, including counseling, can validate children's feelings, help them deal with these feelings constructively, and ultimately help them understand the permanent nature of adoption.

- *Educate and empower the parents to use therapeutic behavior management techniques.* New adoptive parents may lack the experience or confidence to parent a child with special needs. Even if the parents were properly trained dur–ing the preadoption preparation phase, day–to–day parenting is often more challenging than anticipated. Adopted children often test rules and limits. This can be disconcerting, or even threatening to their parents. At times, adoptive parents do not feel "entitled" to parent the adopted child; they may feel and act as if they were parenting a child who belonged to someone else. They may also hold back when disciplining the child, fearful of causing the child further distress or psychological harm, or fearful of rejection. Services that teach and coach parents in parenting strategies, and that promote the development of entitlement, will pro–mote consistency in the family, and clearly establish the parents in their parenting role.

  Additionally, as the child develops, the adoptive parents are likely to be challenged by new behaviors related to the child's developmental stage, or to the child's history. Many families need continuing education and support long after legalization.

- *Build sources of ongoing support for the child and family.* Adoption is a lifelong challenge, and the family can experience stress or crisis at any time. Some developmental periods are more likely to be stressful than are oth–ers. Families are particularly vulnerable when the child reaches adoles–cence, as identity development and emancipation may resurrect feelings and issues related to the child's history, and to the adoption itself. Workers should help the family develop a continuum of supportive resources, and should empower the parents to use these resources to meet their own and the child's needs, both presently and in the future. Supportive resources for the child might include close friends, family members, school counselors, clergy, previous caregivers, and other helpers from his preadoption life.

- *Assist the parents in meeting the child's cultural needs.* Families of children placed transculturally or transracially may need help in recognizing and meeting the child's needs for cultural continuity and affiliation. Services should reinforce the importance of maintaining the child's cultural identity. Parents should be helped to fully understand and appreciate the child's cultural heritage, and should be helped to locate culturally relevant social, recreational, and educational resources in the community. Significant persons from the child's preadoption life can be valuable resources in helping the adoptive family maintain cultural continuity for the child.

- *Provide crisis intervention as needed.* Because of the many changes discussed above, the postplacement adjustment phase can be extremely stressful for both the family and the child. The pervasive changes experienced by all family members create a high vulnerability to crisis. Workers should help families identify potential crisis situations, provide services to prevent crisis, and help families who are experiencing crisis. A thorough assessment, immediate intervention, and the identification of both short- and long–term solutions can stabilize and preserve the adoptive placement, as well as help to prevent future crises.

THE POSTPLACEMENT PHASE— LEARNING TO BE A FAMILY

There is always a period of adjustment for the adoptive family following placement. The family's equilibrium is disrupted by the introduction of a new member(s). The family's immediate tasks after placement include creating a new family system that fully incorporates the adopted child, reestablishing family equilibrium, and developing positive relationships among all family members.

Family adjustment after adoptive placement generally occurs in a predictable sequence of four phases. These have been called Honeymoon, Ambivalence, Reciprocal Interaction, and Bond Solidification [Pinderhughes & Rosenberg 1990].

The "Honeymoon Phase" is characterized by excitement and optimism. Everyone is eager for the adoption. The child is on her best behavior, and all family members get along well. Often, the adoptive parents feel that the caseworker's warnings and cautions were unwarranted, or they believe themselves to be one of the "lucky" families who will have few adjustment problems. In reality, at this stage the child is often emotionally detached and superficial in her relationships. The child gains considerable gratification being the center of attention, and the parents frequently overlook inappropriate behavior, and minimize the importance of problems.

This period of positive feeling is followed by the "Ambivalence Phase." The child's behavior is no longer compliant. Instead, the child begins to test the parents, both to define limits and to test their commitment. The child often struggles with feelings of distrust, divided loyalty, resurrected grief, and fear of attachment. The child may concurrently desire closeness with the adoptive family, yet fear rejection and abandonment, and feel disloyal to biological parents and former caregivers. Consequently, the child may exhibit both attachment behaviors (clinging, whining, neediness), and disengagement behaviors (aggression, hostility, behavioral acting out, and direct rejection of family members). Many children display their "worst behavior," in attempts to determine whether the family will keep them. This is not usually conscious on the child's part, and verbal reassurances will not normally prevent the occurrence of testing behaviors.

Under the circumstances, it is not surprising that the family also experiences ambivalence. As the child's testing behaviors escalate, the parents may question their decision to adopt, or may question whether the agency gave them "the right child." Extended family members may withdraw their support. Siblings may feel resentful or threatened, and their behavior may regress. The parents may fear discussing their ambivalence with the caseworker, or even with each other, as this may exacerbate their feelings of disappointment and failure.

All family members must understand ambivalence to be a normal and expected part of the adjustment process. Their feelings must be aired and validated. The caseworker can remind parents of similar periods of ambivalent feelings they probably experienced early in their marriage, or after the birth of a child, and ask them how they dealt with those. The family must learn to understand and accept what the child is experiencing, and to provide support, while maintaining appropriate discipline and behavioral control. Often, understanding the nature of their own ambivalence minimizes the parents' disappointment, enabling them to sustain their commitment to the child.

When adoptive families can cope with their ambivalence in a constructive manner, they generally progress to the "Reciprocal Interaction Phase." During this period, family members begin to develop feelings of closeness. The adoptive parents feel less threatened, and tend to manage the child's misbehavior with less resentment. They also recognize, and come to appreciate, the child's individuality. Unless the child has serious attachment problems, she typically begins to trust family members, begins to believe she is going to stay, and works to establish a place for herself within the family. Affectionate bonds are strengthened through the reciprocal "give and take" among all family members.

During the "Bond Solidification Phase," family members feel increased satisfaction with family relationships. Attachments between the family and child are strengthened; the family reestablishes its equilibrium; and a new family system emerges, which accommodates to the child's needs, abilities, likes, and dislikes. The family plans a future that includes the adopted child. The child now sees himself as part of the family, and has begun to assimilate adoptive family traits into his identity.

Unfortunately, not all families can tolerate ambivalence, and they do not develop healthy family relationships. In some families, the child's lack of attachment and problematic behaviors prove too disappointing to the parents. They may interpret the child's negative responses as a personal rejection, a lack of commitment, or a lack of appreciation. The child's behaviors may threaten the stability of the marriage, or challenge the parents' self-esteem. These families seem unable to manage the chaos and disorder that typically accompany an adoption. Their family system remains rigid, and they expect the child to conform to their expectations. Some families cope by legally maintaining the adoption, but they have only superficial involvement with the child. The parents may meet the child's physical needs, but they remain emotionally detached. Pinderhughes [1983] refers to this as "pseudo–adoption." At times, the parents will legally maintain the adoption, but will place the child in residential treatment or foster care, or will simply survive until the child emancipates.

Other families may choose to disrupt the adoption. The child is often targeted as the cause of the family's problems, and is ejected. Frequently, the child is returned to his previous foster home or group care setting [Goodman 1993]. However, the child may also be moved to yet another new and strange environment. Disruption for the child is another rejection, which reinforces the child's feelings of worthlessness and low self–esteem. Family members also experience considerable pain, and they often struggle with feelings of loss, failure, and guilt.

THE CONTRIBUTION OF ATTACHMENT DISORDERS TO FAMILY INSTABILITY

Attachment disorders can greatly complicate the process of family adjustment and bonding. Clinical attachment disorders can develop in children who have experienced severe physical abuse, neglect, sexual victimization, multiple separations, and chronic inconsistency in caregivers. These circumstances can profoundly affect a child's ability to trust others, and to establish healthy, reciprocal relationships.

However, an accurate diagnosis of attachment disorder in older children is often difficult. Children in placement, regardless of their age at placement, may exhibit attachment difficulties to greater or lesser degrees, depending upon their early attachment history, the consistency of caregivers in their lives, their temperaments, and the extent of maltreatment or separation trauma they have experienced. Many of these children may exhibit ambivalence or insecurity in their relationships with caregiving adults, particularly in newly formed relationships; however, not all of them have attachment disorders.

Children in adoptive placement may exhibit a wide range of behaviors that suggest insecurity in their attachments, and ambivalence about forming new attachments with their adoptive parents. These behaviors might include the following:

- They may avoid closeness to caregivers, and may remain emotionally aloof. They may behave as if they have learned to meet their own needs, and are physically and emotionally self–sufficient.

- They may exhibit ambivalence in relationships, sometimes seeking parental affection, and at other times, rejecting affection and "shutting out" their parents.

- They may experience excessive anxiety when separated from family members, and may exhibit anger and/or clinging behavior upon reunion. They may strongly react to even short separations, and may "punish" parents with angry, hostile behavior. At other times, they are clingy and inconsolable.

- They may display indiscriminate attachments, and may be more affectionate and engaging with a stranger than with parents and other family members.

Children with clinical attachment disorders exhibit a particular complex of behaviors that reflect fundamental disorders in their social and emotional development. These children generally require intensive therapy, and will not usually respond to attachment-building interventions by their caregivers. (See Section VIII–A, "Attachment and Attachment Disorders," for a more extensive discussion of attachment problems.)

The caseworker plays an important role in helping families recognize and overcome their children's attachment problems, and in facilitating the family bonding process. This includes recognizing serious attachment disorders in children, and referring them for appropriate therapy, as well as helping parents learn and implement attachment-building interventions. Preventing unnecessary losses, and helping the child maintain important relationships from his past can also mitigate the development of attachment problems.

ADOPTION DISRUPTION AND DISSOLUTION

The professional child welfare literature has documented the complicated and interacting effects of multiple factors in precipitating adoption disruption or dissolution. These contributing factors can include:

- A misassessment or an incomplete assessment of the adoptive family and/or the child [Donley 1981];

- Insufficient preparation of the parents and/or the child [Partridge et al. 1986];

- Inappropriate matching and selection [Unger et al. 1981; Partridge et al. 1986];

- Insufficient or inadequate postplacement services [Backhaus 1989; Partridge et al. 1986];

- A lack of postlegalization services [Barth et al. 1986];

- The absence of adoption–specific, community–based mental health services [Goodman 1993];

- A child's anti–social or demanding behavior [Kadushin & Seidl 1971], or other severe behavior problems [Partridge et al. 1986];

- A child's identity confusion [Sorosky et. al. 1975];

- The age of the child at the time of adoption [Rosenthal et al. 1988; Partridge et al. 1986];

- The child's negative preadoption history [Kagan & Reid 1986], particularly, a history of abuse and neglect [Partridge et al. 1986];

- Intellectual impairments of the child [Nelson 1985];

- A child's attachment problems [Brodzinsky 1987; Partridge et al. 1986];

- A lack of adoptive parent flexibility [Kagan & Reid 1986];

- The inability of adoptive parents to meet the child's special needs [Smith & Sherwen 1983];

- Unrealistic parental expectations of the child [Festinger 1986];

- The parent's own negative childhood history [Sack & Dale 1982];

- Lack of parental feelings of entitlement [Bourguignon & Watson 1988];

- The family's inability to manage feelings of ambivalence [Pinderhughes & Rosenberg 1990];

- The absence of concrete help and emotional support from friends and relatives, or the presence of negative influence from them [Partridge et al. 1986];

- A lack of empathy for the child's need for birth information, or to search for members of the child's biological family [Schneider & Rimmer 1984]; and

- Unforeseen circumstances, such as the death or terminal illness of an adoptive parent, or other events which cannot be predicted or prevented.

Disruption is rarely the result of a single factor. One of the challenges of maintaining a family at risk of disruption, or providing appropriate intervention after a disruption, is to identify and understand the effects of these complicated and interacting variables, and to provide supportive or crisis intervention services to the family before, during, and after a disruption.

Research has also identified several steps in the escalation of problems commonly experienced by families during adoption disruption or dissolution [Partridge et al. 1986; Goodman 1993]. Understanding these dynamics can provide social workers with early warning signs of potential crisis, so that services to stabilize the placement and prevent disruption or dissolution can be provided. The sequence begins after the honeymoon, at the time that ambivalence is beginning to emerge.

The Honeymoon

Adoptive families typically experience pleasure and excitement at the onset of the adoption [Pinderhughes & Rosenberg 1990]. They are positive and hopeful about the family's future. The parents feel able to manage the child's behavior. This phase may last several months, or in some cases years, with no major crisis experienced by the family.

Diminishing Pleasures

The adoptive parents begin to feel tension in their interactions with the child. They have difficulty tolerating the child's misbehavior. What may have been "cute" during the honeymoon is irritating now. However, the parents are still hopeful that this is "just a phase," and that it will eventually pass, returning the family to the level of comfort they felt during the Honeymoon Phase.

The Adopted Child Is Seen as the Problem

Despite their best efforts, the parents are unable to tolerate the child's behaviors. They are affected by every tantrum, angry word, or misbehavior by the child. The child senses the parents' tension. This raises the child's anxiety, which increases the child's negative behaviors and emotional withdrawal. The parents often interpret this as rejection, or lack of appreciation, and they may overreact to minor infractions.

"Going Public"

Eventually, the child's behavior impacts the family's public life. The child may experience school problems, or behavioral outbursts may be witnessed by extended family and friends. Prior to this time, the family has likely dealt with the struggle privately. Now the parents turn to others for support and sympathy, and they often air a long list of complaints. Other people may offer advice, may concur with the parents' assessment that the child is a problem, or may unintentionally support the parents' subconscious (or conscious) intent to disrupt. While the adoption at this point is quite tenuous, appropriate services and interventions can still help families reestablish stability, and avoid disruption.

The Turning Point

The family continues to deteriorate. The child is involved in a "critical incident," which was long-expected and dreaded by the parents. The child may act out sexually, steal, assault a family member, or provoke the parents to lose control. In the family's perception, the child has "crossed the line," and there is no hope of reconciliation. The family begins to fantasize about life without the child.

The Deadline or Ultimatum

The adoptive parents establish an ultimatum, and a deadline by which time the situation must drastically improve, or the child must leave. Frequently, these demands are unrealistic, such as demanding that a child earn all "A's" on a report card after the child has earned failing grades during most of the school year.

The Final Crisis

The final crisis erupts within the family. It may occur because the child did not live up to the parents' ultimatum, or a small incident has become "the straw that broke the camel's back." The entire family is in turmoil. Outside interventions generally prove futile.

The Decision to Disrupt

The final crisis results in the decision to displace the child permanently from the family. In most cases, the family requests (or demands) the child's immediate removal. However, this may also be initiated by the child, a therapist, or the caseworker. The caseworker must act quickly to secure an emergency home for the child, and must help the child and family members through the trauma of separation.

The Aftermath

Once the child is removed, it would appear that the crisis is over. Yet, all parties are typically experiencing considerable pain. The child often feels angry, hurt, and rejected. The parents, who generally appear angry, may also be experiencing guilt, feelings of loss, and an overwhelming sense of failure and hopelessness. The caseworker may also feel guilty, and may believe that the disruption was his or her fault. Or, the caseworker may be angry at the family. This pain and anger may be denied or avoided [Partridge et al. 1986]. The caseworker may not want to be in contact with the family because of helplessness in the face of turmoil. The family often does not seek help because of shame and embarrassment. The child's new caregivers or caseworker may not want to broach the topic of the disruption for fear of upsetting the child. Consequently, all must cope with the trauma of disruption without support.

THE ROLE OF THE CASEWORKER IN PROVIDING POSTPLACEMENT SERVICES

The supervising caseworker plays a strategic role during the postplacement phase, as the caseworker may be the only person to have regular contact with the family after the adoptive placement. The caseworker must help the family continually assess their adjustment and their feelings, and to recognize and deal with potential problems. The caseworker can also provide supportive services, or can link the family with appropriate community providers. If the family and caseworker can identify and manage stress before it reaches crisis proportions, the adoption can often be stabilized and maintained.

In practice, workers providing postplacement services often perceive themselves as observers who assure that the placement is going well prior to legalization. They do not recognize the necessity of intensive postplacement interventions, and they often do not see themselves as responsible for initiating such services. When family problems escalate, and crisis occurs, these workers feel helpless, and unable to stop the impending disruption. This is truly unfortunate, since early intervention can often prevent crisis.

The child welfare agency must conscientiously develop a network of postplacement service providers in the community, and must train caseworkers both to support adoptive placements, and to link the family with the most appropriate service providers.

Application

USING HOME VISITS EFFECTIVELY

The caseworker should have frequent contact with the adoptive family during the first 90 days of placement. The initial three months are especially critical, since the seeds of disruption are frequently sown during this time. Optimally, the caseworker should meet with the family weekly for one to two hours each visit. When this occurs, family members are more likely to view the worker's involvement as an expected part of the adoption process. They will feel more relaxed, behave more naturally, and be more forthright in expressing their feelings and concerns.

The caseworker and the family should jointly develop an agenda for each visit. During home visits, the caseworker should meet with family members both as a group and individually to fully understand their perspectives and feelings. Agenda items should directly address the critical objectives of the postplacement period. These might include:

- To develop or strengthen the collaborative relationship between the caseworker and members of the adoptive family, including the adopted child;

- To review the child's adjustment and behavior since the last contact;

- To help the parents assess their responses to the child's behavior, their coping strategies, and the effectiveness of these strategies;

- To identify and assess areas of potential problems;

- To help the parents develop intervention strategies and contingency plans to deal with expected problems; to help them identify the supports and resources available to them;

- To review the adopted child's Lifebook, and to help the parents acquire skills to talk with the child about the child's history; to share adoption books and videotapes, and to help the family utilize them during family meetings;

- To give the parents and the child positive feedback regarding their successes, and to provide reassurance;

- To reassess the parents' spoken and unspoken expectations for themselves and for the child;

- To observe how the parents are meeting the child's cultural needs, and to provide guidance as indicated; and

- To help the family revise the child's Prediction Path based on newly acquired information.

THE PREDICTION PATH

The Prediction Path [Donley 1990], originally introduced during the preplacement phase to assess the child's needs and potential problem areas, can also be used during the postplacement period. The Prediction Path is composed of three sections: the Placement Trail, the Asset/Debit Sheet, and the Prediction Narrative. (See Section XI–B, "Selecting and Matching Families and Children.")

The Placement Trail identifies the child's typical behaviors in response to prior separation and placement. A review of the Placement Trail may help to illuminate the probable causes of current behaviors, or can prepare the parents for future behavior problems. A review of the Asset/Debit Sheet by the caseworker and the family may reveal that the child has actually progressed in the adoptive placement, and has overcome an earlier problem. This is reassuring and empowering to both the child and the parents. The Prediction Narrative should also be reviewed during home visits to refine strategies to manage potential problem behaviors. The Prediction Path can be an agenda item during each home visit. Revisions to the Prediction Path made during home visits should be copied for the adoptive family.

HELPING PARENTS ENCOURAGE THE DEVELOPMENT OF ATTACHMENT

Caseworkers can help adoptive families learn and use parenting strategies that build and strengthen attachment. Because many families believe that attachment will happen naturally or effortlessly over time, they are not prepared for the attachment difficulties typical for children with histories of abuse, neglect, and separation.

Fahlberg [1979; 1991] has identified several strategies that adoptive parents can use to promote attachment with an older child. These are referred to as: 1) the Arousal–Relaxation Cycle; 2) the Positive Interaction Cycle; and 3) "Claiming" Behaviors. (See Section VIII–A, "Attachment and Attachment Disorders," for related discussion.)

The Arousal–Relaxation Cycle is based on our understanding that trust, security, and attachment are strengthened when a consistent adult caregiver repeatedly meets a child's needs. For example, an infant becomes hungry and cries, reflecting a state of tension and arousal. The caregiver meets the infant's need by feeding and comforting the infant, therein relieving tension and promoting a state of contentment. This cycle is repeated multiple times each day.

Children rely on their adult caregivers to meet both their physical and emotional needs. Most parents quickly learn how to recognize and properly interpret their children's cues of need or distress. However, accurately recognizing cues from an adopted child may be more difficult. These children may not give verbal or behavioral indicators that they have needs, or their cues may be missed or misinterpreted by their caregivers. Consequently, adoptive parents must learn to recognize their child's unique signals of physical or emotional need. A thorough preplacement assessment of the child should help identify and record whether, and how, the child is accustomed to signaling for help or comfort.

Once the adoptive parents can identify need states in their child, they can strengthen attachment by becoming a consistent and desired source of need satisfaction for the child. The following case example illustrates this process:

> Becky was a three year old with a history of sexual abuse. She did not like to go to bed, had tantrums at bedtime, and reacted with severe anxiety when left in the dark. She often cried all night, and she claimed there were monsters under her bed. The adoptive parents recognized Becky's emotional need for comfort and security, and they understood the importance of reassuring Becky that "bad things" wouldn't happen to her at night. The adoptive parents responded by taking Becky shopping, and together they selected several night lights. Every night before bed, Becky and her parents inspected the room for monsters. When none were found, Becky and her parents turned on the night lights, and her bedroom door was left open when the room lights were turned off. The parents provided Becky with hugs and reassurance that their bedroom door was always open at night in case Becky needed them. When Becky had a nightmare, her parents comforted her, and stayed with her in her room until she was able to sleep. In this way, Becky's emotional needs were met, and her attachment to her parents was strengthened.

Uninformed or untrained adoptive parents might experience Becky's night time behavior as stubborn, oppositional, or attention-seeking. This could generate a negative response from the parents, such as ignoring her outbursts, chastising her, and punishing or shaming her. Many maltreated children express their emotional needs behaviorally, not verbally. Parents must recognize that tantrums, nightmares, oppositional behavior, refusal to do what is asked, feigning illness, and other outwardly negative behaviors are often expressions of anger, fear, sadness, loneliness, and other emotional need states. Adoptive parents must be trained to identify ways to meet the child's emotional needs, while still being able to control negative and harmful behaviors.

Fahlberg's second technique to promote attachment is called the Positive Interaction Cycle. While the Arousal–Relaxation Cycle is dependent on the child's expression of need, the Positive Interaction Cycle depends upon the parent initiating affirming emotional and social exchanges with the child. The cycle begins when the parent engages the child in a positive interaction. The child enjoys the interaction, and reacts in an affirming manner. Both the child and parent feel a sense of self–worth, and are motivated to continue to interact. This type of interaction greatly augments the attachment process. The following example highlights this process:

> Matthew, age seven, was adopted by David and Su Fong, a child-less couple. During the preplacement visits, they encouraged Matthew to select one of two available bedrooms as his own. They told him he could decide how he wanted to decorate the room. Together they made several trips to the paint store to look at wallpaper books. Matthew finally decided he wanted a

dinosaur room. At each weekly preplacement visit, Matthew was anxious to see the work that had been completed in his room. First it was painted and wallpapered; next it was carpeted with the rug he had chosen. The Fongs thoroughly enjoyed Matthew's delight with the new room.

After Matthew had been placed for two weeks, his adoptive parents woke him one Saturday morning, and told him they were going on a "mystery trip." The first stop was at the pond in the park near their home to feed the ducks. Then they went to the petting zoo–Matthew especially liked the goats. Then the family went to a restaurant for lunch. Matthew was surprised to see that his previous foster parents were waiting for him at the restaurant. On the way home, he gave his new parents each a hug, and told them it was his "favorite day ever."

This example demonstrates how Mr. and Mrs. Fong initiated positive interactions with Matthew. They allowed Matthew to choose his room; they participated with him in the selection of decorations; they took him on an outing, which included his favorite activities; and they involved his former foster parents, who were very important to Matthew. Because of this, Matthew felt important, special, loved, and he had a good time with his family. In return, the parents shared his excitement and pleasure, and were given an affirming emotional response from Matthew. This was encouraging to the parents, and strengthened their attachment to Matthew.

Many adoptive parents wrongly believe that the child should "take the first step" in forming attachments with them. For adopted children, the lack of trust, and their ambivalence about new attachments may make this impossible. Adoptive parents must be encouraged to regularly approach the child in a nonthreatening, gentle manner to initiate social interactions. However, not all children will respond as positively and openly as Matthew did. Parents must be prepared to continue to engage the child in meaningful and pleasurable interaction without expecting the child to reciprocate in kind. Children may resist such involvement at first, or they may participate superficially. Or, they may verbally reject offers while secretly wanting to accept. At times, when parents suspect this might be the case, they might respond, "Well, let's do it anyway; it might be fun." With this type of child, small expressions of pleasure–smiles, brief glances, and unguarded moments of enjoyment–should be interpreted as victories.

"Claiming" is the third technique Fahlberg recommends to promote attachment. Claiming is the process of assimilating the child into the family, and helping the child feel part of the family. Claiming behaviors also promote the development of entitlement by the parents; that is, the firm belief that they have the right to parent the child as their own.

Examples of claiming behaviors are:

- Having a new family photograph taken, which includes the child;

- Adding the child's name to the mailbox; allowing the child to sign greeting cards;

- Sending out announcements to family and friends when the child joins the family;

- Holding a party to celebrate the legalization of the adoption;

- Referring to the child as "my son," "my daughter," "my brother," or, "my granddaughter";

- Including the child's Lifebook with the other family albums;

- Teaching the child old family traditions; incorporating traditions the child remembers from his earlier life into family traditions; involving the child in developing new family traditions; and

- Adding the child's earlier attachment figures to the family's "extended family and friends" list to receive holiday cards, and to be included in family traditions and rituals whenever possible.

Families should also be encouraged to develop their own techniques for claiming the child into the family, and for marking important events and rites of passage.

Caseworkers should actively direct and mentor families in learning to develop positive attachment behaviors. There are several strategies:

1) The caseworker can educate the family regarding the various attachment–building strategies. Seminars, articles, charts, coaching by veteran adoptive families, and regular discussions can help adoptive families understand the importance and challenge of this process.

2) The caseworker can model attachment–building techniques for the family during home visits. For example, the caseworker might ask the adopted child to share and describe pictures from the family's trip to the zoo. Or, the caseworker could ask each family member to think of one thing the family did during the previous week that was fun, assuring that the perspective of the adopted child is included. If an objective of the home visit is to solve a family problem, the adopted child should be encouraged to contribute thoughts and suggestions to the problem–solving process. The caseworker can explain the attachment–building techniques to the parents before the visit, and can help them consider using similar strategies.

3) The caseworker can give the parents "homework" assignments. One or two activities should be selected at a time. The parents may describe a misbehavior. The caseworker should help them recognize an opportunity to promote attachment, and incorporate attachment–building activities into the intervention. The parents can implement the strategy, and report back to the caseworker during the next home visit.

4) The caseworker can ask the parents to keep an "attachment diary." Often, parents do not feel they are progressing with the child, when in reality, they may have made many gains. When parents keep detailed notes in a diary and review them later, they are better able to recognize that the child is having fewer tantrums, that these are lessening in intensity, that

the child is making more gestures of affection toward them, and that the family relationships are beginning to solidify.

5) The caseworker can provide the parents with continual feedback and support. Some parents may become discouraged and frustrated by the slow nature of attachment–building. They may have expected the child to form attachments more quickly. The caseworker should give the parents honest feedback regarding their parenting style and their expectations, and help them make accurate interpretations of the child's behavior. Parents should be given positive reinforcement for appropriate interactions. The caseworker must also assure them that no parent is ever perfect, and that they should be able to learn much from their mistakes.

6) Professional help by therapists who are skilled in treating attachment disorders should be sought for children who demonstrate severe attachment problems, and for children who do not respond over time to attachment–strengthening interventions by their adoptive parents [See Cline 1992; Levy & Orlans 1995; Pinderhughes & Rosenberg 1990].

USING COMMUNITY RESOURCES

Agencies may refer adoptive families to community resources for help with post–placement adjustment issues. Community resources should complement the services provided by the caseworker. The caseworker should work with the family to locate and select services that the family is comfortable using. Through this collaborative selection of services, the caseworker will:

- *Model the skills needed to access services.* This will be useful to the family in the future, should services be needed in the postlegalization period.

- *Empower the parents to meet their own family's needs.* When case planning and service selection are conducted by the family with the worker's input, family members are more likely to feel entitled to provide for their children, and develop the expertise to do so.

- *Access services within the context of the family's culture and community.* The family must feel comfortable and confident with the service provider, and the services must be relevant to them, if services are to be effective.

There are a variety of services that may be useful to adoptive families. Mental health professionals can help the family cope with attachment problems, can promote the development of family relationships, can help families deal with unexpected changes in the family brought about by the adoption, and can help the family manage behavior problems.

The selection of a mental health professional for an adoptive family requires careful consideration. Rosenberg and Franz [1990] recommend that the adoptive family select a therapist who is skilled in family therapy, since the goal of counseling is to build a family, not to create attachment between the therapist and the child. Further, the therapist should have in–depth knowledge and a positive attitude about adoption. The therapist must also be well–versed in the mental health needs of children, particularly children who have experienced abuse, neglect, sexual victimization, and multiple separations. The adoptive family will often need the caseworker's help to identify qualified therapists. A ther-apist the child has previously worked with can provide continuity for the child, and valuable insights about the child to the adoptive family.

Adoptive parent groups are a valuable source of support during the postplacement period. Many groups hold monthly meetings that both parents and children attend. Frequently, the meetings include an educational program, followed by a social or recreational activity. For many families, the support group helps to socialize them to the world of adoption. Adoptees meet other adoptees, and recognize that they are not unique in their adoption experiences. Families are able to develop lasting relationships with other adoptive families, who then form a natural helping network when questions or concerns arise. Information about local support groups can be obtained from adoption agen-cies, telephone directories, and state or national adoption organizations.

Veteran or "buddy" families are adoptive families who have successfully man-aged a special-needs adoption. These families can offer advice and support to new adoptive families. The "buddy" family can assist the new adoptive family by modeling positive parenting behaviors, discussing common issues, identifying adoption resources, or by helping the new family recognize and manage dis-tressing, but expected, adjustment behaviors. Many agencies have a formal "buddy" program. The veteran families are recruited and trained to mentor new families.

PROVIDING CRISIS INTERVENTION SERVICES

There are predictable and typical stressful events for adoptive families. Most adoptive parents experience some level of discomfort when talking with their child about the adoption and about the child's biological family. Many older children experience a difficult adjustment during the postplacement period, as well as just prior to legalization. Adopted children may also react strongly to dif-ficult life events, such as losses or separations brought about by death, divorce, or moving; life changes, such as a new school, teacher, or babysitter; or normal developmental tasks, such as adolescence, sexuality, emancipation, and marriage. In addition, some adoptive families are challenged by the child's special physi-cal, emotional, psychological, or cognitive developmental needs. Many adoptive families are able to handle these events by seeking out community services or support. In other families, these events may escalate into clinical crisis, which can threaten the adoption.

Unfortunately, the caseworker may be the last person the family contacts for help. However, if postplacement support is being properly provided, the case-worker and family should be able to foresee, and sometimes even prevent the crisis. When the crisis cannot be avoided, the caseworker must be prepared to begin crisis intervention services to preserve the family. (Refer to Section VIII-B, "The Effects of Traumatic Separation on Children," and Section VII-D, "Services for Children with Developmental Disabilities and Their Families," for more extensive discussion on crisis intervention theory and strategies to prevent or manage crisis.)

When crisis has occurred or is imminent, the caseworker should pursue the following steps:

1) *The caseworker and family should identify the presenting problem and its source.*

Parents in crisis may be angry, emotional, and anxious, and they may behave in what seem to be overly dramatic ways. They may threaten or blame others, and their behavior may be volatile and erratic. The caseworker must help the family assess the situation to determine the nature of the problem, and how serious it really is. While the parents often describe the problem in terms of the child's faults or behavior, other factors typically contribute to the crisis. The caseworker must fully explore the events that led up to the crisis to identify the "trigger event," and must simultaneously explore both the parents' coping, strategies and their perception of the event. Information may have to be gathered from family members and from sources outside the family to accurately understand what has happened. It is also important to review historical information from the family homestudy and the child's placement history. It is likely that the underlying problem will be related to one of the following issues:

Parents' Misinterpretation of Normal Child or Adolescent Behavior

The child may be acting in ways that are typical for her age and developmental stage, such as a three year old's temper tantrums; an eight year old's desire to avoid chores and homework; a 13 year old who prefers to be with friends instead of the family; and a 16 year old who verbally criticizes his parents, and repeatedly rebels against parental authority. The parent may not have had previous experience with normal child development, and may misinterpret these behaviors as adoption–specific problems.

The Long-Term Impact of Separation, Abuse, and Neglect

Frequently, adoptive parents fail to realize how a child's past history of abuse, neglect, sexual victimization, and separation can impact the child's behavior, even years after the adoption is finalized. The child may still experience feelings of worthlessness, fear of abandonment, rage, and a lack of trust. As children grow, the behavioral expressions of their issues and concerns will evolve and change. For example, while a sexually abused three year old may act out through play, a preteen may become seductive and indiscriminately sexually active. The child's Prediction Path is often useful in assessing the long–term impact of separation, abuse, and/or neglect on the child's behavior.

The child's current behavior could also be part of a recurring pattern, or directly related to past events. An anniversary, birthday, holiday, or other event can trigger a recurrence of negative feelings for the child, and thus affect behavior. For example, an adoptive family reported that their daughter's behavior was uncontrollable during the week prior to summer camp. After careful questioning, the child revealed that she had previously gone to camp, only to be moved to a new foster home when she returned from camp. This child's behavior resulted from fear of being rejected and abandoned by her adoptive family while she was at camp. In many cases the child's Placement Trail can assist the caseworker and parents in identifying potential trigger dates or events.

Issues Related to the Adoption

Every adoptee struggles to understand and come to terms with his adoptive status. Some adoptees need to inquire about their biological family history, and may desire to search for family members. Others may not feel that they "belong" in the adoptive family. Many youth experience loyalty conflicts. The adoptee may have difficulty integrating aspects of identify from both his biological family and his adoptive family into one "self." The adoptee may respond to these stresses by emotionally withdrawing from the adoptive family. Parents may misinterpret the child's interest in his history and biological family as a rejection of them, or a negation of everything they have done for and given to the child.

Adoptive parents often have their own adoption–related issues as well. Bourguignon and Watson [1987] note that adoptive parents often have difficulty believing that they are "entitled," or have the right, to parent the child as if he were their own. They also have difficulty with claiming behaviors that fully integrate the child into the family. Some parents cannot accept the child's failure to live up to their expectations, yet they lack insight into their own issues of loss and grief related to the fantasy child they wish they had had.

To accurately assess the complex variables that contribute to crisis, the caseworker must have a high level of knowledge regarding normal child development, the impact and interaction of abuse and neglect on development, and the unique issues of both children and parents related to adoption. In addition, the caseworker must be prepared before intervening by reviewing the child's and family case histories to gain useful background information. All of this knowledge is critical to obtaining an accurate assessment of the family's issues.

2) ***The caseworker should be part of the solution, not part of the problem.***

When a crisis call is received, the typical reaction of many caseworkers is to panic [Donley 1981]. This often results in an over-reaction, which may lead to the child's immediate removal from the home, often unnecessarily. Or, the caseworker may become immobilized and underreact by denying that the problems exist, or by avoiding contact with the family. Either reaction will serve to exacerbate the crisis.

Caseworkers must avoid becoming caught up in family members' heightened anxiety and emotionalism. The caseworker must view crisis as an expression of unmanageable stress to the family system, and must understand that the crisis cannot be blamed on the child, the family, or their circumstances. The caseworker must also recognize that her own demeanor and attitude will create the atmosphere in which crisis management will occur. If the caseworker is calm, direct, matter-of-fact, and confident that a workable solution can eventually be reached, this helps reduce family members' anxiety, and restores order. The caseworker must help the family fully assess the circumstances, and must validate each family member's concerns, issues, and feelings. Communicating her own observations to the family may also help them gain an increased understanding of their situation. A thorough understanding of the trigger event and the contributing factors to crisis must be achieved prior to any decision-making regarding interventions, particularly decisions about the child's future with the family.

3) *Develop a short-term plan with the family for immediate relief.*

During the crisis, all members of the adoptive family are experiencing intense pain and uncontrollable feelings of fear, frustration, anger, hopelessness, and sadness. These feelings can result in total immobility, or in impulsive behavior and decision making. The caseworker should help the family choose short-term interventions that will provide immediate relief from the stress without forcing a premature solution to their problems. For example:

- The family can be seen on an emergency basis by a mental health professional for supportive crisis counseling. This can help them better understand the situation, identify potential coping strategies, and reestablish a measure of control.

- The child may spend a few days with relatives, a former foster family, or friends, to give the parents and the child a period of respite; or, the parents may leave the home for a short period of time, leaving the child in the care of a grandparent, friend, or a respite care provider.

- If the child is demonstrating what appear to be severe behavioral or psychological problems, an in-patient evaluation may provide short-term relief to the family while providing additional diagnostic information about the child.

- Family members should agree that they will operate, for the next several weeks, on a day-to-day basis, and they will not make any important or permanent decisions. This lessens the family's anxiety about making the wrong decision. Crisis often occurs when people see no options to deal with a serious problem, even though they feel compelled to solve the problem immediately. If they can be helped to recognize that the solution will be identified in time, and, in fact, they should *not* try to resolve it now, this can reduce much of the stress.

The family should be aware that the short–term plan is designed to give family members a respite from emotional stress, and to provide the caseworker more time to help the family assess their situation. The family should be reconvened within a few days to begin to devise an intervention plan.

4) *The caseworker should review the assessment information with an objective adoption professional.*

Crisis is complex and often hard to assess. The caseworker may feel confused and conflicted during the assessment process. This may result from lack of experience, knowledge, or skill; or, it may occur if the caseworker personally identifies and empathizes more readily with either the parent or child. A worker's lack of objectivity can obscure and confuse the assessment. The worker's own feelings of guilt, anger, inadequacy, frustration, or failure may also cloud his judgment.

Discussing the family's situation with a supervisor, a veteran adoption caseworker, a mental health professional or a consultant often provides the caseworker with alternative explanations and insights not previously considered. The caseworker may also gain information about possible referral resources, supports, and interventions to assist the family.

5) *The caseworker should design an intervention plan with the family.*

The initial goal with all adoptive families in crisis is to strengthen, empower, and preserve the family. Consequently, the caseworker should develop the intervention plan in collaboration with the family. (See Chapter IV, Case Planning and Family-Centered Casework.) This assures that the family assumes ownership of the plan, and remains committed to its implementation. Once the origins of the problems have been identified, the family should choose from one to three issues or problems to address. Objectives should be developed for each issue or problem area. It is particularly important that objectives be short-term, observable, and measurable. The plan should involve objectives for all members of the family. For example, the objectives should not all revolve around the child improving his behavior.

The family should then formulate activities and timeframes to achieve the objectives. The caseworker can help the family identify appropriate service providers and facilitate a referral. It is critical that families be referred to providers with special expertise in adoption issues. Service providers who lack knowledge and insight regarding adoption issues may actually facilitate a disruption.

Involving veteran adoptive families who have, themselves, survived similar crisis situations is among the most useful of interventions, and should be included in all family case plans. The caseworker should also link the family to adoptive parent support groups who can provide peer support for the family long after the family's case is closed.

6) ***The caseworker should provide ongoing support to the family.***

The intervention plan may need to be revised several times during the course of crisis intervention work. As some objectives are met, others can be addressed. The caseworker should maintain regular contact with the family through phone calls and home visits to offer regular encouragement, provide positive reinforcement, to further assess the family's level of functioning, and to determine how they are doing.

THE DECISION TO DISRUPT

At times, the adoptive parents may believe they have no choice but to end the adoption. This may occur after a period of crisis counseling, or there may have been no attempt to preserve the adoption. At times, the child may request removal from the family, or may demonstrate this wish by running away or through other acting–out behaviors. Some families may ask the caseworker to make the decision for them. Disruption can also be initiated by the caseworker or therapist, if the child is at risk of physical or emotional harm in the adoptive home. In any case, the decision to disrupt or dissolve the adoption must be made carefully.

The decision to terminate an adoptive relationship can legitimately be made when:

- A through assessment of the family indicates the problems are intractable or of sufficient scope that there is little likelihood of resolving them;

- Concerted efforts to preserve or reunite the family have been unsuccessful; and

- There is clear evidence that the child is at risk of emotional harm, abuse, or neglect should the adoption continue.

If the caseworker has been properly involved with the family during the postplacement period, in the majority of cases, the disruption will not be a surprise. The caseworker will have been aware of the problems and stresses in the family, and will have helped the family evaluate their ability to cope with them. However, some families can successfully hide their ambivalence or distress from the caseworker. Families may hint at problems, but not fully discuss them, or the caseworker may not recognize their importance. If the caseworker is personally invested in the adoption succeeding, the caseworker may deny or minimize signs that the placement is not stable. Of course, if the caseworker provides little postplacement intervention, the caseworker will generally not be prepared for a disruption.

Should a disruption/dissolution be warranted, the caseworker should take steps to manage the situation in ways that minimize trauma for both the child and the adoptive family. Activities at the time of disruption should achieve the following objectives:

Reduce the chaos, confusion, and emotional volatility that typically accompany disruption and dissolution.

Too often, disruption is handled quickly and without prior planning. The caseworker picks up the child at the family's request and re-places the child. The caseworker often has minimal, if any, subsequent contact with the adoptive family. The child often doesn't fully understand what is happening, or why, and often experiences the disruption as simply another failure and rejection. An absence of careful disruption planning actually exacerbates the crisis for the family and the child.

The re-placement of a child after a disruption or dissolution should follow all the principles of "best placement practice," including: preplacement preparation of both the child and the family; involving the parents in preparing the child for the move; preplacement visits; and supportive intervention by the caseworker for both the child and the family. (See Section VIII-C, "Placement Strategies to Prevent Trauma.") Careful planning with the family provides structure and stability during an otherwise chaotic time, which helps them cope with the crisis.

Help the caseworker, family members, and the child gain insight into the factors that contributed to the disruption, and avoid assigning blame to any one party.

At the time of disruption, all family members are likely to be angry, hostile, and uncooperative. The child may be oppositional, may act out behaviorally, or may be stunned and immobilized. Family members typically experience hurt, rejection, fear, guilt, and sadness as well, even though these feelings are often not expressed. They often fear they will be seen as responsible for the disruption, and may feel the need to defensively deflect the blame. They may blame the child, claiming that the child's unruly and unmanageable behavior, lack of responsiveness to affection, lack of appreciation for them, argumentative nature, or other qualities made it impossible to parent the child. The parents may blame the agency for not placing the "right child" with them, or for failing to sufficiently support them. Some parents blame themselves for not having had the skills and stamina to make the adoption work. If one parent chooses to disrupt, and the other wants to maintain the adoption, the parents may blame each other. At times, the caseworker may feel angry at the parents, and perhaps the child, for not "trying hard enough," or the caseworker may blame himself or herself for failing to preserve the placement.

Families need a safe and controlled setting in which to air their feelings, receive emotional support, and be helped to understand the events leading up to disruption more objectively and accurately. This can also help them better understand the reasons for the disruption, thus reducing the need to assign blame.

Help the caseworker gather additional assessment information to be used in future planning for the child and the family.

It is important for workers to remember that adoption of an older child has dynamics more characteristic of a marriage than childbirth. In a broad sense, the adoption worker is a professional matchmaker, whose job is to predict which families and children will form strong attachments and stay together. However, the "glue" that sustains intimate relationships is difficult to quantify. We should not be surprised when, in spite of our best judgments, some families and children cannot remain together.

Research has documented that a high percentage of children who disrupt from adoptive families are re-placed successfully in new adoptive homes [Unger, Dwarshuis, & Johnson 1981; Partridge et al. 1986]. Disruption does not, therefore, indicate that the child is unadoptable. Nor does disruption automatically mean a family is unsuitable to adopt another child. There are many complicated reasons for disruption, but they can often be summarized as the match was not a good one. Perhaps the family homestudy or the child's assessment was incomplete or inaccurate. The family may not have been honest about important issues, or may not have known themselves well enough to identify their strengths and vulnerabilities. Often, the factors that ultimately caused the disruption could not have been predicted.

There is much to be learned from an adoption disruption. If given the opportunity to fully process their experience, the adoptive family can perhaps better understand their strengths and recognize their vulnerabilities. This may alter their decision to adopt, or revise their conception of the kind of child they could successfully parent. The caseworker and family can gain insight into how the family handles stress, and the extent of their coping abilities. The family's experiences with the child can also provide insight into the child's personality, problems and needs. The caseworker may also discern whether, and how, agency practices contributed to the disruption, or how the worker's own actions should have been different. This information is crucial in helping make informed decisions about future placements for the child and the family, as well as to strengthen the agency's ability to support and strengthen future placements.

The adoption disruption is usually emotionally charged, and has the potential to be painful and destructive for all family members. Casework involvement with the family may be difficult. However, quickly moving the child and avoiding subsequent contact with the family can have long–term negative consequences for both the family and the child. A skilled caseworker using crisis intervention strategies can help family members and adopted children cope constructively with the trauma of disruption.

The caseworker should have several contacts with all family members at the time of disruption, and in the weeks that follow, to help family members cope with the disruption. The caseworker may use individual or group meetings, depending upon the case circumstances. Whether or not the adopted child should be included in all or part of family meetings should be determined on a case–by–case basis, depending upon the child's age, maturity, vulnerability, and the level of hostility and antagonism between the adoptee and the adoptive family. When the adoptive parents' anger and blame cannot be effectively controlled during meetings, the child should not be included. In such situations, the caseworker should meet with the adoptive parents and the child at different times.

The caseworker should utilize one family meeting to plan the steps of the child's re–placement, including times for preplacement visits and how family members can help prepare the child to move. The preplacement visits should begin as soon as an alternative placement for the child is located, and generally should be completed within a week. Allowing the child to contribute to the planning process helps the child maintain a sense of control, which can prevent or minimize placement trauma.

Casework with the child is designed to help the child understand the reasons for disruption, and to prevent unwarranted self–blame. Helping the child write a story about the adoption for her Lifebook can be a useful intervention. It gives the child permission to vent anger, disappointment, and fear. The caseworker can also help the child deal with unwarranted feelings of guilt, or feelings of rejection and unworthiness that often result from disruption.

Activities at the time of disruption must be individualized to meet the needs of the child and the family. They must also be appropriate for the circumstances surrounding the disruption. A well–planned and well–timed re–placement is a primary objective of disrupted adoptive placement. However, some families may adamantly refuse to participate in re–placement planning activities. They may not be able to transcend hostility, or they may continue to inappropriately assign blame to the child. Some children may be at risk of emotional or physical harm in the adoptive family. In these situations, the child's need for protection should be the worker's prime concern.

The primary purpose of services at the time of disruption is to prevent lasting emotional harm to either the child or the adoptive family as a result of the crisis of disruption. If these services are provided appropriately, blame can be minimized, self–esteem can be preserved, and both the child and family can be helped to formulate a more positive future.

Case Examples

The following case studies illustrate two approaches to casework activity during the postplacement period. The caseworker in the first scenario provides the family with only perfunctory supervision, while the caseworker in the second scenario provides the family with effective postplacement services.

🚶 The Jones Family

Elizabeth and Ronald Jones and their 15-year-old daughter Michelle have recently adopted Charlie, age eight. Charlie was placed with the family two weeks ago. Ed Tolbert, who had supervised the placement, was also assigned to work with the family after the placement.

Ed called Mrs. Jones to schedule the required monthly home visit. Due to Mrs. Jones' work schedule and other scheduling difficulties, the first postplacement home visit was scheduled on the one-month anniversary of Charlie's placement.

During this visit, Ed asked the family, "Well, how's it going?" Everyone replied, "Fine." Charlie was anxious to show Ed the new football he had been given, and took Ed to the park across the street. Ed tossed the ball with Charlie for about 10 minutes. He then returned to the house and told Mrs. Jones that everything seemed to be going well. He advised Mrs. Jones to call him if she had any questions or concerns. He told her that he would be out to check on the family the next month. As he pulled away from the curb, he waved to Charlie, who was sitting on the front stoop.

Each month, Ed came to see "how the family was doing." He didn't stay very long, and only exchanged pleasantries. Mrs. Jones was hesitant to share any of her concerns, because she didn't know him that well, and she was afraid of what might happen if she told him about the problems with Charlie. A few weeks before the legalization court hearing, Ed sent Mrs. Jones a letter informing her of the date and time. He stated in the letter that he looked forward to seeing the family there. Four days later, Ed received a phone call from an agitated Mrs. Jones, who told him that she and her husband had changed their minds and did not want to legalize the adoption. Ed was caught totally unaware; he thought the placement was going fine.

🚶 The Marks Family

Ms. Marjorie Marks, her 11-year old daughter, Patrice, and her grandmother, Mrs. Bessie Stokes, recently adopted Cindy, age eight. At the time of Cindy's placement, her caseworker, Richard Hobbs, scheduled weekly discussion meetings with the family for the first two months of placement. Ms. Marks agreed to adjust her work schedule, whenever possible, to accommodate these appointments. When she could not, Richard visited the family at dinner time.

For the first visit, Richard arrived at the family's home at 3:30 p.m., about 45 minutes before the girls were to come home from school. During this time, he met with Ms. Marks and Mrs. Stokes to review Cindy's Prediction Path. In the first weeks following her placement, Cindy wet the bed, as had been anticipated. Ms. Marks said that she was ready for that, with a plastic mattress cover and an extra set of sheets. Ms. Marks and Mrs. Stokes had worked out a plan with Cindy to handle wet sheets. Since Ms. Marks must leave for work early, Mrs. Stokes supervised the bed change before Cindy left for school. Richard commended the teamwork of Ms. Marks and Mrs. Stokes. During the meeting, Richard also reviewed other behaviors that were identified in the Predication Narrative, and helped the family develop contingency plans, should the behaviors reoccur.

The girls arrived home from school about 4:15 p.m. Richard taught them the strategy of "thumbs up" and "thumbs down" discussion, where each family member relates their best and worst experiences of the week. This activity was to be used in their weekly meetings. During the meeting, Cindy admitted to a "thumbs down" day at school. She said that she had to stay in at recess because she got in a fight with another girl earlier in the morning. Richard led a discussion with the family about how Cindy could handle this situation in the future. Ms. Marks gave Cindy a hug, and told her she was proud that Cindy shared this experience with the family; then she encouraged her to try talking to the teacher next time.

Richard then asked Cindy if she would talk with him privately on the front steps for a few minutes. Ms. Marks suggested that it would be a good time for Patrice to change clothes, and she went in the kitchen to start dinner. Richard began by asking Cindy how she felt about her new school, and how she was fitting in. Cindy said she liked her new teacher, and that some of the kids were mean, but she had made some friends. Richard told Cindy that fitting into a new school could be scary. He also said it could be hard and scary fitting into a new family! Richard asked Cindy how she was feeling about her new family, and was it as she had expected? Cindy became very quiet and turned away from Richard. Richard asked Cindy what was wrong. She tearfully said she missed her foster family. Richard told Cindy that lots of kids who are adopted are afraid at first, and miss their foster family. Cindy shook her head, "Yes." She said that she wished she could go back and live with her foster family again. Richard told Cindy the Marks' were her family now, but that she could still love her foster parents. He asked Cindy if she had talked to them. She said she had, but only two times. Richard asked Cindy if she had told her mom how she felt. Cindy said, "No." She said she was too scared. Richard asked Cindy if she wanted his help in telling her mom. She nodded, and Richard told her to wait on the steps. He asked Ms. Marks to step outside for a moment. Richard then said, "Cindy misses her foster parents, but she was a little afraid to tell you. I think she would like to talk to them. Would that be all right?" Ms. Marks sat down next to Cindy, put her arm around her shoulders and said, "Of course. They're part of our family now. We'll call them tonight. Maybe in a couple of weeks, we can all get together for a visit. Okay?" Cindy turned and gave Ms. Marks a hug. She told Richard, "Thanks," and went to change her clothes.

During the fourth weekly meeting, it became evident that Cindy was struggling with trust issues. She was having a hard time making friends, and kept saying that she shouldn't bother trying, she was just going to move again. When

Richard met with Ms. Marks and Mrs. Stokes before the girls came home from school, he observed the frustration both of them were feeling. Ms. Marks stated that she hadn't thought it would be this hard, because she had been a parent before. Richard reminded Ms. Marks that giving birth and adoption were two very different ways that a child joins a family. Mrs. Stokes stated that Cindy often accuses her of liking Patrice better, because Patrice is her "real" granddaughter. Richard told them that Cindy's behaviors were not uncommon for adopted children, and he suggested that the family become involved with other adoptive families who could help with solutions. He said they could join a support group, or he could link them with a veteran adoptive family similar to theirs. Ms. Marks and Mrs. Stokes talked for a few minutes, and decided they would prefer to talk with an individual family. Richard said he would have an adoptive parent call them. He then arranged a "buddy family" for the Marks'. Ms. Emma Thomason, also a single parent, had adopted and raised three children through the agency.

Richard continued to meet with the Marks family weekly during the first ten weeks of placement. Sometimes he would ask to see Cindy's Lifebook, and they would talk about where she used to live, and who had cared for her. He encouraged her to continue to work on her Lifebook by adding pictures and stories about her new family and school. Richard also continued to discuss Cindy's adjustment, referring to the Prediction Path, and helping with parenting techniques. Ms. Marks found Ms. Thomason, her "buddy" family, to be a valuable resource, and they were becoming good friends. Ms. Marks learned that many of the adjustment problems the family was experiencing were to be expected, which she found very reassuring.

During the third, fourth, and fifth months of placement, Richard visited the Marks family twice each month. He met with family members both individually and as a group. He encouraged Ms. Marks to use the meetings to discuss her feelings about the adoption, and to resolve any parenting or behavior management problems. At the end of the fourth month of placement, Ms. Marks called Richard and asked him to come over as soon as possible. She stated that Cindy had been sent home from school that day because of her tantrums. She didn't know what to do, but knew that Richard could help.

Richard came to the home later that day. He talked with Ms. Marks and Mrs. Stokes alone. He brought out the Prediction Narrative and reviewed the "expected behaviors" section, where tantrums were identified as a potential problem. Ms. Marks stated that she had managed Cindy's tantrums fairly well at home, but the teacher couldn't. Mrs. Stokes jokingly said that the teacher needed her own copy of the Prediction Narrative! Richard pointed out that it might not be a bad idea for Ms. Marks to talk with the teacher, and discuss how she had handled Cindy's tantrums at home. Ms. Marks agreed. Richard asked how Ms. Marks would discipline Cindy for being sent home from school. Ms. Marks described her plan to use time out, loss of privileges, and parent–child discussions. Richard agreed with her strategies.

Ms. Marks phoned Richard a few days later and told him about her conference with the teacher. She said it had gone very well, and they were working together to manage Cindy's tantrums. Ms. Marks noted that she really felt like Cindy's "real" mother now. Richard commended her efforts, and told her that he would likely call on her in the future to be a "buddy" parent to someone else.

In subsequent visits, Richard initiated discussions with Ms. Marks and Mrs. Stokes about helping Cindy deal with the adoption, and her biological family. Ms. Marks said Cindy had recently begun to talk about her biological mother, whom she referred to as "Alice." Cindy had, at first, given glowing descriptions of her life with Alice, but recently she had begun to share some of the details of the abuse she had experienced. Ms. Marks said even though she had learned during preservice training that this might happen, she was unsure how to handle it. She said she had just let Cindy talk and tried not to look shocked, even though that was how she felt. Richard said listening was very important. He told Ms. Marks that Cindy's willingness to talk suggested she was feeling more comfortable and secure in the family. He also said helping Cindy talk about her traumatic past, and giving her loving support was a good way to strengthen attachment. Ms. Marks seemed reassured.

Richard asked her how she felt when talking with Cindy about Alice. Ms. Marks said it was hard, because hearing about the abuse made her "raging mad." She wondered if it wouldn't be better to "let bygones be bygones," and thought it might make it worse for Cindy to talk about her life with Alice. Richard explained that talking about it was the first step in dealing with it, and, if done properly, could be very helpful for Cindy. He stressed the importance of helping Cindy understand that the abuse was not her fault. He also suggested that Ms. Marks record this information, as at some time in the future, it might help Cindy better understand the circumstances of her removal from her family. Ms. Marks said she'd have to think about it. Richard suggested that Ms. Marks could one day help Cindy develop empathy for her mother's problems, which would further help her avoid self-blame. Ms. Marks said she remembered that from pre-service training. Richard agreed that Ms. Marks should think about it, and they would talk more in later visits.

During the sixth month of placement, Cindy's behavior, which had been steadily improving, deteriorated quickly. She began to wet the bed regularly and had violent temper tantrums. She threatened to run away, and one day she did not come home from school. Patrice said she had looked everywhere, and didn't know where Cindy had gone. After a frantic tour of the neighborhood and a call to the police, the family found Cindy sitting alone in the dark on the school playground. Ms. Marks called Richard, who came out the next day.

Ms. Marks was emotionally distraught and frantic. She and Richard tried to identify what might have happened to prompt this behavior. Ms. Marks said she wasn't sure she could put up with Cindy's running away. She said Cindy wouldn't talk to her about it. She said it made no sense, since the weekend before had been Cindy's birthday, and they had had a big party and had invited Cindy's school friends, the whole extended Marks/Stokes family, and Cindy's foster parents. Richard consulted the Prediction Path and noted that Cindy's negative behaviors always increased just prior to a move, and he noted that a couple of Cindy's placements had lasted less than six months. He speculated that Cindy might be feeling threatened about moving. He also said it was possible that the birthday party made it clear to Cindy that she was truly part of the family, and it may have frightened her. He said while they couldn't know for sure, Ms. Marks should reassure Cindy about the permanence of this adoption, and tell Cindy she was there to stay. He told Ms. Marks helping Cindy recognize how upset she was might also reaffirm her commitment to Cindy. Richard offered to help Ms. Marks talk to Cindy about this.

Ms. Marks called Cindy in and proceeded to tell her firmly how angry and upset she was because Cindy had run away, and that she was angry because Cindy had scared her to death. Ms. Marks said she would never forgive herself if anything happened to Cindy. She also told Cindy that she was part of this family forever now, and she hoped Cindy understood that. Ms. Marks also said that running away was not a solution to anything, and if Cindy had problems, she should talk to her, or to Richard. Cindy cried quietly as Ms. Marks talked. When Ms. Marks had finished, she pulled Cindy onto her lap and held her for the rest of the meeting with Richard. Cindy's negative behaviors diminished. There was no recurrence of running away.

Throughout the sixth, seventh, and eighth months of placement, Richard visited with the family every three weeks. In each session, the entire family talked about the "ups and downs" since their last meeting. They had decided to write important positive events on a calendar in the kitchen, so they could look back and see how many good things had happened. Richard asked what the most recent positive event had been. Mrs. Stokes laughed, and said Cindy and Patrice had tried to cook her breakfast in bed for her birthday. She said it was clear that she would have to teach both of the girls how to cook!

Richard frequently mailed Ms. Marks notices about lectures and classes, and he gave her books about adoption and children with special needs. He also began to help her plan for legalization. The legalization court hearing was scheduled during the ninth month of placement. About a month before the hearing, Richard brought a camera to the visit, and asked to take some pictures of the family. He asked Cindy if he could add some pictures to her Lifebook. He asked Ms. Marks to take two pictures of himself and Cindy, one for him, and one for Cindy's Lifebook. He also asked to take a picture of the family to keep in his office. They posed happily for the portrait.

Richard also spent some time reminiscing about the nine months since placement, and how far they had all come. He explained what would happen at the court hearing, and asked if Cindy and her family would like to visit the courtroom before the hearing date. They all agreed, and met a week before the hearing to take a tour and talk to members of the judge's staff. Cindy asked Ms. Marks if she could invite her foster family to her adoption party. Ms. Marks said, "Of course. Would you like to invite them to the court hearing, too?" Cindy said that she would think about that. Cindy then turned to Richard and invited him to her party.

Before closing the case, Richard met one last time with Ms. Marks and Mrs. Stokes, and reiterated that Cindy might have crises from time to time, and that adolescence could be particularly difficult. He said while no one could predict the future, he knew that it would be important for the family to maintain sources of support. He suggested that Ms. Marks stay in contact with him, and let him know if she or the family ever needed help. He stressed the importance of continuing to seek support for herself from her family, friends, and from other adoptive parents like Ms. Thomason. He also suggested that once Cindy was fully settled in, if Ms. Marks wanted to consider helping another new adoptive family, she should let him know.

SYNOPSIS

In the first scenario, the caseworker maintained minimal supervisory contact with the family and provided no services or support. This did not allow the development of working relationships, or permit an ongoing assessment of the family's adjustment. Consequently, minor problems were not identified, which later became a precipitant for disruption.

In the second scenario, the caseworker provided regular supportive services to the family. He utilized each contact to assess the quality of family relationships, to assist the parents with problem solving, and to help the child adjust to a new home. Richard empowered Ms. Marks and Mrs. Stokes to use what they already knew about child management to handle the difficulties they were experiencing with Cindy. Richard also used the concrete tools of the Prediction Path, the Prediction Narrative, and the Lifebook effectively with the family. He frequently suggested possible interventions, and he offered praise and encouragement to Ms. Marks and Mrs. Stokes.

Richard also planned the termination and case closure, taking into account the many losses that Cindy had experienced, and recognizing the need to gradually withdraw services and support. He did this by slowly increasing the time between contacts during the fourth through ninth months. Richard began discussing closure a month before legalization. He reviewed their work together and used the photo session as an informal closure activity. The legalization hearing and Cindy's adoption party were used as formal rites of passage, where the family "graduated" from postplacement services. Yet, he made certain the family knew he continued to be a resource, if they needed ongoing help, and he encouraged their continued use of support services within their family and community.

BIBLIOGRAPHY

Bibliography

Abel, G.G. & Rouleau, J.L. (1990). The nature and extent of sexual assault. In W.L. Marshall, D.R.Laws, & H.E. Barbaree (Eds.), *Handbook of sexual assault: Issues, theories, and treatment of the offender.* New York: Plenum. As cited in Salter, A.C. (1995). *Transforming trauma: A guide to understanding and treating adult survivors of child sexual abuse.* Newbury Park, CA: Sage Publications.

Abel, G.G., Becker, J.V., Cunningham-Rathner, J., Mittelman, M. & Rouleau, J.L. (1988). Multiple paraphilic diagnoses among sex offenders. *Bulletin of the American Academy of Psychiatry and the Law, 16(2).* As cited in Salter, A.C. (1995). *Transforming trauma: A guide to understanding and treating adult survivors of child sexual abuse.* Newbury Park, CA: Sage Publications.

Abel, G.G., Becker, J.V., Mittelman, M., Cunningham-Rathner, J., Rouleau, J. L., & Murphy, W.D. (1987). Self-reported sex crimes of nonincarcerated paraphiliacs. *Journal of Interpersonal Violence, 2(1).* As cited in Salter, A.C. (1995). *Transforming trauma: A guide to understanding and treating adult survivors of child sexual abuse.* Newbury Park, CA: Sage Publications.

Abel, G.G., Mittelman, M.S., & Becker, J.V. (1985). Sexual offenders: Results of assessment and recommendations for treatment. In M.R. Ben-Aron, S.J. Huckle, & C.D. Webster (Eds.), *Clinical criminology: The assessment and treatment of criminal behavior.* Toronto: M & M Graphic Ltd. As cited in Salter, A.C. (1995). *Transforming trauma: A guide to understanding and treating adult survivors of child sexual abuse.* Newbury Park, CA: Sage Publications.

Abroms, I.F., M.D. (1980). The child with a seizure disorder. In A.P. Scheiner & I.F. Abroms (Eds.), *The practical management of the developmentally disabled child.* St. Louis: C.V. Mosby Co.

Abroms, I.F., M.D. (1980). The child with significant developmental motor disability (Cerebral palsy: Medical and neurological aspects). In A.P. Scheiner & I.F. Abroms (Eds.), *The practical management of the developmentally disabled child.* St. Louis: C.V. Mosby Co.

Ainsworth, M.D.S., & Wittig, B.A. (1969). Attachment and exploratory behaviour of one year olds in a strange situation. In B.M. Foss (Ed.), *Determinants of infant behaviour, (Vol 4).* London: Methuen; New York: Barnes & Noble. As cited in Levy, T.M. & Orlans, M. (1995). Intensive short-term therapy with attachment-disordered children. In L. VandeCreek, S. Knapp, & T.L. Jackson (Eds.), *Innovations in clinical practice: A source book (Vol 14).* Sarasota, FL: Professional Resource Press.

Ainsworth, M.D.S., Blehar, M.C., Waters, E., & Wall, S. (1978a). *Patterns of attachment: A psychological study of the strange situation.* Hillsdale, N.J.: Erlbaum. As cited in Levy, T.M. & Orlans, M. (1995). Intensive short-term therapy with attachment-disordered children. In L. VandeCreek, S. Knapp, & T.L. Jackson (Eds.), *Innovations in clinical practice: A source book (Vol 14).* Sarasota, FL: Professional Resource Press.

Ainsworth, M.S. (1978b). Attachment: Retrospect and prospect. In C. Parkes & J. Stevenson-Hinde (Eds.), *The place of attachment in human behavior.* New York: Basic Books.

Akins, C., Davison, R., & Hopkins, T. (1980). The child with myelodysplasia. In A.P. Scheiner & I.F. Abroms (Eds.), *The practical management of the developmentally disabled child.* St. Louis: C.V. Mosby Co.

American Association for Protecting Children (1988). *Child sexual abuse curriculum for social workers.* Denver: American Humane Association.

American Association of Mental Retardation (1992). *AAMR diagnosis, classification, and systems of supports.* Washington, DC: American Association of Mental Retardation.

American Professional Society on the Abuse of Children (1991). *Guidelines for psychosocial evaluation of suspected sexual abuse in young children.* American Professional Society on the Abuse of Children.

American Prosecutors Research Institute (APRI) (1989). *Investigation and prosecution of child abuse.* Virginia: APRI.

American Psychiatric Association (1994). *Diagnostic and statistical manual of mental disorders (DSM-IV).* (4th ed.) Washington, DC: American Psychiatric Association.

Anday, E.K., Cohen, M.E., Kelley, N.E., & Leitner, D.S. (1989). Effect of in-utero cocaine exposure on startle and its modification. *Dev Pharmacol Ther, 12*(3), 137–145.

Andujo, E. (1988). Ethnic identity of transethnically adopted hispanic adolescents. *Social Work, 33*(6): 531–535.

Annas, G.J. (1989). *The rights of hospital patients.* Carbondale: Southern Illinois University Press.

Arnold, L.E. (1978). *Helping parents help their children.* New York: Brunner/Mazel.

Asch, A., Cohen, C.B., Edgar, H., & Weisbard, A.J. (1987). Section 4: Who should decide? In Imperiled newborns. *Hastings Center Report, 17*(6).

Ashley, B.M., & O'Rourke, K.D. (1978). *Health care ethics: A theological analysis.* St. Louis: The Catholic Health Care Association of the United States.

Avery, M.E., Janeway, C.A., Berenberg, W., & Medearis, D.N. (1978). The Saikewicz decision. *New England Journal of Medicine*, 1208–1209.

Azuma, S.D., & Chasnoff, I.J. (1993). Outcome of children prenatally exposed to cocaine and other drugs: A path analysis of three-year data. *Pediatrics, 92*(3), September, 396–402.

Backhaus, K. (1989). Training mental health practitioners to work with adoptive families who seek help. *Child Welfare, LXVIII*, 61–68.

Baltes, P. & Reese, H.W. (1984). The life span perspective in developmental psychology. In M.H. Bornstein & M.E. Lamb, *Developmental psychology: An advanced textbook.* Hillsdale, NJ: Lawrence Erlbaum Associates.

Barnett, T.J. (1990) Baby doe: Nothing to fear but fear itself. *Journal of Perinatology, 10*(3), 307–311.

Barth, R.P. (1988). Disruption in older child adoptions. *Public Welfare, 46*, p. 23–29. As cited in Petr, C.G. & Barney, D.D. (1993). Reasonable efforts for children with disabilities: The parents' perspective. *Social Work, 38*(3), May, 247–254.

Barth, R.P. (1994). Long-term in-home services. In D.J. Besharov (Ed.), *When drug addicts have children.* Washington, DC: Child Welfare League of America.

Barth, R.P., Berry, M., Carson, M., Goodfield, R., & Feinberg, B. (1986). Contributors to disruption and dissolution of older-child adoptions. *Child Welfare, LXV*(4), 359.

Bartoshesky, L.E. (1980). Genetics and the child with developmental disabilities. In A.P. Scheiner & I.F. Abroms (Eds.), *The practical management of the developmentally disabled child.* St. Louis: C.V. Mosby Co.

Basson, M.D. (1983). Bioethical decision-making: A reply to Ackerman. *The Journal of Medicine and Philosophy, 8*, 181–185.

Battle, C.U. (1987). Beyond the nursery door: The obligation to survivors of technology. *Clinics in Perinatology, 14*(2), 417–427.

Bauchner, H., Zuckerman, B., McClain, M., Frank, D., Fried, L.E., & Kayne, H. (1988). Risk of sudden infant death syndrome among infants with in-utero exposure to cocaine. *J. Pediatrics, 113*(5), November, 831–834.

Beauchamp, T.L., & Childress, J.F. (1983). *Principles of biomedical ethics.* (2nd ed.) New York: Oxford University Press.

Becker, J.V. & Coleman, E.M. (1988). Incest. In V.B. Van Hasselt, R.L Morrison, A.S. Bellack, & M. Hersen (Eds.), *Handbook of family violence.* New York: Plenum. As cited in Salter, A.C. (1995). *Transforming trauma: A guide to understanding and treating adult survivors of child sexual abuse.* Newbury Park, CA: Sage Publications.

Becker, J.V. (1988). The effects of child sexual abuse on adolescent sexual offenders. In G. Wyatt & G. Powell (Eds.), *Lasting effects of child sexual abuse.* Newbury Park, CA: Sage Publications.

Becker, J.V., Cunningham-Rathner, J., & Kaplan, M.S. (1986). Adolescent sexual offenders: Demographics, criminal and sexual histories, and recommendations for reducing future offenses. *Journal of Interpersonal Violence, 1*(4). As cited in Salter, A.C. (1995). *Transforming trauma: A guide to understanding and treating adult survivors of child sexual abuse.* Newbury Park, CA: Sage Publications.

Beckman, P.J. (1983). Influence of selected child characteristics on stress in families of handicapped infants. *American Journal of Mental Deficiency, 88*(2), 150–156.

Beeler, N.G., Rycus, J.S., & Hughes, R.C. (1990.) *The effects of abuse and neglect on child development: A training curriculum.* Washington, DC: Child Welfare League of America.

Beeler, N., Cartwright, P., Ginther, N., King, C., & LeSure, S. (1993). Victim Trauma Treatment Project Curriculum, Ohio Child Welfare Training Program. Columbus, OH; Institute for Human Services and the Ohio Department of Human Services.

Benn, S.J. (1972). Justice. In P. Edwards (Ed.), *The encyclopedia of philosophy.* (Vol. 4). New York: Macmillan, 299.

Berkowitz, S.T. (1986). A committee consults: The care of an anencephalic infant. *Hastings Center Report, 3,* 18–22.

Besharov, D.J. (1994) *When drug addicts have children.* Washington, DC: Child Welfare League of America.

Bornstein, M.H., & Lamb, M.E. *Developmental psychology: An advanced textbook.* Hillsdale, NJ: Lawrence Erlbaum Associates.

Bossard, J. & Boll, E.S. (1966). *The sociology of childhood: Fourth edition.* New York: Harper & Row.

Bourguignon, J. & Watson, K. (1988). *After adoption: A manual for professionals working with adoptive families.* Springfield, IL: Illinois Department of Children and Family Services.

Bourguignon, J. & Watson, K. (1990). *Making placements that work.* Evanston, IL: NBI Press.

Bowlby, J. (1970). *Attachment and loss, Vol. I: Attachment.* New York: Basic Books.

Bowlby, J. (1973). *Attachment and loss, Vol. II: Separation: Anxiety and anger.* New York: Basic Books.

Boyd-Franklin, N. (1989). *Black families in therapy: A multisystems approach.* New York: Guilford Press.

Brecht, B. (1964 translation). Threepenny opera. New York: Grove.

Brennan, T.A. (1986). Do-not-resuscitate orders for the incompetent patient in the absence of family consent. *Law, Medicine and Health Care, 14*(1), 13–19.

Briere, J. & Runtz, M. (1988) Post sexual abuse trauma. In G. Wyatt & G. Powell (Eds.), *Lasting effects of child sexual abuse.* Newbury Park, CA: Sage Publications.

Briere, J. (1992). Child abuse trauma: Theory and treatment of the lasting effects. Newbury Park, CA: Sage Publications.

Brody, H. (1981). *Ethical decisions in medicine* (2nd ed.) Boston: Little, Brown.

Brodzinsky, D.M. (1987). Looking at adoption through rose-colored glasses: A critique of Marquis and Detweiler's "Does adoption mean different?" An attributional analysis. *Journal of Personality and Social Psychology, 52,* 394–398.

Bullen, J. (1991). J. J. Kelso and the "new" child-savers. The genesis of the children's aid movement in Ontario. In R. Smandych, G. Dodds, & A. Esau (Eds.), *Dimensions of childhood: Essays on the history of children and youth in Canada.* Winnipeg, Manitoba: Legal Research Institute of the University of Manitoba.

Butler, S. (1978). *Conspiracy of silence: The trauma of incest.* San Francisco: Volcano Press, Inc.

Byler, W. (1977). The destruction of American Indian families. In S. Unger (Ed.), The destruction of American Indian families. New York: Association on American Indian Affairs. As cited in J. Laird & A. Hartman (Eds.), *A handbook of child welfare: Context, knowledge, and practice.* New York: The Free Press.

Cage, R. (1988). Criminal investigation of child sexual abuse cases. In S. Sgroi, *Vulnerable populations: Evaluation and treatment of sexually abused children and adult survivors. (Vol. I).* New York: Lexington Books.

Canadian Paediatric Society, Bioethics Committee. (1986). Treatment decisions for infants and children. *Canadian Medical Association Journal, 135,* 447–448.

Caplan, A. & Cohen, C.B. (Eds.), Imperiled newborns. *The Hastings Center Report, 17(6).*

Carlson, V., Cicchetti, D., Barnett, D. & Braunwald, K. (1989). Disorganized/disoriented attachment relationships in maltreated infants. *Developmental Psychology, 25,* 525–531. As cited in Lyons-Ruth, K., Alpern, L. & Repacholi, B. (1993). Disorganized infant attachment classification and maternal psychosocial problems as predictors of hostile–aggressive behavior in the preschool classroom. *Child Development, 64,* 572–585.

Caruso, K. & ten Bensel, R. (1993). Fetal alcohol syndrome and fetal alcohol effects. *Minnesota Medicine, 76,* April, 25–29.

Caulfield, E. (1931). *The infant welfare movement of the eighteenth century.* New York: Paul Horker.

Chalnick, M.K. (1989). Compromising positions: Medical treatment for disabled infants. *Maternal-Child Nursing Journal, 18(2),* 167–177.

Chase, H.P., & Martin, H.P. (1970). Undernutrition and child development. *New England Journal of Medicine, 282,* 933–939.

Chasnoff, I.J., Griffith, D.R., MacGregor, S., Dirkes, K., & Burns, K.A. (1989a). Temporal patterns of cocaine use in pregnancy. Perinatal outcome. *JAMA, 261(12),* Mar 24–31, 1741–1744.

Chasnoff, I.J., Hunt, C.E., Kletter, R., & Kaplan, D. (1989b). Prenatal cocaine exposure is associated with respiratory pattern abnormalities. *Am. J. Dis. Child 143(5)* May, 583–7.

Chasnoff, I.J., Lewis, D.E., Griffith, D.R., & Willey, S. (1989c). Cocaine and pregnancy: Clinical and toxicological implications for the neonate. *Clin Chem 35(7),* July 1989, 1276–8.

Chavkin, W., Paone, D., Friedmann, P., & Wilets, I. (1993). Reframing the debate: Toward effective treatment for inner city drug–abusing mothers. *Bulletin of the New York Academy of Medicine, 70(1),* Summer.

Bibliography

Cherukuri, R., Minkoff, H., Feldman, J., Parekh, A., & Glass, L. (1988) A cohort study of alkaloidal cocaine ("crack") in pregnancy. *Obstetrics and Gynecology, 72*(2) August, 147–51.

Child Welfare League of America North American Kinship Care Policy and Practice Committee (1994). *Kinship care: A natural bridge.* Washington, DC: Child Welfare League of America.

Chimezie, A. (1977). Bold but irrelevant: Grow and Shapiro on transracial adoption. *Child Welfare, LIV*(2): 75–85.

Christoffel, K.K., Scheidt, P.C., Agran, P.F., Kraus, J.F., McLoughlin, E., & Paulson, J.A. (1992). Standard definitions for childhood injury research: Excerpts of a conference report. *Pediatrics, 89*, 1027–1034. As cited in National Research Council, Panel on Research on Child Abuse and Neglect, Commission on Behavioral and Social Sciences and Education (1993). *Understanding child abuse and neglect.* Washington, DC: National Academy Press.

Clement, K. (1988). Family builder notes. *Roundtable.* As cited by Ryan, G. (1990). Sexual behavior in childhood. In J. McNamara & B. McNamara (Eds.), *Adoption and the sexually abused child.* Portland, ME: University of Southern Maine, Human Services Development Institute.

Cline, F.W. (1979). *Understanding and treating the severely disturbed child.* Evergreen, CO: Evergreen Consultants.

Cline, F.W. (1992). *Hope for high risk and rage filled children: Reactive attachment disorder: Theory and intrusive therapy.* Evergreen, CO: E.C. Publications.

Coles, C.D. (1993). Impact of prenatal alcohol exposure on the newborn and the child. *Clinical Obstetrics and Gynecology, 36*(2), June, 255–65.

Columbus Dispatch (1991). *Hospital can't remove girl's life support.* Columbus, Ohio: Dispatch Publishing Company, October 18.

Columbus Dispatch (1991). *Is no life better than life of pain, suffering?* Columbus, Ohio: Dispatch Publishing Company, November 30.

Comprehensive Epilepsy Program (1980). Epilepsy and the School Age Child. Minneapolis: University of Minnesota.

Conte, J. & Schuerman, J. (1988). The effects of sexual abuse on children: A multidimensional view. In G. Wyatt & G. Powell (Eds.), *Lasting effects of child sexual abuse.* Newbury Park, CA: Sage Publications.

Copeland, J. Intake Supervisor, Athens County Children Services, personal conversation with author, Nan Beeler,, June, 1994.

Cornford, F.M. (1945). *The republic of plato.* London: Oxford University Press.

Corwin, D. (1988). Early diagnosis of child sexual abuse: Diminishing the lasting effects. In G. Wyatt & G. Powell, *Lasting effects of child sexual abuse.* Newbury Park: Sage Publications.

Costin, L.B. (1985). The historical context of child welfare. In J. Laird & A. Hartman (Eds.), *A handbook of child welfare: Context, knowledge, and practice.* New York: The Free Press.

Council on Social Work Education (1992). *Curriculum policy statement for master's degree programs in social work education.* Alexandria, VA: Council on Social Work Education.

Cowan, E. & Stout, E. (1939). A comparative study of the adjustment made by foster children after complete and partial breaks in continuity of home environment. *American Journal of Orthopsychiatry, 9.*

Coyne, A., & Brown, M.E. (1985). Developmentally disabled children can be adopted. *Child Welfare, LXIV*(6), 607–616.

Coyne, A., & Brown, M.E. (1986). Relationship between foster care and adoption units serving developmentally disabled children. *Child Welfare, LXV*(2), 189–198.

Cranford, R.E. & Doudera, A.E. (1984). *Institutional ethics committees and health care decision making.* Ann Arbor, MI: Health Administration Press.

Cranford, R.E. & Roberts, J.C. (1986). Biomedical ethics committees. *Primary Care, 13*(2) 327–341.

Crittenden, P. (1985). Maltreated infants: Vulnerability and resilience. *Journal of Child Psychology and Psychiatry, 26,* 85–96. As cited in Levy, T.M. & Orlans, M. (1995). Intensive short–term therapy with attachment–disordered children. In L. VandeCreek, S. Knapp, & T.L. Jackson (Eds.), *Innovations in clinical practice: A source book (Vol 14).* Sarasota, FL: Professional Resource Press.

Crossley, M.A. (1987). Selective nontreatment of handicapped newborns: An analysis. *Medicine and Law, 6,* 499–524.

Cunningham, C. & MacFarlane, K. (1991). When children molest children: Group treatment strategies for young sexual abusers. Vermont: Safer Society Press.

Curran, W.J. (1978). The Saikewicz decision. *New England Journal of Medicine,* 1209(b).

Damme, C. (1978). Infanticide: The worth of an infant under the law. *Medical History, 22,* 1–24.

Damon, W. (1977). *The social world of the child.* New York: Jossey–Bass.

Damon, W. (1983). *Social and personality development.* New York: W.W. Norton.

Davis, A. (1986). Informed dissent: The view of a disabled woman. *Journal of Medical Ethics, 12,* 775–776.

Debo, A. (1970). *A history of the Indians of the United States.* Norman, Oklahoma: University of Oklahoma Press.

de Young, M. (1987). Disclosing sexual abuse: The impact of developmental variables. *Child Welfare, LXVI*(3), May–June.

de Young, M. & Corbin, B. (1994) Helping early adolescents tell: A guided exercise for trauma–focused sexual abuse treatment groups. *Child Welfare, LXXIII*(2), March–April.

Doberczak, T.M., Shanzer, S., Senie, R.T., & Kandall, S.R. (1988). Neonatal neurologic and electroencephalographic effects of intrauterine cocaine exposure. *J. Pediatrics, 113*(2) August, 354–8.

Donaldson, M.A. & Gardner, R. (1985). Diagnosis and treatment of traumatic stress among women after childhood incest. In C.R. Figley (Ed.), *Trauma and its wake.* (Vol. 1). New York: Brunner/Mazel.

Donley, K. (1981). Observations on disruption. *Adoption Disruptions.* (DHHS Publication No. 81–30319.) Washington, D.C.: U.S. Department of Health and Human Services.

Donley, K. (1990). A morning consultation with Kay Donley. Workshop conducted at the July, 1990 Conference of The Attachment Center, Golden, Colorado.

Doudera, A.E. (1986). Developing issues in medical decision making: The durable power of attorney and institutional ethics committees. *Primary Care, 13*(2), 315–325.

Drews, K., Salus, M.K., & Dodge, D. (1981). *Child protective services: inservice training for supervisors and workers.* Washington, DC: Creative Associates, Inc.

Driscoll, J. (1982). Mortality and morbidity in infants less than 1001 grams birth weight. *Pediatrics, 69,* 21–26.

Duff, R.S., & Campbell, A.G.M. (1973). Moral and ethical dilemmas in the special care nursery. *New England Journal of Medicine, 289,* 890–94.

Dyson, L. (1991). Families of young children with handicaps: Parental stress and family functioning. *American Journal on Mental Retardation, 95(6),* 623–629.

Egeland, B. & Sroufe, L.A. (1980). Attachment and early maltreatment. *Child Development, 52,* 44–52.

Elbow, M. & Knight, M. (1987). Adoption disruption: Losses, transitions, and tasks. *Social Casework, 68,* 546–552.

Elmer, E. & Gregg, G. (1967). Developmental characteristics of abused children. *Pediatrics, 40(4),* 596–602.

Emmit, D. (1967). Ethics and the social worker. In E. Younghusband (Ed.), *Social work and social values.* London: George Allen & Unwin Ltd.

English, D.J., & Pecora, P.J. (1994). Risk assessment as a practice method in child protective services. *Child Welfare, LXXIII(5),* September/October, 451–73.

Epstein, M.H., Cullinan, D., Lessen, E.I., & Lloyd, J. (1980). Understanding children with learning disabilities. *Child Welfare, LIX(1),* 2–14.

Erikson, E. (1959). Identity and the life cycle. *Psychological Issues. 1* (1) Monograph 1. New York: International Universities Press, Inc.

Erikson, E. (1963). *Childhood and society.* (2nd ed.) New York: W.W. Norton and Co.

Fahlberg, V.I. (1979). *Attachment and separation.* Dearborn, Michigan: Michigan Department of Social Services.

Fahlberg, V.I. (1991). *A child's journey through placement.* Indianapolis, IN: Perspectives Press.

Falconer, J. (1982). Health care delivery problems for the disabled. In M.G. Eisenberg, C. Griggins, & R.J. Duval (Eds.), *Disabled people as second class citizens.* New York: Springer.

Faller, K.C. (1994). Child sexual abuse allegations: How to decide when they are true. *Violence Update, 4(6).*

Faller, K.C. (1990). Sexual abuse by paternal caretakers: A comparison of abusers who are biological fathers in intact families, stepfathers, and noncustodial fathers. In A.L. Horton, B.L. Johnson, L.M. Roundy, & D. Williams (Eds.), *The incest perpetrator; A family member no one wants to treat.* Newbury Park, CA: Sage. As cited in Salter, A.C. (1995). *Transforming trauma: A guide to understanding and treating adult survivors of child sexual abuse.* Newbury Park, CA: Sage Publications.

Fanshel, D. & Shinn, E. (1978). *Children in foster care: A longitudinal investigation.* New York: Columbia University Press.

Festinger, T. (1986). *Necessary risk: A study of adoptions and disrupted adoptive placements.* New York: Child Welfare League of America.

Finkelhor, D. (1984). *Child sexual abuse: New theory and research.* New York: Free Press.

Finkelhor, D. (1986). *A sourcebook on child sexual abuse,* Newbury Park, CA: Sage Publications.

Finkelhor, D. (1988). The trauma of child sexual abuse: Two models. In G. Wyatt & G. Powell (Eds.), *Lasting effects of child sexual abuse.* Newbury Park, CA: Sage Publications.

Fleischman, A.R. (1986). An infant bioethical review committee in an urban medical center. *Hastings Center Report, 3,* 16–18.

Fleischman, A.R. (1988). Ethical issues in neonatology: A U.S. perspective. *Annals of the New York Academy of Sciences, 530,* 83–91.

Fortune, A.E. (1994). Field education. In F.G. Reamer (Ed.), *The foundations of social work knowledge.* New York: Columbia University Press.

Fost, N. (1981). Counseling families who have a child with a severe congenital abnormality. *Pediatrics, 67,* 321–324.

Fox, R. & Swazey, J. (1978). *The courage to fail.* Chicago: University of Chicago Press.

Fraiberg, S. (1977). *Every child's birthright: In defense of mothering.* New York: Basic Books. As cited in Fahlberg, V.I. (1991). *A child's journey through placement.* Indianapolis, IN: Perspectives Press.

Francoeur, R.T. (1983). Biomedical ethics: *A guide to decision making.* New York: John Wiley and Sons.

Fraser, B.G. (1976). The child and his parents: A delicate balance of rights. In R.E. Helfer & C.H. Kempe (Eds.), *Child abuse and neglect: The family and the community.* Cambridge, MA: Ballinger, 315–333.

Freud, A. & Burlingham, D. (1943). *War and children.* New York: Ernest Willard.

Freund, K. (1990). Courtship disorder. In W.L. Marshall, D.R. Laws, & H.E. Barbaree (Eds.), *Handbook of sexual assault: Issues, theories, and treatment of the offender.* New York: Plenum. As cited in Salter, A.C. (1995). *Transforming trauma: A guide to understanding and treating adult survivors of child sexual abuse.* Newbury Park, CA: Sage Publications.

Friedrich, W. (1988). Behavior problems in sexually abused children: An adaptational perspective. In G. Wyatt & G. Powell (Eds.), *Lasting effects of child sexual abuse.* Newbury Park, CA: Sage Publications.

Friedrich, W., Grambsch, P., Damon, L., Koverola, C., Wolfe, V., Hewitt, S.K., Lang, R.A., & Broughton, D. (1992). Child sexual behavior inventory: Normative and clinical findings. *Psychological Assessment,* 4(3), 303–311. As cited in Gil, E. & Johnson, T.C. (1993). *Sexualized children: Assessment and treatment of sexualized children and children who molest.* Rockville, MD: Launch Press.

Fulroth, R., Phillips, B., & Durand, D.J. (1989). Perinatal outcome of infants exposed to cocaine and/or heroin in utero. *Am J. Dis Child,* 143(8), August, 905–910.

Gardner, H. (1978). *Developmental psychology.* Boston, MA: Little, Brown & Co.

Garibaldi (1987). In the matter of Kathleen Farrell, (Case 108 N.J. 335). *New Jersey Supreme Court Reporter, 108.*

Gelman, R. (1979). Preschool thought. *American Psychologist,* October, 900–905.

Gerard, M.W., & Dukette, R. (1953). *Techniques for preventing separation trauma in child placement.* Presentation, Annual Meeting, Illinois Children's Home and Aid Society, Chicago.

Gil, D. (1973). *Unravelling social policy: Theory, analysis, and political action towards social equality.* Cambridge, MA: Schenkman Books.

Gil, E. (1993). Age-appropriate sex play versus problematic sexual behaviors. In E. Gil & T.C. Johnson (1993). *Sexualized children: Assessment and treatment of sexualized children and children who molest.* Rockville, MD: Launch Press.

Ginther, N. Foster parent/child welfare professional. Personal conversation with Sally Cooper, August, 1995.

Goldson, E., & Hagerman, R.J. (1993). "Fragile-X syndrome and failure to thrive. *American Journal of Diseases of Children, 147*, June, 605-6.

Goodman, D. (1993). Here today, gone tomorrow: An investigation of the factors that impact adoption disruption. *Dissertation Abstracts International, 54*, 4259A. (University Microfilms No. 94-11 949).

Greenstein, L.J. (1987). Withholding life-sustaining treatment from severely defective newborns: Who should decide? *Medicine and Law, 6*, 487-497.

Griffith, D.R., Azuma, S.D., & Chasnoff, I.J. (1994). Three-year outcome of children exposed pre-natally to drugs. *Journal of the American Academy of Child and Adolescent Psychiatry. 33*(l), January, 20-27.

Groth, A.N., Nobson, W.F., & Gary, T.S. (1982). The child molester: Clinical observations. In J.R. Conte & D.A. Shore (Eds.), *Social work and child sexual abuse*. Binghamton, NY: Haworth. As cited in Salter, A.C. (1995). *Transforming trauma: A guide to understanding and treating adult survivors of child sexual abuse*. Newbury Park, CA: Sage Publications.

Groze, V. & Gruenwald, A. (1991). Partners: A model program for special needs families in stress. *Child Welfare, LXX*(5), 581-598.

Guroff, G. (1979). Effects of inborn errors of metabolism on the nutrition of the brain. In R.J. Wurtman & J.J. Wurtman (Eds.), *Nutrition and the brain*. (Vol. 4.) New York: Raven Press.

Gustaitis, R. (1988). Right to refuse life-sustaining treatment. *Pediatrics, 81*(2), 317-321.

Hadeed, A.J., & Siegel, S.R. (1989). Maternal cocaine use during pregnancy: Effect on the new-born infant. *Pediatrics, 84*(2), August, 205-210.

Hagerman, R.J., Jackson, A.W. III., Levitas, A., Rimland, B., & Braden, M. (1986). An analysis of autism in fifty males with the fragile-X syndrome. *American Journal of Medical Genetics, 23*, 359-74.

Hartman, A. (1994). Social work practice. In F.G. Reamer (Ed.), *The foundations of social work knowledge*. New York: Columbia University Press.

Haskett, M.E., Wayland, K., Hutcheson, J., & Tavana, T. (1995). Substantiation of sexual abuse allegations: Factors involved in the decison-making process. *Journal of Child Sexual Abuse, 4*(2).

Hasselt, V. (1988). *Handbook of family violence*. New York: Plenum.

Hastings Center Report (1987). Who should decide? Imperiled newborns. *Hastings Center Report, 17*(6).

Hedges, B. Clinical Director, Mid-Ohio Counseling Center, Lancaster, Ohio. Personal conversation with Nan Beeler, June, 1994.

Helfer, R.E., & Kempe, R.S. (Eds.), (1987). *The battered child*. (4th ed.) Chicago: University of Chicago Press.

Helfer, R.E., McKinney, J., & Kempe, R. (1976). Arresting or freezing the developmental process. In R.E. Helfer & C.H. Kempe, *Child abuse and neglect: The family and the community*. Cambridge, MA: Ballinger Publishing Company.

Henderson, D.J. (1975). Incest. In A.M. Freeman, H.I. Kaplan, & B.J. Sadock (Eds.), *Comprehensive testbook of psychiatry*. (2nd ed.) Baltimore: Williams & Wilkins. As cited in Salter, A.C. (1988). *Treating child sex offenders and victims: A practical guide*. Newbury Park, CA: Sage Publications.

Hepburn, J. (1994). The implications of contemporary feminist theories of develoment for the treatment of male victims of sexual abuse. *Journal of Child Sexual Abuse, 3* (4).

Hill, R. (1965). Generic features of families under stress. In H. Parad & G. Caplan (Eds.), *Crisis intervention: Selected readings.* New York: Family Service Association of America.

Holder, W.M., & Mohr, C. (Eds.), (1980). *Helping in child protective services.* Englewood, CO: American Humane Association.

Hollis, E.V. & Taylor, A.L. (1951). *Social work education in the United States.* Westport, CT: Greenwood Press.

Horejsi, C.R. (1979). *Foster family care: A handbook for social workers, allied professionals, and concerned citizens.* Springfield, IL: Charles C. Thomas.

Hosford, B. (1986). *Bioethics committees: The health care provider's guide.* Rockville, MD: Aspen Publications.

Howard, A., Royse, D., & Skerl, J. (1977). Transracial adoption: The black community perspective. *Social Work, 22*(3): 184–189.

Howard, J. (1994). Barriers to successful intervention. In D.J. Besharov (Ed.), *When drug addicts have children.* Washington, DC: Child Welfare League of America.

Howard, J., Beckwith, L., Rodning, C., & Kropenske, M.P.H. (1989). The development of young children of substance–abusing parents: Insights from seven years of intervention and research." *Zero to Three,* June.

Hughes, R.C. (1993). Child welfare services for the catastrophically ill newborn: A confusion of responsibility. *Child Welfare, LXXII*(4), July–August, 323–340.

Hughes, R.C. (1993). Child welfare services for the catastrophically ill newborn: A guiding ethical paradigm. *Child Welfare, LXXII*(5), September–October, 423–440.

Hughes, R.C. (1989). *Ethical paradigms utilized by health care workers in decision making for developmentally disabled neonates with life threatening medical conditions.* Unpublished research.

Hughes, R.C. & Rycus, J. S. (1983). *Child welfare services for children with developmental disabilities.* New York: Child Welfare League of America.

Hughes, R.C. & Rycus, J.S. (1989). *Target: Competent staff. Competency-based inservice training for child welfare.* Washington, DC: Child Welfare League of America.

Hull, C. & Hagerman, R.J. (1993). A study of the physical, behavioral, and medical phenotype, including anthropometric measures, of females with fragile x syndrome. *American Journal of Diseases of Children, 147,* November, 1236–41.

Human Policy Press. (1976). *Handicapism.* Syracuse, NY: Human Policy Press.

Hunter, W.M., Coulter, M.L., Runyan, D.K., & Everson, M.D. (1990). Determinants of placement for sexually abused children. *Child Abuse and Neglect, 14.*

Hutchinson, J.R., Lloyd, J.C., Landsman, M.J., Nelson, K., & Bryce, M. (1983). *Family centered social services: A model for child welfare agencies.* Oakdale, Iowa: National Resource Center on Family Based Services, The University of Iowa School of Social Work.

Imai, S., Logan, K., & Stein, G. (1993). *Aboriginal Law Handbook.* Scarborough, Ontario: Carswell.

In Re Quinlan, 70 N.J., L0, 355 A.2d647 (New Jersey, 1976).

Institute for Child Advocacy. (1987). *Children in out-of-home care.* Cleveland, OH: Institute for Child

Advocacy.

Isabella, R.A. (1993). Origins of attachment: Maternal interactive behavior across the first year. *Child Development, 64,* 605–621.

Jarvis, P.A. & Creasey, G.L. (1991). Parental stress, coping, and attachment in families with an 18–month–old infant. *Infant Behavior and Development, 14,* 383–395.

Jenkins, J.L., Salus, M.K., & Schultze, G.L. (1979). *Child protective services: A guide for workers.* Washington, D.C.: National Center on Child Abuse and Neglect; Children's Bureau; Administration for Children, Youth and Families; U.S. Department of Health, Education, and Welfare. (DHEW Publication No. (OHDS) 79–30203).

Johanek, M.F. (1988). Treatment of male victims of child sexual abuse in military service. In S.M. Sgroi (Ed.), *Vulnerable populations: Evaluation and treatment of sexually abused children and adult survivors.* Lexington, MA: Lexington.

Johnson, C.F. (1995). Personal consultation. Columbus, Ohio: Children's Hospital Child Abuse Program.

Johnson, L.C. & Schwartz, C.L. (1991). *Social welfare: A response to human need.* Boston: Allyn & Bacon.

Johnson, P., Shireman, J., & Watson, K. (1987). Transracial adoption and the development of black identity at age eight. *Child Welfare, LXVI*(1), 45–56.

Johnson, T.C. (1991). Identification and treatment approaches for children who molest other children. *Journal of Interpersonal Violence.* 4(4).

Johnson, T.C. & Feldmeth, J. (1993). Sexual behaviors: A continuum. In E. Gil & T.C. Johnson, *Sexualized children: Assessment and treatment of sexualized children and children who molest.* Rockville, MD: Launch Press.

Johnson, T.C. (1990). Important tools for adoptive parents of children with touching problems. In J. McNamara & B. McNamara (Eds.), *Adoption and the sexually abused child.* Portland, Me: University of Southern Maine, Human Services Development Institute.

Johnson, T.C. (1991). Understanding the sexual behaviors of young children. *Seicus Report.* Aug–Sept.

Johnson, T.C. (1993). Childhood sexuality. In E. Gil & T.C. Johnson, *Sexualized children: Assessment and treatment of sexualized children and children who molest.* Rockville, MD: Launch Press.

Jones, C.E. & Else, J.F. (1979). Racial and cultural issues in adoption. *Child Welfare, LVIII*(6), 373–382.

Jones, E.D. (1972). On transracial adoption of black children. *Child Welfare, LI*(3): 156–164.

Jones, K.L. (1988). *Smith's recognizable patterns of human malformation.* Philadelphia: W.B. Saunders Company.

Jones, K.L. & Smith, D.W. (1973). Recognition of the fetal alcohol syndrome in early infancy. *Lancet, ii,* 999–1001.

Jones, L. (1983). Appalachian values. In B. Ergood & B. Kuhre (Eds.), *Appalachia: Social context past and present.* Dubuque, Iowa: Kendall/Hunt.

Jones, R. (1970). Social values and social work education. In K.A. Kendall (Ed.), *Social work values in an age of discontent.* New York: Council on Social Work Education, Inc.

Kaak, H. O. (1977). Unpublished Lecture. Columbus, Ohio: Children's Hospital.

Kadushin, A. & Martin, J. (1988). *Child welfare services.* (4th ed.) New York: MacMillan.

Kadushin, A. & Seidl, F. (1971). Adoption failure: A social work post mortem. *Social Work, 16*, 32–38.

Kadushin, A. (1980). *Child welfare services.* (3rd ed.) New York: Macmillan.

Kagan, J., & Klein, R.E. (1973). Cross–cultural perspectives on early development. *American Psychologist*, November, 947–961.

Kagan, R.M. & Reid, W.J. (1986). Critical factors in the adoption of emotionally disturbed youths. *Child Welfare, 65*(1), 63–73.

Kanner, L. (1973). *Childhood psychosis: Initial studies and new insight.* Washington, DC: V.H. Winston and Sons.

Kant, I. (1959). *Foundation of the metaphysics of morals.* L.W. Beck, Trans. New York: Liberal Arts Press. (Original work published in 1785).

Katz, L. & Robinson, C. Foster care drift: A risk–assessment matrix. *Child Welfare, LXX*(3) May–June, 347–358.

Katz, L. (1974). Transracial adoption: Some guidelines. *Child Welfare, LIII*(3): 180–188.

Kaye, K., Elkind, L., Goldberg, D., & Tytun, A. (1989). Birth outcomes for infants of drug abusing mothers. *N Y State J. Med 89*(5), May, 256–61.

Kearney, M.H., Murphy, S. & Rosenbaum, M. (1994). Mothering on crack cocaine: A grounded theory analysis. *Soc. Sci. Med. 38*(2), 351–361.

Kempe, C.H. & Helfer, R.E. (1972). *Helping the battered child and his family.* Philadelphia: J.B. Lippincott.

Kempe, R.S., & Goldbloom, R.B. (1987). Malnutrition and growth retardation ("failure to thrive") in the context of child abuse and neglect. In R.E. Helfer & R.S. Kempe (Eds.), *The battered child.* (4th ed.) Chicago: University of Chicago Press, 312–335

Kerby, D.S., & Dawson, B.L. (1994). Autistic features, personality, and adaptive behavior in males with the fragile x syndrome and no autism. *American Journal on Mental Retardation, 98*(4), 455–62.

Keyserlingk, E.W. (1987). Against infanticide. *Law, Medicine and Health Care. 14*(3–4), 154–157.

Kim, S.P. (1980). Behavior symptoms in three transracially adopted Asian children: Diagnosis dilemma. *Child Welfare, LIX*(4): 213–224.

Kinlaw, K. (1990). Is it ethical to provide futile care?" *Journal of the Medical Association of Georgia,* 79(11) 839–842.

Knoles, G.H. & Snyder, R.K. (Eds.), (1968). *Readings in western civilization.* (4th ed.) Philadelphia: J.B. Lippincott Co.

Knopp, F.H. (1984). *Retraining adult sex offenders: Methods and models*, Orwell, VT: Safer Society Press.

Korbin, J.E. (1987). Child abuse and neglect: The cultural context. In R.E. Helfer & R.S. Kempe (Eds.), *The battered child.* (4th ed.) Chicago: University of Chicago Press, 23–41.

Kubler-Ross, E. (1972). *On death and dying.* New York, MacMillan.

Kuhse, H. & Singer, P. (1987). For sometimes letting – and helping – die. *Law, Medicine and Health Care,* 14(3–4), 149–153.

Kuhse, H. & Singer, P. (1989). The quality/quantity–of–life distinction and its importance for nurses. *Int. J. Nurs. Stud., 26*(3) 203–212.

Kurtz, P.D. (1979). Early identification of handicapped children: A time for social work involvement. *Child Welfare, LVIII*(3), 165–176.

Laird, J. & Hartman, A. (Eds.), (1985). *A handbook of child welfare: Context, knowledge, and practice.* New York: The Free Press.

Lamb, M. (1994). The investigation of child sexual abuse: An interdisciplinary consensus statement. *Journal of Child Sexual Abuse, 3*(4).

Lang, G.C. (1985) Baby doe – a medical ethical issue. *Western Journal of Medicine, 142*(6), 837–841.

Larson, D. (Ed.), (1990). *The Mayo Clinic family health book.* Minneapolis, MN: Mayo Foundation for Medical Education.

Leigh, J.W. Jr. (1985). The ethnically competent social worker. In J. Laird & A. Hartman (Eds.), (1985). *A handbook of child welfare: Context, knowledge, and practice.* New York: The Free Press.

Leland, H. & Smith, D.E. (1974). *Mental retardation: Present and future perspectives.* Worthington, OH: Charles A. Jones Publishing.

Levine, M.D. (1980). The child with learning disabilities. In A.P. Scheiner & I.F. Abroms (Eds.), *The practical management of the developmentally disabled child.* St. Louis: C.V. Mosby Co.

Levy, T.M. & Orlans, M. (1995). Intensive short–term therapy with attachment–disordered children. In L. VandeCreek, S. Knapp, & T.L. Jackson (Eds.), *Innovations in clinical practice: A source book (Vol. 14).* Sarasota, FL: Professional Resource Press.

Lindemann, E. (1965). Symptomatology and management of acute grief. In H. Parad & G. Caplan (Eds.), *Crisis intervention: Selected readings.* New York: Family Service Association of America.

Lister, D. (1986). Ethical issues in infanticide of severely defective infants. *Canadian Medical Association Journal, 135,* 1401–1404.

Little, B.B., Snell, L.M., Klein, V.R., & Gilstrap, L.C. (1989). Cocaine abuse during pregnancy: Maternal and fetal implications. *Obstetrics and Gynecology, 73*(2), February, 157–60.

Littner, N. (1956). *Some traumatic effects of separation and placement.* New York: Child Welfare League of America.

Littner, N. (1975). The importance of the natural parents to the child in placement. *Child Welfare, LIV*(3).

Liu, A.N.C. (1987). Wrongful life: Some of the problems. *Journal of Medical Ethics, 13,* 69–73.

Lloyd, J.C., & Bryce, M.E. (1980) *Placement prevention and family unification: A practitioner's handbook for the home-based family centered program.* Iowa: University of Iowa School of Social Work.

Longo, R.E. & Groth, A.N. (1983). Juvenile sexual offenses in the history of adult rapists and child molesters. *International Journal of Offender Therapy and Comparitive Criminology, 27*(2). As cited in Salter, A.C. (1995). *Transforming trauma: A guide to understanding and treating adult survivors of child sexual abuse.* Newbury Park, CA: Sage Publications.

Longo, R.E. & McFadin, J.B. (1981). Inappropriate behavior development in the sexual offender. *Law and Order Magazine, 19.* As cited in Salter, A.C. (1995). *Transforming trauma: A guide to understanding and treating adult survivors of child sexual abuse.* Newbury Park, CA: Sage Publications.

Longo, R.E. (1982). Sexual learning and experiences among adolescent sex offenders. *International Journal of Offender Therapy and Comparative Criminology, 26.*

Lorber, J. (1971). Results of treatment of myelomeningocele. *Developmental Medicine and Child Neurology, 13,* 300.

Lubove, R. (1965). *The professional altruist: The emergence of social work as a career – 1880-1930.* Cambridge, MA: Harvard University Press.

Lyon, J. (1985). *Playing god in the nursery.* New York: W.W. Norton.

Lyons–Ruth, K., Alpern, L. & Repacholi, B. (1993). Disorganized infant attachment classification and maternal psychosocial problems as predictors of hostile–aggressive behavior in the preschool classroom. *Child Development, 64,* 572–585.

Lyons–Ruth, K., Connell, D., Zoll, D., & Stahl, J. (1987). Infants at social risk: Relations among infant maltreatment, maternal behavior, and infant attachment behavior. *Developmental Psychology, 23,* 223–232.

Maccoby, E.E. (1980) *Social development: Psychological growth and the parent-child relationship.* New York: Harcourt Brace Jovanovich, Inc.

MacGregor, S.N., Keith, L.G., Chasnoff, I.J., Rosner, M.A., Chisum, G.M., Shaw, P., & Minogue, J.P. (1987). Cocaine use during pregnancy: Adverse perinatal outcomes. *Am J. Obstet Gynecol, 157*(3), 686–69.

Magura, S. & Moses, B.S. (1987). *Outcome measures for child welfare services: The child well-being scales.* Washington, DC: Child Welfare League of America.

Mahon, M.M. (1988). Nursing involvement in treatment decisions regarding newborns with congenital anomalies. *Holistic Nursing Practice, 2*(2), 55–67.

Main, M. & Hesse, E. (1990). Lack of resolution of mourning in adulthood and its relationship to infant disorganization: Some speculations regarding causal mechanisms. In M. Greenberg, D. Cicchetti, & N. Cummings (Eds.), *Attachment in the preschool years: Theory, research, and intervention.* Chicago: University of Chicago Press. As cited in Levy, T.M. & Orlans, M. (1995). Intensive short–term therapy with attachment–disordered children. In L. VandeCreek, S. Knapp, & T.L. Jackson (Eds.), *Innovations in clinical practice: A source book (Vol 14).* Sarasota, FL: Professional Resource Press.

Main, M. & Solomon, J. (1990). Procedures for identifying infants as disorganized/disoriented during the Ainsworth strange situation. In M. Greenberg, D. Cicchetti, & N. Cummings, (Eds.), *Attachment in the preschool years: Theory, research, and intervention.* Chicago: University of Chicago Press. As cited in Levy, T.M. & Orlans, M. (1995). Intensive short–term therapy with attachment–disordered children. In L. VandeCreek, S. Knapp, & T.L. Jackson (Eds.), *Innovations in clinical practice: A source book. (Vol. 14.)* Sarasota, FL: Professional Resource Press.

Maletzky, B.M. (1991). *Treating the sexual offender.* Newbury, CA: Sage Publications.

Mallucio, A.N., Fein, E., & Olmstead, K.A. (1986). *Permanency planning for children: Concepts and methods.* New York: Tavistock Publications.

Marshall, W.L., Barbaree, H.E., & Eccles, A. (1991). Early onset and deviant sexuality in child molesters. *Journal of Interpersonal Violence, 6*(3). As cited in Salter, A.C. (1995). *Transforming trauma: A guide to understanding and treating adult survivors of child sexual abuse.* Newbury Park, CA: Sage Publications.

Martin, H. (1972). The child and his development. In C.H. Kempe & R.E. Helfer, (Eds.), *Helping the battered child and his family.* Philadelphia: Lippincott, 93–114.

Martin, J.E. & Laidlow, T.T. (1980). Implications of direct service planning, delivery and policy. In A.R. Novak & L.W. Heal, (Eds.), *Integration of developmentally disabled individuals into the community.* Baltimore: Paul H. Brooks.

Mason, J.K. & Meyers, D.W. (1986). Parental choice and selective non-treatment of deformed newborns: A view from mid-atlantic. *Journal of Medical Ethics, 12,* 66–71.

Mathews, R. (1987). *Preliminary typology of female sexual offenders.* Unpublished document. As cited in Mathews, R., Matthews, J.K., & Speltz, K. (1989). *Female sexual offenders: An exploratory study.* Orwell, VT: Safer Society Press.

Mathews, R., Matthews, J.K., & Speltz, K. (1989). *Female sexual offenders: An exploratory study.* Orwell, VT: Safer Society Press.

McCarthy, D. (1981). *Women who rape.* Unpublished manuscript. As cited in Matthews, R., Matthews, J.K., & Speltz, K. (1989). *Female sexual offenders: An exploratory study.* Orwell, VT: Safer Society Press.

McCarty, L. (1986). Mother–child incest: Characteristics of the offender. *Child Welfare, 65*(5). As cited in Matthews, R., Matthews, J.K., & Speltz, K. (1989). *Female sexual offenders: An exploratory study.* Orwell, VT: Safer Society Press.

McCormick, R. (1978). The quality of life, the sanctity of life. *Hastings Center Report, 8*(1), 30–36.

McCubbin, H. & Patterson, J. (1983). Family stress adaptation to crises: A double ABCX model of family behavior. In H. McCubbin, M. Sussman, & J. Patterson (Eds.), *Social stresses and the family: Advances and developments in family stress theory and research.* New York: The Haworth Press. As cited in Wikler, L.M. (1986). Family stress theory and research on families of children with mental retardation. In J.J. Gallagher & P.M. Vietze (Eds.), *Families of handicapped persons: Research, programs, and policy issues.* Baltimore: Paul Brookes, 167–195.

McNamara, J. (1988). *Tangled feelings.* Ossining, NY: Family Resources. As cited by Ryan, G. Sexual behavior in childhood. In J. McNamara & B. McNamara (Eds.), *Adoption and the sexually abused child.* Portland, ME: University of Southern Maine, Human Services Development Institute.

McNamara, & J., McNamara, B. (Eds.), (1990). *Adoption and the sexually abused child.* Portland, Me: University of Southern Maine, Human Services Development Institute.

Meinig, M.B., & Bonner, B.L. (1990). Returning the treated sex offender to the family. *Violence Update, 1*(2).

Mill, J.S. (1987). *Utilitarianism.* London: London Press.

Morgan, M. (1995). *How to interview sexual abuse victims, including the use of anatomical dolls.* Thousand Oaks, CA: Sage Publications.

Morin, R. (1977). Black child, white parents: A beginning biography. *Child Welfare, LVI*(9): 576–583.

Mortland, C. & Egan, M. (1987). Vietnamese youth in American foster care. *Social Work, 32*(3): 240–245.

Murphy, L.B. & Moriarty, A.E. (1976) *Vulnerability, coping and growth from infancy to adolescence.* London: Yale University Press.

Murphy, W.D., Rau, T.J., & Worley, P.J. (1994). Offender treatment: The perils and pitfalls of profiling child sex abusers. *The APSAC Advisor, 7*(1).

Murphy, W.D., & Peters, J.M. (1992). Profiling child sexual abusers: Psychological considerations. *Criminal justice and behavior, 4,* 24–37.

Murray, T.H. The final anticlimactic rule on baby doe. *Hastings Center Report, 15*(3) 5–9.

Mussen, P.H., Conger, J.J., Kagan, J., & Huston, A.C. (1984). *Child development and personality. Sixth edition.* New York: Harper & Row.

National Research Council, Panel on Research on Child Abuse and Neglect, Commission on Behavioral and Social Sciences and Education (1993). *Understanding child abuse and neglect.* Washington, DC: National Academy Press.

National Resource Center for Special Needs Adoption [Undated]. *What to look for in assessing parents for the placement of children with developmental disabilities.* Southfield, MI: National Resource Center for Special Needs Adoption, Spaulding for Children.

Neilson, J. (1976). Tayari: Black homes for black children. *Child Welfare, LV*(1): 41–50.

Nelson, K.A. (1985). *On the frontier of adoption: A study of special needs adoptive families.* New York: Child Welfare League of America.

Nunes–Dinis, M. & Barth, R.P. (1993). Cocaine treatment and outcome. *Social Work,* 38(5), September.

O'Connell, M.A., Leberg, E., & Donaldson, C. (1990). *Working with sex offenders: Guidelines for therapist selection.* Newbury Park, CA: Sage Publications.

O'Connell, M.A. & Associates (1994). *Reuniting incest offenders with their families.* Unpublished paper.

Ohio Coalition for the Education of Handicapped Children (1987). *Family ties: Early intervention, early childhood education, "The law."* Marion, Ohio: Ohio Coalition for the Education of Handicapped Children.

Ohio Department of Human Services (1989). *The Ohio child abuse and neglect investigation decisions handbook.* Columbus, Ohio: Ohio Department of Human Services.

Ohio Department of Human Services, Children's Protective Services. (1980). *Open the door on child abuse and neglect: Prevention and reporting kit.* Columbus, Ohio: Ohio Department of Human Services.

Olson, R.G. (1967). Deontological ethics. In P. Edwards (Ed.), *The encyclopedia of philosophy.* (Vol. 2.) New York: Macmillan.

Ornitz, E.M., & Ritvo, E.R. (1976). The syndrome of autism: A critical review. *American Journal of Psychiatry, 133*(6), June.

Osterloh, J.D. & Lee, B.L. (1989). Urine drug screening in mothers and newborns. *Am. J. Dis. Child 143*(7), July, 791–3.

Ostrea, E.M., Brady, M.J., Parks, P.M., Asensio, D.C., & Naluz, A. (1989). Drug screening of meconium in infants of drug–dependent mothers: An alternative to urine testing. *J. Pediatrics 115*(3), September, 474–477.

Pahl, J. & Quine, L. (1984). *Families with mentally handicapped children.* Kent: University of Kent.

Parad, H.J., & Caplan, G. (1965). A framework for studying families in crisis. In H. Parad & G. Caplan (Eds.), *Crisis intervention: Selected readings.* New York: Family Service Association of America.

Paris, J. (1982). Terminating treatment for newborns: A theological perspective. *Law, Medicine, and Health Care, 10.*

Partridge, S., Hornby, H., & McDonald, T. (1986). *Learning from adoption disruption: Insights for practice.* Portland, ME: University of Southern Maine.

Peikoff, T., & Brickey, S. (1991). Creating precious children and glorified mothers: A theoretical assessment of the transformation of childhood. In R. Smandych, G. Dodds, & A. Esau (Eds.), *Dimensions of childhood: Essays on the history of children and youth in Canada.* Winnipeg, Manitoba: Legal Research Institute of the University of Manitoba.

Pence, D., & Wilson, C. (1994). *Team investigation of child sexual abuse: The uneasy alliance.* Newbury Park, CA: Sage Publications.

Pernell, R. (1970). Social work values on the new frontiers. In K.A. Kendall (Ed.), *Social work values in an age of discontent.* New York: Council on Social Work Education, Inc.

Peters, S.D. (1988). Child sexual abuse and later psychological problems. In G. Wyatt & G. Powell (Eds.), *Lasting effects of child sexual abuse.* Newbury Park, CA: Sage Publications.

Petr, C.G. & Barney, D.D. (1993). Reasonable efforts for children with disabilities: The parents' perspective. *Social Work, 38*(3), May, 247–254.

Pianta, R.C., Egeland, B., & Erickson, M.F. (1989). The antecedents of maltreatment: Results of the mother–child interaction research project. In D. Cicchetti & V. Carlson (Eds.), *Child maltreatment: Theory and research on the causes and consequences of child abuse and neglect.* New York: Cambridge University Press.

Pinderhughes, E.E. (1983). Older child adoptions and families' participation in postplacement supports. Paper presented at the 91st Annual Convention of the American Psychological Association, Anaheim, CA, August 1983.

Pinderhughes, E.E. & Rosenberg, K.F. (1990). Family–bonding with high risk placements: A therapy model that promotes the process of becoming a family. *Journal of Children in Contemporary Society, 21*(3–4), 209–230.

Pine, B.A., Warsh, R., & Maluccio, A.N. (1993). *Together again: Family reunification in foster care.* Washington, DC: Child Welfare League of America.

Polansky, N.A., De Saix, C., & Sharlin, S.A. (1972). *Child neglect: Understanding and reaching the parent.* New York: Child Welfare League of America.

Popkin, R.H. & Stroll, A. (1956). *Philosophy made simple.* New York: Doubleday.

Porter, F.S., Blick, L.C., & Sgroi, S.M. (1985). Treatment of the sexually abused child. In S.M. Sgroi, *Handbook of clinical intervention in child sexual abuse.* Lexington, MA: Lexington Books.

Powell, M.B., & Merrick, I.J. (1992). Assessing the incestuous family's readiness for reconstitution. *Families in Society: The Journal of Contemporary Human Services.* Families International, Inc., September.

Prater, G, & King, L. (1988). Experiences of black families as adoptive parents. *Social Work, 33*(6), 543–545.

President's Commission for the Study of Ethical Problems in Medicine and Biomedical and Behavioral Research. (1983). *Deciding to forego life-sustaining treatment: Ethical, medical, and legal issues in treatment decisions.* Washington, DC: U.S. Government Printing Office, 82–90.

Provence, S., & Lipton, H. (1962). *Infants in institutions.* New York: International University Press.

Public Children Services Association of Ohio (1994). *Standards for child welfare practice.* Unpublished.

Ragan, C.K., Salus, M.K., & Schultze, G.L. (1980). *Child protection: Providing ongoing services.* National Center on Child Abuse and Neglect, Children's Bureau, Administration for Children, Youth and Families, Office of Human Development Services, U.S. Department of Health and Human Services.

Rapoport, L. (1965). The state of crisis: Some theoretical considerations. In H. Parad & G. Caplan (Eds.), *Crisis intervention: Selected readings.* New York: Family Service Association of America.

Reamer, F.G. (1994). Social work values and ethics. In F.G. Reamer (Ed.), *The foundations of social work knowledge.* New York: Columbia University Press.

Rice, E. (1990). *Captain Sir Richard Francis Burton*. New York: Charles Scribner & Sons.

Richardson, M., West, M.A., Day, P., & Stuart, S. (1989). Children with developmental disabilities in the child welfare system: A national survey. *Child Welfare, LXVIII(6)*, 605–614.

Rieser, M. (1991). Recantation in child sexual abuse cases. *Child Welfare, LXX(6)*, November/December.

Rodriguez, P., & Meyer, A. (1990). Minority adoptions and agency practices. *Social Work, 35(6)*: 528–531.

Rogoff, B., Gauvain, M., & Ellis, S. (1984). Development viewed in its cultural context. In M.H. Bornstein & M.E. Lamb, *Developmental psychology: An advanced textbook*. Hillsdale, NJ: Lawrence Erlbaum Associates.

Rooke, P. T., & Schnell, R. L. *Discarding the asylum: From child rescue to the welfare state in English-Canada (1800-1950)*. Lanham, MD: University Press of America, Inc.

Rosen, M., Clark, G.R., & Kivitz, M. (Ed.), (1976). *The history of mental retardation: Collected papers*. Vol. I and II. Baltimore, MD: University Park Press.

Rosenberg, K.F. & Franz, K. (1990). *Using the mental health system*. Unpublished manuscript.

Rosenthal, J., Groze, V., & Curiel, H. (1990). Race, social class, and special needs adoption. *Social Work, 35(6)*: 532–539.

Rosenthal, J.A., Schmidt, D., & Conner, J. (1988). Predictors of special needs adoption disruption: An exploratory study. *Children and Youth Services Review, 10*, 101–117.

Rosenthal, R. & Jackson, L. (1968). *Pygmalion in the classroom: Teacher expectation and pupils' intellectual development*. New York: Holt, Rinehart, and Winston.

Rosner, F. (1983). The traditional jewish physician and modern biomedical ethical problems. *The Journal of Medicine and Philosophy, 8*, 225–241.

Ross Laboratories (1989). Cocaine Babies. *Special Currents*. Columbus, Ohio: Ross Laboratories.

Ross, J.W., Bayley, C., Michel, V., & Pugh, D. (1986). *Handbook for hospital ethics committees*. Chicago: American Hospital Publishing, Inc.

Russell, D. (1983). The incidence and prevalence of intrafamilial and extrafamilal sexual abuse of female children. *Child Abuse and Neglect,7*.

Russell, D. (1984). *Sexual exploitation: Rape, child sexual abuse and sexual harrassment*, Newbury Park, CA: Sage Publications.

Ryan, G. (1990). Sexual behavior in childhood. In J. McNamara & B. McNamara (Eds.), *Adoption and the sexually abused child*. Portland, ME: University of Southern Maine, Human Services Development Institute.

Rycus, J.S., & Hughes, R.C. (1989). *Casework process and case planning in child protective services: A training curriculum*. Washington, DC: Child Welfare League of America.

Rycus, J.S., Hughes, R.C., & Garrison, J.K. (1989). *Child protective services: A training curriculum*. Washington, DC: Child Welfare League of America.

Rycus, J.S., Hughes, R.C., & Ginther, N.L. (1988). *Separation and placement in child protective services: A training curriculum*. Washington, DC: Child Welfare League of America.

Sack, W.H. & Dale, D.D. (1982). Abuse and deprivation in failed adoptions. *Child Abuse and Neglect*, 6, 443–451.

Salter, A.C. (1988). *Treating child sex offenders and victims: A practical guide.* Newbury Park, CA: Sage Publications.

Salter, A.C. (1995). *Transforming trauma: A guide to understanding and treating adult survivors of child sexual abuse.* Newbury Park, CA: Sage Publications.

Sarles, R.M. (1975). Incest. *Pediatric Clinics of North America, 22(3),* 633–642. As cited in Salter, A.C. (1988). *Treating child sex offenders and victims: A practical guide.* Newbury Park, CA: Sage Publications.

Sassaman, E.A. Ethical considerations in medical treatment. In J.L. Matson & J.A. Mulick (Eds.), *Handbook of mental retardation.* New York: Pergamon Press, 1983.

Saywitz, Karen (1994). Questioning child witnesses. *Violence Update, 4(7).*

Scheiner, A.P. (1980). The high risk mother and infant. In A.P. Scheiner & I.F. Abroms (Eds.), *The practical management of the developmentally disabled child.* St. Louis: C.V. Mosby Co.

Scherling, D. (1994). Prenatal cocaine exposure and childhood psychopathology: A developmental analysis. *American Journal of Orthopsychiatry, 64(1),* January, 9–19.

Schild, S. (1968). Counseling with parents of retarded children living at home. In F.J. Turner (Ed.), *Differential diagnosis and treatment in social work.* New York: The Free Press.

Schilling, R.F., Kirkham, M.A., & Schinke, S.P. (1986). Do child protection services neglect developmentally disabled children? *Education and Training of the Mentally Retarded, 21(1),* 21–26.

Schmitt, B.D. (1979). *Child abuse/neglect: The visual diagnosis of non-accidental trauma and failure to thrive.* Produced by the University of Colorado Medical Center in cooperation with the American Academy of Pediatrics. Elk Grove, IL: American Academy of Pediatrics.

Schneider, S. & Rimmer, E. (1984). Adoptive parents' hostility toward their adopted children. *Children and Youth Services Review, 6,* 345–352.

Schoeman, F. (1985). Parental discretion and children's rights: Background and implications for medical decision-making. *The Journal of Medicine and Philosophy, 10,* 45–61.

Schottenfeld, R.S., Viscarello, R.R., Grossman, J., Klerman, L.V., Nagler, S.F., & Adnopoz, J.A. (1994). A comprehensive public health approach. In D.J. Besharov (Ed.), *When drug addicts have children.* Washington, DC: Child Welfare League of America.

Sgroi, S.M. (1982). *Handbook of clinical intervention in child sexual abuse.* Lexington, MA: Lexington Books, D.C. Heath & Co.

Sgroi, S., Bunk, B., & Wabrek, C. (1988). Children's sexual behaviors and their relationship to sexual abuse. In S.M. Sgroi (Ed.), *Vulnerable populations: Evaluation and treatment of sexually abused children and adult survivors.* Lexington, MA: Lexington.

Shapiro, J.P., Burkey, B.M., Dorman, R.L., & Welker, C.J. (1994). *An investigation of factors related to burnout among child sexual abuse professionals: Final report.* Cleveland, OH: Research and Training Department, Child Guidance Center of Greater Cleveland.

Shapiro, J.P., Director of Research and Training Department, Child Guidance Center of Greater Cleveland; personal conversation with author Nan Beeler, June, 1994.

Shaw, A. (1973). Dilemmas of 'informed consent' in children. *New England Journal of Medicine, 17(289),* 885–890.

Shaw, D.S.. & Vondra, J.I. (1993). Chronic family adversity and infant attachment security. *Journal of Child Psychology and Psychiatry, 34(7),* 1205–1215.

Shelp, E.E. (1986). Born to die? Deciding the fate of critically ill newborns. New York: Free Press.

Sheperd, J.R., Dworin, B., Farley, R.H., Tressler, P.W., & the National Center for Missing and Exploited Children (1992). *Child abuse and exploitation: Investigative techniques.* (2nd ed.) U.S. Department of Justice, Office of Justice and Delinquency Prevention.

Shreeve, J. (1994). Terms of estrangement. *Discover,* 15(II), November.

Siegler, M. (1986). Ethics committees: Decisions by bureaucracy. *Hastings Center Report, 3,* 22–24.

Simms, M. (1986). Informed dissent: The views of some mothers of severely mentally handicapped young adults. *Journal of Medical Ethics, 12,* 72–74.

Simms, M.D. & Bolden, B.J. (1991). The family reunification project: Facilitating regular contact among foster children, biological families, and foster families. *Child Welfare, LXX(6),* November–December, 679–689.

Simon, R. (1993). Should white families be allowed to adopt African American children? Yes. *Health,* 7(4). July–August, 22.

Singer, P. & Kuhse, H. (1988). Resolving arguments about the sanctity of life: A response to Long. *Journal of Medical Ethics, 14,* 198–199.

Smith, D.W. (1982). *Recognizable patterns of human malformation: Genetic and embryologic and clinical aspects.* (3rd ed.) Philadelphia: W.B. Saunders Co.

Smith, D.W. & Sherwen, L.N. (1983). *Mothers and their adopted children: The bonding process.* New York: Tiresias Press.

Smith, S.L., & Howard, J.A. (1994). The impact of previous sexual abuse on children's adjustment in adoptive placement. *Social Work,* 39(5), September.

Sorensen, B. & Snow, B. (1991). How children tell: The process of disclosure in child sexual abuse. *Child Welfare, LXX(1),* Jan–Feb.

Sorosky, S.D., Baron, A., & Pannor, R. (1975). Identity conflict in adoptees. *American Journal of Orthopsychiatry, 45,* 18–27.

Spaulding for Children (1989). *Characteristics of Successful Adoptive Families.* [Video]. Southfield, MI: National Resource Center for Special Needs Adoption.

Spohr, H.L., Willms, J. & Steinhausen, H.C. (1993). Prenatal alcohol exposure and long–term developmental consequences. *The Lancet,* 341(8850) April 10, 907–11.

Stark, G.D. (1977). *Spina bifida: problems and management.* London: Blackwell Scientific Publications.

Steele, B. (1987). Psychodynamic factors in child abuse. In R.E. Helfer & R.S. Kempe (Eds.), *The battered child.* (4th ed.) Chicago: University of Chicago Press.

Stehno, S.M. (1982). Differential treatment of minority children in service systems. *Social Work,* 27(1), January, 39–45.

Stehno, S.M. (1990). The elusive continuum of child welfare services: Implications for minority children and youths. *Child Welfare, LXIX(6),* Nov–Dec., 551–562.
Steinhausen, H.C., Willms, J., & Spohr, H.L. (1993). Long–term psychopathological and cognitive outcomes of children with fetal alcohol syndrome. *Journal of the American Academy of Child and Adolescent Psychiatry.* 32(5) September, 990–994.

Stewart, E.C. & Bennett, M.J. (1991). *American cultural patterns: A cross-cultural perspective.* Yarmouth, Maine: Intercultural Press.

Stone, L.J., Smith, H.T., & Murphy, L.B. (1973). *The competent infant: Research and commentary.* New York: Basic Books, Inc.

Subramanian, K.N.S. (1986). In India, Nepal, and Sri Lanka, quality of life weighs heavily. *Hastings Center Report, 4*, 20–22.

Summit, R. (1983). The child sexual abuse accommodation syndrome. *Child Abuse & Neglect, 7*.

Sumner, W. (1959). *Folkways*. New York, Dover Publications.

Taft, C. (1987). Baby doe decisions: A hospital manager's perspective. *Health Care Management Review, 12*(2), 61–68.

Task Force on Permanency Planning for Foster Children, Inc. (1990). *Kinship care: The double-edged dilemma*. Rochester, NY: Task Force on Permanency Planning for Children. As cited in Child Welfare League of America North American Kinship Care Policy and Practice Committee (1994). *Kinship care: A natural bridge*. Washington, DC: Child Welfare League of America.

Telsey, A.M., Merrit, T.A., & Dixon, S.D. (1988). Cocaine exposure in a term neonate: Necrotizing enterocolitis as a complication. *Clin Pediatr 27*(11), November, 547–550.

Thain, W.S., Casto, G. & Peterson, A. (1980). *Normal and handicapped children: A growth and development primer for parents and professionals*. Littleton, MA: PSG Publishing Co., Inc.

The Crack Children. Newsweek, February 12, 1990.

Thomas, A. & Chess, S. (1977). *Temperament and development*. New York: Bruner/Mazel.

Thompson, A. (1993). Should white families be allowed to adopt African American children? No. *Health, 7*(4). July–August, 22.

Thompson, L. (1990). Working with alcoholic families in a child welfare agency: The problem of underdiagnosis. *Child Welfare*, LXIX(5) September–October.

Thompson, R.W., Authier, K., & Ruma, P. (1994). Behavior problems of sexually abused children in foster care: A preliminary study. *Journal of Child Sexual Abuse*, 3(4). The Haworth Press, Inc.

Thorton, J.L. (1987). An investigation into the nature of kinship foster homes. DSW dissertation. As cited in Child Welfare League of America North American Kinship Care Policy and Practice Committee (1994). *Kinship care: A natural bridge*. Washington, DC: Child Welfare League of America.

Todres, I. (1977). Pediatricians' attitudes affecting decision making in defective newborns. *Pediatrics, 60*, 197–201.

Trépanier, J. (1991). The origin of the Juvenile Deliquents Act of 1908: Controlling delinquency through seeking its causes and through youth protection. In R. Smandych, G. Dodds, & A. Esau (Eds.), *Dimensions of childhood: Essays on the history of children and youth in Canada*. Winnipeg, Manitoba: Legal Research Institute of the University of Manitoba.

Turner, M.T. & Turner, T.N. (1994). *Female adolescent sexual abusers; An exploratory study of mother-daughter dynamics with implications for treatment*. Brandon, VT: Safer Society Press.

U.S. Commission on Civil Rights. (1989). *Medical discrimination against children with disabilities*. September.

U.S. Congress, Senate (1975). Subcommittee on Children and Youth of the Senate Committee on Labor and Public Welfare, and the House of Representatives Select Subcommittee on Education, December 1.

U.S. Department of Health and Human Services, Office of Human Development Services. (1985). Child abuse amendments. (45 CFR Part 1340). *Federal Register, 50*(72)(April): L4878, L4880, L4889, L4893–L4901.

U.S. Department of Health and Human Services. *Permanent planning for children in foster care.* (1977). DHHS Publication No. (OHDS) 80–30124. Washington, DC: US Department of Health and Human Services.

U.S. Department of Health, Education and Welfare. *Protective services for abused and neglected children and their families.* Publication (SRS) 77–23042. Washington, DC: US Department of Health, Education and Welfare.

Unger, C., Dwarshuis, G. & Johnson, E. (1981). Coping with disruption. *Adoption Disruptions.* (DHHS Publication No. 81–30319). Washington, DC: US Department of Health and Human Services.

Veatch, R.M. (1981). *A theory of medical ethics.* New York: Basic Books.

Victoroff, M.S. (1986). The ballad of baby doe: Parental discretion or medical neglect? *Primary Care, 13*(2), 271–283.

Wald, M.S. (1994). Termination of parental rights. In D.J. Besharov (Ed.), *When drug addicts have children.* Washington, DC: Child Welfare League of America.

Walters, J.W. (1988). Approaches to ethical decision making in the neonatal intensive care unit. *American Journal of Diseases of Children, 8*(142) 825–830.

Washington, V. (1987). Community involvement in recruiting adoptive homes for black children. *Child Welfare, LXVI*(1), 57–68.

Webster's new universal unabridged dictionary (1983). (2nd ed.) New York: New World Dictionaries/Simon & Schuster.

Weil, W.B. (1986). The baby doe regulations: Another view of change. *Hastings Center Report, 2,* 12–14.

Weiner, I.B. (1962). Father–daughter incest: A clinical report. *Psychiatric Quarterly, 29,* 1–27. As cited in Salter, A.C. (1988). *Treating child sex offenders and victims: A practical guide.* Newbury Park, CA: Sage Publications.

Weinrott, M.R., & Saylor, M. (1991). Self-report of crimes committed by sex offenders. *Journal of Interpersonal Violence, 6*(3). As cited in Salter, A.C. (1995). *Transforming trauma: A guide to understanding and treating adult survivors of child sexual abuse.* Newbury Park, CA: Sage Publications.

Weinstein, E.A. (1960). *The self-image of the foster child.* New York: Russell Sage Foundation.

White House Conference on Children (1909). *Proceedings of the Conference on the Care and Protection of Dependent Children,* Jan 25–26. Senate Document #13, 60th Congress, 1908–9. Washington, DC: US Government Printing Office.

Wiebe, E. & Wiebe, A. (1994). Fragile–X syndrome. *Canadian Family Physician, 40,* February, 290–295.

Wikler, L.M. (1986). Family stress theory and research on families of children with mental retardation. In J.J. Gallagher & P.M. Vietze (Eds.), *Families of handicapped persons: Research, programs, and policy issues.* Baltimore: Paul Brookes, 167–195.

Williams, B.E. (1987). Looking for Linda: Identity in black and white. *Child Welfare, LXVI*(3): 207–216.

Wimmer, J. & Richardson, S. (1990). Adoption of children with developmental disabilities. *Child Welfare, LXIX*(6), November–December, 563–569.

Wolf, S.M. (1986). Ethics committees in the courts. *Hastings Center Report, 3,* 12–15.

Wormith, J.S. (1983). A survey of incarcerated sexual offenders. *Canadian Journal of Criminology, 25*(4). As cited in Salter, A.C. (1995). *Transforming trauma: A guide to understanding and treating adult survivors of child sexual abuse.* Newbury Park, CA: Sage Publications.

Wyatt, G. & Mickey, M. (1988). The support by parents and others as it mediates the effects of child sexual abuse. In G. Wyatt & G. Powell (Eds.), *Lasting effects of child sexual abuse*. Newbury Park, CA: Sage Publications.

Wyatt, G. & Powell, G. (1988). *Lasting effects of child sexual abuse*. Newbury Park: Sage Publications.

Young, E.W.D., & Stevenson, D. K. (1990). Limiting treatment for extremely premature, low-birth-weight infants (500-750 G). *American Journal of Diseases of Children, 144*(5), 549-552.

Zamosky, J., Sparks, J., Hatt, R., & Sharman, J. (1993). Believing in families. In B. Pine, R. Warsh, & A. Maluccio (Eds.), *Together again: Family reunification in foster care*. Washington, DC: Child Welfare League of America.

Zeanah, C.H., Benoit, D.B., Barton, M., Regan, C., Hirshberg, L.M., & Lipsitt, L.P. (1993). Representations of attachment in mothers and their one-year-old infants. *Journal of the American Academy of Child and Adolescent Psychiatry, 32*(2), March.

Zigler, E., & Berman, W. (1983). Discerning the future of early childhood intervention. *American Psychologist*, August, 894-904.

Zuckerman, B. (1994). Effects on parents and children. In D.J. Besharov (Ed.), *When drug addicts have children*. Washington, DC: Child Welfare League of America.

Zuckerman, B., Frank, D.A., Hingson, R., Amaro, H., Levenson, S.M., Kayne, H., Parker, S., Vinci, R., Aboagye, K., & Fried, L.E. (1989). Effects of maternal marijuana and cocaine use on fetal growth. *New England Journal of Medicine 23, 320*(12) March, 762-768.

INDEX

Index

A

O

P

T